Byron's WOMEN

ALEXANDER LARMAN is a historian and journalist. He is the author of *Blazing Star* (2014), the life of Lord Rochester, and *Restoration* (2016), and writes for the *Observer*, the *Telegraph* and the *Guardian*, as well as the *New Statesman* and the *Times Literary Supplement*.

Byron's WOMEN

ALEXANDER LARMAN

First published in the UK in 2016 by Head of Zeus Ltd

Copyright © Alexander Larman, 2016

The moral right of Alexander Larman to be identified as the author of this work has been asserted in accordance with the Copyright, Designs and Patents Act of 1988.

1 3 5 7 9 8 6 4 2

A catalogue record for this book is available from the British Library.

ISBN (HB) 9781784082024
ISBN (E) 9781784082017

Designed and typeset by Lindsay Nash

Printed and bound by CPI Group (UK) Ltd, Croydon, CR0 4YY

Head of Zeus Ltd
Clerkenwell House
45–47 Clerkenwell Green
London EC1R 0HT

WWW.HEADOFZEUS.COM

For my own women, Nancy and Rose,
who would have *shunned* Byron

❧

'Alas, the love of women! It is known
To be a lovely and a fearful thing'

BYRON, *DON JUAN*

CONTENTS

Contents

PART IV: CLAIRE AND MARY

PART V: TERESA

PART VI: ADA AND MEDORA

DRAMATIS PERSONAE
in order of appearance

Part I

George Gordon, Lord Byron, *a poet and lover of women*

Catherine Gordon, *his mother, weighed down by troubles*

John 'Jack' Byron, *his father, a man unencumbered*

Augusta Leigh, *Jack's daughter and Byron's much-loved half-sister*

John Hanson, *a lawyer, much put-upon*

May Gray, *a nurse of unusually affectionate character*

Mary Ann Chaworth, *Byron's cousin: a first love*

Lord Carlisle, *Byron's guardian, no friend to Catherine*

Dr Glennie, *Byron's first headmaster*

Margaret Parker, *another cousin, and muse*

Lord Grey de Ruthyn, *tenant of Newstead, friend to both mother and son*

Dr Drury, *Byron's Harrow headmaster*

Henry Drury, *his son and Byron's housemaster, a frustrated man*

Elizabeth Pigot, *a friend and neighbour of Byron's*

John Edleston, *a choirboy, and lover of Byron's*

John Cam Hobhouse, *a writer and intimate friend of Byron's: a rogue*

Scrope Davies, *another friend of Byron's: a dandy*

Robert Rushton, *Byron's page, a great help to his master*

John Murray, *Byron's publisher, a canny man*

Part II

Lady Caroline Lamb, *a woman given to giddiness of spirit*

Lady Harriet Spencer, *her mother, a legendary beauty, dancer and socialite*

Lord Ponsonby, *her father, a less happy figure*

Lady Margaret Spencer, *her much-beloved grandmother*

Georgiana, Duchess of Devonshire, *her aunt, a woman of repute*

Charles Fox, *Foreign Secretary and legendary orator: lover of life high and low*

Lord Granville Leveson-Gower, *Harriet's inamorata*

Lady Harriet 'Harryo' Cavendish, *Caroline's cousin and confidante*

William Lamb, *Caroline's husband, a long-suffering man*

The Prince of Wales, later George IV, *England's finest*

Lady Melbourne, *William's mother, and trusted friend to Byron*

George Augustus Frederick Lamb, *Caroline and William's son, beset by fits*

Sir Godfrey Webster, *a soldier and familiar of Caroline's: unblessed with brains*

Lady Holland, *his mother and society hostess, no admirer of Caroline*

Lady Morgan, *writer and friend of Caroline's*

Samuel Rogers, *art collector, writer and gossip*

Douglas Kinnaird, *banker, politician and confidante of Byron's*

Robert Dallas, *a friend of Byron's*

Thomas Moore, *friend and subsequent biographer of Byron's*

Thomas Medwin, *poet and friend of both Byron and Shelley's*

Annabella Milbanke, *intellectual and correspondent of Byron's: later his unhappy wife*

Lady Jane Harley, *an amusement of Byron's*

Part III

Ralph Milbanke, *Annabella's father, somewhat advanced in years*

Judith Milbanke, *her mother, ambitious for her daughter*

Mrs Clermont, *her redoubtable governess*

George Leigh, *Augusta's husband, a soldier: of little use domestically*

Elizabeth Medora Leigh, *Augusta's daughter, believed to be Byron's*

Ada Lovelace, *Annabella and Byron's daughter, destined for greatness*

Stephen Lushington, *Annabella's capable solicitor*

Part IV

Claire Clairmont, *Byron's mistress, one hardened by experience*

Mary Clairmont, *her forthright mother*

William Godwin, *her stepfather: novelist and political philosopher*

Mary Shelley, *his daughter by the feminist Mary Wollstonecraft: prone to dreams*

Fanny Imlay, *his stepdaughter*

Percy Bysshe Shelley, *a poet and adventurer*

Harriet Shelley, *his first wife, all but unacknowledged*

Eliza Westbrook, *her sister*

John William Polidori, *a doctor, and would-be writer*

William Shelley, *Shelley and Mary's son*

Matthew 'Monk' Lewis, *an author of Gothic tales*

Clara Shelley, *Mary and Shelley's daughter*

Allegra Byron, *'natural' daughter of Claire and Byron*

Richard Hoppner, *English consul-general in Venice*

Percy Florence Shelley, *Mary and Shelley's second son*

Part V

Teresa Guiccioli, *Byron's last attachment, and aware of that fact*

Count Ruggero Gamba, *her father, of liberal political thinking*

Count Alessandro Guiccioli, *her husband: a much-married man*

Countess Maria Benzoni, *the means of introducing Byron and Teresa*

Fanny Silvestrini, *Teresa's former governess: a great help*

Lega Zambelli, *Byron's secretary and consigliere*

Count Giuseppe Alborghetti, *Secretary-General of Ravenna*

Pietro Gamba, *Teresa's brother, given to revolutionary ideas*

Hippolito Gamba, *Teresa's younger brother, of fiery temperament*

Marchese Cavalli, *Teresa's uncle*

Edward John Trelawny, *sailor and adventurer*

Lady Marguerite Blessington, *novelist and hostess*

Leigh Hunt, *critic and essayist*

Marianne Hunt, *his wife*

Paolo Costa, *Teresa's literary tutor and mentor*

Ignazio Guiccoli, *Guiccoli's unimpressed son*

Part VI

Theresa Villiers, *a confidante of Annabella, and former friend of Augusta*

Charles Babbage, *a mathematician and engineer, blessed with ideas*

Mary Somerville, *mentor to Ada, scientist and mathematician*

William King, *Ada's husband, later Earl of Lovelace*

Woronzow Greig, *King's friend*

Byron King-Noel, *King and Ada's eldest son*

Annabella King-Noel, *their daughter*

Ralph King-Milbanke, *their youngest son*

Augustus de Morgan, *logician and instructor to Ada*

Georgiana Leigh, *Medora's sister*

Henry Trevanion, *her husband: a wicked fellow*

Marie Leigh, *Medora's daughter by Trevanion*

M. Carrel, *Medora's doctor and guardian*

Natalie Beaurepaire, *Medora's maid, and Annabella's spy; given
    to snobbery*

Victor Beaurepaire, *her husband, of similar mind*

Captain Joseph Barrallier, *a rare friend of Medora's*

John Crosse, *an acquaintance of Ada's, and aficionado of the turf*

Jean-Louis Taillefer, *Medora's admirer, later husband*

Jean-Louis Elie Taillefer, *Medora and Taillefer's son*

BYRON FAMILY TREE

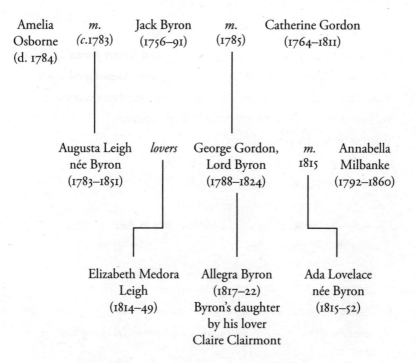

Amelia Osborne (d. 1784) *m.* (*c.*1783) Jack Byron (1756–91) *m.* (1785) Catherine Gordon (1764–1811)

Augusta Leigh née Byron (1783–1851) *lovers* George Gordon, Lord Byron (1788–1824) *m.* 1815 Annabella Milbanke (1792–1860)

Elizabeth Medora Leigh (1814–49)

Allegra Byron (1817–22) Byron's daughter by his lover Claire Clairmont

Ada Lovelace née Byron (1815–52)

INTRODUCTION

In October 1819 Lord Byron wrote to his banker and literary agent Douglas Kinnaird from Italy to reflect on the fortunes of the first two cantos of *Don Juan*. Though published anonymously, the mixture of social and literary satire and unapologetic sexual content had, as with most things Byronic, led to scandal. Few were unaware of the identity of the author, although sales had been slower than those of his autobiographical poem *Childe Harold's Pilgrimage*, published to ecstatic reception in 1812. The character of Don Juan, in particular, seemed to have overtones of his creator, and it was these that Byron reflected on to Kinnaird:

> As to 'Don Juan' – confess – confess – you dog and be candid that it is the sublime of *that there* sort of writing – it may be bawdy – but is it not good English? It may be profligate – but is it not *life*, is it not *the thing*? – Could any man have written it – who has not lived in the world? – and tooled in a post-chaise? – in a hackney coach? – in a gondola? – against a wall? – in a court carriage? – in a vis a vis? – on a table? – and under it? I have written about a hundred stanzas of a third Canto – but it is damned modest – the outcry has frightened me. I have such projects for the Don – but the *Cant* is so much stronger than the *Cunt* – nowadays, – that the benefit of experience in a man

who had well weighed the worth of both monosyllables – must
be lost to despairing posterity.

Since Byron's death in 1824, 'despairing posterity' has been
generous, on the whole. Lady Caroline Lamb's measure of the man
as 'mad, bad and dangerous to know' has stuck, not as condemnation but swaggering affirmation. The adjective 'Byronic' has
entered the language in a way that the names of few other writers
have, bestowed as a rule as a mark of approval. Many men, and
not a few women, would regard being described thus as a badge
of honour; it seems to convey dash and panache, coupled with a
liberal political stance and peerless artistic achievement. The less
savoury aspects of Byron's character – the often callous treatment
towards his lovers; the violence of his mercurial temper; an attitude towards friends that alternated between reckless generosity
and equally reckless dismissal – have not been ignored, but have
become part of the Byronic myth. It is time to delve beneath its
surface and to be prepared for what we may find there.

Byron's Women is not a cradle-to-grave biography of Byron,
a crowded field in which several excellent titles (not least Leslie
Marchand's legendary three-volume offering) have already established strong claims to being definitive. Nor is it a literary text; while
the poetry and literature of the age are often germane to the discussion, I have tried to steer the narrative away from questions that
would more usefully be asked in lecture halls and seminar rooms
and to concentrate instead on telling a diverse sequence of stories of
emotional, sexual and familial attachment, spanning many decades
and myriad places, and characterized variously by casual cruelty,
warm affection, unbridled carnality – and perhaps even true love.
We begin with the birth of a scion of a grand family in a haunted
Scottish castle and end with the funeral of the pioneer of computing
almost ninety years later. This saga is nothing if not varied.

Although Byron is the glue that binds the threads of this narrative, he is not the central focus of this book. Instead, my intention

is to tell a series of intertwined stories about nine significant women in his life, from his mother Catherine Gordon to the daughter he never had the chance to know, Ada Lovelace. Some of the *dramatis personae* – such as Mary Shelley and Caroline Lamb – will be familiar to a great number of readers. Others, such as Byron's ill-treated mistress Claire Clairmont and the daughter of his half-sister Augusta, Elizabeth Medora Leigh, have been neglected by biographical history.

It is my intention to give all of these women the dignified and compassionate treatment that they deserve, and also to explore their relationships with one another. The book may be structured around nine discrete emotional stories, but to ignore the synchronicity of the relationships would be to present them in unnatural isolation. One of the principal attractions in examining these women's lives in a single volume was to explore the unexpected ways in which they encountered and dealt with each other, and how the emotional tie to Byron that they had in common could lead to both alliance and hostility.

This is a long book, but it could have been longer. There are many fascinating women with whom I would have liked to have spent more time, from the all-powerful 'spider' Lady Melbourne, Byron's confidante and possible lover, to Jane Harley, Countess of Oxford; their own scandalous private lives and political interests would provide material enough for fine biographies in their own right.* I am as interested in, and even more sympathetic to, the innumerable chambermaids, servants and acolytes who were, as Byron describes so colourfully, 'tooled in post-chaises' and other such seduction sites at his immediate, impatient disposal. I spent a great deal of time trying, and ultimately failing, to find a hitherto untold tale of an anonymous discarded lover who had had a liaison with Byron, fallen pregnant and produced an unacknowledged,

---

* Such as Jonathan David Gross's edition of *Byron's 'Corbeau Blanc': The Life and Letters of Lady Melbourne* (Rice, 1997).

unloved infant. The closest I came is the servant girl, Lucy, who Byron impregnated when he was 21, and provided an allowance for; tantalizingly, no further evidence exists of Byron's illegitimate son or daughter. In the end it must be the naïve young Claire Clairmont, Mary Shelley's stepsister, who speaks for these women, and whose experience of emotional and physical neglect and, eventually, personal tragedy through Byron's callousness will, I hope, place the cliché of Byron the great lover of women into some form of relief.

I have tried, as far as possible, to tell the stories in this book through the protagonists' own words. In Byron's case, it was all too easy to plunder the voluminous archives of his brilliant correspondence; the greatest challenge was, inevitably, deciding what to omit. But I was equally keen for the voices of those around him to be heard, whether the precise, cold decisiveness of Annabella Milbanke; the worried but fiercely loyal bustling of Catherine Gordon; the warm affection of Augusta; and even the bewildered tenacity of Medora Leigh. The distinctive voice of Mary Shelley is, of course, heard through her own correspondence and through her principal literary creation *Frankenstein*, conceived in the summer of 1816 at the Villa Diodati by Lake Geneva, with Byron, Percy Shelley and John Polidori in attendance. I hope that, in telling the stories of all nine women, I have shone light on some unjustly neglected lives, and examined other, better-known, ones in a fresh and clear-eyed manner.

What is plain to see in the people I have spent so much time with is how extraordinarily independent-minded and tough they were, each in her own way. Catherine Gordon, abandoned by her feckless, debt-ridden husband, doggedly brought up her son to be worthy of the title that he inherited; Caroline Lamb took revenge on Byron by publishing a *roman-à-clef* that was nearly as scandalous as anything her lordly lover ever wrote; the unlikely trio of Mary, Claire and Shelley travelled through Italy and Switzerland as free agents, casting off the shackles of respectability they were expected to wear in favour of intellectual and sexual emancipation; and Ada played a pioneering role in the development of computing science. All nine of 'Byron's women' are a remarkable reminder, decades before universal suffrage and the concept of women's rights, that intelligent women could and did expect a life considerably richer than merely as serving wives and dutiful producers of children. These lives might often have been difficult, unconventional, or short. They were seldom uneventful.

And then there is 'the Manager' himself, as Annabella nicknamed Byron. At times, as I have written about his grotesque cruelty towards his wife and Claire, I found myself loathing him so much that it was almost an ordeal to continue to chart his misdeeds. Yet I must confess that I have, like so many others, been at least half-seduced by Byron. Like the women with whom he associated, he was a pioneer in thought and deed. Of all the Romantic poets, it is his writing that speaks most clearly to us today, as his hatred of 'the cant' will find a warm reception with readers who have themselves long since wearied of being told what they should think and feel. His personal legacy is undeniably a tarnished one, and many readers may have some sympathy with the manner in which Annabella attempted, without success, to bring up her daughter in ignorance of what her father represented. But there can be little doubt that Ada's fierce protectiveness of him should find an echo in all but the most dogmatic of hearts. Unlike the Roman, I have come here neither to praise him, nor to bury him.

With this in mind, in the Prologue that follows, I wish to offer a cameo of an event that took place a month after Byron's death. Its aim was to preserve his name and reputation through well-intended censorship, and, had it never taken place, I imagine that this book – and any other written about him – would have turned out altogether differently. We would have a fuller picture of his thoughts and impressions about most, if not all, of the people who feature in this narrative, as well as another perspective on the man who linked them all. Yet the material destroyed is lost to us, and we must, instead, make the most of what we have as we attempt to decipher the tantalizing clues that have been left to us in search of, in Byron's words, 'a selfish prayer for light'.

PROLOGUE

On 17 May 1824 a small and purposeful group of men gathered at 50 Albemarle Street, Mayfair. The elegant rooms of Byron's publisher John Murray had seen their share of incident, not least when, eleven years previously, Byron's mistress Lady Caroline Lamb had visited, armed with a forged letter, and subsequently departed with a much-prized portrait of the poet by George Sanders.* Murray, a successful and careful businessman whom Byron nicknamed 'the most timid of God's booksellers', had made his reputation and money in the creation of property, not its destruction. However, an altogether different matter now awaited those assembled.

Since Byron's death in April, the matter of his memoirs had concerned those who wished to defend his posthumous reputation against the obloquy that would, inevitably, be levelled at him by his many enemies. His recollections began in 1818 in Italy; he had written to Murray to inform him that 'I think of writing (for your full edition) some memoirs of my life… without any intention of making disclosures or remarks upon living people, which would be unpleasant to them: but I think it might be done, and well done.

---

* Relations between Caroline and Murray were good (see Chapters 5 and 6 for details) and he considered publishing *Glenarvon*; it is also possible that he showed her Byron's memoirs, although he denied it, 'looking red as fire', to Hobhouse.

However, this is to be considered.'¹ If the memoirs were begun with tactful intentions, such diplomacy did not last the course. By August, Byron described his reminiscences as 'full of many passions and prejudices, of which it has been impossible for me to keep clear – I have not the patience'.²

As to the nature of these 'passions and prejudices', it is relatively easy to speculate. We know with certainty that he discussed his failed marriage to Annabella Milbanke. He wrote a letter to his ex-wife in late 1820 to ask her to proofread the memoir and describing its unsparing contents. 'You will find nothing to flatter you, nothing to lead you to the most remote supposition that we could ever have been, or be happy together,' he warned, with unflinching candour.*³ He may also have attempted to answer (or to admit) some of the charges publicly levelled at him. There could have been discussion of his high-profile love affairs, most notably with Caroline Lamb and his current inamorata Teresa Guiccioli. And it is possible that he even discussed his 'unnatural relations' with his half-sister Augusta Leigh, a matter considered so scandalous that he only referred to it by code in letters to his closest friends.

Byron added more material to his memoirs in 1820, and asked his friend Thomas Moore to ensure their posthumous publication. Moore noted in his diary that:

> I see that Byron in his continuation says that I advised him to go
> into the details of his loves more fully, but if I recollect right, it
> was only his adventures in the East I alluded to, as in recounting
> these there could be but little harm done to anyone.⁴

Moore was being disingenuous. The content of these memoirs was potentially so explosive that, on 27 July, he was able to record that

---

* Unsurprisingly, she declined the opportunity, on the grounds that 'I consider publication or circulation of such a composition at any time as prejudicial to Ada's future happiness.'

Murray had offered two thousand guineas* for them on condition that Moore would act as their editor. Upon hearing this news, Byron was so thrilled at the prospect that he briefly considered publishing immediately, before being gently dissuaded by Murray.

Although a few friends of Byron saw the memoirs in his lifetime – Kinnaird gushed to its author and protagonist that 'it is excellent – your [sic] curse & swear occasionally in the second part'⁵ – and it was copied in Paris in the expectation of later publication, it was kept essentially secret. This, in view of its substance, was probably wise; Byron observed to Moore that 'a man always *looks dead* after his Life has appeared, and I should certes not survive the appearance of mine'.⁶ Moore was permitted free rein to cut what he liked from the second part, but was made to promise that the first, which dealt with Byron's marriage to and subsequent separation from Annabella, was to be published unexpurgated. He gave his word, no doubt believing that he would not be called upon to act for decades, by which time the events described would seem distant indeed.

Byron's untimely death was therefore both a personal and literary tragedy for Moore, who found himself in the unfortunate position of having to defend his intentions to the late poets's friends. The reaction of John Cam Hobhouse, one of Byron's closest companions, was typical. He wrote:

> After the first access of grief was over I then determined to lose no time in doing my duty by preserving all that was left to me of my friend – his fame – my thoughts were turned to the Memoirs of his life given to Thomas Moore & deposited by him in Mr Murray's hands for certain considerations.⁷

He believed that no 'rumours prejudicial to his fame' should escape, and most of those to whom he spoke, including Augusta, agreed;

---

* In order to obtain a rough equivalence for a value today, multiply the sum by around seventy.

they promised their own discretion on the matters that might be contained. The memoirs had to be disposed of. Even Murray, of whom Hobhouse stated 'I did him the injustice to think that he might prove the obstacle to their destruction',[8] was prepared to countenance the potential loss of a huge sum in revenue; ever the businessman, he calculated that the damage to Byron's reputation and consequent hit to sales probably outweighed the short-term profit. He was influenced in this by the literary critic William Gifford, editor of the *Quarterly Review*. Gifford read the memoirs at Murray's request and announced grimly that they were 'fit only for a brothel and would doom Lord B to everlasting infamy if published'.[9]

All seemed unanimous, with the exception of Moore, who wished to copy out extracts from the memoir to use in his proposed biography of Byron. Hobhouse also reported Moore's (possibly disingenuous) comments that 'the first part of the memoirs contained nothing objectionable except one anecdote… the second part contained all sorts of erotic adventures'.[10] It was suggested that Moore surrender the manuscript to Augusta, for her to do with as she wished, but he continued to argue that 'this would be throwing a stigma upon the work, which it did not deserve.'[11] Had he been able to talk with Augusta, he might have obtained a partial stay of execution that allowed him time to accomplish his purpose. Unfortunately, Hobhouse had got there first and successfully persuaded her that the memoirs should be destroyed, and as quickly as possible.

Moore and Hobhouse met in the early morning of 17 May by The Albany, where Byron had once lived. Here, Hobhouse bullied Moore into giving his consent, on the grounds that 'I was certain that in this case there was but one line for a man of honour & for a friend of Lord Byron to take'.[12] Once this was accomplished, he gathered Moore, Murray and his friend Henry Luttrell in his rooms, where an argument broke out between Moore and Murray; the former still wished for extracts to be published; the latter, fearing scandal, 'in a very determined voice and manner protested that the MSS should be burnt forthwith', as the would-be biographer himself had earlier agreed. Moore argued somewhat weakly that Byron had entrusted him with the memoirs and that it should therefore fall to him to determine what became of them. But it was Murray who wielded the final blow, when he declared 'you have acted anything but like a man of honour'.

The implication that Moore had a greater interest in pecuniary profit than protecting his friend's reputation was both strong and fatal, particularly since he found himself unable to refute it satisfactorily. He was the sole person who attempted to safeguard at least some of the memoirs for posterity, but that did little to count in his favour. The company adjourned to Murray's offices, where they were joined by Augusta's representative Wilmot Horton and Colonel Doyle, Annabella's proxy. Moore made a final but feeble attempt to appeal to their better nature and asked that the manuscript be sealed and kept under lock and key until some indeterminate date in the future; as the only man who opposed the destruction of the memoirs, he was outnumbered and outvoted, despite his pleas with Hobhouse that 'I told you I would be no party to the burning'. Byron's friend, implacable in his desire to see the act done, replied, 'you did not – you only said you would not be present at the burning'.[13] The assembled company then set about tearing up the memoirs, as Moore looked helplessly on. The scraps were placed inside the fireplace and burned, and the assembled company, Moore notwithstanding, parted with the sense of worthy accomplishment. The friendship between Moore and Hobhouse, however, never recovered.*

Despite suggestive clues, we will almost certainly never encounter the contents of Byron's memoirs. It is not impossible that a

---

* Although this story might seem to indicate that Hobhouse was to blame for the destruction of Byron's legacy, it is he who should be credited with ensuring the survival of many of Byron's letters and papers; Moore, meanwhile, destroyed the ones in his possession.

copy was secretly made in Paris or elsewhere, whether at Byron's instigation or at Moore's, and still survives today, lurking unacknowledged in the corner of some great library or dusty archive. However, in its absence, one can only speculate what reputation-wrecking scandal they contained.

∾

Byron's Women is not intended to recreate the contents of the memoirs. Yet, through careful reconstruction, fresh consideration of little-known letters and journals and an alternative approach to the subject, I hope to suggest why, exactly, his friends and literary executors were so desperate to destroy a work that would have deepened our understanding of an enigmatic figure, as well as the women that played so crucial a role in his life. The fire in Albemarle Street destroyed Byron's writing. It did not destroy his legacy.

PART I

Catherine

1

Trust in Byron.

BYRON FAMILY MOTTO

I t was always said that the Gordons walked with the devil. Their ancestral seat, Gight Castle in Scotland, was a bleak, miserable place that had been built in the sixteenth century and had been the target of whisperings of witchcraft and ill-doing ever since. The family inhabiting it were said to be notorious for defying law and order.[1] The grimmest of all the stories about Gight came from the time of the Covenanters' Wars in 1644, when the laird, Lewis Gordon, hid his jewels in a natural well close to the castle known as Hagberry Pot. When Gordon asked one of his factotums to retrieve the jewels, the shaken young man returned and claimed that Satan himself guarded the treasure. However, the laird was no less intimidating a figure than Lucifer, and so the hapless diver was sent back once again to Hagberry Pot. The jewels were never seen again, but the young man's body reappeared a few minutes later, neatly cut into four pieces. His spirit was said to roam the castle, desperately seeking his missing body and lasting peace.

It was at this unsettled and frightening place that, just over a century later, in April 1764, Catherine, the latest in the Gordon line, was born. Her father George died when she was only fourteen, and her mother and sisters had predeceased her,* meaning

---

* Catherine never mentioned their deaths to Byron, who believed all his life that she had been an only child.

that she inherited a substantial portion of the family fortune – around £30,000 – and Gight Castle itself, as well as becoming the 13th Laird of Gight. Her grandmother Margaret Duff Gordon brought her up in isolation, instilling in the impressionable girl a mixture of histrionic emotion and a rough understanding of what her position was to be. Described by her friend Pryse Gordon as 'a romping, good-humoured girl… inclined to corpulency',[2] she was frustrated and bored by the austerity of her surroundings. Although not academically gifted, she had a keen interest in her family's macabre history. Clairvoyance and the supernatural were an everyday part of Catherine's existence, and she stimulated herself by revelling in sensationalist books.

She lived at a time when the first Gothic novels were appearing, and knew the prototype of the genre, Horace Walpole's Romantic horror of 1764, *The Castle Of Otranto*, which combined a mysterious and intrigue-laden storyline with a forbidding location. She had first-hand experience of haunted castles and the secrets that their walls contained, so there were no revelations. However, she had never encountered a man like Walpole's nefarious but charismatic antagonist Manfred, who, by the end of the first chapter, had embraced 'the next transition of his soul to exquisite villainy'.[3] Living in the depths of the Scottish countryside, with no friends or confidantes, she believed – or feared – that she would never encounter a Manfred in real life.

She soon discovered otherwise.

❧

John Byron was better known by his nickname of 'Mad Jack'. Colourful appellations ran in the family. His father, another John, had served with distinction in the navy as a vice-admiral, but had become better known for his unreliable and often violent behaviour, possibly caused by syphilis. His heroic sobriquet of 'Foul-weather Jack' was consequently bastardized into 'the wicked Lord'.[4] The elder John made the family name synonymous with scandal on

26 January 1765 when he killed his neighbour Viscount Chaworth in a brawl in a Pall Mall tavern. This forced his retirement to his family seat, the tumbledown estate of Newstead Abbey in Nottinghamshire, which was rumoured to be haunted by the ghosts of the monks who had been evicted during the Reformation. Here he went half-mad, and rumours were heard of everything from spousal abuse to the murder of his coachman. It was an unimpressive example for the chaotic Jack to set, and an unfortunate place for his eldest son and namesake to grow up. The family's ancestral motto, *Crede Byron* ('Trust in Byron'), therefore took on an ironic taint.

Born on 7 February 1756, Jack had an undistinguished early career at Westminster School and at a military academy in Paris, where he achieved little other than becoming notorious for 'pastimes and prodigalities'.[5] Handsome and charismatic, but self-obsessed and venal, he cut a dash through society, enchanting beautiful women by the score. He even acted as a gigolo; clearly his conquests were sufficiently captivated by the handsome young man to have considered their pleasures worth paying for.[6] Yet the money that he received was barely sufficient to cover his gambling debts, let alone keep him in the style that he believed he deserved. His father, disgusted by the prodigal's extravagances, disinherited him, leaving him penniless. As a result, Jack set about looking for a wife: ideally one who was malleable, wealthy and beautiful. The last was negotiable, but the other two were not.

First, he entangled himself with Amelia Osborne, Lady Carmarthen, whose £4,000 a year beguiled as much as her other charms. She was already married, and the mother of three young children, but Jack's swashbuckling charisma enraptured her. After she obtained a divorce from her appalled husband, the two were married on 9 June 1779, and moved to France in a 'vortex of dissipation'[7] to avoid the censure of a society that had been disgusted by their love affair. It would not be the last time that a Byron fled England with the shocked whispers of his country pursuing him. Once Jack and Amelia were settled in France, where they moved between Paris and Chantilly, he attempted to provide himself with a heir; she bore three children in five years. Only the youngest, Augusta, who was born on 26 January 1783, survived; Amelia died on 26 January 1784 of what was said to be everything from consumption or fever to 'ill usage' by her husband.*[8] In any case, Jack was now left a penniless widower with a young child and little else. Leaving Augusta in the care of his sister Frances, he puffed himself up once more and set about searching for his next wife, or victim.

&

The place to which fortune hunters, ladies of pleasure and the *beau monde* in general headed in the late eighteenth century was Bath. The dandy and man-of-taste Beau Nash, who had died two decades before, had succeeded in turning a small spa town into the most fashionable resort in England, and one that had much scandal and gossip attached to it. The previous decade, the young playwright Richard Sheridan had eloped with his lover Elizabeth Linley after defending her honour in a violent duel with his rival Captain Thomas Mathews, and had nearly died in the process. It was undoubtedly a beautiful place, thanks to the grand architectural schemes of the John Woods *père et fils*, but lust and intrigue flowed through the town just as freely as the spa waters.

It was in Bath's crescents and salons that Catherine Gordon and Jack Byron first met in early 1785. He was nearly thirty, both an experienced man of the world and a penniless widower drowning in debt. She was on the cusp of twenty-one, and had never left Scotland before; she was in Bath to visit her uncle, Admiral Robert Duff, and her aunt: representatives of the grander circles of Bath society. Her stay there was intended to be brief. It would allow the young

---

* Byron defended his father against these accusations, claiming 'so far from being brutal, he was, according to the testimony of all those who knew him, of an extremely amiable and joyous character'. One might argue that his father's downfall lay entirely in this 'amiable and joyous character'.

heiress to see how the English conducted their pleasures, to buy a few trinkets and perhaps to be flirted with at some of the dances and salons to which her relatives would chaperone her. Duff and his wife knew that the inexperienced Catherine was an easy target for fortune-hunters. She was far from attractive, being 'awkward in her movements, provincial in her accent and manner',[9] as well as overweight and plain. Additionally, she possessed a sense of vanity engendered by her wealth and birth; like all her family, she was said to be 'as proud as Lucifer' of being a Gordon.[10] Her arrival in Bath stirred up some unwelcome memories, as it was here that her father had died by drowning, in what was widely believed to be suicide.*[11]

Nonetheless, murmurs of her wealth soon reached Jack's ears, helped by her donning expensive (if ill-suited) clothes. Her father's death had led to the local newspaper describing her as 'possessed of a considerable estate'[12] and he set about trying to impress the naïve young woman with his charm, elegant dancing and good looks. He succeeded entirely. Ignoring the advice of her aunt and uncle, Catherine agreed to marry the captain virtually immediately, and the two were wed at St Michael's church in Bath on Friday, 13 May 1785. Both ignored the unlucky connotations of the date. Catherine, thrilled to be marrying a real-life incarnation of the handsome heroes that she had encountered in her novels, was overjoyed by what seemed like extraordinary good fortune on her part. It was to be the last time in her life that she felt such uncomplicated happiness.

The nuptials were not entirely to Jack's advantage. While he had achieved his aim of marrying another wealthy heiress, he had consequently pledged himself to a woman altogether less attractive than those to whom he was used to making love. It also became clear that he was not to be allowed untrammelled access to her finances. Her parents had known enough of their daughter's fecklessness to place severe restrictions on her financial autonomy, meaning that Jack, debt-ridden and impoverished as ever, was unable to do

* Catherine's grandfather had also died in a similar way.

anything other than pass his debts on to his wife, and try his best to
find new lenders who were sufficiently impressed by his new standing to offer him credit. He had even been compelled to add his
wife's name to his own, thanks to a clause in Catherine's parents'
will that had stipulated either that she should marry a Gordon or
that her husband should take her name; as a result, he was now
known as John Byron Gordon, a necessity if he was to be allowed
any money. With his new wife and identity, he reluctantly headed
up to Scotland and Gight Castle with her shortly after their marriage. His son later sardonically referred to the few weeks between
their wedding and arrival at Gight as a 'treacle-moon', hinting at
difficulties from the beginning.[13]

If either had false expectations of the other, they were soon
dispelled. Catherine was horrified by her husband's financial profligacy and his belief that it was his new wife's duty to pay his vast
debts. In the early months of their marriage she was forced to sell
farms, fisheries and shares just to accommodate her husband's
extravagances and exhausted the £3,000 cash that formed her
dowry, as well as taking out an £8,000 loan against Gight.[14] Jack
fancied himself as something of a grandee, and began to entertain
political ambitions, none of which came to anything. The locals
regarded him as a laughing stock. They were never well disposed
towards Englishmen, especially one who had spent time in France
and carried dandyish airs. A satirical ballad began to circulate that
mocked both him and the 'bonnie and braw' Catherine:

> O whare are ye gaeing, bonny Miss Gordon?
> O, whare are ye gaeing, sae bonnie and braw?
> Ye've married, wi' Johnny Byron
> To squander the lands o'Gight awa'.
> This youth is a rake, frae England is come,
> The Scots dinna ken his extraction ava;
> He keeps up his misses, his landlords he duns,
> That's fast drawn the lands o'Gight awa.[15]

It soon became clear that neither Jack nor Catherine was going to be able to maintain a life in the miserable surroundings of Gight. A year after their marriage they returned to England, having heard of the death of his father. Perhaps, the ever-optimistic Jack reasoned, the admiral had forgiven him his earlier profligacies and remembered him in his will now that he was a respectably married man, and to a Scottish heiress to boot. He was to be disappointed; there was to be no forgiveness for Mad Jack and only £500 left to him in the will,[16] meaning that his financial state remained desperate. Initially, he took advantage of the excitements of London, but a brief spell in a debtor's prison reminded him that his difficulties remained pressing, and, in between trying to charm or bully money from his remaining relatives, he gave notice that Gight should be sold, and the proceeds remitted to him.

Catherine was soon resigned to her husband's faults. When she wrote to her cousin Mary Urquhart later in 1786, it was with a mixture of distrust, resignation and fear:

> The best that I could wish or expect (from the sale) would be £10,000... I would have that settled in such a manner that it would be out of Mr Byron's power to spend, and out of my own power to give up to him... I should not wish [that] Mr Byron should know that I wrote or spoke to anybody upon the subject, because if he did he would never forgive me... for God's sake mention [this] to nobody but who is necessary.[17]

There was nowhere else that she could turn. She and her husband were pitched upon one another, devoid of money, family or friends. As Jack attempted to flee his creditors, moving from home to home, Catherine saw the ruin of her romantic dreams of the previous year. Her Manfred had indeed appeared, in the most disappointing of forms.

Their marital relations, at least, continued, and in early 1787 Catherine became pregnant with her first child. By then, Gight had been bought by the 3rd Earl of Aberdeen for £17,850 ,[18] but the vast majority of the cash had either been swallowed up by Jack's debts or was kept in trust in Scotland by Catherine's agents, who knew that she was incapable of refusing her husband's demands. Jack kept running about England, spending what little he was allowed on his dissipated pleasures; typically, when he was given £700 by Catherine in July, he headed off on a two-month trip to Paris, during which time he spent every penny of it and ran up extra debts as well. To put this into contemporary context, the money that he took with him would today be worth around £50,000 – enough for all but the most committed of reprobates.

Pitching up at Chantilly, where his brother George lived, Jack summoned his heavily pregnant wife and asked that she bring her stepdaughter Augusta to join them in France. His motives in unifying his family lay less in a desire for harmony and more in a desire to cajole what little money he could from his spouse. The long-suffering Catherine headed to France for a short time, nursing the sickly Augusta while her husband racked up new expenses with a gaiety that belied his poverty and her pregnancy. Eventually, she returned to England, placed Augusta in the charge of her grandmother Lady Holderness – whose attitude towards her second daughter-in-law was one of contemptuous dismissal – and in mid-December 1787 rented lodgings in the respectable surroundings of 16 Holles Street, a small street adjacent to Cavendish Square. It was here that she would give birth to her first child, and she prepared for her confinement with a glum stoicism. When one of her Scottish agents offered her money out of the little that remained she responded, 'I don't want much and if there was to be large sums it would only be thrown away as it was before.'[19]

The instigator of this waste arrived in the capital at the beginning of 1788, fresh from his latest revels. He resumed his previous existence of moving across the country at speed, avoiding his creditors wherever he went; while he was occasionally in London, he was not present at the birth of his son on 22 January. As it was a Tuesday, it was not subject to the amnesty that debtors were allowed on the Sabbath, and he spent the day in hiding, a state to which he had become accustomed. By now, Jack Byron was far from the devil-may-care figure who had sold his body for wealthy women's pleasure a few years before.

Had he attended the birth of his heir, he was unlikely to have enjoyed the event. As Catherine was unable to afford a midwife and nurse of good quality, and had no friends who could offer advice, she was obliged to rely on the inferior staff engaged by her solicitor John Hanson. These wretches, a man called Combe and a woman called Mills, proved unequal to the task, and so her son's birth was a botched affair. Whether or not the delivery itself resulted in damage to the boy's right foot, the amateurs had no idea what to do after the complex labour. A nearby surgeon, John Hunter, was called in for advice, and suggested that the boy would only be able to walk with the aid of an orthopaedic shoe when he was older, but that nothing could be done for the time being. This advice, and lack of medical treatment, hung over Byron for the rest of his life. On a more positive note, the boy was born with a caul, which was seen as a sign of good fortune and a harbinger of greatness.*

The boy was baptized at St Marylebone Parish Church on 29 February 1788, with Jack again absent. By now, his debts amounted to around £1300. Their son was given the name George Gordon Byron, acknowledging both Catherine's father and his own father's yoked-together surnames. By now, Catherine had somehow got word to her profligate husband of both her delivery and of their son's damaged foot, and he nonchalantly remarked to his sister Frances,† 'for my son, I am happy he is well, but for his walking,

* A piece of membrane covering the face. Others born with a caul include the eclectic mix of Byron's idol Napoleon Bonaparte, Sigmund Freud, Liberace and George Formby.
† It is likely that Jack and Frances had an incestuous relationship, judging by the letters that they sent one another; this, of course, had a sequel.

'tis impossible, as he is club-footed'.[20] If this does not smack of any great interest, it is perhaps unsurprising: Byron was Jack's fourth child and, after two of them had died, he was resigned to the likelihood of it happening again. He had written to Catherine's land agent James Watson in a similar vein the previous month, noting that 'she was brought to bed of a son on Monday last, and is far from well.'*[21] The letter was sent from Edinburgh; Jack's fortunes showed no signs of amelioration.

His wife, meanwhile, was beset with worries, both about her son's health and her parlous state. She informed Watson that her husband should not be allowed to fritter away any money earmarked for paying his debts: 'he will only pay what he is obliged to pay and there will be still more debts coming in and more demands for money'. But she remained helpless in the face of his extravagance, and remarked, 'I am sorry he is getting a new carriage.' Knowing her husband's invincible lack of financial acumen, she added briskly that 'I want money to be sent to me while in town and I must have it as if Mr Byron gets it it will be thrown away in some foolish way or other and I shall be obliged to apply for more.'[22] That Catherine – still only twenty-two – had grown up extremely quickly was undeniable, and the naiveté of the young girl swept off her feet by a dashing suitor had quickly ceded to bitterer feelings.

Although Jack remained persuasive, either through force of personality or simple force – a London attorney, Thomas Becket, told Watson that 'Mrs Byron is afraid she has not the resolution to refuse any request Mr Byron may make her personally'[23] – his appearances at home were fleeting and brief. He wrote to Frances on 21 March in melancholy mood, and mourned that 'my father and now my sister† dying within a few years really makes me reflect that it will be my turn soon, and I am quite depressed'. Mindful as ever of money, he complained that 'my income is but small, and

* Byron was actually born on a Tuesday.
† Jack is referring to his other sister, Julianna, Lady Wilmot, who had died on 15 March in Derbyshire.

what there is of it is settled on Mrs Byron and the child, therefore I am obliged to live in a narrow circle which I need not have done'.[24] A more intelligent or sophisticated man might have exercised some restraint or common sense when it came to his debts, but Jack, hopelessly weak-willed, simply wondered whether he 'might run again into extravagance… by buying horses and perhaps hounds… in short I cannot answer for myself'.[25] He contemplated a return to France, but even that was beyond his meagre income, and he feared that his more persistent creditors would pursue him across the Channel. He continued to roam the country, pathetically asking what few friends and relatives he had remaining for 'loans'.

He had seen his wife and son in early March 1788, and, when they headed up to Aberdeen in 1789, he briefly accompanied them to Catherine's lodgings in Queen Street. While their new home was hardly the cosmopolitan centre that London and Bath had been – Catherine complained that a bonnet 'was out of fashion in London before it arrived here'[26] – it was not devoid of culture, boasting playhouses and bookshops and a thriving port that brought trade and money to the city. Perhaps Catherine hoped that the relative lack of opportunities for wilder excitements would curtail Jack's spendthrift tendencies and enable the three of them to live together as a family, or maybe Jack thought that he would be able to extract money from Catherine more easily if they lived under the same roof.

He was to be disappointed. From the wealthy young heiress who had arrived in Bath with an estate and plentiful money in hand, Catherine had been reduced to an annual income of £150 from the sale of Gight, an adequate enough amount for her and her son, but nowhere near enough to support her extravagant husband as well. Their relations descended into arguing and scolding, partially remedied when Jack took a house at the other end of the street, but there was no ultimate reconciliation. Once, in an effort to prove his worth as a father, Jack offered to look after his son for a night. The experiment was not a success and the child was returned early the next morning. Shortly after this, in September 1790, Jack left his wife and son and Aberdeen for good, heading to his sister's house in France, leaving a trail of bills and debts totalling around £300 in his wake. He never saw either of them again, and, after a few months of further self-indulgence and affairs with actresses and local girls ('I believe I have had one third of Valenciennes,' he wrote to the apparently unshockable Frances in December), he ran out of money for the final time. He developed tuberculosis, the same illness that had killed his first wife, Amelia, and despite his protestations that it was little more than a cold, died on 2 August 1791 at the age of just thirty-five. His last thoughtless act of cruelty was to leave nothing to his wife or children, but instead to saddle the three-year-old Byron with his funeral expenses.

Catherine spent the final months of her husband's life fruitlessly trying to appeal to Frances for a much-needed loan of £30 or £40, on the doubtful grounds that she was responsible for her brother's extravagance. Frances, who had received similar begging letters from Jack, made an attempt to reconcile the family. She suggested a meeting in France, but Catherine demurred; she wrote that 'it will not be possible for me to leave Scotland for some time', due to a lack of funds and the difficulty of taking her young son with her. Instead, she asked if Frances could deliver a letter to the surgeon John Hunter concerning a 'proper shoe' for her son. Poignantly, she alluded to her isolation by asking 'pray, what is going on in the world for I am quite out of it here? Are we to have war? Do you ever hear anything of little Augusta and how she is?'[27] When her sister-in-law replied, Catherine learned of Jack's death, and was said to have howled so violently and piteously that her lamenting for her 'dear Jonnie' could be heard in the street.[28] He might have been inconstant and useless as a husband, but he had at least *been* a husband, and now another member of her family was no more. Frances's letter has been lost, but it is clear that it did not anticipate the strength of reaction that it would provoke. Catherine therefore wrote back to her on 23 August to set the record straight. She stated

that 'necessity, not inclination, parted us, at least on my part…
notwithstanding all his foibles… I ever sincerely loved him… I do
not think I shall ever recover the severe shock I have received'.
As for his son, he was only three, but Byron later claimed to be
able to remember Jack well, saying to his friend Thomas Medwin
that '(he) had very early a horror of matrimony from the sight of
domestic broils – he seemed born for his own ruin and that of the
other sex'.[29] Like father, like son.

At least her errant husband's death now meant that no further
debt could be incurred on his part, and so Catherine's attention
turned to providing for her small son. The two of them moved
from Queen Street to the main road, Broad Street, and lived on the
first floor of a house there along with their maid, Agnes Grey. Byron
was proving to be troublesome even from a young age; already
self-conscious about his lame foot, he once attacked another nurse
who spoke patronizingly of his deformity, crying 'Dinna speak of
it!'[30] At this age, the boy spoke with his mother's strong Scottish
accent, something that would later cause him embarrassment. A
happier occurrence was that Catherine joined the local subscription
library, and encouraged her son to read widely and inquisitively.
This nascent interest in learning was helped by Byron's being sent
to a local school run by a man named Bower; it was 'a mixed school
of good esteem though small pretentious [sic]'. Catherine, recog-
nizing that her son could potentially be troublesome, asked the
master to make sure that Byron was 'kept in about',[31] or in check.
It would be Bower who was responsible for his early spiritual education, in thought, word and deed. He did not quite succeed, and
Byron was soon transmitted to the care of a new tutor, a clergyman
named Ross, under whom he made what he modestly called 'an
astonishing progress'.[32]

While the relationship between Byron and Catherine would
soon be less easy, he was initially a charming and curious boy
whose greatest wickedness was his habit of pricking his mother's
arms with a hatpin when they attended the local church together.

Despite the undistinguished circumstances in which they lived, Catherine took pride in reminding her son about his aristocratic background and about the high breeding that she had enjoyed. She also implied that the Byron family were disreputable; he later told John Murray that she set great store by her descent from 'the old Gordons, not the Seyton Gordons, as she disdainfully termed the Ducal branch... [and she reminded me] how superior her Gordons were to the Southern Byrons'.[33] Byron soon discovered the less savoury side of the Gordon dynasty, something that gave him amused pleasure rather than shock. The mother instilled her liberal political sympathies into her son; Catherine had been a Whig sympathizer from an early age. She supported the French Revolution, and wrote to Frances to say that 'I am quite a Democrat and I do not think the King, after his treachery and perjury, deserves to be restored'.*[34]

Although she was living in near poverty, Catherine still believed her aristocratic background to be an integral part of her bearing. She was aided in this by a reconciliation with her grandmother Lady Gight, who had despaired of her marriage to Jack Byron, but was now a neighbour in nearby Banff. Lady Gight doted on her great-grandson, who was allowed to play tricks and create mayhem and get away with it. On one occasion he created a dummy dressed in his clothes and let it fall out of a window to the accompaniment of his own shrieks. His mother was so relieved that he was not injured that she forgave him his transgression.

Catherine adored her son, who was beginning to grow up into a very striking boy. A portrait painted of him by William Kay when he was seven shows a confident-looking youth holding a bow and arrow, with a keen eye on the bullseye before him. However, an altogether different sort of target had been placed before mother and son a few months before, when, in July 1794, Byron had

* She had her wish; Louis XVI was executed less than two months later, on 21 January 1793.

become the heir-but-one to the estates of his paternal grandfather John, after his cousin (and John's other grandson) was killed at the Siege of Calvi in Corsica during the French Revolutionary Wars. At last, it seemed possible that the fortune of the Byron Gordons might be about to return to their previous heights.

As a result, the boy was removed from his tutors and sent to the local grammar school, where he was given the rudiments of a classical education – or as he described it later, 'Latin, Latin, Latin'. It suited a young aristocrat to know his way around some famous texts, but it was not a life that he relished; he later claimed that as a young boy, he hated poetry.[35] Catherine, however, had grand ambitions for her son, and Aberdeen Grammar School did not have the cachet that the English public schools possessed. She asked Frances whether the last remaining Lord Byron might be prepared to pay for his relative's education and to pay for it by selling unwanted parts of the estate. She enquired earnestly, 'Do you think he will do anything for George, or be at any expense to give him a proper education, or, if he wish to do it, is his present fortune such a one that he could spare anything out of it?'[36] Unsurprisingly, given the low reputation that Jack had enjoyed with his family, no help was forthcoming for his heir. In the meantime, the eight-year-old Byron contracted a dose of scarlet fever, and developed what would be the first of many *grand amours*, this one for his cousin, Mary Duff, who lived nearby in Aberdeen and whom he encountered at a dancing school. He would later say, 'How odd that I should have been so utterly devoted to that girl at an age when I could neither feel passion or know the meaning of the word.'[37]

Catherine also attempted to instruct Byron in the arts. Mother and son visited the local playhouse from his earliest years, and at the age of nine he saw a production of *Romeo and Juliet*, with an excerpt from *The Taming of the Shrew* appended to it. Byron, already showing a tendency to challenge expected norms, responded to the actor playing Petruchio's line 'Nay, then, I swear it is the blessed sun' by standing on his chair and shouting, 'But I say it is the moon, sir!'[38] Yet relations between mother and son became fraught, because a boy of great intelligence and rebelliousness enjoyed causing trouble for its own sake. Byron later recalled that, while still in Aberdeen, '[my mother and the maid] once in one of my silent rages wrenched a knife from me, which I had snatched from table at Mrs Byron's dinner... and applied to my breast'.[39] The dramatic force of the image is only undermined by its absurdity. But then, the young Byron had by that time fully absorbed his mother's sense of entitlement. When Catherine read one of her friends a rousing political speech, she tried to include and flatter the boy by saying 'we shall have the pleasure of reading your speeches in the House of Commons'. Byron was said to pause, and then remarked, contemptuously, 'I hope not... if you read any speeches of mine it will be in the House of Lords.'[40]

Byron did not have long to wait before joining the ranks of the English nobility. Old Lord Byron died on 19 May 1798, and the ten-year-old boy became the 6th Baron Byron of Rochdale, an event that was celebrated at his school with gifts of cake and wine. He greeted the change in his fortunes firstly by bursting into tears, and then by asking his mother 'whether she perceived any change in him since he had become a lord for he perceived none himself'.[41] After Catherine managed to sell what few pieces of furniture she possessed, out of which she paid for the previous Lord Byron's funeral, they left for the ancestral seat of the Byrons, Newstead Abbey in Nottinghamshire, in August. They were accompanied by the boy's nanny, May Gray. As they travelled down through the country, neither of them had any idea that their lives were about to change forever.

2

I will cut myself a path through the world
or perish in the attempt.

BYRON TO CATHERINE GORDON,
I MAY 1804

C atherine knew nothing of her son's erotic awakening. An inexperienced woman when it came to sex, she had few admirers after Jack's death.* While she was first enraptured and then disappointed with her husband, her energies initially went into keeping herself and Byron at the periphery of respectability, and then, when her son came into his expectations, ensuring that he would behave with the dignity and decorum that his new place in society merited. However, while she was not a stupid woman, her unworldliness when it came to carnal matters sometimes showed itself in unfortunate fashion.

Catherine, Byron and May Gray arrived at Newstead Abbey after an exhausting journey of nearly 400 miles that took several days on the public coach, the Aberdeen and Edinburgh Fly; Byron's ennoblement had not yet resulted in any money being released from the estate of his grandfather. Nonetheless, all of them were in high spirits, as George Moore recounts in a revealing anecdote in his *Life of Byron*. Arriving at a tollgate near the Abbey, Catherine asked the keeper if there was an estate nearby, and upon being told there was, asked who owned it. The keeper responded that 'it was Lord Byron, but now he's dead'. Catherine disingenuously asked

* With one possible exception, Monsieur Saint-Louis; see pp. 38.

who the current heir was. When he replied 'they say a little boy that lives in Aberdeen', May Gray pulled Byron on to her knee, caressed and kissed him demonstratively and said 'this is him, God bless him'.[1] The incongruity of a not-so-little ten-year-old being embraced in this fashion by his nanny should have alerted Catherine to the possibility that their relationship was not normal, but she either chose to ignore it, or genuinely saw nothing untoward.

In any case, their arrival at Newstead in August 1798 put such considerations out of their minds. Earlier in the century, Horace Walpole had said in admiration that 'Newstead is the very abbey',[2] and its ruined grandeur excited Byron's imagination from the first moment he saw it. Despite the fact that it was barely habitable as it stood, with roofs missing, animals grazing inside rooms and little in the way of comfort, it offered Catherine a second chance to inhabit somewhere on the scale of Gight. On their arrival they were given a cautious welcome by the solicitor John Hanson, newly arrived from London. Hanson, who would become a crucial figure in Byron's life, was all too aware of the task ahead of them. He was keen to deal with the legal complexities as quickly as possible, meaning that Byron could inherit both his title and the Abbey without any threat of a challenge from some disgruntled distant branch of the family. Hanson became his guardian, given the young lord's status as a minor. Catherine, meanwhile, was faced with the pleasing prospect of her minuscule income of £150 increasing as much as tenfold, even if immediate money was lacking, and legal fees threatened to swallow much of the legacy; the new overseer, Owen Mealey, was told that there were no funds available to buy him a bed.[3] Newstead was reputedly worth £90,000, but its selling points were well concealed by its state of disrepair.

Nonetheless, there was pleasure to be had in exploring the Abbey in the late summer weather, and the boy enjoyed both the spaciousness and novelty of his new surroundings. His sense of *joie de vivre* rubbed off on his mother. Hanson told another lawyer, James Farquhar, that 'Mrs Gordon (Mrs Byron)… has a great wish to live at Newstead – I doubt very much the prudence of it at least at first, it strikes me it would be better for her to take a house or lodgings in or near London til the affairs are arranged.'[4] But Catherine, who remembered the grim time that she had spent there previously, refused to return to the capital, preferring to stay at Newstead. Hanson also had a clear idea of what the young Byron was like; he described him as 'a fine sharp boy not a little spoiled by indulgence but that is scarcely to be wondered at'.[5]

Catherine, meanwhile, was enjoying her new life, especially as she had managed to regain some of the respectability that she had lost after her marriage. Some of her husband's relatives lived nearby in Nottingham, including the previous lord's brother's widow, Frances, whose eccentricity and querulousness led the young Byron to mock her in a poem:

> In Nottingham county there lives at Swine Green
> As cursed an old lady as ever was seen,
> And when she does die, which I hope will be soon,
> She firmly believes she will go to the moon.[6]

Despite his distaste for his aunt, Byron was soon uprooted from the congenial surroundings of Newstead to stay with Frances and the other Byrons in Nottingham in the winter of 1798, leaving his mother at the Abbey to attempt to impose order there. One of her first actions was to raise the estate's income by increasing the rents paid by the tenant farmers, which led to resentment and some grumbling about the new owners. But people did not underestimate Catherine. Necessity had toughened her from the romantic, silly girl who had married hastily thirteen years before. Now, aided by Hanson, her priority was to restore Newstead, and then her family's fortunes. In order for her to concentrate on this endeavour, she needed to place her son in the hands of others for a short while.

Byron had his second brush with a girl of around his own age when he was introduced to his cousin Mary Ann Chaworth; his grandfather had murdered her great-uncle twenty years before.[7] The macabre overtones to their encounter did not stop him from conceiving an affection for her. This was so clear that, when she reappeared at Newstead for a second visit, Hanson lightly teased Byron by saying 'here is a pretty young lady – you had better marry her'. Byron, however, was equal to his lawyer's mocking, responding, with an unusually advanced sensitivity to his family's bizarre situation, 'what, Mr Hanson, the Capulets and the Montagues intermarry?'[8] His youthful assurance was obvious in a letter that he had written from Newstead in November to his aunt Charlotte: 'My mamma being unable to write herself desires I will let you know that the potatoes are now ready and you are welcome to them whenever you please.' The note of largesse being dispensed – as if from on high – is reinforced by his concluding sentence: 'My mamma desires her best compliments to you all in which I join.'[9]

Byron and his mother spent the next few months apart as she attempted to extract more money from the tenant farmers at Newstead; he remained in Nottingham with neighbours of his aunt, the Parkyns. In a letter to Catherine written in mid-March 1799 from their house, Gridlesmith Gate, he remarked: 'upon my word I did not expect so long a letter from you'. Catherine was missing him and had written to him at some length to alleviate the tedium. Byron, however, was anything but bored. He asked to be given a new tutor, Mr 'Dummer' Rogers, and asserted, pertly:

> I am astonished you do not acquiesce in this scheme which would keep me in mind of what I have almost entirely forgot...
> if some plan of this kind is not adopted I shall be called or rather branded with the name of dunce which you know I could not bear.[10]

A postscript to Byron's letter included the words: 'May desires her duty'. When he had moved to Nottingham, the attentive May had accompanied him. One of her duties was to make sure that, among other things, his foot was looked after, to which end he visited a nearby surgeon, Lavender. In fact, it was his entire body that was taken care of by May Gray, against his wishes. While she presented a persona that was pious and loving, urging Byron to follow his Bible studies and to grow up with *mens sana in corpore sano*, she was systematically abusing the boy. The details of the abuse are unclear, but it seems to have begun in Aberdeen and continued after the move to Newstead. Byron later wrote that 'my passions were developed very early – so early, that few would believe me, if I were to state the period, and the facts which accompanied it'. It was to Hanson that Byron first confided what he was suffering at her hands, and the solicitor later described it to Byron's friend Hobhouse, who commented after Byron's death both that it was 'much less romantic and more satisfactory than the *amour* with Mary Duff' – satisfactory for both parties, or for one? – and that 'when [Byron was] nine years old at his mother's house, a free Scotch girl used to come to bed to him & play tricks with his person'.[11]

May's bad behaviour was not restricted to the bedroom. Intoxicated and frustrated, she beat Byron savagely, so much so that Hanson later informed Catherine that 'his bones sometimes ached from it', and that, when she was not molesting the boy, 'she brought all sorts of company of the lowest description into his apartments... was out late at nights, and he was frequently left to put himself to bed'. Casting her apparent gentility and respectability aside, she kept company with the familiars of the local tavern. Hanson told Catherine gravely that, in her drunken state, 'she has even – traduced yourself'.[12]

In September 1799, Byron travelled from Nottingham to London to visit various doctors, who were attempting to find an appropriate treatment for his damaged foot. These he saw on the advice of Lord Carlisle, Jack's cousin, who had become an informal mentor to the boy. During his stay, Byron was a guest of Hanson's, and was accompanied by May, allowing his guardian to see her

activities at first hand, as well as her ward's fear of her. Appalled by
her true character, he banished her back to Newstead and informed
Catherine, who had been ignorant of the situation until Hanson
illuminated her; May was dismissed soon afterwards.* Matters
were soon sufficiently transparent for Byron to write to Hanson
from his new school in Dulwich, Dr Glennie's Academy, to say
'since you are going to Newstead I beg if you meet Gray send her
a-packing as fast as possible.'[13]

There are no surviving letters between Catherine and Byron that
record the activities and subsequent ousting of his erstwhile nurse.
But Catherine's reaction must have been one of profound shock
and embarrassment, not least since she would have believed that
her son's newly elevated position in society – and her own by association – rendered him above such indignities. And she must also
have felt anger that a woman she had trusted entirely had proved
capable of such actions.

In the summer of 1799, at Hanson's behest, she wrote to court
officials to ask for recognition of her and her son. A typical letter
is the one she wrote to the Tory leader in the House of Commons,
the Duke of Portland, in which, after describing her loss of fortune, she asked for charity by saying, 'I am myself descended from
an ancient and noble family… it has been mentioned to me that
persons in my situation have been thought [the] object of His
Majesty's bounty.'†[14] Her request was successful, and she received
£300 a year out of the Civil List, with immediate effect. She wrote
gratefully to Hanson:

> As you have been so very friendly to me in the business which
> I shall ever remember with gratitude, I have lost no time in

---

* The removal was not immediate; there was at least a six-week gap
between May Gray's return to Newstead and subsequent journey back to
Scotland.
† The letter was actually ghosted by Hanson, and Catherine filled in
points of detail.

sending you a copy of the Duke's letter as I am sure from the friendship you have shown me you will rejoice at it.[15]

To be closer to Byron, Catherine headed to London and took lodgings in Sloane Terrace, near the Hansons. But relations between mother and son were far from smooth. Byron, whose undoubted intelligence was combined with a tendency to be precociously annoying, misbehaved and defied his mother. Hanson's son Newton later wrote that 'Mrs Byron showed a great fondness for her son, but it was occasionally interrupted by a contrary disposition. She was certainly fickle in her humour and treatment of him but on the whole they were very fond of each other.' Newton also noted that 'Byron had a sad trick of biting his nails which sometimes used to call forth from his mother sudden and violent ejaculations of disgust accompanied by a box on the ear or hands.'[16]

It was not a happy time for Catherine. When she first encountered Lord Carlisle on 16 January 1800, her lack of manners, coupled with her plain speech and strong Scots accent, horrified him. She meddled in her son's life and education, removing him from Glennie's school for up to a week at a time, as she believed that he learned more at home than there. Catherine made as poor an impression on Dr Glennie as she had on Carlisle, thanks to her 'audible fits of temper as it was impossible to keep from reaching the ears of the scholars and of the servants'.[17] He eventually gave vent to his anger, and suggested that not only was she ruining her son's education, but she had surrounded him with ill-natured boys who were likely to corrupt him.*[18] Catherine's response is not recorded, but Byron was soon removed from Glennie's institution (which he would later dismiss as 'a damned place'). From

---

* There is also the following telling exchange between Byron and one of his classmates, who had witnessed Catherine in full flow: 'Byron, your mother is a fool', to which the perhaps inevitable reply was '*I* know it, but *you* shan't say so' (my italics).

now on, Hanson took sole responsibility for Byron's education. As for Carlisle, he had had enough of Catherine; he wrote testily to Hanson that 'I can have nothing more to do with Mrs Byron – you must manage her as best you can'.[19]

A charitable view of Catherine's behaviour while in London was that she was clumsily trying to do what was best for her son, and, feeling guilty about his mistreatment by May Gray, attempting to ensure that he would not fall into bad company again. Unfortunately, not only was she no diplomat, but her inclination to loudness and vulgarity did not charm those whom she encountered. Glennie later stated that:

> Mrs Byron was a total stranger to English society and English manners; with an exterior far from prepossessing, and understanding where nature had not been bountiful, a mind almost wholly without cultivation and the peculiarities of northern opinions, northern habit and northern accent. I trust I do no great prejudice to the memory of my countrywoman if I say Mrs Byron was not a Madame de Lambert,* endowed with powers to retrieve the fortune, and form the character and manners of a young nobleman, her son. [20]

While May had run her reputation through the Nottingham dirt, Catherine was capable of doing the same on her own account in the capital. She had conceived an inappropriate passion for a French dancing master known as Monsieur Saint-Louis; Hanson reported in conversation with Hobhouse that she 'fell in love with a French dancing master at Brompton and laid a plan for carrying Byron to France... but (Glennie) would not let him go'.[21] If true, it is a mark of Catherine's inability to see beyond her own narrow focus; not only was Byron a minor and subject to the guardianship

* This is an allusion to the French writer Anne-Thérèse de Marguenat de Courcelles, better known as Madame de Lambert; she achieved fame with her 1726 book *Advice from a mother to her son.*

of Carlisle and Hanson at the time, but England was then at war with France. To have removed an English lord and taken him to the enemy's country would have been the height of stupidity at best, treachery at worst.

&

Byron began his education at Harrow in April 1801, having left Glennie's school a few months before. Now thirteen, he was maturing into a handsome boy, albeit an insecure one owing to his crippled foot and his fluctuating weight. The previous year, he had met and fallen in love with another of his cousins, Margaret Parker, while at Newstead for the summer. He said that she inspired his 'first dash into poetry' and called her 'one of the most beautiful of evanescent beings'.[22] Byron claimed that he could not eat, rest or sleep while apart from her – a separation which he was sufficiently self-aware to note could last as long as *twelve hours*.

While Byron wished to carry on his flirtation, his mother intended to return to London and solicit Hanson's advice on how to make Newstead financially solvent. While her son began his studies, Catherine lingered in Sloane Terrace until May, hoping to settle her financial affairs. However, they were more complex than she had believed. A peremptory letter to Hanson stated:

> It is five months since I came to town for no other purpose than to get myself settled... I am now at a loss to account for the delay. I desire that you will fix a day when you will come to my house, or I come to yours to settle accounts.

The letter ends: 'I also want thirty pounds immediately.'[23] Her stay in London had not improved Catherine's manners. When summer came, she and Byron headed to Cheltenham, where she visited a fortune-teller, who correctly discerned that she was a widow and that her son was lame, and went on to say that he would marry twice, face near-death from poisoning, and encounter great

misfortune when he was twenty-seven. This proved to be perceptive, if not entirely accurate.

After Byron returned to Harrow, Catherine headed to newly
fashionable Brighton, where she faced further difficulties. Not only
was the cost of Byron's treatment for his foot exorbitant at over £50
a year, which led her to complain to the doctor, Laurie, that 'I
think [your bill] comes extremely huge',[24] but she was involved in
a *contretemps* with a cab driver and suffered the indignity of being
summoned to a magistrate's court over an unpaid fare, which was
only resolved by the intervention of Hanson. While he knew how
difficult and demanding she could be, he was still her lawyer and
her son's legal guardian, and responsible for her as much as he was
her boy. But his help was seldom met with gratitude.

In October 1801, Catherine discovered that Augusta's grandmother Lady Holderness had died. She contacted her stepdaughter,
attempting to end a semi-estrangement that had arisen. Her
motives may have been selfless, but the hope that Augusta had now
become an heiress – and therefore was in a position to assist her
family – was uppermost. She offer condolences for her loss: 'I take
up my pen now however to console with you on the melancholy
event that has happened… [and] to assure you of the unutterable
regard and friendship of myself and son.' She reminded Augusta of
her own care of her during her earlier sickness, and stressed Byron's
love for her, saying 'although he knows so little of you, he often
mentions you to me in the most affectionate manner'. Catherine
concluded her letter with the words: 'your brother is at Harrow
school and if you wish to see him I have now no desire to keep you
asunder'.[25]

It transpired that Lady Holderness had left Augusta £350 a year
as an income. This was a considerable amount for a seventeen-
year-old, but hardly enough to allow her to be regarded as a great
heiress and insufficient to allow her to assist her half-brother
or Catherine in any meaningful way. However, there was to be
some good news for Catherine's wilting finances shortly, as her

grandmother Margaret Duff Gordon, Lady Gight, died in early December, leaving her £1200, which raised her annual income to £190; no fortune, but enough to allow her to ask Dr Laurie to continue his much-needed visits to Byron at Harrow. Laurie told her on 7 December 1801 that 'I found his foot in a much worse state than when I last saw it… I have only to add that with proper care and bandaging, his foot may still be greatly recovered; but any delay further than the present vacation would render it folly to undertake it.'[26] Her son's future mobility remained uncertain.

In early 1802, Catherine moved from Brighton back to London, taking lodgings at 23 George Street, near Portman Square. Byron stayed with her for the Easter holidays, at one point terrifying her by taking part in a horse race with his mother's friend Pryse Gordon* in Hyde Park. Gordon later recounted that, when the two had a subsequent race to Kensington Gardens, '[Catherine] would on no account permit the course… but the ride was not to be abandoned, and he gave his word he would not gallop, and kept religiously to it.' He also provided a useful insight into the fourteen-year-old Byron's relationship with his mother by quoting her comment that 'though he was a spoiled child and had too much his own way, he never did anything intentionally to disoblige or vex me'. This seems unlikely, but Gordon's words reveal Catherine's wish to save face at all times as far as her son was concerned. Gordon also described the boy, who became a lifelong friend, as being 'a fine, lively, restless lad, full of fire and energy, and passionately fond of riding'.[27] He was every bit a Byron.

Later in 1802, Catherine continued her wanderings across England, travelling from London to Cheltenham, and then returning to the scene of former glories at Bath, where she lodged at 16 Henrietta Street in late October. Newstead was by now being let to a nearby landowner, Lord Grey de Ruthyn, whom Hanson persuaded to take responsibility for the repairs and pay rent of £50

---

* Gordon was not related to Catherine.

a year until Byron came of age. This brought in welcome further income for Catherine, but Lord Grey failed to fulfil his agreement to keep Newstead in order, meaning that it sank further into disrepair.

Meanwhile, the headstrong Byron was creating difficulty at Harrow. Although the headmaster Dr Drury made allowances for Byron's foot, and saw to it that he had as easy a time of it at school as possible, Byron took to rebellion and disorder with grim pleasure, defying the teachers just as he had his mother. He initially refused to return to school at the beginning of 1803, leading Catherine to tell Hanson that 'he says he has been used ill for some time past'. She believed that his behaviour was no longer her concern, whether from a lack of care or a surfeit of it: 'you may perhaps be surprised that I do not force him to return, but he is rather too old and has too much sense for that'.[28]

Byron had a particular disdain for his housemaster (and headmaster's son), Henry Drury, and although he changed houses and eventually returned in mid-February to a new housemaster, Evans, antagonism between Byron and Henry remained.* A long and vituperative letter that he sent Catherine shortly afterwards claimed that the younger Drury had 'abused me in a most violent manner, called me *blackguard*, said he *would* and *could* have me expelled from the school… better let him take away my life than ruin my character'. He ended by an appeal to Catherine's maternal instincts, saying 'I am sure *you* will not see me *ill treated…* I believe you will be tired by this time of reading my letter, but if you love me, you will now show it… pray write me immediately.'[29] Whether or not Henry deserved such vitriol from his pupil, the tone and language of the letter was designed to arouse feelings of protective outrage from Catherine and to ensure that she remained on his side. As emotional manipulation it worked. She asked Hanson to

---

* This antagonism may have been a result of Drury being angered by his father's favouritism of Byron.

intervene, and the headmaster formally apologized on behalf of his son. Dr Drury said of Byron: '[he] possesses... a mind that feels, and that can discriminate reasonably on points in which it conceives itself injured'. Byron soon wrote to his mother cheerfully, saying that he was in a higher form and that 'Dr Drury and I go on very well'.*[30] His stratagem had succeeded.

∽

Catherine, tiring of London life again, decided to return to Nottinghamshire, taking Burgage Manor in the minster town of Southwell. A considerable step up from previous rented properties, it was a handsome manor house of the sort that a family of means might merit. However, it was not to Byron's taste. He first saw his new house in July 1803, and found it disappointing. It lacked the romance and Gothic mystery of Newstead, or the sophistication of the houses in Bath or London. He saw himself as an alien among people he did not understand or like – he described the locals as no better than 'old maids and parsons' – and they, in return, viewed him as haughty and distant. At fifteen, he was no longer the winsome boy on whom his mother had doted, but an adolescent whose impulses to roam and explore were kept in check by both his situation and his parent.

After rowing furiously with Catherine for the first few days of his return, Byron left Southwell and returned to Newstead, where Lord Grey welcomed him as an honoured guest rather than a troublesome schoolboy. Byron soon set about behaving as the lord-in-waiting. He invited the local farmers to a grand dinner (Catherine contributed £5, which proved to be entirely inadequate)[31] and resumed his acquaintance with the now eighteen-year-old Mary Chaworth, who lived at nearby Annesley Hall. Talk of the Montagues and Capulets no longer seemed so ridiculous as he conceived a desperate love for

* Ironically, Henry Drury and Byron later became good friends, and Byron was invited back to Harrow's Speech Day as an honoured guest before his travels in 1809.

her, even though she was engaged to a nearby squire, John Musters. As a result of this passion, he not only travelled the four-mile journey from Newstead to Annesley and back every day, but refused to return to Harrow in the autumn, despite saying to Catherine that 'it will make me *unhappy*; but I will *obey*'.[32]

Obedience, however, was not Byron's forte. He remained in Nottinghamshire, drifting between Newstead and Burgage, where he mooned after Mary and defied both his school and his mother. Weary and irritated, Catherine told Hanson in October that 'you may well be surprised... that Byron is not returned to Harrow. But the truth is, I cannot get him to return to school, though I have done all in my power for six weeks past.' She knew exactly why he refused to resume his studies – 'love, desperate love, the worst of all maladies in my opinion' – but frowned upon the flirtation. 'It is the last of all connections that I would wish to take place; it has given me much uneasiness.' She ended by suggesting that she had had enough of her troublesome son: 'I am determined he shall not come here again til Easter... I wish Dr Drury would keep him.'[33]

The only comfort for both Catherine and her son was the presence of Lord Grey at Newstead. Byron and the young aristocrat became intimate; his servant Mealey wrote to Hanson to report that 'they go out those moonlight nights and shoot pheasants... [Grey] kills all the game in the county',[34] and Catherine, in her visits to the Abbey, conceived an affection for him as well. Not only did he have charm and good looks, but his politics – unusually for a Tory-leaning area – were Whiggish, a point of agreement between them. The three of them got along, and a besotted Catherine wrote to Hanson on 7 November to say 'Byron is really so unhappy that I have agreed, much against my inclination, to let him remain in this county til after the next holidays'.[35] Lord Grey seemed a force for good in the lives of both mother and son, a father-figure to the boy and a friend – and possibly more – to the woman.

Or so it appeared. In the winter of 1803–4, something occurred between Byron and Lord Grey that led to the former's abrupt departure from Newstead and a return to Harrow for the spring term of 1804. Precisely what happened remains unclear, as Byron refused to discuss it with anyone explicitly. Moore's biography suggested that 'an intimacy had sprung up between Byron and his noble tenant',[36] and Byron's friend John Cam Hobhouse noted in his copy – presumably as a result of a confidence being placed in him by Byron – that 'a circumstance occurred during [this] intimacy which certainly had much effect on his future morals'.

The obvious inference is that Grey, presuming on more than just a close friendship, made a pass at Byron, who, shocked and disturbed by the suggestion, rebuffed him angrily and left Newstead immediately. A later letter that he wrote to Augusta contains substantial hints as to why this was the case; he said that 'I am not reconciled to Lord Grey *and I never will* [be]', and that 'he was once my *greatest friend*... [but] my reasons for ceasing that friendship are such as I cannot explain... they are good ones, for although I am *violent* I am not *capricious* in my *attachments*.' After bemoaning his mother's continuing friendship with him – Catherine remained unaware of whatever had passed between them, 'and she never will know' – he venomously spat 'he has forfeited all *title to my esteem*, but I hold him in too much *contempt* ever *to hate him*'.[37] Grey, meanwhile, was hurt at Byron's abrupt rejection of him; a later letter stated that 'I can only say it will ever be the farthest from my wish to assume any character your lordship but that of friend... under all these events, you cannot wonder at my being somewhat surprised'.[38]

Meanwhile, a degree of intimacy had begun to develop between Byron and Augusta, and Catherine was pleased that a relationship between the two half-siblings had finally come into being. Now that Byron had resumed his studies, he was in favour with his mother once more; she threw a party for him in April that was designed to prepare Byron for his coming of age. While he seemed amused by the idea, and told Augusta 'I intend to fall violently in love, it will serve as an amusement *pour passer le temps* and it will at least have the charm of novelty to recommend it',[39] the festivities were not a success. Byron behaved in a distant and superior fashion, either out of arrogance or shyness.[40] In an attempt to find Byron some nearby friends, Catherine introduced him to her neighbours, the Pigots, and their daughter Elizabeth. She described the sixteen-year-old Byron as 'shy and formal' in his manners on first meeting, although he soon warmed up when a play by Frederick Reynolds was discussed. Elizabeth jokingly referred to Byron as 'Gaby', an allusion to the clueless character of Gabriel Lackbrain. It was to be the beginning of a lasting friendship between the two. Catherine, for all her tactlessness, had at least some success in integrating her son into local society: possibly too much so in the case of Lord Grey.

When Byron returned to Harrow, he found himself in what he referred to as 'two or three scrapes', and was accused of having made his house 'a scene of riot and confusion'. It was unclear how he had done this, but he complained that he did not receive his due as an aristocrat ('I have as much money, as many clothes, and in every respect of appearance am equal if not superior to most of my schoolfellows') and then declared his overarching ambition by saying 'the way *to riches, to greatness* lies before me… I will cut myself a path through the world or perish in the attempt.'[41] Catherine's response to her son's declaration of intent was to sigh and tell Hanson that he was a 'turbulent unruly boy that wants to be emancipated from all restraints', even if his sentiments were 'noble'.[42]

The question of how Byron was to be emancipated concerned Catherine throughout the year. After his time of riot, he discovered a talent as an orator, and redeemed himself by reciting a speech from the *Aeneid* at Speech Day on 5 July 1804. Catherine happily informed her cousin Miss Abernathy that 'I long to see him, he is much improved in every respect. He is truly amiable and passes his time I am informed very differently from most young people, he writes a great deal (of) poetry.'[43] The main source of friction between them at this time was Catherine's friendship with

Lord Grey; Mealey told Hanson that the relationship between 'Mrs Byron and [Grey] is greater than ever… he has dined with her several times since you left here, and whatever he says is right with her… when he writes to her it is "my dear Mrs Byron"'.[44] Her feelings towards him were fond and affectionate, his tempered more with politeness than passion, although it is possible that few women could have inspired more, given his probable homosexual (if not pederastic) inclinations.*

When Byron returned home, he had few kind words for Catherine. He referred to her ironically to Augusta as 'my *amiable* mother' and said 'I can send nothing to amuse you, excepting a repetition of my complaints against my tormentor, whose *diabolical* disposition… seems to increase with age, and to acquire new force with time.' Even allowing for partiality, Byron's remarks offer a valuable insight into Catherine's outbreaks of temper; he compares her mood swings to storms, saying '[the] hurricane, which threatens to destroy everything… [until] exhausted by its own violence, it is lulled into a sullen torpor which, after a short period, is again roused into fresh and renewed frenzy, to me most terrible, and to every other spectator astonishing.' He had similarly caustic words for the county of Nottinghamshire: this 'more stupid place', he said, was 'the region of dullness itself, and more stupid than the banks of Lethe'. He concluded with the observation: 'I wander about hating everything I behold, and if I remained here a few months longer, I should become, what with *envy, spleen and all uncharitableness*, a complete *misanthrope*.'[45] This anger was entirely on Byron's side; the day before he wrote these words to Augusta, Catherine had praised her son to Hanson, and said 'never was a boy more improved in every respect… I shall not know how to part with him'. Had she read his letters, the parting might have been an easier one.

---

* Lord Grey did marry, and produced a daughter in 1809 shortly before his premature death in 1810. Byron wrote sneeringly to Catherine that 'Lord Grey is married to a rustic. Well done!'

Nonetheless, Byron's feelings towards Catherine were mercurial, alternating between irritation and fondness. When he returned to Harrow for the autumn term in 1804, he admitted some responsibility for their difficult relations. He referred to her in a letter to Augusta as 'the old lady', and went on to say, in self-critical vein: '[we] don't agree like lambs in a meadow, but I believe it is all my own fault, I am rather too fidgety, which my precise mama objects to, we differ, then argue, and to my shame be it spoken fall out a *little*... however after a storm comes a calm'.[46] His correspondence with Augusta was now a good deal more frequent, and from this point onwards was laden with jokes and digs at his mother. He was both ashamed of what he perceived as her coarseness and vulgarity and sufficiently canny, like anyone writing to entertain, to know that exaggerating Catherine's defects made him a funnier correspondent.

As he decried her 'eccentric manner', Byron allowed that she 'supplies me with as much money as I can spend', but criticized her for being 'so hasty, so impatient, that I dread the approach of the holidays'. 'For the most trifling thing,' he wrote, 'she upbraids me in the most outrageous manner.' Byron noted that a key barrier to their good relations was 'that object of my cordial, deliberate detestation, Lord Grey de Ruthyn', and sneered that 'once she let drop such an odd expression that I was half inclined to believe the dowager was in love with him'.[47] Augusta held similar opinions about Catherine, which led Byron into ever-greater sallies of abuse; highlights of a later tirade included 'she has an excellent opinion of her personal attractions, sinks her age a good six years, avers that when I was born she was only eighteen' and, when Byron had offended her in some way, '[she] flies into a fit of frenzy, upbraids me as if I was the most undutiful wretch in existence, rakes up the ashes of my father, abuses him, says I shall be a true Byrrone [sic], which is the worst epithet she can invent'.[48]

Such outbursts on Byron's part should not be taken as a true record of either Catherine's behaviour towards him, nor of his true feelings about her. A subsequent letter makes the grudging admission that 'I do not however wish to be separated from *her* entirely… for I do believe she likes me.' In a letter to Augusta in November 1804, he notes her 'most *ungovernable appetite* for scandal' – something that he shared and revelled in – and announced his intention of avoiding Southwell when term finished in a fortnight.[49] The impression given is of a bright, mature young man whose aim is to amuse and (metaphorically) seduce his intended reader, and who chose to use a sharp, cruel wit in order to do so. This tendency would find greater expression in his later satires.

Nonetheless, Byron needed to find a new playground. Harrow no longer seemed enough for him, and both Catherine and Dr Drury concurred. Drury wrote to Hanson on 29 December to say that 'during his last residence, his conduct gave me much trouble and uneasiness – if we part now, we may entertain affectionate dispositions towards each other, and his lordship will have left school with credit'.[50] Drury suggested that Byron be placed in the hands of a private tutor, but the boy would not accept this. Instead, he stayed with Hanson, refusing to return to Catherine and Southwell, and planned his next step. He had already outgrown his school and his mother's home. Soon, he would outgrow her altogether.

3

That boy will be the death of me.

CATHERINE GORDON TO HANSON,
4 MARCH 1806

Over the course of the year 1804, Byron had transformed from a boy into a man. The changes wrought on his personality were complex: too complex for Catherine to appreciate. She pleaded with Hanson early in 1805: 'as soon as there is a tolerable day, I hope you will send Byron down. I shall be quite unhappy til I see him',[1] but her previous attitude towards him, of a fond, often put-upon, but affectionate mother, now met a more developed degree of resistance. It had not helped that Byron, lingering in London, had met his erstwhile mentor Lord Carlisle and his family on 26 January and had charmed them. The feeling was mutual; Byron, eschewing the witty snobbery with which he described Catherine, told Augusta that 'I like them very much… his Lordship too improves upon further acquaintanceship.'[2]

If Carlisle wished to be reassured that his protégé was more socially competent than his mother, the aim was achieved. Along with Hanson, he convinced Byron that the first half of the year would be better filled by his returning to Harrow, rather than flitting about Nottinghamshire, and Byron, who had no great wish to see his mother, agreed. When he did next visit her, it was not until April, an absence of over six months. She had been ill in February, but her first concern was to pay her son's Harrow bills, a generous gesture unappreciated by him. Instead, he took the usual opportunity to rant about her to Augusta, referring ironically to her 'sweet and amiable temper'. He recounted how, after he had told Catherine he found Southwell dull, he had been subject to 'an oration in the *ancient style*… unequalled by anything of modern or antique date… one would really imagine, to hear the good lady, that I was a most treasonable culprit'.[3] Even allowing for his usual exaggeration, it is clear that Byron's talk of her 'blackest malevolence' and 'outrageous conduct' was due to an argument between the two, and that she resented her son's casual contempt for her and her home. Byron left Southwell on 1 May, and the parting was far from sorrowful on either side.

It was around now that Catherine changed her mind about the relationship between Augusta and her son. After having supported their rapprochement, she became uneasy about the greater intimacy that had developed between them, fearing that she was the butt of their mockery. When she discovered that Byron had been visiting Augusta in London without her knowledge, she reacted furiously, venting spleen in which Augusta saw, as Byron later put it, 'a specimen of one of the dowager's talents for epistles in the *furioso* style… she is, as I have before declared, certainly mad'.[4] This coincided with Catherine forbidding Byron to see Lord Carlisle and his family again, but he, believing that Carlisle was likely to be a more useful ally than his mother, simply ignored her.[5]

Byron left Harrow at the beginning of July 1805, having shone in two Speech Days, one on 6 June (in which he recited a speech from Edward Young's *The Revenge*) and the final one on 4 July, when he took on the persona of Lear, raging at the storm so passionately that he was overcome by exhaustion and had to leave the stage.[6] Neither Catherine nor Augusta attended either event; his half-sister was unable to come, and his mother was not invited. Byron later claimed that his time at Harrow had changed him immeasurably, saying in his *Detached Thoughts** that '[it was] one

* This was a later journal that Byron kept between 1821 and 1822.

of the deadliest and heaviest feelings of my life to feel that I was no longer a boy'.[7]

Reluctantly, he returned home to Southwell on 3 August, having put his mother off visiting him in London the previous month so that he might spend time with Augusta instead. He airily told Hanson, 'I cannot conceive what the deuce she can want at this season in London', and took on a conspiratorial note when he asked 'if… you can by any means prevent this mother from exe-cuting her purposes [of coming to London], believe me, you will greatly oblige'.[8] While in town, he decided that his next move should be to attend Trinity College, Cambridge (his preferred choice of Christ Church, Oxford having no vacant rooms), and planned his matriculation for the autumn of 1805.

Catherine, angered by his absence, took revenge by informing him of the imminent marriage of his former would-be *inamorata* Mary Chaworth. Moore recounted that, when Byron was told this, 'an expression, very peculiar, impossible to describe, passed over his pale face, and he hurried his handkerchief into his pocket, saying, with an affected air of coldness and nonchalance, "Is that all?"' Catherine attempted to bait him further by sneering 'why, I expected you would have been plunged into grief!', but he ignored her and swiftly changed the subject.[9] Mary's nuptials clearly stung him – a poem he wrote that summer contains the lines 'Now no more my Mary smiling/Makes ye seem a heaven to me'[10] – but he was determined not to show weakness in front of his mother.

He began his studies at Cambridge on 24 October 1805, aged seventeen and a half. A few days earlier, Lord Nelson had won a great victory at the Battle of Trafalgar, but neither Byron nor Catherine refer to this in any of their correspondence: a degree of self-absorption had enveloped them both. He would later say to his publisher John Murray that he was 'miserable and untoward to a degree' at this time, and alluded to 'private domestic circum-stances of different kinds'.[11] These could have been disagreements with Catherine, his disappointment at Mary's betrothal, or both.

However, when he wrote to Augusta around this time, he showed little sign of misery. Instead, he boasted of his '*super*excellent rooms' and how he felt 'so independent as a German prince who coins his own cash, or a Cherokee chief who coins no cash at all'. He neglected to mention that his new-found liberty was as a result of Catherine's generosity, and claimed cheerfully that 'I am not in the least obliged to Mrs B. for it, as it comes off my own property.'[12] This was not true, as Byron had no income of his own while still underage. In fact, Catherine had been keen to ensure that he was well provided for at college, and informed Hanson in September that 'I gave up the five hundred a year [from my income] to my son and you will supply him with money accordingly'. She also noted that 'my house will always be a home for my son whenever he chooses to come to it'.[13]

Byron had no intention of returning to Southwell. He told Augusta after he had been at Cambridge for a few weeks that 'in future, I shall avoid her *hospitable* mansion, though she has the folly to suppose she is to be mistress of my house when I come of age'.[14] So caustic was Byron's attitude towards Catherine that it seems a surprise he did not wish to see her reduced to beggardom. Hanson, the de facto go-between, was informed that 'the horror of entering Mrs Byron's house has of late years been so implanted in my soul, that I dreaded the approach of the vacations as the harbingers of misery'.[15]

As Byron embraced a fast existence of dissipation and high living at Cambridge (he demanded Hanson send him '4 dozen [bottles] of wine, port – sherry – claret & madeira, one dozen of each'),[16] Catherine remained in Southwell, kept at arm's length* and increasingly worried about him. She believed that his servant Francis Boyce was dishonest and likely to be given to theft, and asked Hanson to use his influence to have Byron fire him,

---

* Byron went so far as to write to Hanson on 30 November claiming that he had visited 'the plains of *merry Sherwood*' for the final time and talked of his horror at his mother coming to Cambridge to visit him.

only for her request to be refused.* Lonely and isolated, with only Lord Grey for occasional company, she was mainly occupied with attempting to pay her son's debts. Hanson pleaded Catherine's case in a letter to Byron, in which he wrote 'I have felt uneasiness myself at the treatment I have at times received from your mother, but it has grown into compassion and there I am disposed to let it rest.'[17] Hanson's mediatory efforts bore some fruit. Byron remarked to Augusta later in the month that 'the Dowager (Mrs B) has thought it proper to solicit a reconciliation, which in some measure I have agreed to', although he criticized her 'impertinent and unjust proceedings' against Augusta.[18]

It was soon after this that a schism arose between Byron and Augusta. The cause was not love, but money. Even with Catherine's assistance, Byron remained in debt, to an extent that he felt embarrassed to admit either to his mother or to Hanson. He alluded to his penury offhandedly to Augusta – 'like all other young men just let loose, and especially one as I am, freed from the worse than bondage of my maternal home, I have been extravagant, and consequently am in want of money' – but asked that she be joint security for a sum of a few hundred a moneylender had offered to lend him. Augusta, despite her affection for her half-brother, felt unable to involve herself in his scheme. She initially offered him a one-off gift, and then informed Hanson and Carlisle of his request. When Byron discovered what he regarded as her duplicity in February 1806, he felt betrayed by one of the few people that he had trusted, and would not write to her for several years thereafter.

❧

Catherine, meanwhile, was surprised to receive a rare letter from her son in late February 1806, and even more alarmed by the contents. In it, Byron stated:

* Catherine was right; Boyce ended up being transported to Australia for stealing.

I find it inconvenient to remain at college, not for the expence [sic] as I could live on my allowance, (only I am naturally extravagant), however the mode of going on does not suit my constitution, improvement at an English university to a man of rank is you know impossible, and the very idea ridiculous.

The letter drips with the mixture of arrogance and patronage that had become the eighteen-year-old Byron's default way of treating those he considered his inferiors, including his lawyer and mother. In a further mocking remark, he described Southwell as an '*execrable* Kennel', and demanded that Catherine employ a manservant, as otherwise he would be unable to bring his horses on a forthcoming visit.[19] He did not mention another reason for wishing to leave university; he was hundreds of pounds in debt to a moneylender who was pursuing him doggedly.

His mother knew of her both her son's tendency to be evasive when it came to financial matters, and his profligacy. After all, she had seen it all before with Jack Byron. When she told Hanson that 'I much fear he has fallen into bad hands not only with regard to money matters but in other respects',[20] she was more perceptive than she knew, although her belief that 'he has inveigled himself with some woman that he wishes to get rid of but finds it difficult' was wide of the mark. At Cambridge, Byron's lovers were predominantly male, most notably a fifteen-year-old choirboy, John Edleston, of whom he later sighed to Elizabeth Pigot: 'I certainly *love* him more than any human being.'[21] Augusta had been usurped. Byron's actions were typically reckless, and dangerous as well, for sodomy was a capital crime; in 1806 more people were executed for buggery than for murder.[22] Had Catherine known of his activities, she might have expired of shock on the spot, thereby fulfilling a subsequent prophecy that she made, in which she said 'that boy will be the death of me and drive me mad!'[23]

While her sanity was not in doubt, her patience certainly was. Writing to Hanson in early March, she wailed in despair that

'I much fear he is already ruined at eighteen! Great God I am distracted I can say no more.'[24] Another letter to Hanson refers to some new outrage that her son had visited on her; she growled that 'I will no longer submit to insults from a boy, if it were possible to die of grief, he would kill me', and instructing him not to pay Byron's allowance until he returned to Southwell for a dressing-down.[25] The threat worked; an agreement was reached that he would return to Cambridge after Easter. Byron seemed more interested in finding yet new avenues for expenditure, including horses, servants and lavish crockery; he hosted drunken parties and soirées by the score. After running out of money, he was compelled to return to Southwell in July. He reappeared every inch the prodigal son, in a coach and four with the family crest on the doors, and with a Newfoundland dog in tow; it was called Boatswain, and it immediately attacked Catherine's terrier Gilpin. The symbolism – that the young master had returned to take charge of his exhausted, fearful mother – was clear. Her words to Hanson later that month hint at a certain resignation: 'My son has been with me some time… I am perfectly satisfied with his conduct indeed I have no reason to be otherwise.'[26] She had again been defeated and worn down by a Byron.

The atmosphere of calm could not last. A row erupted between the two of them, and Byron abruptly departed on 7 August assisted by his friends the Pigots. Writing from his lodgings at No. 16 Piccadilly a couple of days later, he thanked them for their 'kind connivance at my escape from Mrs Byron *furiosa*',[27] and begged them not to reveal his new address to Catherine. He boasted to his Cambridge and Harrow friend Edward Long the same day that 'I took the liberty of departing in my carriage and four without "beat of drum" in the "dead of night"'.[28] He was proud of his dramatic exit; the only thing concerning him was the safety of his first collection of poems, *Fugitive Pieces*, which he was then revising. However, Catherine was not content to remain at Southwell while her son mocked her, and headed down to London in pursuit. While her son had driven down in his coach and four, she was compelled to trail behind in her rather humbler chaise and pair. When Byron discovered her means of transport, he sneered 'Poor soul'.[29]

This story encapsulates the differences between Catherine and Byron. He saw himself as the brilliant exemplar of a new world, where looking back into the past was only worthwhile if it was a noble recollection of a romanticized glory. This, at least, he shared with his mother, but she clung on to her belief in her lineage with a fervour that her son – always far more attuned to irony – could only mock. Catherine remained hidebound by the values and beliefs that she had grown up with. Tales of Gight Castle were of little use when it came to restraining a defiant young man whose charm and wit barely concealed a temperament that combined callous selfishness and a determination to see his own name become immortalized at all costs.

Their encounter, when Catherine eventually obtained Byron's address from Hanson and arrived at his lodgings, was an unequal one. Byron, at home in the suave London milieu, was relaxed and dismissive; Catherine, exhausted from a long and tiring journey, could discover little about her son's activities, and returned to Southwell almost immediately. Byron announced triumphantly to Elizabeth Pigot's brother John that:

> I cannot exactly say with Caesar 'Veni, vidi, vici'… though Mrs Byron took the trouble of '*coming*' and '*seeing*', yet your humble servant proved the victor – after an obstinate engagement of some hours, in which *we* suffered considerable damage, from the quickness of the enemy's fire, *they* at length retired in confusion… their defeat is decisive of the *present* campaign.[30]

In jovial spirits, Byron headed to Worthing, where he continued to ridicule Catherine, but he eventually returned to Southwell. Here, he amused in amateur theatricals with the Pigots, endured his mother's presence, and continued to revise *Fugitive Pieces*,

which was finally finished in November and privately produced by
the Newark printers Samuel and John Ridge. Elizabeth proved a
particularly useful amanuensis, carefully transcribing the printer's
copy of the verses from Byron's original manuscript. It included
love poems about Mary Chaworth and Margaret Parker, as well
as what Byron termed 'a whole bevy' of other local women with
whom he had been infatuated.*

As with Harrow, so with Cambridge: Byron seemed to be in no
hurry to return to his studies. The only irritation was that he was
placed on a strict diet, with 'animal food' limited and no alcohol
taken apart from two glasses of port after dinner; he had grown portly
through good living, with his bad foot restricting his movement.

After the rows of the summer, the relationship between Byron
and Catherine had become calmer. She hoped that he would settle
down, complete his studies and then marry a wealthy heiress –
or a 'golden Dolly' as he later wrote sardonically. She was to be
disappointed in this; his major female entanglement at the time
was with a local girl named Julia Leacroft, whose family's financial
situation was even worse than the Byrons'. He was also heavily in
debt to moneylenders, and used his sometime landlady Elizabeth
Massingberd as a go-between with them. Catherine wrote despairingly to Hanson at the beginning of 1807 that '[Massingberd] is
now trying to get my son into another scrape that is to borrow
more money. She is certainly a dupe herself or wishes to make him
one.'[31] Owing to his financial problems, a return to Cambridge
seemed impossible; Catherine complained to Hanson in March
that 'Lord Byron has been with me seven months with two men
servants for which I have never received one farthing.'†[32]

---

* The collection was thought to be too scandalous, due to its amorous
content, and ended up being destroyed and reissued, with additional
poems to replace the controversial ones, as *Poems On Various Occasions*.
† Byron claimed in return that he had lent Catherine £60 the previous
year, and that he was responsible for the payment of his servants and
upkeep of horses.

After Byron managed to obtain a loan of £1,000, supposedly to pay off his debts, he finally headed back to university in late June. There, he resumed a libertine life, as well as associating with his young lover Edleston. His correspondence with Elizabeth Pigot continued, and he portrayed himself as a man-about-town, following 'one continued routine of dissipation – out at different places every day, engaged to more dinners etc than my *stay* would permit me to *fulfil*'.[33] Catherine was not mentioned in his letters to Elizabeth, and was dealt with dismissively when he corresponded with Hanson; Byron responded to his suggestion that she be made guardian of his funds by saying of her that 'Mrs Byron has already made more *free* with my *funds* than suits my convenience, and I do not (propose) to expose her to the danger of temptation.'[34] That this was both untrue and unfair did not appear to bother him at all.

Despite the acquisition of a tame bear that he named Bruin – for which, he quipped to Elizabeth, his plan was that 'he should *sit* for a *fellowship*' – university life was of little interest to him as he prepared for the June publication of his new edition of poetry, *Hours of Idleness* – his first to be publicly sold – and he eventually left Cambridge at the end of 1807, still heavily in debt, even as his collection was 'praised by *reviewers*, admired by *Duchesses* and sold by every bookseller of the metropolis'.[35] Catherine, still loyal to her son despite everything, declared to Hanson that 'I have as high an opinion of my son's abilities as anyone can have, yet I am sensible that clever people are not always the most prudent in regard to money matters.' She also echoed Byron's dismissal of Lord Grey, saying 'I am glad that Lord Grey de Ruthyn leaves Newstead at Midsummer… I have not seen [the house] myself but I must inform you that almost every person I meet informs me of the shameful state it is in.'[36]

Ironically, given Byron's dismissal of her as a potential reader of his poetry (he sardonically asked Catherine's local vicar, John Becher, to warn her of some potential bad reviews – 'I trust that

her mind will not be ruffled'),*[37] she had a more level-headed attitude towards hostile critics than he did. A posthumously printed
letter of hers indicated that he took any harsh comments extremely
ill; in it, she states, 'he says if I have any regard for him I will never
mention his poetry to him more as he wishes to forget it... he has
really no opinion of his talents in that way and has now no pleasure
in the employment'. This reveals another side of the relationship
between Byron and Catherine. Gone is the superiority and arrogant dismissiveness that the young man so enjoyed displaying in
front of her, replaced by a deep plunge into melancholy. When she
wrote that 'he is really discouraged and depressed... I am really
grieved to the heart of all this',[38] the relationship between them
seemed to have reverted to its status a decade before, with Byron
little more than a petulant schoolboy denied some new toy, and
Catherine fulfilling the maternal role of soothing and reassuring
her disappointed son.

Byron consoled himself by moving into Newstead, complete
with horses, dogs and bear, when Lord Grey left it in the summer
of 1808. Byron intended to restore it to the glories of former years –
a house fit for a lordly poet. Yet the absence of funds bedevilled his
attempts and it remained ramshackle, with the rain frequently drip-
ping through on to the lavish furnishings that Byron had acquired.
Nonetheless, a state of détente now existed between Catherine and
her son. He was friendlier to her than before, and expressed a wish
to aid her: 'I have taken care you shall have the house and manor
for life, besides a sufficient income [in the case of his death]... so
you see my improvements are not entirely selfish.'[39]

Even a brief outbreak of hostilities, revolving around Catherine's opposition to his continued infatuation with the now married
Mary Chaworth, was dealt with gracefully, when he proclaimed
that 'if you please we will forget the things you mention, I have no

* Becher had acted unofficially as Byron's touchstone for the poem's lewd
content, describing some of the sexual material as 'rather too warmly
drawn'.

desire to remember them'. Byron then announced his intention to travel the world: 'if we see no nation but our own, we do not give mankind a fair chance'.[40] He had decided to voyage abroad in the spring of 1809. In the meantime, he amused himself by writing *English Bards and Scotch Reviewers,* an acidic satire on those who he believed had not appreciated *Hours of Idleness.* The work had been particularly poorly received by the influential *Edinburgh Review*, which stated: 'it is a sort of privilege of poets to be egotists; but they should "use it as not abusing it"; and particularly one who piques himself... of being "an infant bard"... should either not know, or should seem not to know, so much about his own ancestry'.[41] His mood was helped by his discovery of a skull in the grounds of Newstead, which he had polished, set in silver and used as a drinking vessel. Catherine was not informed of this latest foray into decadence.

Had she known, she would have been appalled, but other matters were distracting her. She had suffered from poor health since late August, and was prescribed a mixture of powders, ointments and bleeding by leeches. None of these had the desired effect, and she was sufficiently unwell to tell Hanson later in the year that she was 'very ill indeed, and I do not expect ever to be better'.[42] Even as Byron, resuming contact with Augusta to congratulate her on the birth of her daughter, contemptuously claimed, 'Mrs Byron I have shaken off for two years, and I shall not resume her yoke in future',[43] his mother's health was irreparably broken. Byron makes no allusion to her illness in his letters of the time; either he was unaware, or he believed that she was exaggerating her infirmity to gain sympathy. He appeared more affected by the ill health of his dog Boatswain (who died of rabies in November 1808) than he was by that of his mother; indeed, Boatswain's demise led him to write the poem 'Epitaph To A Dog'. He exhibited no such compassion to the forty-four-year-old Catherine, who was worn down after trying to keep what remained of her family and estate together.

She still believed the best of her son, or at least adopted a public façade of maternal pride and loyalty. She praised him to Hanson in generous terms at the start of 1809: 'his heart is good and his talents are great, and I have no doubt about his being a great man', although she had seen enough of his behaviour over the last decade to add a note of caution to her encomium: 'may God grant that he may be a prudent and happy one also'.[44] This 'prudent and happy' man was nearly twenty-one, and had celebrated the imminence of his majority by making one of his servant girls, Lucy, pregnant. As he confided to Hanson: 'I need not tell you by whom... I cannot have the girl on the parish.'*[45] Catherine was not informed of the arrival of her first grandchild, although such events were far from uncommon in houses of 'quality', and she might have greeted the news with equanimity.

As Byron celebrated his coming of age in London on 22 January 1809 with bacon, eggs and beer – more lavish celebrations took place at Newstead for the tenant farmers and servants – Catherine's health remained too poor for her to take part in either set of festivities. She lingered at Southwell, dosing herself with pills and potions. She lamented to Hanson that 'I was very sorry to hear of the great expense the Newstead fete would put him to... I see nothing but the road to ruin in all this, which grieves me to the heart and makes me still worse than I would otherwise be.'[46] Her health and mood were not helped by her son writing to her to claim that he was now ruined, because of constant payments to his creditors; Catherine robustly replied that she hoped he would marry an heiress immediately. Perhaps remembering her own marital experiences and disappointments, she added the cynical observation: 'love matches is all nonsense'.[47]

Now that he had attained manhood, Byron had no interest in tarrying. He took his seat in the House of Lords on 13 March, after having proved the legitimacy of his grandfather's marriage and

---

* Byron provided an annuity of £100 a year, half for Lucy and half for the child. It is unknown as to what happened to the boy or girl, although he later referred to having 'two natural children' to provide for.

thereby confirming his right to be considered the 6th Lord Byron. Despite debts that amounted to around £12,000,[48] he continued with his plans for a foreign trip. Byron intended to make Newstead his home when he returned; as he wrote in a letter to Catherine: 'Newstead and I stand or fall together, I have now lived on the spot, I have fixed my heart upon it, and no pressure past or future shall induce me to barter the last vestige of our inheritance.' That the income raised by a sale would have been enormously helpful for both him and his mother did not influence his wishes.

Byron visited Catherine once more before he departed on his travels, though not before holding a riotous party at Newstead where he and his friends, including Hobhouse, James Wedderburn Webster and his fellow Cambridge student Charles Matthews, sat drinking out of the skull-cup while dressed in monks' habits; Byron, naturally, was known as 'abbot', and persistent rumours suggested their newly adopted vows of celibacy had been tested by servant girls in Paphian garb.* The last encounter between Catherine and her son was far from a happy one; Byron later remarked to his friend Lord Sligo that 'she, in one of her fits of passion, uttered an imprecation upon me, praying that I might prove as ill-formed in mind as I am in body!'[49] Even allowing for exaggeration, it seems likely that Catherine, both angered and frightened by her son's looming absence, lashed out at him by attacking his vulnerability, and the reminder of his fiscal and physical infirmities alike clearly stung Byron. Returning to London, he made the final preparations for his grand tour, which was to encompass visits to the Mediterranean countries; the Napoleonic wars made a trip to northern or western Europe impossible at that time. In a will drawn up on 14 June, he left £500 a year to Catherine in the event of his death: the same sum that she had allowed him as a student at Cambridge. A few days later, she complained to Hanson that he was 'unsteady and thoughtless' in his actions. 'The grief I feel at my

* These rumours were denied by Hobhouse.

son's going abroad and the addition of his leaving his affairs in so unsettled a state… I think altogether it will kill me.'[50]

Byron, meanwhile, departed England on 2 July 1809 in a state of some excitement,* having obtained funds for his journey by a reckless series of loans, one of which involved his friend, the dandy Scrope Davies, standing surety for the impressive sum of £6,000. Shortly before he left for Lisbon with Hobhouse and four servants, including his page and occasional lover Robert Rushton, he wrote to his mother at Newstead: 'the world is all before me, and I leave England without regret, and without a wish to revisit anything it contains, except *yourself*, and your present residence'.[51] The final clause is the most telling; Byron loved Newstead and all it represented considerably more than anything, or anyone, else.

After travelling from Lisbon to Seville, Byron revelled in the freedom that his European release offered him. He swan across the Tagus river, which bisected Portugal and Spain, in two hours; had relations with a Spanish woman, Donna Josepha Beltram, in Seville; and visited a bullfight near Cadiz. By the time he arrived in Malta in August 1809 Byron had become something of an aristocratic celebrity, a fact he used to his own advantage when he seduced 'some absurd womankind', the twenty-four-year-old Constance Spencer Smith; she had achieved her own fame three years earlier when she had been abducted by a Sicilian nobleman before she could be imprisoned by Napoleon's government in Italy. Byron wrote to Catherine to say that 'her life has been from commencement so fertile in remarkable incidents, that in a romance they would appear improbable'.[52]

He wrote sporadically to his mother throughout the year; she was to be his most regular correspondent. Byron's letters to Catherine were long; they gave a fluent and witty account of his travels, and

---

* Byron expected to be able to enjoy a more liberated sexual outlook upon the continent. He joked to his former housemaster Henry Drury that he would write a treatise entitled 'Sodomy simplified or Paederasty proved to be praiseworthy, from ancient authors and modern practice'.

compared the countries in which he found himself favourably with England; he took particular relish in describing his autumn visit to Greece and Albania and his encounter there with the local potentate, Ali Pasha, whose cruelty co-existed with a strange courtesy.* Byron told Catherine that 'he treated me like a child, sending me almonds & sugared sherbert, fruit & sweetmeats 20 times a day'.[53] What his correspondence lacked was any affection or warmth towards her; his first letter contained a half-hearted statement of apology for not having written before: 'I have been so much occupied since my departure from England that til I could address you at length I have forborne writing altogether.'[54] Distracted by his new horizons, Byron was much more interested in describing his exploits than in making any attempt to forge a closer relationship with his mother. The only first-hand contact that Catherine would have with anyone associated with her son came in October 1809, when Rushton and his butler Old Joe Murray returned to Newstead, bearing stories of their – and their master's – exploits and a letter from Gibraltar. Byron had sent Rushton home 'because Turkey is in too dangerous a state for boys to enter'; Byron noted '*you know* boys are not *safe* amongst the Turks'. She responded in a fond if faintly bemused manner, advised him not to embroil himself with Spanish women ('they make nothing of poisoning both husbands and lovers if they are jealous of them') and alluded to her poor health: 'I have been very ill but Dr Marsden of Nottingham has been of great service to me.' She ended, poignantly: 'do dear Byron write to me often & wherever you go if you wish me to be happy, indeed not miserable.'[55]

As her son continued his journeys through his 'dearly beloved Greece', showing the first signs of his interest in Greek independence, Catherine sank further into debt and despair. She suffered the ignominy of having bailiffs visit Newstead for the first time in February 1810, demanding the repayment of £1,600 owed

* This might have been due to a rumoured love affair between the two.

to a Nottinghamshire upholstery firm, Brothers, in addition to Byron's other debts, which were now well over £10,000. She did not tell him, but her next letter to him was drenched in anguish and worry; she beseeched him to tell her of his wellbeing, asking 'Good God where are you? I hope & trust in God you are safe', and mentioned that she was 'unhappy on your account'.[56] Even as she hoped that the funds that Byron was receiving from *English Bards and Scotch Reviewers* might defray the debts that he owed, she was unaware that he, snobbish about the idea of being 'a paid author', had munificently gifted the proceeds to its publisher, James Cawthorn. Despite frequently begging Hanson for money, Catherine remained isolated, impoverished and ill. That Byron appeared not to have received any of her letters grieved her; she wrote to him in May to say 'it is lamentable that we cannot hear from each other more regularly', and referred to her continuing poor health.[57] To add to the woes of the house, Byron's bear had died earlier that month; he, enjoying the 'loveliest spots on earth', in Constantinople, remained unaware. Instead, on 3 May 1810, he swam the Hellespont in imitation of Leander swimming to his lover Hero. In later life, Byron would sometimes state that this was his greatest achievement.

Despite his apparently blasé attitude towards his mother, Byron at least paid passing attention to her wellbeing while on his travels, instructing Hanson to let her have any funds she needed at his expense. When he next wrote to her from Athens, in July, he adopted a lightly mocking but affectionate tone; he referred to her as 'northern gentry' and a 'vixen' and asked her to take care of his books and papers – 'and pray leave me a few bottles of champagne to drink, for I am very thirsty'.*[58] He was in no hurry to return to England, not least because he had fallen in love with another boy, Eustathius Georgiou, but he expressed his surprise at Hanson's

* This was written at around the same time that Byron vehemently criticized Catherine to Sligo.

silence. Perhaps the solicitor, exhausted by his dealings with the Byron family, wanted little more to do with any of them.

Catherine had at least been given a portrait of her son, commissioned as a parting gift. Painted by George Sanders, the picture depicts him and his page Rushton on a rocky seashore with a backdrop of mountains. The young lord is portrayed as self-assured, devilishly handsome and on the cusp of a great adventure, the great Romantic embarking upon on his travels; no indication is made of his bad foot, nor does any hint of his former corpulence remain. It was magnificent and striking, and gave his mother at least a small amount of comfort. She said of the depiction of Byron that 'the countenance is angelic and the finest I ever saw and it is very like'.[59] Her son, suffering from a bad case of malaria that he described as a 'tertian fever', did not respond, but he at least recovered, unlike his erstwhile friend Lord Grey, who died on 29 October of 'a violent haemorrhage', which killed him in five days.*[60]

Byron continued to dally around Greece in early 1811 with the adventuress Lady Hester Stanhope and Hobhouse (who described Stanhope as a 'violent, peremptory person'),[61] seeking to emulate the classical heroes he admired and hoping that the Greeks would once more rise 'to their pristine superiority'. Meanwhile, Catherine's health continued to decline. Tormented with fear at the thought of the bailiffs coming and carrying out an 'execution' on Newstead, she sought to keep Byron's most beloved possessions intact, even if this meant selling what scraps of furniture and jewellery she had managed to retain. Her son made only the vaguest of gestures of concern about her wellbeing, asking Hanson to apprise him of any news about her, but he was more concerned about the future of Newstead. In a letter to Catherine in February 1811 he admonished her for even hinting that it might be sold, and

---

* When Byron recovered, his first reaction was to say, with pleasure, 'how pale I look! – I should like, I think, to die of a consumption'. When asked why, he responded 'because then the women would all say "See that Byron – how interesting he looks in dying!"'

threatened not to return if it was no longer his property: 'my only tie in England is Newstead, and that once gone neither interest nor inclination lead me northward'.[62] The unspoken hint that he considered his house more important than her was enough to send Catherine into a self-pitying spiral of drunkenness and loneliness. Without friends, money or her son, her life was bleak and empty.

Whether or not she knew that she was seriously ill, her last letters took on a valedictory tone. Telling her son that 'if you are unfortunate, it will bring down my grey hairs with sorrow to the grave', she supported his plan of retaining Newstead at virtually all costs, but trusted in the illusory belief that there would be £100,000 left after Byron's substantial debts were paid, were it to be sold. Such a sum would have made him a wealthy man, but it remained a fanciful dream. She had also become as disgruntled with Hanson as the solicitor was with his clients: 'I am neither satisfied with his activity or his diligence.'[63]

She ended her letter by expressing the wish that Byron would return to England to make things right at the estate. In fact, unbeknown to her, he had arrived in Malta on 30 April and was making plans for his return voyage, which had been delayed due to his poor health, but which would eventually begin from the port of Valetta on 1 June 1811. He agreed with his mother that Hanson was negligent and was irritated by his insistence that Newstead should be sold to clients of his. 'I will see them damned first,'[64] he wrote to Hobhouse. Whether Hanson was trying to assist the Byrons, or wished to be rid of them, he had roused the animosity of both mother and son, and saw his role change from trusted family confidante into mistrusted enemy. Catherine's attitude towards him oscillated between anger and a pathetic sense of need, as when she wrote to him in late May begging 'for God's sake do not let me live in this state'.[65]

Meanwhile, her son, still unaware of the gravity of Catherine's illness, prepared to head back to Newstead, complete with cantos one and two of *Childe Harold's Pilgrimage*. His penultimate letter to her boasted of his good health and his hopes for his return. He neglected to mention his recent poor health, and continued to stress that Newstead was Catherine's home, and that he should only be considered a temporary guest. This was either done out of a sincere desire to submit to Catherine's authority, or as a feint designed to disclaim responsibility for the considerable debt that attached to Newstead: probably the latter. Suspecting that she was unlikely to recover, Catherine remarked to her maid, 'if I should die before Byron comes down, what a strange thing it would be'.[66]

Her prophecy was to prove accurate. Catherine died on 1 August, having had her doctor Hutchinson summon another medic, Marsden, from Nottingham. The precise cause of her last illness and death remains elusive. Byron's friend and biographer Thomas Moore speculated that she perished 'as the result of a fit of rage brought on by reading over an upholsterer's bill',[67] but this seems fanciful. Instead, alcohol, obesity and perhaps cancer would have been the causes that appeared on a modern birth certificate. Catherine was forty-six when she died, utterly miserable, and devoid of everything other than the hope that her wayward son would go on to achieve the fame and greatness that he seemed to be on the verge of attaining. But this hope was not enough to keep her clinging on to life.

⤍

After a long and gloomy journey, Byron's ship docked in Sheerness in Kent on 14 July 1811. His glum mood, exacerbated by the anti-climax of his return, was soon worsened when Hutchinson informed him that Catherine was gravely ill. Having no knowledge of her indisposition, his final letter to her had given instructions for his return to Newstead, in which he wrote 'I expect a powerful stock of potatoes, greens, & biscuit, I drink no wine'.[68] He cancelled his other engagements in London to head to her bedside. After borrowing £40 from Hanson, he made it to a coaching inn at Newport Pagnell, where Rushton informed him of his mother's death. As he wrote to John Pigot immediately afterwards, he clung to the little comfort that he was offered: 'her last moments were most tranquil... I am told she was in little pain, and not aware of her situation.'[69]

When Byron arrived at Newstead, his self-control at last gave way to remorse and self-reproach; the final straw was coming across a book that Catherine had dutifully kept of all his reviews and notices, with her own comments in the margins.[70] His mother's servant recounted a story of him sitting by his mother's deathbed in tears, and crying 'I had but one friend in the world and she is gone!'[71] Even as he made arrangements for the funeral, writing in businesslike terms to Hanson about the potential value of Catherine's remaining jewels and clothes, he was in a state of distress. When he told Scrope Davies that 'some curse hangs over me', he articulated his belief that he was not as other men, and that his fate was doomed to be an unhappy one. His sadness was exacerbated by the news of the death of his first boy-lover, John Edleston, from consumption in May; he wrote to his friend Francis Hodgson to bemoan that 'I had not a tear left for an event which five years ago would have bowed me to the dust'.

Although he made careful preparations for Catherine's interment in the family vault at Hucknall Church, Byron felt so stricken by grief on 9 August that he was unable to attend the funeral itself. Byron instead watched as the cortege headed towards nearby Hucknall, where his mother's body joined that of the ancestral Byrons. When Rushton suggested some light sparring as a distraction, he roughly attacked the page, before returning to Newstead to brood in melancholy. He mourned both Edleston and his 'amiable mamma', but also the idea of loss itself; he saw himself as an orphan, miserable that he had missed a chance to bid her farewell by one day. It was this feeling that he poured out to Hobhouse the day after the funeral, when he described there being:

Something to me so incomprehensible in death, that I can neither speak or think upon the subject – indeed when I looked

on the mass of corruption, which was the being from whence I
sprang, I doubted within myself whether I was, or she was not...
I have lost her who gave me being.

He referred to both loneliness and 'a kind of hysterical merriment'
overtaking him, and summed up his state as 'wretched but not
melancholy or gentlemanlike'.*[72] Later in the month, he told
Hodgson, 'I am yet stupid from the shock, although I do eat, and
drink, and talk, and even laugh at times.' But he also struck a note
of reinvigoration: 'I shall now waive the subject – the dead are at
rest, and none but the dead can be so.'[73]

Byron, at the age of twenty-three, was on the cusp of a new
life. The publication of the first stanzas of his autobiographical
narrative poem *Childe Harold's Pilgrimage*, which introduced the
original Byronic protagonist in its account of a young man† seeking for greater fulfilment in his life by travelling the world, was less
than a year away. When John Murray published it on 10 March
1812, the first edition of 500 copies sold out within three days, and
his reputation was elevated from satirist-of-note to one of the most
famous men in England. He would obliquely reference Catherine
and his guilt at leaving her in the tenth stanza of the first canto,
saying of his alter ego 'Childe Harold had a mother – not forgot/
Though parting from that mother he did shun', before referring to
her in more general terms as being bound up with the existence
that he was abandoning:

> Yet deem not thence his breast a breast of steel;
> Ye, who have known what 'tis to dote upon

---

* Hobhouse was also in a state of deep mourning for their Cambridge
friend Charles Matthews, who had drowned while swimming earlier that
month. His death may have been suicide.
† 'Childe' is a medieval term for a nobleman who had not yet become a
knight.

A few dear objects, will in sadness feel
Such partings break the heart they fondly hope to heal.

Greater adventure would soon consume the rest of his life. And yet, as he contemplated his mother's death, musing on his heart-sickness and melancholy, he cast off the last ties of family. From then, he would succeed or fail on his own terms, as the last scion of the Byrons, and it would be he who would be associated with the name forever.

PART II
Caroline

4

Mad, bad and dangerous to know.

CAROLINE LAMB'S DIARY,
MARCH 1812

There is irony in a man who was the most famous poet of his age taking for his most infamous lover a woman said to be illiterate until she was a teenager. Like so many aristocratic ladies, she was uneducated. Yet virtually everything in the relationship between Byron and Lady Caroline Lamb was unusual. He was the author of the most celebrated work of the day, *Childe Harold's Pilgrimage*, which, since it first appeared on 10 March 1812, had enraptured and scandalized his readers,* leading him to quip 'I awoke one morning and found myself famous'. She was the wife of an aristocratic Whig MP who had already attracted attention – and scandal – by her affair with a Tory, Sir Godfrey Webster. Yet this was nothing compared to the notoriety that she and Byron would court by their very public entanglement. Although it only lasted for a matter of months, it would became one of the most scandalous of the century, thanks to the high-profile fashion in which it was conducted.

❧

---

* Byron noted that his rooms were 'loaded with letters from critics, poets, authors, and various pretenders to fame of different walks, all lavish in their raptures'.

Caroline Ponsonby was born on 13 November 1785. She was the daughter of Frederick Ponsonby, Viscount Duncannon and sub-sequently 3rd earl of Bessborough, and Lady Henrietta Frances Spencer, countess of Bessborough. Her parents' union was a turbu-lent and unhappy one. Bessborough, despite being well thought of by most of his friends and familiars – and described by Horace Walpole, perhaps condescendingly, as 'so gentle and very amiable a man'[1] – was an undynamic husband and a father, owing to a simplicity of character that made him feel uneasy in the grand circles of society in which he mixed. He was happier spending time at his country seat in Northampton riding and shooting; when he did attempt to take part in such urban pursuits as gambling and financial speculation, he invariably lost money. His aesthetic sense was so poor that he was prevailed upon by unscrupulous art dealers to pay huge prices for prints that he was assured would become hugely valuable: they did not.[2]

Lady Bessborough, or Harriet as she was known, was worldlier. Well known for her elegant dancing, beauty and personal charm, she was a Whig, and a keen supporter of her distant cousin, the Foreign Secretary Charles James Fox. Fox's brilliance in oratory was matched by his extravagant private life; he drank heavily and racked up crippling debts (said to be 'like Caesar's') as if they were badges of honour. This cavalier attitude endeared him to both Harriet and to her sister Georgiana, duchess of Devonshire, the legendary beauty and socialite; compared to their dull husbands, Fox's iconoclasm and wit made him hugely entertaining company.

Bessborough's main goal in his marriage was to produce children, and in this he was not disappointed. Harriet gave birth to two boys, John and Frederick, and Caroline was her third child; according to her daughter, she had always wanted a girl. When Caroline was born in Cavendish Square, her grandmother Lady Spencer described her as 'a lovely little girl – who seems very lively and in perfect health'.[3] 'Lively' was a term often used about Caroline in later life: 'lovely' less frequently. She was a puny child when she was born, so much so that it was initially feared that she would not survive, but she soon flourished. Christened Caroline, her mother nicknamed her 'Caro', meaning 'dear' or 'beloved' in Italian.

She was always a headstrong child. Born into great privilege and indulgence, she was doted on by Lady Spencer; so much so that, as a young child, Caroline refused to sleep unless she was in her grandmother's bed. The relationship between the two was always close; Lady Spencer instructed her in Biblical studies and in how to be a lady of good breeding. Caroline was precocious in her knowledge of languages, speaking a little French and Italian by the age of five, and studied music from the age of six onwards. She was also small for her age (three feet three inches at the age of four and a half) and was unable to speak normally, alternating between baby talk and a lisping, drawling drone.[4] She had all the tutors and governesses usual for a girl of her background, but fared badly in her formal education because she was unusually strong-willed and refused to work unless the subject at hand interested her.

The peripatetic nature of her early years did not help. While her father preferred to stay at home slaying the local wildlife, her mother and aunt stayed at the grandest houses in the country, and Caroline spent much of her childhood at Brocket Hall and Chatsworth, her aunt Georgiana's home. With the adults present uninterested in discipline, the children were given licence to run riot. Caroline later told her friend Lady Morgan that she had done as she pleased from the age of three until nine; she lived in a fantastical world of whimsy and make-believe, where bread came freshly buttered, where horses ate beef and where there was no social class other than dukedom or beggardom.[5]

Her unconventional upbringing was mirrored by her family's unorthodox romantic lives. Georgiana's marriage to William Cavendish, duke of Devonshire, was one that gave rise to a great deal of gossip and intrigue on account of the flirtations – and more – of both parties, and Caroline grew up surrounded by her legitimate and illegitimate cousins, all of whom she unquestioningly accepted as her relations. Harriet was culpable in this regard too; in addition to running up gambling debts of tens of thousands of pounds, she mixed with a loose and often louche set of witty, hard-drinking young men that included the playwright Richard Sheridan, whose intimacy with her was such that he was rumoured to have been Caroline's real father.[6] When asked why she courted scandal, she was said to have shrugged and said 'I could never love *a little*'.

In an attempt to escape from scandal and to give Caroline a broader perspective on life, Harriet travelled with her daughter to Naples when she was four. After a short time there they moved to France, where they remained until the execution of Louis XVI on 21 January 1793, at which point they returned to Italy. It was here that Harriet fell in love with the twenty-one-year-old Lord Granville Leveson-Gower, who was witty, handsome and charismatic and set his sights on her with passionate determination. As she became his mistress, the welfare of her daughter became a secondary concern to her happiness. But a serious bout of illness, which caused a fever from which Caroline nearly died, necessitated her return to England. Reluctantly, Harriet accompanied her, with the family reaching their home in August 1794.

Caroline was now a mixture of learning and utter ignorance. She spoke European languages, could ride a horse and probably had a wider knowledge of political – and sexual – affairs than virtually any other eight-year-old girl in the country. Yet she had received no formal education and, in October 1795, concentrating momentarily on her daughter rather than her own business, Harriet decided to send her to a 'dame school' in Knightsbridge. These establishments specialized in a basic education for anyone whose parents could pay the fees. The school that Caroline attended at 22 Hans Place – whose former pupils included Jane Austen[7] – specialized in a range of instruction that included everything from French and Italian lessons to classes in deportment, in which the girls were marched around by an off-duty drill sergeant.

If this regime was supposed to instil discipline and obedience in Caroline, it failed. She rebelled against her teachers from the beginning, threw hysterical fits and refused to submit to the school's discipline. Something had to be done. With her ineffectual father more interested in countryside carnage than his children and her mother following her own pursuits, it became expedient to hire a governess who would instil order and respectability in her; Harriet openly desired someone who would 'take charge of [her] til somebody else can be found'.[8] That the problems lay less with Caroline and more in her louche and unsettled domestic milieu seemed not to occur to her mother. The family physician, Dr Warren, diagnosed Caroline as suffering from an over-active brain and, in an attempt to relax and calm her, recommended that no further attempts be made to educate her.[9] This led to her being sent to live with Georgiana at Chatsworth and their London home, Devonshire House, in the hope that these would provide a more stable family environment.

Devonshire House could hardly be said to offer the calming atmosphere that Dr Warren had prescribed. It was a Bacchanalian place in which all-night parties were the norm, regularly attended by such pleasure-seeking members of the *haut ton* as Fox and the Prince of Wales. Caroline became an entertaining addition to the ménage, and endeared herself to her cousins by her bold-faced contempt for propriety. She was a hyperactive child, exhausting her grandmother when she attempted to care for her; Lady Spencer despairingly said to her notional governess, Selina Trimmer, 'I feel incapable of doing anything with the Dear Child, the little attempt I made at opposing the questions today has quite discouraged me.'[10]

As both Harriet and Georgiana suffered from ill health as a result of their social over-exertions, Caroline was left to her own devices, and became increasingly wild. A letter that she wrote to her cousin 'Little G' Georgiana paints a picture of a household where 'mama reads Shakespeare in the evening, when she goes… upstairs to sleep [my brothers] and I generally rail out a song with a machine that would frighten you in the great hall while the men drink in the dining room'.[11] She was able to quote poetry and talk to adults on near-equal terms, but refused to be ministered to or to study. She ate and went to bed when she wanted to, and any attempts to curtail her fun led to hysterical outbursts that were more troublesome than the original act of indiscipline.[12]

Unsurprisingly, given the sexualized households in which she grew up, Caroline matured quickly. She was volatile and flirtatious, given to manic episodes and ostentatious displays of coquetry. Her nicknames included Ariel, Squirrel and Young Savage.[13] She looked like a young boy when she was in her early teens, with slim hips, cropped hair and an unusually low voice, but she was adept at dealing with men from an early age. A favourite technique that she adopted was to take hold of an arm, or a hand, and pout in a seductive fashion, and accuse whoever she was talking to of finding her insufficiently attractive to pay her court.[14] She adopted a lisping little-girl-lost voice, which many men found irresistible but other girls derided; a particularly scathing comment was 'Lady Caroline ba-a-a-as like a little sheep'.[15] She paid attention to virtually any man in sight, most embarrassingly to her mother's suitor Lord Granville; she once stated to her cousin Lady Harriet 'Harryo' Cavendish, who was besotted by him,* that, had it not been for her mother's attachment to him, she would have happily considered becoming his mistress. That her mother had had an illegitimate child by Granville in 1800 did nothing to lessen the attraction.

As Caroline prepared to come out into society in 1803, at the age of eighteen, she had already met her future husband. William Lamb had been born on 15 March 1779 into an aristocratic Whig family. His mother, Elizabeth Milbanke Lamb, Lady Melbourne, was well known both for her boundless political influence and her tendency to pick the most influential men of the time as her lovers. This meant that William's putative father, Lord Melbourne, was

---

* Harriet Cavendish would eventually marry Granville, on Christmas Eve 1809.

unsure of the paternity of his younger son, and was accordingly suspicious of him.* Lady Melbourne was a close friend of Georgiana, and the two were sufficiently intimate to be immortalized, along with the sculptor Anne Seymour Damer, in Daniel Gardner's 1775 picture 'The Three Witches From *Macbeth*'. William was brought up in the style that any young aristocrat would expect, educated at Eton and then Trinity College, Cambridge, the same college that Byron would attend a decade later. Like the Bessboroughs, he was a committed Whig, with an especial loathing for the Tory minister George Canning.

At the age of twenty, he encountered Caroline for the first time at his family's country estate, Brocket Hall. She was just fourteen, but the chemistry between the two was obvious; Harryo described 'an extraordinary flirtation between William Lamb and Caro Ponsonby, and they seem, I hear, mutually captivated… [though] he did not captivate anyone else'.[16] After meeting her, he said 'of all the Devonshire House girls, she is the one for me'.[17] As for Caroline, she was impressed by the handsome yet shy man, and had been so ever since she had read some of his juvenile poems two years previously.[18] Her family were less enraptured because, as the second son, William had few prospects and, given their gambling debts, the Bessborough clan needed someone who could provide both for their headstrong, difficult daughter and, by extension, themselves. They had high hopes for her; it was even suggested that the Prince of Wales might be an appropriate suitor.[19]

If nothing had changed, the likelihood was that Caroline would have been married to another, wealthier, aristocrat, and William compelled to pursue a respectable profession in law; he was called to the Bar in 1804 and began his career on the northern circuit. However, in late 1804 his elder brother Peniston, who was to have inherited the estate, fell seriously ill with consumption, and

* William Lamb's actual father was rumoured to be the art collector Lord Egremont, patron to Turner and Constable.

so William became a more attractive candidate for marriage; it helped that Caroline had taken the initiative and already hinted that, were he to propose to her, she would accept. However, when the proposal did take place at the beginning of 1805, Caroline, mindful of her parents' dislike of him, turned him down, claiming that she was too wilful and independent to become anyone's wife, although she did offer, semi-seriously, to dress up as a clerk and accompany him while he practised law.[20]

Caroline was not short of admirers, despite (or perhaps because of) her eccentricities of manner and person. Sometimes these admirers expressed themselves in equally eccentric ways, not least a 'Mr Hill', who wrote her a letter that was, as her mother later complained to Granville, 'filled with every gross, disgusting indecency that the most depraved imagination could suggest – worse, indeed, than anything I ever heard, saw, read or could imagine among the lowest class of the most abandoned wretches'.[21] Given her own far from chaste behaviour, the letter – of which, regrettably, no copy survives – must have been strong stuff indeed, although it was also said to be 'very well written', as well as 'nasty and disgusting'. Harriet claimed that Caroline 'luckily only read the first few lines, when she was so shocked that she flew to me and gave me the horrid letter'. But Harriet had not always thought ill of Caroline's libidinous admirer. When Hill had, on an earlier occasion, described Caroline as 'the cleverest and prettiest girl in London', Harriet had purred 'dear Mr Hill, I shall set about admiring him whenever I meet him'.[22]

The identity of 'Mr Hill' remained a mystery. Caroline encountered a man of that name at a ball, but he was not privy to many of the intimate details that were described in the letter, or, as Harriet described them, 'conversation and jokes that passed at my sister's a very few days ago'. The writer had to be someone closely connected with the family, who either had desperate carnal designs upon Caroline or was keen to offend her family by pretending that he did. 'Mr Hill' has been variously rumoured to be Sheridan (which, given that there were those who thought the playwright was Caroline's father, gives matters an incestuous spin), the unfortunate Hill whom Caroline encountered at the ball, or even Caroline herself. Her motives, were this to be the case, would have been to cause a stir and shock her mother by producing an exaggeratedly sexual letter that would indicate that her daughter was now thought of not just as potential material for marriage, but also a corruptible prospect. Had she wished to force Harriet's hand and accept any reasonable suitor, writing such a letter might have been the perfect means of doing so, whether of her own volition or in cahoots with a family friend who was willing to co-operate.

William renewed his courtship again after his brother's death in late January 1805, although he was still without funds, owing to Lord Melbourne's continuing antipathy towards him. Therefore, he turned his back on the law and sought a parliamentary seat instead. He also decided that it was high time that he was married. He proposed to Caroline a second time, this time by letter. 'I have loved you for four years,' he wrote, 'loved you deeply, dearly, faithfully – so faithfully that my love has withstood my firm determination to conquer it when honour forbade my declaring myself.'[23] When she received his letter, she showed it to her mother, who was ambivalent about the idea of the match. She wrote to Granville: 'in some things I like it… he has a thousand good qualities, is very clever… and [Caroline] is now so much in love with him that before his speaking, I dreaded it affecting her health'. While she allowed that William had behaved honourably and that his letter had been beautifully written, Harriet saw him as much worldlier than her daughter, and had serious doubts about his character: 'I dislike the connection extremely, I dislike his manners, and still more his principles and his creed, or rather no creed.'*[24] After some soul-searching, aided by Georgiana, Harriet

---

* These qualities did, at least, make Lamb well suited to his career in politics.

reluctantly agreed to the match, and the marriage was 'settled and declared' four days later.[25]

The couple wed soon afterwards, on 3 June 1805. The Prince of Wales was said to have been delighted, exclaiming 'I am *so* happy, oh! But so very happy.'[26] Whether he was saying this out of joy for the couple's union or relief that he had escaped marrying Caroline can only be guessed at. The allowance settled on them at their nuptials was not huge – £400 pin money for Caroline and £1,500 a year (subsequently £1,800) for William.*[27] He was thrilled by their match, and remained so, writing in his autobiography that 'a passion that I had long cherished but had repressed, while prudence forbade the indulgence of it… [it] broke forth and became my master'.[28] The same could not be said for his bride. On her wedding day, nervous at the prospect of marriage and commitment, Caroline threw a hysterical fit: she screamed, she tore her wedding dress and finally fainted.[29] Even a lavish party could not restore her spirits, and she remained unwell for some time afterwards.

Despite this inauspicious start, the marriage was initially a contented one. Harriet commented that her daughter was 'amazingly improved' and that she was 'as gentle and *posée* as if she had been a matron in the country for 20 years rather than days'.[30] She was certainly in love, but not without reservations; she told Little G soon after their marriage that '[I] am very much contented with my present state & yet I cannot say I have never felt happier', which she put down to separation from her family rather than her 'more delightful & more attentive' husband.†[31]

Although Caroline was a virgin when they married, William was an experienced man of the world. She suffered a miscarriage at the beginning of the year, but was pregnant by the end of 1806. They divided their time between Brocket Hall and rooms at Melbourne

* By way of comparison, Peniston had received an allowance of £5,000 per year.
† William had also formed an attachment to Little G and Caroline was bothered for some time with the question of where his affections truly lay.

House in Whitehall, where William could pursue his political ambitions. What he lacked in funds for greasing palms, he made up for in charm and likeability, and he became the Whig member for Leominster on 31 January 1806, helped by 2,000 guineas his father provided for his campaign.[32] While William ingratiated himself at London's finest salons, Caroline was left to amuse herself and to worry about her pregnancy. She asked Little G anxious questions about whether the symptoms that she felt were normal – 'were you very nervous, apt to be frightened, very hungry, very dry, very sleepy & very languid?'[33] Violent arguments with William were followed by emotional reconciliations, in which Caroline continued to fight but also flirted with her husband. When she said to him 'you must not contradict me in anything', it was a simple statement of fact.

Caroline gave birth to her first child, George Augustus Frederick, known as Augustus, on 28 August 1807. He was 'a very fine boy' and a big one too, which made the diminutive Caroline's labour a difficult one, although William noted in a letter to their friend Lady Holland that 'it was very short lasting'.[34] The child was one of the most notable aristocratic births of the year – the Prince of Wales, after whom he was named, was his godfather – and was an attractive baby; Harryo described him as 'really beautiful, [with] a degree of strength, animation and vivacity'.[35] Yet Caroline, suffering from what would now be classed as post-natal depression, exhibited alarming mood swings. Sometimes she could be quiet, gentle and good-natured, and at other times, she would shout and scream at anyone who was around, most often William. Her family referred to her as 'the little beast'[36] and her husband began to devote increasing amounts of time to his political career. William was certainly fond of his son, but Caroline claimed that he was 'less so than I am in outward demonstrations'.[37] It may be the case that William, like many men of his class and era, was emotionally repressed, but it is also more than likely that Caroline's 'outward demonstrations' were histrionic in nature; if William's displays of parental affection did not match Caroline's, it would hardly be remarkable.

By the middle of 1808, it was increasingly clear that Augustus was ill. He frequently suffered frighteningly violent fits and sometimes blacked out completely. Caroline was initially assured that such episodes were natural, but the regularity of the fits led her doctors to suspect that the child had inherited the condition from his mother, who had suffered from a similar affliction during her pregnancy. William, disappointed by the thought that his son and heir would not grow up to be normal, increasingly withdrew into his own circle, spending little time with his wife. They conceived a girl late in 1808, but Caroline suffered a miscarriage on 29 January 1809, which affected both parents greatly. As William distracted himself with politics, Caroline determined that Augustus would be her focus. She wrote a saccharine poem in her commonplace book that celebrated both her son and her husband:

> His little eyes like William's shine
> How great is then my joy,
> For while I call this darling mine,
> I see 'tis William's boy.[38]

After her miscarriage, Caroline threw herself into happier activities. She hosted dinner parties, rode and played at being a loving and dutiful wife; she referred to her husband as 'dearest Mannie' and 'my own dearest sweetest man'.[39] William, however, had begun to lose interest in his wife, and Caroline herself hinted that all was not well between them when she said: 'we have been very troublesome to each other'.[40] William wrote in his commonplace book: 'before I was married, whenever I saw the children and the dogs allowed… to be troublesome… I used to lay it all to the fault of the master… since I have married I find that this was a very rash and premature judgement'.[41]

Caroline took delight in scandalizing London. She attended one masked ball dressed up as a boy, having dyed her hair red, and 'laughed heartily and had no mercy on anyone'. She impersonated a Yorkshire clergyman and Scots literary critic – perhaps from the *Edinburgh Review* – at the same event. In an age when lavish parties and masquerades were designed to cater to the pleasure of several hundred guests, and when champagne and wine were drunk in Bacchanalian quantities, it took a great deal to be noticed, whether for beauty or conversation, or simple bad behaviour. But Caroline's public antics gained her a notoriety that resonated far beyond the elegant venues of the balls and soirées she frequented. She appeared to embrace the sneers of her contemporaries and revel in her infamy. Her husband – who eschewed the wild parties that she patronized and preferred to spend time at his club or at his patrons' houses – could only despair.

Although their marriage had cooled, neither party was openly unfaithful to the other at this stage. In the case of William, his sexual tastes were somewhat specialized in nature, and increasingly focused on *le vice anglais,* flogging and whipping.[42] To have pursued this and been exposed for it would have led to disgrace and shame, and so during Caroline's lifetime he followed his inclinations with great discretion, if at all. She, meanwhile, liked to flirt with other men in an attempt to make her husband jealous, most notably with Sir Godfrey Webster, a dim-witted but handsome young man who had served heroically in the Peninsular War, as had her brother Frederick. Among Webster's more decadent habits was drinking wine out of the skull of a French soldier, which he had had turned into a gold-encrusted drinking vessel. Caroline was attracted to the valour he represented as much as the man himself, and, in early 1810, she began to conduct her first extra-marital liaison, consisting of kisses 'snatched up with a great deal of fear'[43] in back alleys, and exchanges of love letters and tokens of affection, such as gold chains and a puppy.

It remains uncertain whether the affair was consummated, but Caroline's behaviour in public continued to be provocative and attention-seeking, as she switched from wearing boys' attire to loose-fitting bodices that exposed her breasts. While William was either unaware of or unconcerned by such conduct, others took sharper notice. Webster's mother Lady Holland, one of the grandest society hostesses of the day, asked for an explanation of Caroline's relationship with Webster, and was assured that theirs was nothing more than a friendship; Caroline insisted that 'I am not lost enough to break everybody's heart & my own by abandoning my husband & child.'[44]

However, her mother-in-law, Lady Melbourne, was appalled, and, after seeing Caroline and Webster at a party, wrote her a furious letter in which she said 'your behaviour last night was so disgraceful in its appearances and so disgusting in its motives that it is quite impossible it should ever be effaced from my mind'.[45] Lady Melbourne was a significant figure in society and to be ostracized by her – 'do not drive me to explain the meaning of the cold civility that will henceforth pass between us' – was the kiss of death as far as being received in respectable households went. The unspoken point she made was that she was not against the traditional aristocratic pursuit of infidelity, but found the brazen flaunting of it to be deeply offensive.

Caroline belatedly realized the gravity of her actions, and so she grovelled to Lady Melbourne, stressing that 'I am indeed very miserable [and] very repentant… Good God I tremble when I think of it, I was indeed on the brink of perdition & about to encounter misery, infamy and ruin with perfect levity.' She promised to give up Webster, although she blamed William in part, claiming that he 'taught me to regard without horror all the forms & restraints I had laid so much stress on… he is superior to those passions and vanities which mislead weaker characters and which I may be ashamed to own it, are continually misleading me'.[46] She also wrote to Lady Holland in early May to say 'I am more innocent than I appear',[47] but this was dismissed by Lord Holland, who described the letter as 'monstrous silly… the common cant of every woman in similar circumstances'. Caroline's repentance was not sincere; she continued to see Webster until June 1810, and would probably have prolonged the affair had parental pressure not been exerted upon him to leave the country and return to soldiering.

Webster's absence did not check Caroline's increasingly unseemly behaviour. Her attempts at being conciliatory and well-behaved were token. Even as she declared that she would be 'silent of a morning, entertaining after dinner, docile, fearless as a heroine in the last volume of her troubles, strong as a mountain tiger',[48] she remained drawn to scandal and controversy. She began to practise waltzing, a new dance believed to be immoral because of the closeness between partners; she defended herself in an otherwise conciliatory letter to Lady Holland by professing:

> I have always been of [the] opinion and still am that those who like [waltzing] like it because it is doubtful – those good young women who shudder at the thought of vice like to venture to the edge of the precipice down which so many of their frail companions have been thrown.[49]

Her family were unimpressed. Lady Spencer believed both that she acted 'not from vice but vanity' – the implication was that vice at least had a purpose – and that she 'lowers her character by such improprieties'.[50]

Her marriage to William grew increasingly miserable, but few took Caroline's side. On their sixth wedding anniversary in June 1811 they attended a ball and seemed to be all but estranged already; he left early and she continued to cavort wildly. While he remained controlled and contained, others were happy to intercede on his behalf and make it clear to Caroline that she was bringing disgrace on her family. Defensive by nature, she fought back. Lady Holland told her that 'in our last reconciliation, you vexed me more than during our quarrel – you said hard things to me under the appearance of kindness'.[51] Caroline justified herself with the retaliation that 'my passions have so long been used to master my reason that although it exists it is not everybody who knows it does'.[52] She then continued the feud when she wrote to Lady Holland in a fit of pique after being barred from a party. Angry, Caroline mocked her for her poor treatment of Webster ('you do well to renounce a mother's name') and averred that 'neither by writing or by conversation or by any other means will I from this hour hold the smallest communication with you'.[53]

Although she realized that she had been rash and foolish – even by her previous standards – and made desperate attempts at reconciliation with Lady Holland, she looked ridiculous. A truce of sorts was eventually brokered months later, although this was more out of deference to William's status as the rising star of politics than out of forgiveness on Lady Holland's part. A tough and determined woman, described by her friend the wit Sydney Smith as 'formidable' and famous for what the actress Elizabeth Kemble called her 'domineering rudeness', her cold control was the opposite of Caroline's emotional instability.

~&~

The year 1812 seemed, at first, to promise better things for Caroline. She had befriended the poet and writer Sydney Owenson, later Lady Morgan, and Caroline was pleased that someone cared about her. Sydney described her as 'gifted with the rarest powers, at once an artist, a poetess, a writer of romance, a woman of society and the world', and even went so far as to praise her as 'a woman of genius', even as she acknowledged her 'sublime discontent' and restless nature.[54] This sense of affirmation and approval had been sorely lacking from Caroline's life for years, probably since her miscarriage; the previous year, she had complained to a pre-schism Lady Holland that 'no time will ever bring me back the perfect innocence & enjoyment I once possessed, nor shall I ever hear William's name or meet his eyes without feelings of bitter reproach'.[55] She had disappointed as a wife, failing to comply with the tradition that political wives should be excellent hostesses and little more, and Augustus showed no signs of improvement as he grew older. After the trauma of Caroline's last miscarriage, the couple would have no other child.

Under Sydney's influence, Caroline began to read more widely, studying the classics and contemporary poets alike. Her literary interests became known, and the wealthy art collector, banker and occasional writer Samuel Rogers believed that she would make a receptive reader and potential publicist for a brilliant yet scandalous work that he had encountered, the first two cantos of *Childe Harold's Pilgrimage*. He gave her an early proof copy in February 1812. His instincts were correct. Caroline was enraptured by the depiction of the dashing, world-weary protagonist, misunderstood and maligned but able to rise above his materialistic and drab surroundings and contemporaries – the 'heartless parasites' of society – in order to display his heroic individuality. Sensing a kindred spirit, she eagerly demanded an introduction to the poet from Rogers, who demurred, perhaps realizing what an unholy union he risked engineering. It did not help that Byron, who had delivered his first speech to the House of Lords at the end of February to what he called 'many marvellous eulogies',[56] had become a celebrity and the most invited man in town. In an attempt to cool Caroline's interest, Rogers described him as 'a nail biter with a club foot'. It was no good; she responded 'if he is as ugly as Aesop, I must see him'.[57]

To stress her point, she wrote to Byron anonymously, shortly after the publication on 3 March. In gushing terms, she addressed him as 'Childe Harold' and claimed: 'I have read your book and cannot refrain from telling you that I think it… beautiful… do not throw away such talents as you possess in gloom and regrets for the past and above all live here in your own country which will be proud of you.'[58] In the last sentiment, she was correct. Byron's friend Thomas Moore wrote of how 'his fame had not to wait for any of the ordinary gradations, but seemed to spring up, like the palace of a fairy tale, in a night'.[59] Female admirers besieged him; many of them took to verse to express their admiration for the coming

man.* Caroline was no exception, using iambic pentameter to
illustrate both her poetic ability and her understanding of Childe
Harold's sentiments. Some of what she said was ambiguous:

> Strong love I feel for one I shall not name –
> What I should feel for thee could never be the same –
> But admiration interest is free –
> And that Childe Harold may receive from me.[60]

Byron, sensing both a kindred spirit and a challenge, was intrigued.
He made enquiries of his friend Robert Dallas, and was informed
that his correspondent was none other than the notorious Lady
Caroline Lamb. By now both parties were on the hunt for one
another, and Caroline saw Byron at a society ball at Lady Westmoreland's. She noted both his dark good looks and pallor, as if
he was suffering from a fever. As the young literary lion of the
day – by his self-description, 'a ball-room bard – a *hot-pressed*
darling'[61] – he was surrounded by eager young women, either
fawningly sycophantic or determinedly forward in their attentions.
Rather than cheapen herself, Caroline spurned an introduction
to him and left, claiming that she 'looked earnestly at him, and
turned my heel'.[62] Writing in her diary that evening, she famously
dismissed him as 'mad, bad and dangerous to know'.[63] Had matters rested there, then the hint of a flirtation would have remained
nothing more than that. Yet neither Byron nor Caroline were
satisfied with hints of flirtation.

---

* A recently discovered collection of such letters includes one correspondent writing of how she felt 'trembling' when she looked at Byron's
portrait and asked 'Why, did my breast with rapture glow/Thy talents to
admire?/Why, as I read, my bosom felt/Enthusiastic fire?'

5

That beautiful pale face is my fate.

CAROLINE LAMB, IN HER COMMONPLACE BOOK,
24 MARCH 1812

Byron, in the first thrill of fame, was not used to being rebuffed. When Caroline had walked away from Lady Westmoreland's soirée without acknowledging him, he was both surprised and intrigued by this curious, scandalous and apparently ungovernable woman. While she was not the most attractive prospect in London, she was aristocratic, and Byron, a relatively new arrival to the upper classes, saw an authenticity in her that he aspired to. Even the rumours of her inconstancy and histrionic behaviour did little to dispel his curiosity; bad behaviour, after all, was the privilege of those at the pinnacle of society.

The first official meeting between Byron and Caroline took place at Holland House on 24 March 1812. Caroline's lack of favour with Lady Holland, due to her flirtation with the latter's son, coloured the encounter. When Byron arrived at the house, Lady Holland announced, 'I must present Lord Byron to you.' Caroline greeted him politely, but Byron, piqued by her behaviour, said 'this offer was made to you before; may I ask why you rejected it?'[1] Caroline was embarrassed and flustered by his directness, stammering that she had felt uncomfortable and tired; the truth was that she had not wished to be one of a giggling gaggle of acolytes. Byron then, devastatingly, delivered his 'underlook', a smouldering glance that he had practised to his own satisfaction for years, and which he

believed made him irresistible to women and men alike. It worked
as he intended. That evening, Caroline confided in her commonplace book that 'that beautiful pale face is my fate'.[2]

Byron, with the avidity of a predator sighting its prey, asked for
and received permission to call on her again, which he did the next
day at Melbourne House. As a confidante of William Lamb's parents, especially Lady Melbourne, he had the usual privileges of an
ami de maison, but his interest lay in the awkward, boyish Caroline.
Appearing with Samuel Rogers, they were greeted by her coming
'filthy and hot' from riding, and she was surprised by Byron's visi-
tation; she wondered, 'should I go up to my room and tidy myself
before confronting him as I was? No, my curiosity was too great and
I rushed in to be introduced to this portent.'[3] She invited him to a
ball on 26 March, and he asked if he could see her the following evening. From that time forth, there was no escaping her destiny; she
later reflected that 'Lord Byron wished to come and see me at eight
o'clock, when I was alone; that was my dinner hour. I said he might.
From that moment, for more than nine months, he almost lived
at Melbourne House.'[4] Byron knew what he could expect when he
headed there; as he told Thomas Moore, who accompanied him,
'you will meet with a civil reception and decent entertainment'.

'Decent entertainment' was just one of the things that could be
found at Melbourne House. It housed what Moore described as
'the whole splendid interior of the High Life', and everyone from
politicians and artists to writers and aristocrats enjoyed intoxi-
cating debate and wine in equal quantities. The building itself
featured a mixture of grand public spaces and enclosed and dark
private staircases and corridors; it was as ideal for assignations and
snatched kisses as it was for the daily waltzing that took place for
the *beau monde*. Byron, never a comfortable dancer due to his lame
foot, was more interested in the backstairs intrigues that could be
partaken of there instead.[5]

When he arrived at Melbourne House on 26 March, he bore
a well-chosen gift for Caroline, a rose and carnation, as well as a

poem he had written about the death of his dog Boatswain. When she received them with pleasure, he smiled half-sarcastically and said, 'your Ladyship, I am told, likes all that is new and rare for the moment'.[6] The parallel with the 'new and rare' man standing before her was irresistible. She treasured the rose, keeping it long beyond the end of her acquaintance with Byron, perhaps because it represented something pure and beautiful – yet still subject to inevitable decline and decay. When it faded, she responded histrionically, saying that it had 'died in despite of every effort made to save it; probably from regret at its fallen fortunes', and seized the chance to compare herself to a sunflower that 'having once beheld in its full lustre the bright and unclouded sun that for one moment condescended to shine upon it, never while it exists could think any lower object worthy of its worship and admiration'.[7]

Initially, Byron and Caroline's relationship was platonic. Each feigned a lack of physical attraction to the other (Byron later called her 'too thin… wanting that roundness that grace and elegance would vainly supply')[8] and claimed that their friendship was one of shared intellectual interests. Caroline's mother Harriet, who realized the peril at hand, tried to dissuade him, which Byron later commented to Lady Melbourne spurred him on: 'she piqued that vanity (which it would be the *vainest* thing on earth to deny) by telling me she was certain "I was not beloved"'.[9] He nicknamed her 'Lady Blarney', a reference to Goldsmith's wittering society woman in his novel *The Vicar Of Wakefield* and 'the hack whore of the last half century', a gesture of misogynistic contempt. Nonetheless, her daughter retained his interest. Although Caroline was not a conventional beauty, she had a seductive 'soft, low, caressing voice' and dark eyes that had first drawn William to her, and also lacked the conventional and stilted manners of high society, remaining free-spirited.

The sexual tension between her and Byron became inescapable, however, and they consummated their affair in early April. They first had sex in a carriage; she later claimed 'you drew me to you like a magnet and I could not… have kept away'.[10] Enraptured, she wrote to him afterwards to declare: 'never while life beats in this heart shall I forget you or that moment when first you said you loved me – when my heart did not meet yours but flew before it – & both intended to remain innocent of greater wrong'.[11] Byron appeared to reciprocate her affections. He addressed her by her pet name of 'Caro' and praised her as 'the cleverest, most agreeable, absurd, perplexing, dangerous fascinating little being that lives now or ought to have lived 2000 years ago'; a hint of equivocation could be found when he mused 'every word you utter, every line you write proves you to be either *sincere* or a *fool*'.[12] His friend Dallas believed Byron was sincere in his affection towards her, and described him as 'so enraptured, so intoxicated, that his time and thoughts were almost entirely devoted to reading her letters and answering them',[13] which he was said to do with 'a peculiar smile on his lips'.

Caroline made little secret of her attachment to Byron, and behaved with even less discretion than she had during her liaison with Webster. Proud to have snared the most talked-about man in London society, she showed off her prize and made it clear to all interested parties that their relationship was a sexual one. Rogers, for one, was incredulous at her boldness. He later wrote that 'she absolutely besieged him' at public events, waiting outside if she had not been invited and Byron had, and that 'I saw her – yes, saw her – talking to Byron, with half of her body thrust into the carriage which he had just entered'.[14] Harryo, meanwhile – no stranger to the outrageous entanglements of her family – summed up the situation with admirable economy, remarking dryly that 'Lord Byron is still upon a pedestal, and Caroline [Lamb] [is] doing homage.' Harryo was far from smitten by Byron, saying that 'his countenance is fine, when it is in repose, but the moment it is in play [it is] suspicious, malignant and consequently repulsive'.[15]

The 'play' between Byron and Caroline was thoroughly adult in nature. As far back as 1808 he had enjoyed a liaison with another Caro, the sixteen-year-old Caroline Cameron. She was a blue-eyed and 'charming' prostitute whom Byron liked to have sex with in the persona of a boy. A kinky twist much appreciated by him was that she posed as his brother, on the pretext that 'my mother might not hear of my having such a female acquaintance',[16] but in fact because cross-dressing excited Byron's pan-sexual appetites. Such was the frequency and enthusiasm of his activity with Caroline at first that he was obliged to obtain a doctor's prescription for what he unblushingly described as 'a debility occasioned by too frequent connection'.[17] Now, the second Caroline donned breeches as well, partly to avoid detection when she appeared at Byron's rooms in St James's Street, but also because it stimulated him. Her disguise was, according to Dallas, wholly convincing; she was described as looking like 'a fair-faced delicate boy of thirteen or fourteen years old… dressed in scarlet hussar jacket and pantaloons'. The resemblance between her and Byron's late boy-love John Edleston may well not have been a coincidence.[18]

Despite his fame and adulation, Byron was not without worries, mainly financial ones; the sales of *Childe Harold's Pilgrimage* were strong, but he had given the royalties to Dallas, just as he had gifted the proceeds from *English Bards and Scotch Reviewers* to James Cawthorn. He discussed his money woes with Caroline, who pledged him financial support should he need it, even offering to sell her jewellery. This depth of involvement was new territory for Byron, who, even as he continued his dalliances with other women, was smitten by Caroline and told her stories of his past. He confessed to his dalliance with Rushton (although not that with Edleston) and his liaisons with everyone from foreign ladies to washerwomen. They staged a mock marriage, exchanging wedding rings, and Byron wrote Caroline a love poem in thanks for a gift of a gold chain:

> Since gifts returned but pain the giver
> And the soft band put on by thee
> The slightest chain, will last forever.[19]

He even did his best to be avuncular towards Augustus, although his natural *métier* was not one of bouncing a small child on his knee.[20]

The relationship between the two was nonetheless compromised from the start by the lovers' conflicting personalities. Byron was sexually insatiable, yet keenly aware of the thoughts and attitudes of those around him. Whether he took any notice of them was another matter entirely. Caroline, who was experiencing an awakening that rendered anything that she had felt before indifferent, was obsessed by her conquest, and damned propriety with her every action. When Byron wrote to Caroline to describe her heart as 'a little volcano',[21] he knew, as well as she did, that volcanoes simmered before erupting with a remarkable and deadly force, laying waste to everything in their path. This proved prescient.

◆

If Caroline was content to ignore others and wallow in the luxury of new love, Byron had no desire to cut himself off from the society that seemed, finally, to have accepted him. He felt jealous of Caroline's husband, comparing himself to William in sardonic terms as the devilish adulterer to the angelic politician (he was presumably unaware of William's kinkier interests), and flirted with other women in front of her to make her feel envious. In the case of the heiress and intellectual Annabella Milbanke, with whom Byron had recently begun a correspondence,* the flirtation would lead elsewhere, but she had an unexpected rival in the impressive form of Lady Melbourne. Although the queen of London society was sixty-two and old enough to be Byron's mother, if not his grandmother, she was his confidante and friend. She had always loathed her daughter-in-law – and Harriet, who responded by christening her 'The Thorn' – and so her loyalty in the affair lay, bizarrely, with the man cuckolding her son. Caroline

---

* A fuller account of Byron's relationship with Annabella is contained in Part III.

feared, possibly with good reason, that Byron's friendship with her also had a physical aspect; she sneered 'if I feel jealous of her, I will remember her age and respect her… she is wholly without sentiment and romance'.[22]

Caroline and Byron's relationship was driven by furious quarrels from the beginning. When Caroline admitted that she still loved her husband, it was met with contempt. She declared that Byron 'did abuse me & scorn me & mock me so and called me such horrid names', before he announced that 'you shall pay for this… I will wring that obstinate little neck'.[23] However, what Rogers called 'the insanity of her passion for Byron' meant that the violent rows were soon made up in equally violent lovemaking. Sometimes this lovemaking – or 'connection' – transgressed the bounds of decency. Byron's friend Medwin reported that Byron remarked that one of their quarrels 'was made up in a very odd way, and without any verbal explanation. She will remember it.'[24] This 'very odd way' was almost certainly anal intercourse, instigated by Byron in an attempt to do with Caroline, the sometime pageboy, what he had previously enjoyed with young men. His behaviour would mean scandal and ruin were it to be made public, given the notoriety in which sodomy was held.

For all their rowing, it was widely believed that Byron and Caroline would elope together, and so it became obvious that action had to be taken to forestall this, otherwise scandal would overwhelm them both. Accordingly, Caroline left for Brocket Hall on 18 May 1812, after a lengthy farewell lovemaking session that saw Byron joke to Moore that 'at three… I saw her launched into the country'.[25] Before her departure, Caroline made Lady Melbourne three promises: that she would never let the affair end badly; that she would never elope; and that she would never claim that she preferred Byron to her husband. At least two of these were eventually broken. The day that she left, Byron witnessed the hanging of John Bellingham, the murderer of Prime Minister Spencer Perceval, and he was profoundly disturbed by it; Caroline later referred to 'your being deeply so [affected] yourself'.[26] Beneath his assurance and charm, the ever-present possibility of disgrace, even execution, shook Byron deeply.

Perhaps not coincidentally, he now attempted to end the affair as kindly as he could. Writing to Caroline, he acknowledged that rumours and gossip had become pervasive – 'people talk as if there were no other pair of absurdities in London' – and that 'it is hard to bear all this without cause, but worse to give cause for it'. As a public figure, and a bachelor, the onus was on him to end matters ('I conformed & could conform'), but he was moved by her plight, saying 'I can't bear to see you look so unhappy and am always on the watch to observe if you are trying to make me so.' Summing up their romance as 'this delirium of two months', he counselled finishing it cleanly, claiming 'we have both had 1000 previous fancies of the same kind and shall get the better of this and shall be ashamed of it'.[27]

Byron's efforts failed, and, on 29 July, matters worsened considerably.

❧

Caroline received Byron's attempt at severance with both distress and renewed determination. She knew that it would be easy for him to walk away from her and find himself another lover, but considerably harder for her to retain her dignity in such circumstances. Therefore, she wrote to Byron in conciliatory fashion, addressed him as 'my dearest', and claimed that 'I am exceedingly grieved I gave you so much uneasiness'. She also referred to the resolution of a quarrel by saying, 'I will endeavour by all possible means to avoid a return of anything so painful between us.'[28] She alluded to her 'present circumstances' as being the cause of this difficulty; this was a reference to both her strained marriage to William, and her much-discussed position as a scandalous woman.

When the two were in London again, Caroline seemed hell-bent on forcing a lasting union. Offering a placid exterior, she managed to convince Harriet that she and William were as close as ever on 24 July, assuaging her worries that she was planning to abscond with Byron. In a matter of days, things changed dramatically. Byron, knowing that Caroline had potentially ruinous designs, planned to leave London for Harrow with his friend Hobhouse,* knowing of 'the threatened visit of a Lady'.[29] They were at Byron's rooms in St James's Street at midday when they heard 'several thundering taps' on the door, and then a 'person in most strange disguise walked upstairs', past Hobhouse, into Byron's bedroom. It was Caroline, dressed in her customary disguise of pageboy attire. For Byron to be seen publicly in the company of a married woman – and in the most compromising of positions – would have been deeply embarrassing at best, socially ruinous at worst. Aided by Hobhouse, Caroline was persuaded to don more feminine clothing, borrowed from the servants, but showed no signs of leaving. Instead, she revealed that the purpose of her visit was nothing less than an elopement, saying 'we must go off together, there is no alternative'.

Hobhouse, blessed with greater presence of mind than anyone else, asked Caroline to leave, but she threatened that 'there will be blood spilt' if anyone attempted to intercede. 'There will indeed, unless you go away,' responded Hobhouse, to which Byron nodded assent. Caroline, frustrated and angry, seized a dress sword from the sofa nearby and attempted to tussle with the men, but Byron managed to restrain her. Eventually, they persuaded her to leave St James's Street, which she agreed to as long as she could have a further rendezvous with Byron before she returned to Brocket Hall at the end of the week. Hobhouse later described his role as being 'to prevent a public disclosure and an elopement'. He succeeded.

The failure of the scheme did nothing to limit Caroline's ardour. In what would become one of her most notorious actions, she sent Byron an intimate letter in early August, containing a tuft of her

* Hobhouse was no admirer of Caroline, referring to her as 'the Lamb that taketh not away the sins of this world'. It is thanks to him that we have such an unusually detailed account of the day.

pubic hair. She had cut rather too close to the skin, so the hairs came stained with blood; the accompanying letter stated 'I asked you not to send blood, but yet do – because if it means love I like to have it.' Asking him not to put scissor points near where '*quei capelli*'* grow, she signed herself 'your wild antelope'. Byron's response was poised and careful; although he did not reciprocate with any intimate clippings of his own, he sent her a gold locket bearing the family crest of *Crede Byron*, or 'have faith in Byron'. The potential for faithlessness was not remarked upon.

Byron's attitude towards Caroline at this time oscillated between obsession and realization that their affair had to end. He told Hobhouse that 'he could only do what she pleased', but also that 'a few weeks absence would cure him'. The upshot of any ending of the dalliance in an elopement would be, he joked grimly, 'that he should blow his brains out a week after'.[30] In his desire to sever relations, he was inadvertently aided by both Harriet and William, keen to avoid potentially career-threatening scandal. In one especially vitriolic row on 12 August, after Caroline threatened to leave him for Byron, William called her bluff, wishing both that she should 'go, and be damned!' and openly doubting that Byron would have her.[31] Caroline's response was to flee to an unknown destination; while it was thought that she would have run to St James's Street, she was not to be found there. Instead, she had pawned a ring to hire a coach with the intention of heading to Portsmouth and catching the first boat, wherever it travelled.

Caroline's actions at this time were more influenced by mental disturbance than any romantic ideals. She did not leave London, instead taking refuge at the Kensington house of a surgeon she knew, Dr Thomas. Sending farewell letters to her husband and lover care of the coachman who delivered her there proved her undoing. Byron, always determined when it came to pursuing women, bribed and bullied the coachman to let him know where

---

* Literally, 'those hairs'.

Caroline had fled to, and headed to Thomas's house. Once there, he dramatically announced that he was Caroline's brother, there on a mission of mercy to retrieve her. When she was returned to the Bessborough's home in Cavendish Square, it was quickly agreed to hush the matter up, for fear of ridicule and public exposure. The stress and upset had the added and unfortunate effect of reducing Harriet to a state of nervous collapse, in which she coughed up blood; it transpired that she had suffered a mild stroke. Caroline was scolded for this by Harriet's maid, Mrs Petersen, who criticized her for her 'cruel and unnatural' behaviour towards her mother, and told her to 'pray to God for strength of mind and resolution to behave as you ought for this is dreadful'.[32]

It seemed clear that Caroline should leave London immediately before she could cause any more trouble, and it was proposed that she be taken to the Bessborough family house in County Kilkenny in Ireland. Byron, knowing that her actions left her vulnerable and exposed, wrote her a letter that cunningly mixed expressions of apparent endearment – 'no other in word or deed shall ever hold the place in my affection which is & shall be most sacred to you' – with statements of belief that their affair would end shortly, either of his own volition or through the agency of her mother and husband.[33] Thus, he adopted the persona of the ardent lover who was being forced by cruel fate to quit his beloved forever, without having to commit to anything more lasting. He might have declared 'I was and am *yours,* freely and most entirely, to obey, honour, love', and promised a future elopement 'when, where & how you, yourself *might and may* determine', but his fine words were mere window dressing, designed to absolve him of any guilt he was feeling. This was in keeping with a witheringly cynical statement he made to Medwin that 'I made every effort to be in love, expressed as much ardour as I could muster, and kept feeding the flame with a constant surprise of *billets doux* and amatory verses.'[34]

However, Caroline had learned from him over the previous few months, and one area that she now excelled was in subterfuge.

Accordingly, she announced to Harriet that she believed herself to be pregnant, and that she feared that the journey to Ireland would bring on a miscarriage. Whether or not this was true – or whether the child was William's or Byron's – her plea not to be forced to travel carried weight. Rather more than she did, it soon transpired; by the end of August, it was clear that she was not expecting a child, and so she, William and her parents left for Bessborough House in County Kilkenny in early September. Before she left, she wrote Byron several letters, in which she swore that she would love him more than any wife he took, tried in vain to suggest 'accidental' rendezvous locations, and confessed her disappointment at not seeing him at a party, saying that 'when I came out last night, which was of itself an effort, and when I heard your name announced, the moment after I saw nothing more, but seemed in a dream'.[35]

When Caroline departed for Ireland, she consoled herself with the belief that her parting from Byron was one that neither had wished for, and that he would be as despondent at her absence from his side as she was about his. This was unreciprocated. Byron, who was in the process of trying to sell his beloved Newstead Abbey to realize some necessary funds,* headed out of London for some relaxation; as he wrote to Lord Holland, 'by the waters of Cheltenham, I sat down & *drank*'.[36] He had enlisted Lady Melbourne's assistance in attempting to calm Caroline. He knew that he was in sufficient favour to be able to say that 'if she is to be persecuted for my faults – to be reproached with the consequences of a misplaced affection but too well returned... I cannot & will not bear it, without at least taking my own just share of the consequences'.[37] The 'consequences', such as they were, involved nothing more onerous than his fashionable sojourn; Lady Melbourne, and others, even joined him in Cheltenham, strengthening the bond between them.

* Byron was eventually offered £140,000, by a Lancashire lawyer named Thomas Claughton; Claughton subsequently defaulted on the sale.

While Byron flirted, and possibly more, with his confidante, Caroline continued to pine for him. Amid the damp and dull surroundings of Bessborough House, she tried to entertain herself as best she could with dinners and dancing, among her ever-watchful family, but she believed that she was being punished for her behaviour and that she had not deserved her exile. Harriet even went so far as to write to Lady Melbourne to ask her to maintain her hold on Byron, something that the poet was swiftly informed of by his amused patron.[38] Not only was he delighted by the power that he had over Caroline – only kept in check by one of London's grandest women – but it added another layer of magnetism and intrigue to his ever-increasing reputation. When he announced that 'I do not believe in the existence of what is called love',[39] it was Childe Harolde's renunciation of traditional human attachment made flesh. Caroline was reduced to little more than a pawn.

Nonetheless, unwilling to give up the game, he continued to correspond with her, albeit with less frequency than her near-daily epistles. While he occasionally privately entertained the idea of marriage to Caroline,[40] if only to provide himself with an aristocratic wife, a more telling display of his intentions was a letter he sent to Lady Melbourne in which he casually betrayed his lover by telling her that 'C is suspicious of our counter plots', and revealed his allegiances when he said 'I am obliged to be as treacherous as Talleyrand, but remember that *treachery is truth* to you',[41] before he boasted of his lies to Caroline and stated that 'my amatory tropes and figures are exhausted'. He concluded, boastfully, by claiming 'her worst enemy could not wish her such a fate as *now* to be thrown back upon me'.[42]

Even as Byron attempted to extricate himself from his troublesome lover, his thoughts turned to marriage to a more appealing (and unmarried) prospect as a way out; as he told Lady Melbourne, 'nothing but a marriage and a *speedy one* can save me… [I would marry] the very first woman who does not look as if she would spit in my face'.[43] As a result of this, his attentions turned to Annabella,

whose gentler urgings to him to embrace virtue seemed an altogether safer matrimonial option than the scandalous consequences
of embracing a woman who would have to obtain a very public
divorce. He remained confused about his feelings for Caroline,
alternating between (increasingly rare) private rapture and public
dismissal. His confusion and cruelty was summarized by an apparently sincere paradox that he outlined in relation to Harriet, when
he claimed he wished to spare her the hurt of seeing her daughter
abandoned abruptly; he commented that 'she will *hate* me if *I* don't
break my heart'.[44]

By October, sensing that Lady Melbourne was in the ascendant
both in influence and proximity, Caroline felt that she had to call
her less-than-ardent swain's bluff and find out whether he really
did have any affection for her. She blamed Lady Melbourne's influence, and drafted an angry letter that lambasted her for talking
'harshly and unkindly' and stated that her 'savage words' had forced
her to a point where she could neither eat nor sleep, and that her
influence on Byron had been a harsh and unfair one.[45] The letter
was unsent, and instead she wrote a more temperate one in which
she praised her mother-in-law for her 'generous' behaviour and
blamed herself for the 'madness and excess' that her attachment to
Byron had driven her to.

Caroline made the perceptive judgement of him that, while he is
'amiable, generous & full of talents', 'he is of a character to desire
those who love him most', which he exercised with 'violence and
rashness'. While she claimed to 'love & admire & believe in him
from my heart & soul', she was not so foolish as to believe that
his behaviour towards her stemmed from love. She remarked that
'being talked of with one man is also a nice excuse for all others to
seek you', but contrasted the 'generous noble kind husband' she had
with the doomed and wicked affair on which she had embarked.
Everything about the letter spoke of misery and hurt, with the
abiding sense that Byron had started their entanglement and had
been slapped on the back by society for his *élan* in conducting it,

whereas she had been roundly condemned and exiled to Ireland. Like Ophelia,* she was the more deceived, and felt helpless as a result.

Caroline finally wrote to Byron to ask him, as calmly as she could, whether there was any future for the two of them. He was atypically lost for words in his reply, destroying his original response and justifying it on the grounds that all his answer would do would lead to 'endless recapitulation, recrimination, *bother*ation… accusation, & all other –ations but *sal*vation'.[46] Lady Melbourne's advice was by turns brutal *realpolitik* ('whatever step you take to break off this affair has my full concurrence')[47] and apparent kindness, as when she stated that 'I would not have you say a harsh sentence to her for the world, and anything that could be deemed insulting'. This was soon undercut by her coldly Machiavellian judgement that 'how much more kind to give her a little present pain, and avoid her total ruin'.[48]

It did not help Caroline that Byron had become infatuated with a friend of hers, Jane Harley, countess of Oxford. Lady Oxford was the opposite of Caroline in many regards, being 'gentle and kind', as well as a conventional feminine beauty. Two characteristics that she did share with Caroline (as well as Byron) were an interest in liberal politics – she was an ardent Whig and supporter of the Reform movement – and an unwillingness to be discreet about her love affairs, which was tolerated as long as she remained popular. Byron had begun a fling with her shortly after Caroline's departure for Ireland, and found himself in the delicate situation of juggling her, Caroline and Lady Melbourne in an especially exhausting *ménage à quatre*. Nonetheless, his life could be simplified by at least removing Caroline from the complex equation, and so he wrote to her with as much finality as he could manage to bring about a very definite end of the affair. Although no finished copy of the letter

* Caroline identified with the Shakespearean heroine: she would refer to Ophelia's line 'Shake not your heads, nor say the lady's mad' in her 'bonfire poem' at Christmas that year.

itself exists, Caroline reproduced a version of it in her *roman-à-clef* about her and Byron's love affair, *Glenarvon*, and it exists in a couple of manuscript drafts.*

In attempting to 'undo the knot', Byron told her that 'our affections are not in our own power', and that his were engaged elsewhere; as he bluntly said, 'I am attached to another'. Byron had recently become betrothed to his previous correspondent Annabella, who was his 'public' amour, but the attachment might just as easily have been Lady Oxford, Lady Melbourne or one of the many others who he was involved with at this time. His refusal to give the name of the woman 'to whom I am now entirely devoted & attached' merely exacerbated the situation. Either in an attempt to show kindness or out of a cruel desire to taunt her, Byron claimed '[I shall] ever remember with gratitude the many instances I have received of the predilection you have shown in my favour'. His truer intentions were shown by the faux-amity of his statement that 'I shall ever continue your friend... and, as a first proof of my regard, I offer you this advice; correct your vanity, which is ridiculous; exert your absurd caprices upon others; and leave me in peace.' As a final piece of cruelty, the letter was sent under Lady Oxford's seal, reaching Caroline at the Dolphin Hotel in Dublin just before she departed for England at the beginning of November.

The effect was devastating. Caroline later claimed that 'it destroyed me: I lost my brain... I was in great prostration of mind and spirit',[49] and even made a feeble attempt at suicide, grasping a razor and grappling with her mother for control of it. Upon her return to England, she was sequestered in a 'filthy' inn in Rock, Cornwall for a fortnight,† and found herself at her lowest point, fearing for both her sanity and her health. Anything that she wrote Byron merely reinforced his resolve not to see her, even a letter

* I am indebted to Paul Douglass for his reconstruction of it, as found on pp. 135–6 of *Lady Caroline Lamb*.
† Coincidentally also called the Dolphin.

that begged piteously for a final meeting between the two. He dismissed her to Lady Melbourne as 'the most contradictory, absurd, selfish & contemptibly wicked of human productions'.[50]

As she returned to Brocket Hall with William, any hope of reconciliation with Byron seemed entirely lost. A request that her letters and gifts be returned was partially honoured; many of her presents to him had been given away to other women he had wished to impress. In a spirit of revenge, she destroyed what she was given on a Christmas bonfire, as her pages, all dressed in buttons saying 'Ne crede Byron',* recited a poem that contained these lines:

> London, farewell; vain world, vain life adieu!
> Take the last tears I e'er shall shed for you.
> Young tho' I seem, I leave the world for ever,
> Never to enter it again; no, never, never!

Anyone who had listened to her might have been forgiven for thinking that Caroline had planned her own spectacular immolation on the bonfire. However, she refused to do so, perhaps fearful of giving her enemies the satisfaction of ridding themselves of her so easily. Byron was both horrified and flattered by the conflagration. Hobhouse, responding to his account, compared Caroline to the ancient courtesan Phryne, saying '*me Phryne macerat... nec uno contenta*', which can be roughly translated as 'not content with one man, Phryne torments me'.[51] Tormented though Byron was by Caroline – he rhetorically asked Lady Melbourne 'what can she do worse than she has done?'[52] – there was a theatricality to her actions that suggested there remained a perverse attachment on her part, despite the extremity of her professed animosity. Only the least curious would have wondered how this particular drama would play out its final act.

They would not be disappointed.

* A perversion of the family motto *Crede Biron*.

6

To the latest hour of my life I shall
hate that woman.

BYRON TO LADY MELBOURNE,
5 APRIL 1813

If 1812 saw Caroline humiliated and rejected by Byron, 1813 saw her gain revenge. As he tried to distract himself by writing his Oriental epic *The Giaour*, she forged a letter, ostensibly from Byron, to his publisher John Murray that demanded that his much-treasured portrait by the artist George Sanders should be handed over to her. Murray, a good-natured and canny businessman, had been involved with Byron since publishing *Childe Harold's Pilgrimage* in 1811, and regarded him as one of his most valued authors; nonetheless, he was equally liable to fall for the wiles of a cunning woman. She then visited Murray's offices in Albermarle Street in January and boldly removed the picture, using the fake letter as justification for her actions. It was a brilliantly unscrupulous way of allowing her to achieve her aims, and worthy of her former lover in its boldness.

When she told him what she had done, Byron was more annoyed by the forgery than the theft itself, and commented wryly on her 'wild way and *Delphine* language' before expressing the half-hearted hope that the picture might be recovered.[1] She hoped to use it as a bargaining tool, telling him that she would return it if he would agree to meet her; Byron, anxious to repel her advances, refused. However, his unconcern of the previous year had given way to increasing worry as to what Caroline unbound was capable of. Writing to Lady Melbourne, he expressed horror at her forging capabilities, saying 'what is to prevent her from the same imitation for any less worthy purpose she may choose to adopt?'[2] He later declared scornfully that 'to the latest hour of my life I shall hate that woman'.[3] Hobhouse received a similar, if more vitriolic, epistle, in which Byron described her as 'that little maniac', comparing her unfavourably to 'the Devil, Medea & her dragons to boot'.[4]

Caroline's obsession with Byron was not restricted to obtaining his likeness. In late January, after sending him a letter in which she alluded to the possibility of blackmailing him for his excursions into sodomy, she broke into his rooms in Bennet Street. Unable to find him, she contented herself by defacing a copy of *Vathek*, a Gothic novel by the bisexual art collector and politician William Beckford, writing the meaningful phrase 'Remember me!' Not only did this allude to her literary interests – they are the Ghost's words in *Hamlet* – but it also made the implicit point that she was not to be ignored; the association made between Beckford and Byron hinted at both men's sexual tastes. Byron, angered by the intimate intrusion, wrote a furious poem in response. Addressed 'To Bd' (or 'Biondetta', his erstwhile pet name for Caroline), it has an impressively caustic charge:

> Remember thee! Remember thee!
> Till Lethe quench life's burning stream
> Remorse and shame shall cling to thee,
> And haunt thee like a feverish dream!
>
> Remember thee! Aye, doubt it not.
> Thy husband too shall think of thee:
> By neither shalt thou be forgot,
> Thou false to him, thou fiend to me!

The allusion to William and her infidelity to him was comically hypocritical, but an incensed Byron did not care about the niceties of propriety. Ironically, given the sentiments that the poem expressed, it was never sent to Caroline, and only published post-humously. Some moments of self-expression, however deeply felt, could not be expressed publicly.

As Byron seethed, Caroline enjoyed the feeling of control, having taken the initiative for the first time since her affair with Webster. When Lady Spencer said of her on 12 February that her grand-daughter looked 'certainly better & happier',[5] it is likely that her mischievous antics had inspired her. She even began writing a short semi-autobiographical novel, dealing with 'George Morrison', a charming but wicked young man whose natural tendency towards crime is both checked and exacerbated by the manipulative and intelligent gypsy girl Bessy. Resemblance to anyone living or dead was purely coincidental.

Inevitably, Byron agreed to a meeting with Caroline. The pretext that she gave was that she wished to say goodbye to him, knowing his intention of leaving England again soon. As a gesture of good faith, she had agreed to return the purloined picture to him, in exchange for a copy by the artist and a lock of Byron's hair. In a perverse attempt to take revenge, he sent her a lock of Lady Oxford's instead, on the grounds that 'I have a long arrear of mischief to be even with that amiable daughter of Lady Bessborough's… I con-sider this as payment for the first bonfire'.[6] Nonetheless, Lady Melbourne convinced Byron that a final encounter between the two might resolve the contretemps between them. Byron wrote to Caroline on 29 April 1813 in businesslike manner: 'If you still persist in your intention of meeting me in opposition to the wishes of your own friends & of mine – it must even be so – I regret it and acquiesce with reluctance.'[7]

Caroline hoped that, when she saw Byron once again, she would cajole him into reigniting the affection that had once existed between them. If so, when they eventually met on 10 May, she was disappointed, although her later account of the meeting was that 'he asked me to forgive him… he looked sorry for me; he cried;

I adored him still… would I had died then!'[8] Byron had failed to convey the firm resolution of his letters, and had instead taken pity on her. Whatever happened between the two in May was pathetic and anti-climatic, rather than a grand encounter between two antagonists. Caroline was sufficiently moved to write a letter in which she declared both that 'you have raised me from despair to the joy we look for in heaven' and that 'I wish you had never known me or that you killed me before you went.'[9] For some, this might have been a cathartic moment of mutual forgiveness. Unfortunately, buoyed by what she hoped was the beginning of a campaign rather than its end, Caroline was unable to leave the battlefield with dignity.

Matters reached their apogee on 5 July. A few weeks previously, Byron and Caroline had, by chance, attended the same ball. He had attempted to avoid her, only to be berated by William, who had discovered an upset Caroline and believed (correctly) that the man cuckolding him was the source of his wife's misery.[10] That this situation was 'really laughable' seemed to occur only to Byron, but he knew that it would inevitably lead to further scandal if the person he termed 'the *correct & animated* waltzer' elicited sympathy from others, as well as making him look like nothing more than a heartless seducer. Both he and Caroline knew that a public showdown was anticipated, and, inadvertently, they provided it at a ball of Lady Heathcote's.

It was a small society gathering that had attracted many of their friends and foes alike, including Lady Melbourne, and, as was customary, waltzing was the dance of choice for the evening. Byron, himself no dancer, was miserable and out of sorts from his arrival, whereupon he encountered Caroline again. She pointedly remarked to Byron, 'I conclude I may waltz *now*', only for him to parry, saying she might do it 'with everybody in turn… you always did it better than anyone'. From this point on, the accounts of what happened differ. She provided a more thrilling version of events, claiming that she felt faint, and had to sit down in the supper room, whereupon Byron entered and sneered 'I have been admiring your dexterity'. In a fit of pique, she seized a knife and made as if to stab herself, only for him to respond, 'do, my dear, but if you mean to act a Roman's part, mind which way you strike with your own knife – be it at your own heart, not mine – you have struck there already'. According to Caroline – albeit in a much later account told to Medwin – she then yelled Byron's name, still holding the knife, and was caught in a mêlée as those surrounding tried to disarm her, leaving her cut and bloodied.[11]

However, according to both Byron and Lady Melbourne, who witnessed the affray, nothing so dramatic occurred. Byron's account was simply that, while he accompanied the society beauty Lady Rancliffe, Caroline pressed a sharp object into his hand, and said, meaningfully, 'I mean to use this', to which he, hoping that she had not been overheard, muttered 'against me, I presume',[12] and then swiftly moved on. Lady Melbourne informed him later that Caroline had made a clumsy attempt at harming herself with a broken glass and a pair of scissors, Byron being the perceived cause of her distress. Unfortunately for both of them, the incident was greatly to their public discredit. Caroline, who had already been pilloried by the press for an apocryphal story in which she had had herself carried into Melbourne House naked in a silver soup tureen,* was similarly mocked in the scurrilous newspaper *The Satirist*, which carried an account of how she had tried to commit suicide with a dessert knife. As Lady Melbourne put it, 'she is now like a barrel of gunpowder, and takes fire with the most trifling spark'.[13]

Byron, meanwhile, was damned by his association with her. The incident, which became the idle chatter of every soirée and salon in London, drove him to expedite his planned odyssey overseas with even greater haste. In the meantime, he distracted himself by accompanying his half-sister Augusta to many of the city's most

---

* A piece of fiction immortalized in the dubious 1972 biographical film, *Lady Caroline Lamb* (directed by Roger Bolt and starring his wife Sarah Miles as Lady Caroline).

high-profile receptions and parties. Some noted that his behaviour towards her was more like that of a fond lover to his long-lost beloved than a brother to his sister. He seldom had eyes for anyone else.

However, Caroline refused to slide meekly into obscurity. She began writing an autobiographical *roman-à-clef* about her relationship with Byron, *Glenarvon*, which she hoped that Murray would publish. She began a correspondence with the publisher in late 1813, allowing him to act as a go-between between her and Byron. Her tone oscillates between lightly scolding ('Why did you not answer my letter?')[14] and gratitude ('I have to thank you for an attention which I feel most extremely').[15] She continued to read Byron's work, praising his verse tale *The Corsair* to Murray, who published it on 1 February 1814, as 'in his very best style', although she was not without criticism of it, especially what she saw as some of his more high-blown indulgences. She carped that Byron ought to 'speak English – it is a goodly language'.[16] Nonetheless, 10,000 copies were sold on the first day alone; Byron's continued celebrity was assured.

His feelings towards Caroline had softened after the disastrous evening at Lady Heathcote's. He told Lady Melbourne that he had written her 'a very earnest but not *savage* letter' in late November,[17] and went so far as to ask Murray to send her an early copy of his poem *The Bride Of Abydos* on 28 November, indicating a residual desire to impress her. However, his attitude towards her was one of ongoing uncertainty. He told Lady Melbourne on 8 January 1814 that 'there is little to dread from her love & I forgive her hatred',[18] and then contradicted himself just days later, when he begged 'don't talk of her – for I am really advancing fast to an utter detestation', which 'I try to curb – and which I must curb',[19] as he mused the following day that 'she will never rest til she has destroyed me in some way or other… if it comes to that point – she will regret it'.[20]

His ongoing uncertainty as to how to deal with Caroline made him vulnerable. Her letters to him exploited this uncertainty by praising him as 'very generous and kind' for his discretion,[21] alluding to his close relationship with Augusta ('as a sister feels as your Augusta for you')[22] and even sending him letters in French attempting to pimp two 'servant girls', and calling herself his 'forsaken mistress'.[23] The implication – that she would be happy to become his lover once again, regardless of what had passed between them before – was a dangerously seductive one.

External events intruded upon the love–hate relationship. As Byron dealt with his conflicting emotions of admiration and disappointment towards 'my poor little pagod' Napoleon, who was exiled in April 1814, Caroline was distraught at the death of Lady Spencer on 18 March. She became frightened that, without her greatest supporter in the family, she would be ostracized. She wrote to her uncle Lord Spencer on 13 May, and tried to excuse herself, saying 'I have been made mad, & then the acts to which I was driven are coldly brought against me', and 'I never wish to allude to what has passed'.[24] She was not acting out of unjustified paranoia; her actions over the previous couple of years were seen as unacceptable, and pressure had been placed on William to estrange himself from his embarrassingly unpredictable wife, for the sake of his political career.

Even as she begged for her family to forgive her, she could or would not give up Byron. She continued writing to him in desperation, with as little consistency in her feelings towards him as his towards her. They met a handful of times in the spring of 1814, mainly at formal social functions, and he tried his best to be polite and civil towards her, but it was of little use. Her obsession with him knew little restraint, which drove him to tell Lady Melbourne on 26 June, dramatically, that 'she may hunt me down – it is the power of any mad or bad woman* to do so by any man… I am already almost a prisoner; she has no shame, no feeling, no one estimable or redeeming quality'.[25]

---

* Perhaps he had in mind her own description of him as 'mad, bad and dangerous to know'.

Caroline visited Byron's new rooms at the Albany in Piccadilly uninvited, occasionally in her time-honoured pageboy garb, and he complained, sardonically, 'I can't throw her out of the window.'[26] In her letters, she took a different tack. She portrayed herself as a piteous outcast from society, writing 'when any friend of yours speaks kindly to me – I dread what they must think of me – for I am about ready to fall at their feet', and claimed 'I will be such as you may not despise'.[27] A subsequent letter, sent on 3 June, boldly announced 'you never have or will be as loved by another', and then compared Byron to a parade of anti-heroes and villains, including 'Mephistocles [sic]… Valmont, Machiavelli [and] Napoleon'.[28] She combined sadness, saying that 'you are a man any woman might live with forever & until she tired you – you could not tire her', with clear-sightedness, when she exclaimed 'whatever the crime be of loving that which by our vows we have reverenced, I only say this one thing for my vindication & also for that of the hundreds who have & the thousands who will fall by the same light'.[29]

Judged by contemporary standards, Caroline would be regarded as mentally unstable. Yet this is a harsh way of viewing an unhappy woman who, in her fixation on the most famous man in Britain, attempted to elevate herself above the level of a casual love affair. She had given herself to a man who, as she accurately surmised, was as seldom short of partners, of either sex, as he was of a well-turned phrase or pithy insult. It was not her fault that she fell in love with her worst possible match, nor his that her entreaties and obsession lasted far longer and more intensely than either might have thought possible.

Even as she wrote grandiose and rambling 'farewell' epistles, some part of Caroline remained convinced that she and Byron were fated to remain together forever. That Byron, for all his stern words about 'breaking off the connection'*[30] between the two to Lady Melbourne, was unable to extricate himself did not help

* See p. 97 for the (possibly intentional) *double entendre* that this suggests.

matters; he described how at a masked ball at Burlington House on 1 July 1814 Caroline appeared, typically clad in green pantaloons, and, although he claimed that she was 'growing actually & seriously disordered in her intellects' and that 'she can not be in her senses', he still stayed until 7am talking to her. The twitch upon the thread remained: regrettably, for both parties.

Finally, Byron ended the uneasy stalemate. As he was about to marry Annabella, he realized that an obsessive former lover was unlikely to be a welcome addition to the wedding ceremony. Therefore, he took the dramatic step of being as candid as he dared with her about his 'true' nature, shortly before his engagement was made public. According to a later account of the conversation that she gave Medwin, Byron kissed her and said, 'poor Caro, if everyone hates me, you, I see, will never change. No, not with ill usage!' His confessions appalled even Caroline, who claimed that she replied 'Yes, I *am* changed, & shall come near you no more.'[31] She sent him a letter shortly afterwards in September 1814, claiming 'women who walk in the streets alone in pagan clothes must encounter insult & barbarity but from you – henceforward you are safe – the means you took to frighten me from your door are not in vain'.[32] After some businesslike queries and formalities, the façade finally cracked, as Caroline launched into a stream of emotive rhetoric that would not have disgraced the most ardent Romantic writer:

> I am not in a state of mind to bear it – cruelty – oh beyond all others – no man ever suffered a woman to bear so much – pray send back those rings & the drawings and book, all shameful witnesses of my misery and eternal disgrace – farewell for ever oh for ever – I will nor see nor write nor think of you again – but I pray God to bless you & your wife & to grant you both every possible happiness & delight – only this – if you have a child – once let me see him, only once just to see him I never can see his father no never more.[33]

Taken literally, this is pitiful, representing the desperate longing of the disappointed lover who now bitterly accepted her lot. However, the floridity of the sentiments might have led an impartial observer to suspect that Caroline was enjoying the opportunity for self-dramatization. A subsequent letter to Murray hinted at this, as she knowingly announced:

> I assure you [the weather] was remarkably warm and pleasant, besides no drizzly rain that falls on me can wash my misarray, as the Lady says to the Friar* – I was reflecting all the way home upon a new cause of misery which I have conjured up.[34]

The self-awareness is strengthened by her comments that 'I think I shall live to see the day – when some beautiful & innocent Lady Byron shall drive to your door – & I picture to myself the delight with which you will receive her'.[35]

Byron, meanwhile, had feared Caroline discovering his engagement, as he believed that she would commit some new atrocity against him. Murray reported to his wife Annie, not without compassion, that Byron believed Caroline was 'the fiend who had interrupted all his projects and who would do so now if possible'.[36] It seemed as if Byron's worst fears were confirmed when the *Morning Chronicle* published an article denying that his engagement was real. After attacking the editor of the paper, James Perry, he suspected that Caroline had made another attempt at forging his signature on a document; as he said to Perry, 'I suspect mischief (and consequently a woman) to be your authority.'[37] His suspicions were proved to be baseless. Whoever was responsible for the addendum, it was not Caroline, and Byron had to concede that she had been 'quiet and rational' when she learned of his engagement.

It is more likely that Caroline, knowing Byron as she did,

---

* An allusion to Thomas Percy's poem 'The Friar Of Orders Gray', rather than a nineteenth-century version of 'as the actress said to the bishop'.

suspected that the marriage would be so disastrous that she did not need to aggravate matters by her own intervention; she quipped sardonically to Murray that Byron was incompatible with 'a woman who went to church regularly, understood statistics and had a bad figure'.[38] In any case, her attentions lay more in the realms of her own writing at this time, not least because her relationship with William continued to be one of polite if icy distance, and because her parents had embarked on a lengthy trip to the south of France, ostensibly for Harriet's health but also to escape the sulphurous whiff of scandal with which her daughter was indelibly tarred.

Caroline hoped that her autobiographical novel *Glenarvon* would interest Murray, and many of her letters of late 1814 and early 1815 concern 'the agony which you know must arise from suspense'.[39] Knowing that she was not a great writer, she allowed Murray a way out, assuring him 'if it is execrable in your estimation you can say gently that it is not so happy as you expected – I shall not be offended'; she went on to insist 'the conceit of an author, particularly one new to the name – can stand much humiliation, therefore if you would knock me down, at once prepare the blow as you would for an ox'.[40] A subsequent letter of early 1815 did little to sell the book, when she declared 'it is very incorrect, very dull, very full of faults but I shall persevere til I finish it'.[41]

A distraction from literature came in June, shortly after the Battle of Waterloo. Caroline's brother Frederick, by now a colonel, had been one of the combatants and had been seriously wounded in the fighting. Caroline and William made a rare journey together to Paris to visit him, but Caroline, excited by attracting male attention in a new country, soon sought more appealing company than that of the sickbed. She conducted a flirtation with a friend of Byron's, Michael Bruce, who she referred to as her 'Star of the East' and her cousin Harryo even believed that she was 'primed for an attack on the Duke of Wellington, and I have no doubt that she will to a certain extent succeed, as no dose of flattery is too strong for him to swallow or for her to administer'.[42] Despite the political differences between them – Wellington was a committed Tory who entered politics in 1818, rising to the office of Prime Minister in 1828 – a friendship grew up between them; Harryo speculated that 'I see she amuses him to the greatest degree, especially her *accidents*, which is the charitable term he gives to all her sorties.'[43]

Although there were suggestions, partially fuelled by Bruce, that Byron would appear in Paris, he never did, even though wild rumours circulated of romantic lakeside assignations between him and Caroline and flight to Switzerland, with William in pursuit.[44] Instead, the newly married man wrote to his friend James Wedderburn Webster,* who was in France and had asked him for some comments on her person, which were disparaging. Byron referred to her as 'a villainous intrigante' and 'mad and malignant', as well as 'that wretched woman'.[45] In a subsequent letter of 18 September, he sought to correct some of the impressions that he had given – 'I wrote rather hurriedly and probably said more than I intended or that she deserved', but remained scathing. While allowing that '[I] did love her very well – til she took abundant pains to cure me of it', and that 'she is such a mixture of good and bad', his attitude towards her remained cautiously detached, exemplified by a piece of advice he gave Webster – 'she is most *dangerous* when *humblest* – like a centipede she *crawls* & *stings*'. William, meanwhile, was praised for his good qualities, 'and his misfortune is having her'.[46]

When Caroline returned from Paris in October 1815, she was intrigued to hear whispers that Byron's marriage to Annabella was on the verge of collapse on account of abhorrent cruelty on his part. She cultivated a friendship with Annabella, sending her manuscripts of a play that she had written – in the hope that Byron would read them – and believed that she would become a valuable go-between, much as Murray had been with her and Byron. Her motives remained opaque; while her fixation with Byron had persisted, it was beginning to dawn on her that he would never love

* No relation to Caroline's previous paramour Godfrey Webster.

her, and could barely be bothered to be polite towards, or about, her. Therefore, when rumours spread of his bisexuality, profligacy and demonic character, she kept her counsel, only smilingly remarking to Hobhouse at a dinner in December 1815 at Holland House that truth was 'what one thinks at the moment'.[47] Rarely pure and never simple, Caroline's revenge continued.

~

At the beginning of 1816, with Byron's fortunes in decline, Caroline took the guise of comforter, writing to him in faux-modest terms ('it is not for me to presume to hope that any thing I can say will find favour in your sight') to claim, disingenuously, 'I have (no interest) but the wish to save you'. She took care to deny that she had spread 'injurious reports' about him, all the while noting his former unkindness to her, and then announced 'oh Lord Byron, let one who has loved you with a devotion almost profane – find favour so far as to incline you to hear her'.[48] However, she made it clear to Hobhouse in March 1816 that, after renouncing Byron ('[he] has behaved almost barbarously towards me & I can never feel any thing towards him again but resentment'), her loyalty lay with his abandoned wife, saying 'in this quarrel too I differ from you and take her part, not his'.[49]

She then informed Murray that 'I no longer am Byron's friend or admirer', and talked scathingly of his 'mean and atrocious' conduct towards Annabella, calling him nothing more than 'a villain, a coward & contemptible'.[50] Murray had shown Caroline Byron's poetic reflection on Annabella and himself, 'Fare Thee Well', which he had written on 18 March , and this aroused Caroline's interest; as a result, she approached Annabella for a meeting, claiming that she was in possession of secret information that would ruin Byron if it were to be revealed. She promised 'I will tell you that which if you merely menace him with the knowledge shall make him tremble… I could not have hated & despised him as from my soul I do now & will.'[51]

The first formal meeting between Annabella and Caroline took place on 26 March 1816. Caroline, who was 'greatly agitated' – whether with guilt, excitement or nerves – proceeded to tell Annabella everything that Byron had ever confided in her, sparing nothing. Whether it was his 'unnatural crimes' with men and boys or the dubiousness of his relationship with her nemesis Lady Melbourne (whom she dubbed, along with Byron, 'two of the greatest hypocrites and most corrupted wretches that were ever suffered to exist on this earth'),[52] Caroline provided Annabella with all the ammunition that she needed to ruin the man who had tormented them both.

Nonetheless, Caroline was not exempt from the whispers of society. Her erratic behaviour included, unbelievably in the light of her alliance with Annabella, writing to Byron in April to inform him that she, 'though your enemy, though forever alienated from you, though resolved never more while she lives to see or speak to or forgive you, yet would perhaps die to save you'.[53] If this smacked of distraction, then it was inevitable that her family, both embarrassed and concerned by her ungovernable actions, sought to have her declared insane and institutionalized. Lady Melbourne, unsurprisingly, was the genius behind this idea, which led Caroline to protest 'any promises I may have been forced to make when a straight waistcoat and a mad doctor are held forth to view – they cannot expect I should think them binding'. She did not do herself any favours with her continued absurdities and inability to govern herself; one incident in April saw her throw a cricket ball at a page who had irritated her, which struck him on the head. She then ran into the street, shouting manically 'Oh God, I have murdered the page!'[54]

Caroline was not institutionalized, although there were plenty around her who believed that she should have been. One who did not was the steadfast William. Although he was embarrassed by his wife's behaviour, he was also compassionate enough to realize that her instability stemmed from fear and panic, rather than dangerous insanity, and so he rejected his family's entreaties for a separation and for Caroline to be locked away. Whatever she had done or said, she remained his wife, and the mother of his son, and, to his credit, he retained his sense of honour. Nonetheless, he still managed, under stress, to refer to his wife as a 'drunken little bitch'.[55]

Caroline's battle with Byron now moved into its closing stages. Murray showed her Byron's poem 'Stanzas to Augusta', and Byron reacted with a fury that appeared to hint at a guilty conscience,* as he wrote Murray an irate letter on 15 April in which he castigated him with vigour: 'really you must not send anything of mine to Lady C L – I have often sufficiently warned you on this topic – you do not know what mischief you do by this'. Nonetheless, beset by scandal, Byron knew that the forces of society were arrayed against him, and that there was nothing else that he could do. On 23 April, he left England forever. He would never see her again.

Whether she saw his departure as a victory or a lost opportunity, she had little time to dwell on his absence, as *Glenarvon* was finally published on 9 May 1816. Despite her entreaties, Murray had eventually decided against publishing the book, either to avoid offending his most lucrative author, or simply because it lacked literary merit. Snapped up by the publisher Henry Colburn, a sharp commercial operator who published Caroline's friend Lady Morgan and had scored success with the periodical *New Monthly Magazine*, he paid Caroline £200 as an advance with the promise of a further £300 on publication. This was less a decision based on literary merit and more a straightforward piece of commerce; Colburn, for £500, now owned the right to publish nothing less than the fictionalized account of Byron's most notorious mistress, in three volumes. It was published anonymously, for the sake of appearances, but leaving Caroline's name off the title page fooled nobody; the world knew of her creation of the book, and prepared to judge it accordingly.

* See Part III, 'Annabella and Augusta'.

Glenarvon was certainly sensational. Byron later described it to Murray as a 'fuck-and-publish' novel,[56] but its commercial success lay in the prurient way in which its characters and settings related to the protagonists of Caroline's own life. Thus, she painted herself as Lady Calantha Delaval, who, like her namesake, blossoms when she encounters the dashing but wicked stand-in for Byron, Glenarvon himself, an Irish rebel who has a magnetic ability both to repel and seduce all who he encounters and 'unites the malice and petty vices of a woman, to the perfidy and villainy of a man'.[57] Glenarvon combines passion and heroism with double-dealing and opportunism, and eventually is driven mad by visions of those he has wronged. Society, meanwhile, in the form of the absurd and infirm Princess of Madagascar (Lady Holland) and the cruel Lady Margaret (Lady Melbourne) is satirized as a place of false bonhomie and hypocrisy, where only the Earl of Avondale (William) rises above the mire, despite his 'general laxity of morals'.[58]

Lady Melbourne came in for particularly withering criticism, with Lady Margaret described as possessing an understanding that 'had so adapted itself to her passion, that it was in her power to give, in her own eyes, a character of grandeur, to the vice and malignity, which offered an inexplicable delight to her depraved imagination'. Nor could Caroline be accused of sparing herself; Calantha is described as possessing 'the pettishness of a spoiled and wayward child'. The Irish setting, meanwhile, offered both an expression of Caroline's Whiggish politics in its sympathetic portrayal of the Irish rebel movement, and also recalled her time spent there in enforced exile, pining for Byron.

When the book was published, it became an instant bestseller, not least because those who had been depicted eagerly bought it to see what their fictional representation consisted of. While Byron was said to be indifferent to it, writing to Moore later in the year that 'if the authoress had written the *truth*, and nothing but the truth – the whole truth – the romance would not only have been more *romantic*, but more entertaining' and 'as for the likeness, the

picture can't be good – I did not sit long enough',[59] others were less
sanguine. Hobhouse, outraged at what he perceived was his friend's
ill treatment, formally called on the woman he labelled 'the little
vicious author' to criticize her on 10 May 1816, and she responded
by threatening to publish Byron's letters, which, she hinted, were
far more scandalous and shocking than anything she had written.
Faced with proof, he was forced to withdraw, humiliated.*

If Caroline had ever had any intention of remaining in society,
Glenarvon finished it forever. Although she claimed that William
had enjoyed it, everyone else was horrified by the casual exposure
of their peccadilloes and secrets by a woman who, for all her eccentricities, knew exactly what she was writing about. Lady Holland, a
particular target of scorn, dismissed the book as 'a strange farrago',
and Lady Melbourne claimed that 'I was so disgusted with the
spirit in which it was written that after reading the first 20 pages I
declared I would read no more' and that she was 'ignorant' of its
contents.[60] Nonetheless, upsetting powerful *grande dames* was a haz-
ardous business. Caroline was cut dead at a party at the Marquess
of Anglesey's Staffordshire estate Beaudesert after the book's publication, and, despite trying to claim – disingenuously – that she had
meant no harm by its presentation of London's great and good, she
had finally managed to achieve what her affair with Byron had not;
expulsion from society. At the age of thirty-one, she had become
persona irrevocably *non grata* throughout London, and would never
be able to cast off her association with Byron again.

৵

The remaining years of of Caroline's life were sad ones. As *Glenarvon* attracted little in the way of critical acclaim – although
the twenty-year-old Edward Bulwer-Lytton, later of 'a dark and

---

* Another reason for Hobhouse's dislike of Caroline was simple literary
jealousy. *Glenarvon* was a bestseller, whereas his own book, a collection of
his letters, sold barely a dozen copies.

stormy night' fame, was an admirer[61] – she had to churn out further works virtually to order, like many hack writers before or since. She wrote several other turgid and unreadable books, including *Graham Hamilton*, *Penruddock* and *Ada Reis*, as well as a long poetic response to Byron's *Don Juan*, *Gordon: A Tale: A Poetical Review of Don Juan*, which she described as 'partly a burlesque parody… partly a sacrifice of praise offered at the shrine of talent, and partly arguments proving its immoral tendency'. Unlike the real *Don Juan*, it attracted little in the way of attention, and was more notable for demonstrating Caroline's continued attachment to Byron, to whom she occasionally continued to write, without response. She was still capable of the odd outlandish flourish – such as appearing at a masquerade in 1820 dressed as Don Juan, attended by pages in devilish attire – but her moment had passed.

Beset by ill health and dropsy, not helped by her increasing drinking, she was devastated when she learned of Byron's death in 1824, claiming to the society hostess Lydia White that 'I have lost the dearest friend & the bitterest enemy any one ever had'.[62] She wrote a piteous letter to Murray, with whom she had continued to correspond, on 13 July 1824, claiming to have seen Byron's hearse pass by Brocket Hall's gates, and saying 'you may judge what I felt'.[63] Lonely and unwell, she and William eventually separated in 1825, leaving her to live out the last few years of her life in increasingly pathetic isolation, still pining for Byron. Lady Morgan claimed she described him as 'that dear, that angel, that misguided and misguiding Byron, whom I adore, although he left that dreadful legacy on me – my memory'.[64] Caroline eventually died of dropsy, with William, concerned to the last, returning to her side on 26 January 1828. She was forty-two. One of her final acts was to bequeath to Lady Morgan the Sanders portrait of Byron that she had gone to such extraordinary lengths to obtain.

William, who went on to become Prime Minister in 1834, wrote to his mistress Lady Brandon after Caroline's death that he felt:

In a manner which I have often heard others describe, but in which I have never felt before myself, and did not think I could feel, a sort of impossibility of believing that I shall never see her countenance or hear her voice again, and a sort of sense of desolation, solitude and carelessness about everything, when I forced myself to remember that she was really gone.[65]

A contemporary obituary in the *Literary Gazette* said of her that she was 'wild and impatient of restraint, rapid in impulses' but also allowed that she was 'generous and kind of heart'. It perhaps offered the kindest epitaph on her turbulent relationship with Byron by stating that their love, and the scandal that grew out of it, arose 'from imagination, not depravity'.[66]

The truer form of Byron's depravity was instead to manifest itself elsewhere.

PART III

Annabella
&
Augusta

7

I am quite the fashion this year.

ANNABELLA MILBANKE TO SIR RALPH MILBANKE,
9 APRIL 1810

'Lord Byron, married.' The words seem to radiate impossibility and suggest the most bizarre of cosmic jokes. That Byron's brief marriage would end in failure was not unexpected. And yet the central reason for its breakdown was unpredictable even by the standards of his quixotic existence. If his entanglements with Caroline and others were scandalous, his disastrous union would be catastrophic for his reputation, and would lead to him voluntarily exiling himself. The reason for this exile lay with two entirely different women, both of whom, in their own ways, led to his downfall and departure.

∿

Anne Isabella Milbanke was born on 17 May 1792 at Elemore Hall, near Durham, and was soon known as Annabella. Although she described her upbringing as a simple one, where 'I was born in the house of my father, a respectable tradesman',[1] this was disingenuous. Not only was Elemore, which belonged to their neighbour George Baker, a grand country house, but her father Ralph was knighted when she was two, meaning that she had joined the ranks of the gentry at a young age. Her Milbanke cousins were angered by the birth, as they were displaced as the heirs apparent to the property. To have made some significant enemies even before she was able to speak was an inauspicious beginning to a career in society, even if she was fortunate in having none other than Lady Melbourne as her aunt.

Ralph Milbanke and his wife Judith were unusually enlightened parents, as well as old ones; both were over forty when Annabella was born.[2] Not only were both of them Whigs, but Ralph was an ardent abolitionist who made his first speech against slavery in 1792, in which he strongly supported the views of his friend Charles James Fox. He was a principled man who nonetheless had difficulty rising to the highest office; he was defeated in an election to become an MP in 1790 in which he had spent as much as £15,000.[3] Annabella later said that 'he could not deal with men, though he could gain their love', and Hobhouse described him as 'an honest, red faced spirit, a little prosy, but by no means devoid of humour'.[4] Both Ralph and Judith saw to it that Annabella grew up inquisitive and socially aware, with her mother taking a particular interest in the local poor on the estate; she even founded a school in nearby Seaham for them.

Annabella's first mentor was her nurse, Mrs Clermont, who took control of the child. She used her formidable personality to subjugate any opposition, and taught her how to master her feelings and hide her natural inclinations towards 'childish' behaviour beneath a carefully cultivated façade of seriousness and maturity far beyond her age.[5] Judith had realized this as early as 1794, saying of her infant daughter in April that 'she gets very saucy and is *governess in chief* of Papa, Mama & the whole family & does not seem to give up her authority... she says every thing & speaks remarkably plain'.[6]

While Annabella never wanted for attention, traditional girlish pleasures, such as toys and dolls, were of far less interest to her than academic study. She became especially engrossed in the study of mathematics and astronomy with her tutor William Frend, a Cambridge don who had been banished from the university for publishing a pamphlet in which he attacked the Napoleonic Wars and argued Britain should seek peace. Frend was politically liberal, hugely intelligent and humourless; he had a lasting impact on his student, who became an avid, if precocious, reader. In her intellectual advancement she took after her mother, who was sharper than her pleasant but slightly limited father. She soon acquired a reputation for refusing to be talked down to by her elders, and developed an independent streak, refusing to perform the duties of a girl of her class and age. Her parents encouraged this, believing that the virtues of having a miniature adult in the family outweighed the pitfalls of not allowing her a childhood.

By 1810, this meant that Annabella was expected, at the age of eighteen, to present herself in London at her first season. It was not a success; she later said 'I was anxious to postpone my entrance into the world, of which I had formed no pleasing conception… but my "hour was come"'.[7] She was right to be concerned. The 'season' was a protracted affair that took place between February and 12 August, only ending when the grouse season – a second round of bagging a desirable trophy – began. The months were devoted to showcasing an annual generation of sequestered young women, all of whom were in search of a husband, and who inevitably criss-crossed the functions, dinners and receptions of Mayfair and St James with a metronomic frequency that led to a sense of a few thousand people in the *beau monde* being cooped up in the most gilded of cages.

Annabella, accompanied by her mother, regarded the entire rigmarole with a sardonic detachment that would have done a Jane Austen protagonist credit, and refused to involve herself in what was, for all the fine words and rigid etiquette, a meat market that paired flesh and money off together. Knowing that she was more intelligent and, in her own estimation, 'better' than those around her, she felt no need to ingratiate herself, much to her parents' disappointment. She did allow that 'I met with one or two who, like myself, did not appear absorbed in the present scene, and who interested me to a degree',[8] and received the occasional proposal, from such suitors as the MP and barrister (and subsequent Governor-General of India) George Eden. However, she found these offers irrelevant; she said of one would-be beau that 'one of my smiles would encourage him, but I am niggardly of my glances'.[9]

Instead, she occupied herself with writing poetry, which eventually reached Byron via Caroline Lamb; Annabella's aunt, Lady Melbourne, was Caroline's mother-in-law. In May 1812, Byron would say to Caroline that Annabella's poems displayed 'fancy, feeling' and said that 'a little practice would soon induce facility of expression'.[10] Intrigued by someone he described as 'a very extraordinary girl', he went on to wonder 'who would imagine so much strength and variety of thought under that placid countenance?' However, in an attempt to forestall the jealousy of Caroline, he did not seek to explore this 'strength and variety', claiming disingenuously that 'I have no desire to be better acquainted with Miss Milbank [sic], she is too good for a fallen spirit to know or wish to know, & I should like her more if she were less perfect'.[11] He was not alone in this assessment of her character; the mother of one frustrated suitor described her as 'so odd a girl: she is good, amiable and sensible, but cold, prudent and reflecting'.[12]

This perfection was to be put to the test during Annabella's third season in 1812, when she arrived in town against her parents' wishes. Her father was ill and her mother, with whom she had an increasingly strained relationship, asked her to remain at home. However, on the pretext of visiting a sick friend, she headed to the city unchaperoned, and, for the first time, found herself having fun. She noted in her diary, with a mixture of irony and genuine surprise, that she went to a ball and stayed there until dawn.[13] Perhaps as a result of this miniature emancipation, she began to behave like a lady of fashion rather than an outsider observing a peculiar scene. She had her portrait painted by George Hayter, a young artist beginning to develop a reputation (it cost her twenty guineas, but 'I can't get myself done decently for anything less'),[14] and donned fine dresses, attempting to cultivate the appearance of a great lady. Although she was no great beauty, she was petite, had lustrous brown hair and a faintly detached demeanour that could convey either gentle amusement or boredom, depending on whom she was with. She wrote to her father in half-ironic, half-pleased fashion in April to say 'I am quite the fashion this year. Mankind bow before me, and the women think me somebody.'[15] Not quite all women were as impressed by her as she believed; Elizabeth, Duchess of Devonshire wrote of her that 'she really is an icicle'.[16]

One man who was genuinely taken with her was the cavalry officer and major-general Edward Pakenham, Wellington's brother-in-law and the great military man of his generation. She knew that he was well regarded by everyone around her, with Wellington's aide-de-camp Colonel Hervey-Bathurst speaking of him 'with very great approbation both as a soldier and a man',[17] and it became necessary for her to reject him without appearing to be ungrateful for his advances. In a letter that she wrote to her mother, she said she wished 'to prevent his increasing his malady by a conduct that could only proceed from his unconsciously cherishing a remain of hope... I am quite satisfied with the part I have acted in regard to him. I meant it for his good, and I am sure that it has proved so.'[18] The fact that a strain of insanity was said to run in the Pakenham family undoubtedly had a bearing on her decision.*

While voyaging on the turbulent seas of the social circuit, Annabella encountered Caroline for the first time. She was unimpressed, describing her as 'unmeaning' and seeming 'clever in every thing that is not within the province of common sense', and would later dismiss her relationship with Byron as being characterized by 'the reluctance he manifests to be shackled to her'.[19] Already gleaning an idea of the situation, she viewed Caroline's long-suffering husband William as 'self-sufficient', as well as making the astute judgement that Lady Holland had a 'countenance [that] says that she is capable

* The unfortunate Pakenham would eventually die in the largely forgotten battle of New Orleans in January 1815 – the final clash of arms between the USA and Britain in the so-called War of 1812.

of determined malice'.[20] Nonetheless, she was invited to a morning party of Caroline's on 25 March 1812, where she encountered Byron, whom she described as 'the subject of universal attention', for the first time. As for so many others, their first meeting, at a scene 'calculated to show human absurdities', was auspicious.

Annabella read *Childe Harold* in late March, like most of London, and was impressed; while criticizing Byron for being 'a *mannerist*... he wants variety in the turns of his expressions', she allowed that it 'contains many passages in the best style of poetry' and that 'he excels most in the delineation of deep feeling, and in reflections relative to human nature'.[21] In a perceptive journal entry of 25 March, she described him reacting to his fame in society in his own, inimitable fashion:

> His mouth continually betrays the acrimony of his spirit. I should judge him sincere and independent – *sincere* at least in society as far as he can be, whilst dissimulating the violence of his scorn... it appeared to me that he tried to control his natural sarcasm and vehemence as best he could, in order not to offend, but at times his lips thickened with disdain, and his eyes rolled impatiently.[22]

That he was described by her mother's friend Selina Gally Knight as possessing 'feelings dreadfully perverted' was simultaneously exciting and a warning. She wrote to her mother on 27 March in an attempt to describe her confused feelings about 'a very independent observer of mankind'. Allowing that 'it is said that he is an infidel, and I think it probable from the general character of his mind', she nonetheless defended him from accusations of wickedness by saying 'his poem sufficiently proves that he *can* feel nobly, but he has discouraged his own goodness.' She found him handsome – 'his features are well formed' – but Annabella noted that 'his upper lip is drawn towards the nose with an expression of impatient disgust'. As Caroline had found on her first encounter with him, he was surrounded by women 'absurdly courting him', meaning that they did not speak. Yet Annabella, even as she attempted to dis-associate herself from this magnetic man ('I cannot worship talents that are unconnected with the love of man, nor be captivated by that genius which is barren in blessings'), was more attracted than she cared to admit. Her final statement that 'I made no offering at the shrine of Childe Harold, though I shall not refuse the acquain-tance if it comes in my way' was equivocal: once more, the trap had been baited.[23]

She spent the next few weeks investigating Byron, discovering anecdotes of both his supposed licentiousness, but also of his recklessly impetuous generosity towards servants and casual acquaintances, such as large cash gifts readily pressed into eager hands. That he was engaged in an affair with Caroline – whom Annabella mocked for her 'childish manner' – did not stop her from writing to her mother after seeing Byron for a second time in April to say 'I have met with much evidence of his goodness', and defending him against the accusations he had been presented with by saying 'you know how easily the noblest heart may be perverted by unkindness – perhaps the most easily a *noble* heart, because it is more susceptible to ungenerous indignities'.[24]

She took the opportunity of discovering this noble heart's secrets for the first time in person by discussing the cobbler-poet Joseph Blackett, whom Byron had written about in *English Bards and Scotch Reviewers*, and to whom both she and her mother had been patrons. Byron, typically, was generous about Blackett, who had died young at twenty-three, and Annabella pronounced her-self 'pleased with the humanity of his feelings' about him. It was not long until she was calling him 'the comet of this year', who 'shone with his customary glory' at a party, and saying that she had enjoyed 'some very pleasing conversation – at least I thought it such'.[25] Byron adopted the persona of a discerning man-of-letters with Annabella, taking care to denigrate the moral character of Blackett's editor Samuel Pratt 'of whose roguishness he had had personal experience', and thereby presenting himself as a wise and benevolent counsellor, rather than the libertine of reputation.

Annabella was too intelligent not to know the risks, but too enraptured to be sufficiently cautious. While she took care to tell her mother that 'Lord Byron is certainly very interesting, but he wants that calm benevolence which could only touch my heart', a more rapturous note was struck by her breathless announcement that 'he is very handsome & his manners are in a superior degree such as one should attribute to nature's gentlemen'. Interrupting her letter to head to a morning party of Caroline's, she returned 'additionally convinced that [Byron] is sincerely repentant for the evil he has done, though he has not resolution (without aid) to adopt a new course of conduct & feeling'.[26] Perhaps the infamous underlook was deployed, because even these qualifications and doubts were disappearing by the following day; she breathlessly announced 'Lord B is without exception of young or old more agreeable in conversation than any person I ever knew', and went on to claim that he was 'softened at times by the more humane feelings', as well as being 'most truly an object of compassion'. The subtext seemed to be clear; Judith, a kind-hearted woman who had taken great interest in assisting the unfortunate, was now being steered in the direction of a man who, despite his previous lapses, was more sinned against than sinning. Annabella's letters have an energy and interest absent from her earlier droll commentaries on the vagaries of the city's failings. For the first time, she was in love.

Whether or not she knew of the level of Byron's entanglement with – and attempts to extricate himself from – Caroline, Annabella cultivated her as a friend, taking suppers and walks with her and obtaining introductions to the artistic circles of the day. At one of these, she recorded in another journal entry that she participated in a lively debate about whether a poet was required to experience the relevant feelings him- or herself in order to arouse such feelings in readers. As she noted, 'Lord Byron asserted the negative'.[27] While her mother continued to doubt his suitability as a match for Annabella, she defended him by claiming that 'he is indeed persecuted to the greatest degree by those who know nothing of him except what they have learned from prejudice', and that, while he was 'violently & unjustly exalted', 'he has too much penetration not to perceive that his *talent* alone is considered, and that there is no *friendship* in all this *mouth-honour*'.[28] It was this mental and social penetration that he used in conversation with her a few days later, when she recorded his railing against there being 'scarcely one person who on returning home dared to look into themselves', and made a slighting comment about 'the caprice natural to your sex', which Annabella described as 'if it were an acknowledged truth which I had too much sense to deny'.[29]

When Byron, intrigued by Annabella, sent her verses to Caroline, he knew that he was creating the potential for jealousy and discord between the two women, but he either did not care or found it exciting. Caroline, however, wrote Annabella a lengthy letter from Brocket Hall that feigned sisterly kindness while continuing to assert her own primacy in Byron's affections. Advising her to 'shun friendships with those whose practice ill accords with your principles', Caroline, although never naming Byron, referred to those who 'may unfortunately be more amiable, more interesting than others, but they will by degrees do you harm'. She might have been better taking her own advice, but she had first-hand experience; as she said, 'if I live longer, the bitter bitter pains will no doubt likewise be mine'. Tacitly acknowledging that Annabella was her romantic rival, Caroline nevertheless offered her the backhanded compliment that 'you seem to me... very superior to those I have the honour of associating with... it is the more pity that you are come to London, for everything that enters into this fair city is tainted more or less'. In an innuendo that the virginal Annabella may or may not have understood, she offered:

One infallible rule of judging others... whenever you see a man or a woman, & particularly the latter, galloping through the parks as hard as horse can go... set that lady or gentleman down immediately for a fool, and ninety-nine times out of a hundred you will not be wrong.[30]

If the letter had any effect on Annabella, it was that she now believed Caroline was little more than a hysteric; she dismissed the letter in her journal as 'very remarkable'. Although she was now fully aware, even if she had not been before, that an affair existed between Byron and Caroline, she was not to be deterred from her lordly poet. During the next few months she privately sounded out her intimates as to his suitability, publicly associated with him at the grand salons and parties (his refusing to waltz notwithstanding), and all the while attempted to ascertain whether a proposal was likely to be made.

As Byron turned away from the demanding Caroline after a succession of public rows and displays of temper, he decided that Annabella would make a better match. He informed Lady Melbourne accordingly, saying 'I know little of her & have not the most distant reason to suppose that I am at all a favourite in that quarter, but I never saw a woman whom I *esteemed* so much'.[31] He spelled out his reasons for matrimony in tongue-in-cheek fashion:

> [Annabella] I admire because she is a clever woman, an amiable woman & of high blood, for I have still have a few Norman & Scotch inherited prejudices on the last score... as to *LOVE,* that is done in a week... besides marriage goes on better with esteem & confidence than romance, and she is quite pretty enough to be loved by her husband, without being so glaringly beautiful as to attract too many rivals.[32]

His only apparent fear – that she would want to waltz with him – was soon allayed, and, on 8 October, she received a formal proposal of marriage, sent via Lady Melbourne, the thinking man's pander.

When she received his offer, she did not act hastily, but instead wrote a 'Character of Lord Byron', in which she attempted to form a detached statement of his strengths and weaknesses. She took as her text a line from *Hours of Idleness*, 'I love the virtues which I cannot claim', and tried, perhaps in vain, to analyse his mercurial character. As she allowed for his chivalry, generosity and lack of ostentation, she also attempted to explain what she saw as his occasionally malevolent disposition, volatile temperament and inconsistent attitudes. If, at times, Annabella's naiveté and lack of wider knowledge of men was exposed – few others who had known him would sincerely comment on 'his love of goodness in its purest form', or claim that it managed to 'prove the uncorrupted purity of his moral sense' – then it was balanced by her willingness to consider Byron's marriage proposal.[33] At last, she made her decision. She would not be his wife, and wrote to Lady Melbourne to say so, stating 'he never will be the object of that strong affection which could make me happy in domestic life... I willingly attribute it more to the defects of my feelings than of his character that I am not inclined to return his attachment.' Had Byron taken her rejection at its face value, the matter would have been at an end. But, as Annabella was to discover, he was not a man comfortable accommodating the wishes of others.

His initial response to her refusal to marry him was sanguine and reserved. While staying in Cheltenham, he replied to Lady Melbourne, who took pride in her enhanced status as go-between. He expressed both relief and a desire to stay on amicable terms:

> I am sure we shall be better friends than before & if I am not embarrassed by all this I cannot see for the soul of me why *she* should – assure her *con tutto rispetto** that the subject shall never be renewed in any shape whatever... were it not for this embarrass[ment] with C, I would much rather remain as I am.[34]

* Literally 'with all respect'.

However, the perceptive might have detected that beneath Byron's worldly bravura there lurked the petulant disappointment of a frustrated boy surprised and angered at not getting his own way. He scornfully described Annabella as 'the fair philosopher' and disingenuously pretended that he barely knew her. Even as he argued 'the present *denial* will lessen me in her estimation as an *article of value*',[35] he brooded on the perceived slight. A subsequent letter, written after he had read a copy of her 'Character' of him received from the ever-helpful Lady Melbourne, defiantly announced 'I do not regret what has passed' but, now that he had a clearer insight into the near-idolatry with which Annabella regarded aspects of him, he mused 'though it was not accepted, I am not at all ashamed of my admiration of the amiable *mathematician*'.[36]

Marriage to Annabella was not Byron's overriding concern at this time. He was busily attempting to extricate himself from Caroline's affections, concerned for the welfare of his former page (and occasional catamite) Robert Rushton* and continuing to harass his endlessly patient lawyer John Hanson with demands for money that he believed he was owed. He also intended to publish his follow-up to *Childe Harold's Pilgrimage*, a long poem ironically entitled 'The Waltz'. Yet he was unable to let go of his *idée fixe* of marrying 'the clever mathematician'.

He had his next chance the following year. She saw him again on 7 May 1813 at a party in London, and again three days later, but she did not speak to him. Nonetheless, Byron remained in her thoughts; she noted the envy of Samuel Rogers at a party when the great man's name was mentioned, writing in her journal, 'I always thought Rogers mean, but I did not think him capable of such petty artifices as he used on this occasion to blast a rival's fame.' While he was no longer the coming man of the day – his fame was at least partially eclipsed by the publication of Austen's *Pride and Prejudice* on 27 January – Byron nevertheless enjoyed an exalted position.

* Rushton was then working as a valet to Byron's friend James Webster.

He was lionized by high society as a great writer, especially when his next major work, the Oriental romance *The Giaour*, appeared in early June. The consequence of his reputation was that he was able to take his pick of the high-born women, most notably Caroline's friend Lady Oxford. He continued an affair with her throughout the first half of 1813, bringing it to an end in late June when she left England for the Mediterranean. Rumours circulated that he had had designs on her thirteen-year-old daughter Charlotte as well.

Around this time, Annabella and Byron finally met again. She later described the event in detail, noting that she was 'extremely agitated' when she saw him, and that, as she offered him her hand, 'he turned pale as he pressed it'. She was sufficiently impressed by the strength of his apparent feeling that, as she later ruefully said, 'perhaps, unconscious as I was, the engagement was then formed on my part'.[37] As a result of this meeting, Byron recommenced his suit, although in guarded terms; when she wrote and coun- selled virtue and 'the principles of unwearied benevolence',[38] he replied to her in August and addressed what had passed between them before, saying 'many years had occurred since I had seen any woman with whom there appeared to me a prospect of rational happiness'. He even claimed, disingenuously, that Lady Melbourne had 'in some degree exceeded my intentions when she made the more direct proposal'.

Apologizing for his presumptuousness in this '*first* & *nearest* approach to that altar', he hedged his bets by allowing that 'Lady M. was perfectly correct in her statement that I preferred you to all others – it was then the fact – it is so still' but also insisted 'I feel a kind of pride even in *your rejection*'. Even as he continued to denigrate himself – 'if you hear ill of me, it is probably not untrue, though perhaps exaggerated' – he deployed a verbal equivalent of the 'underlook' when he swore 'I must be candid with you on the score of friendship – it is a feeling towards you with which I cannot trust myself – I doubt whether I could help loving you'. Ending with a vaguely expressed desire to leave the country ('probably to

Russia'),[39] Byron offered himself, once again, to Annabella, daring her to overcome her doubts and reservations and to accept his suit.

Although Annabella was not yet fully convinced of his sincerity, she was intrigued by the thought of Byron – *the* Lord Byron! – appearing to throw himself at her feet as a supplicant. When she replied in early September, her letter was both measured ('my esteem for you is confirmed by our recent intercourse') and, by her standards, daring ('there is no reason for constraint on our correspondence, which is sanctioned by the concurrence of my father & mother').[40] She requested, in vain, that he should not involve Lady Melbourne in their affairs, but her aunt derived little enjoyment from her earnest and worthy appeals to Byron's higher instincts and immortal soul. Not that he did either; in one brisk retort, he wrote 'you don't like my "restless" doctrines. I should be very sorry if *you* did but I can't *stagnate* nonetheless.'[41] The wit and irony of his correspondence was barely appreciated by Annabella, who stuck to her text of purity and morality. This approach, so carefully indoctrinated by Mrs Clermont, was wasted on Byron, who continued to dabble with other women, including Lady Frances Annesley, whom he seduced while enjoying her husband James Webster's hospitality, an act he explained, with unblushing candour, that he undertook 'to vanquish my demon'.*[42] Fidelity seemed an unlikely step for the devilish one to take.

Byron was both intrigued and perplexed by Annabella, who he began to suspect was more interesting than her prolix letters suggested; he described her as 'either the most *artful* or *artless* of her age I ever encountered'.[43] Even as he wrote to Lady Melbourne in deliberately disinterested style to muse 'I wonder who will have her at last',[44] he continued a correspondence with his potential inamorata that soon took on a settled pattern. She urged him to study religion and philosophy, in order that he might acquire a

* Webster himself was far from a virtuous husband, and he even involved himself with 'a foolish nymph' while he and Byron were on a visit to Newstead together.

greater degree of understanding, and he deflected her with a mixture of jokes and apologies, and all the while described himself in self-deprecating terms as a 'very gloomy personage' and 'a facetious companion'.[45] Eventually, even Annabella had to respond in a less high-minded fashion, when she confessed 'I have received more pleasure from your poetry than from all the QEDs in Euclid… though I think mathematics eminently useful, they are by no means what I like or admire most, & I have not a friend more skilled in them than yourself'. Finally, she cast off propriety, and declared 'I look forward to meeting you next spring in London as one of the most agreeable incidents which my residence there can produce.'[46]

Byron now knew that her full capitulation was imminent, although an invitation to visit her was not immediately forthcoming. As he waited, he continued to pursue other matrimonial options, such as Lady Melbourne's suggestion, Lady Charlotte Leveson-Gower, of whom he said 'whatever she loves I can't help liking',[47] and he might well have spurned Annabella for her, had she not been proposed to by Henry Howard, the future earl of Surrey. Nonetheless, Annabella remained the consistent prospect, and eventually he decided 'after all, Miss Milbanke is to be the person; – I will write to her', and so, after a further flurry of correspondence, he was invited to visit her at her family home in Seaham in April 1814. Flighty to the last, he stalled, quibbling to Lady Melbourne that 'I don't know what to make of her.'[48]

After further indecision, he finally wrote to her in September 1814 to ask 'are your "objections" – to which you alluded – insuperable? – or is there any line or change of conduct which could possibly remove them?' Rather than tiresomely reprise his previous proposal – 'if I do not repeat [my sentiments] it is to avoid – or at least not increase – your displeasure' – he instead believed that he was in little danger of being turned down, and so it proved. Annabella now accepted his proposal with joyful haste, and wrote to him at both Newstead and his rooms at the Albany to say 'I am and have long been pledged to myself to make your happiness my first object in life… I *dared* not believe it possible… there has in reality been scarcely a change in my sentiments.'[49]

Annabella had, at last, secured her poetic prize. As Byron said to Thomas Medwin, 'I was the fashion when she first came out; I had the character of being a great rake, and was a great dandy – both of which young ladies like.'[50] However, as Byron also claimed that she was never in love with him and had instead married him out of a mixture of vanity and a desire to reform and fix him, he had few illusions as to what her motives were. If this strikes one as a reductive way of analysing Annabella's relationship with Byron, especially given his sneer that she was nothing more than 'a spoiled child, and naturally of a jealous disposition',[51] then it should be remembered that Byron was talking to Medwin nearly a decade later, when the marriage had soured disastrously.

The potential failure of their union could be discerned in the scene at Newstead when Byron received Annabella's acceptance of his proposal. Turning to his guest, he was not happy, or excited, but instead turned so pale that it seemed he might faint. He seemed highly agitated and even fearful, saying 'it never rains but it pours'.[52] His mother's wedding ring, long believed lost, reappeared in the dining room; it seemed like the most unwelcome harbinger of ill fortune. His companion had good reason to receive the news of his impending marriage with a similar lack of equanimity. She was his half-sister Augusta, who had been conducting a love affair with him since the previous year, during which time she had given birth to a daughter.

The child was believed to be Byron's.

8

It is unlucky we can neither live with
nor without these women.

BYRON TO THOMAS MOORE,
22 AUGUST 1813

Portraits of Augusta Leigh do not show someone obviously capable of driving Byron to incestuous distraction. Two of the most famous, a miniature painted by James Holmes and a drawing by George Hayter, show a woman whose dark ringlets, slightly protruding lower lip and large eyes bear more than a passing similarity to the features of her half-sibling. She adopts a faintly cautious expression as she looks at the spectator, as if expecting that something scandalous is expected of her. Given what occurred throughout 1813 and 1814, perhaps greater caution might have been justified.

Byron and Augusta had enjoyed a close relationship during his younger years, although a perceived breach of confidence between them led to a lessening of contact from 1806 onwards. Thereafter they had exchanged mainly formal letters, and he had not seen her or written to her at all since 1809. She had therefore missed out on his rise to fame, and on his reaction to his growing literary celebrity, although she had been aghast at an attack that Byron had made on his mentor, Lord Carlisle, in the first edition of *English Bards and Scotch Reviewers*.[1] Without informing her brother, she had married her cousin Colonel George Leigh in 1807, but despite his prestigious posting in the 10th Hussars and his royal connections – he had been the equerry to the Prince of Wales – their union was an unhappy one. This was predicted by the duke of

Buckingham and Chandos,* who wrote on her wedding day that 'I pity her connecting herself with such a family, and such a fool! However she has nobody to blame but herself.' The two resided in Six Mile Bottom near Newmarket, and she gave birth to three children, Georgiana, Augusta and George, in quick succession. Unfortunately, the marriage was dogged by Leigh's financial profligacy, not least at the nearby Newmarket races. As had been the case for her stepmother, a feckless and dashing charmer had beguiled Augusta, and the consequences after the initial rapture had expired were undesirable.

She did not see Byron again until July 1813, although they had resumed their correspondence in 1811. She wrote to him affectionately; she addressed him as 'my dearest brother', suggested opportunities to meet and teased him 'I shall be daily expecting to hear of a *Lady Byron*'.[2] Less happily, she had been forced to write to him to beg for money earlier in the year, which the continuing delay in the sale of Newstead had made impossible. Fleeing from the demands of family life, she sought to enjoy herself in London, in the company of the man of the hour. Initially, Byron's attitude towards Augusta was one of light condescension, mixed with residual affection; he had sent her a copy of *Childe Harold* the previous year inscribed to 'my dearest sister, and my best friend, who has ever loved me better than I deserved'.[3] He promised 'I will watch over you as if you were unmarried',[4] and, as he wrote to Lady Melbourne to ask for an additional ticket to a prestigious society ball, the Almack's Masque in St James's, he remarked of her that 'I wish she were not married for – (now I have no house to keep) she would have been so good a housekeeper… poor soul – she likes her husband.'[5]

However, when Augusta arrived their old amity returned, undimmed by the ill feeling that had passed between them and by

---

* The excellently named Richard Temple-Nugent-Brydges-Chandos-Grenville.

her marriage. Even the fact that she, unlike the rest, had little interest in his poetry did not matter. Seeing themselves as the last scions of an ancient name, the bond that had always existed between them strengthened and grew, aided by Byron's man-about-town fame. He found himself enjoying his new role as seasoned Virgil to Augusta's naïve Dante in the inferno of London society, guiding her to the best soirées and balls with authority and aplomb. For the first time in years, he was genuinely enjoying himself, not least because he was with the person he had always cared about most. Other, that is, than himself.

Their early days in town seemed like a renewed courtship between two lovers who had long been separated. Byron gave her the affectionate nickname 'Guss', which was soon bastardized into 'Goose', a reference to her speaking quickly and unintelligibly when excited. Writing to Moore the week after Augusta arrived, he described her presence as being 'a great comfort', and claimed that this was because 'never having been much together, we are naturally more attached to each other'.[6] As he later said to the Irish writer Lady Blessington, 'Augusta knew all my weaknesses, but she had love enough to bear with them.'[7] Even the occasional incursions of Caroline, and the scandalous incident at Lady Heathcote's ball,* were unable to shake his enjoyment of the situation. He would later say of Augusta that one of her chief talents was in making him laugh, especially in flawless impersonations of others, and he boasted in return that 'I can make (her) laugh *at any thing*'.[8]

He celebrated her ability to create an elaborate and amusing fuss, which he termed 'her damn'd crinkum-crankum'; he was well aware that 'crinkum-crankum' was also low slang for vagina.[9] They spent three weeks together before Augusta had to return to the tiring duties of hearth and home; Byron, relishing his sister's company, accompanied her to Six Mile Bottom to play the role of uncle and patron. Whatever occurred there led to his returning to London

---

* This incident was explored in Chapter Six; see pp. 113–4.

almost immediately, accompanied by Augusta. When rebuked by Lady Melbourne for being a less assiduous correspondent than hitherto, he explained that 'under the existing circumstances of her lord's embarrassments, she could not well do otherwise', and that, suggesting a potential self-imposed exile, 'she appears to have still less reluctance at leaving this country than even myself'.[10]

When she eventually returned to the country, Byron was both bereft and confused by the extremity of his feelings. The two had become lovers during the summer, and even he was aware that this was as much a blow against society as it was against decency itself (had he known that his father had enjoyed a similar relationship with his own sister, Byron might have been either amused or horrified). Even as he boasted to Moore that the seduction had been little trouble, he dissimulated.[11] He was not master of his emotions, and his desperate feelings for Augusta, his 'more than sister', were hard to explain. He attempted to make light of it in a letter to Lady Melbourne, in which he jocularly exclaimed 'when I don't write to you or see you for some time you may be very certain I am about no good',[12] but there was a limit to how far he could confide his desires to the society *grande dame*, whose lack of judgement had its unbreachable limits.

An accurate representation of how Byron felt can be gleaned by the confused tone of his letters to Moore. After wondering whether Sligo or St Petersburg might be a more fitting berth for him, he apologized for having written 'a flippant and rather cold-hearted letter', but explained it saying 'I am, at this moment, in a far more serious, and entirely new, scrape than any of the last twelve months – and that is saying a good deal.' After inserting three asterisks (hinting at a complicity that could not be openly stated in a letter), Byron expressed what was, by that stage, becoming his defining dilemma – 'it is unlucky we can neither live with nor without these women'.[13]

Eventually, he was unable to keep his secret from Lady Melbourne any longer, and, in a letter now unfortunately (or intentionally) lost, she counselled him against his actions, which now included a plan to leave the country and elope with Augusta. However, he was unwilling, or unable, to take her advice, and responded by saying 'your kind letter is unanswerable – no one but yourself would have taken the trouble – no one but me would have been in a situation to require it'.[14]

Even as he corresponded with Annabella, in an attempt to distract himself from the matter in hand, he felt despondent. He joked bleakly to Moore that 'I almost wish I were married, too – which is saying much', and, commenting on the apparently endless demands of 'friends, seniors and juniors' for him to be godfather to their children, he mused that this was 'the only species of parentage which, I believe, will ever come to my share in a lawful way'. Ironically, Annabella had sent Lady Melbourne a list of the qualities she wished for in a husband, which she, in an attempt to remove temptation from Byron's path, delivered to him. His casually dismissive response – 'I return you the plan of A's spouse elect of which I shall say nothing because I do not understand it' – indicated that matrimony was not seriously on his mind. Instead, his current *magnum opus,* his romantic poem *The Giaour,* offered an outlet for his turbulent and contradictory feelings about love, and some of its lines can be read as an autobiographical account of the mixture of pleasure and guilt he felt at the sweet sin he was committing:

> I grant *my* love imperfect, all
> That mortals by the name miscall;
> Then deem it evil, what thou wilt,
> But say, oh say, *hers* was not guilt!*

In this, he was matched by Augusta, who took the attitude that their unconventional affair was, at best, simply a demonstration

* The autobiographical nature of the poem was made explicit in a letter he wrote to Lady Melbourne in which he commented that she might 'perceive in parts a coincidence in my own state of mind with that of my hero'.

of the great love that could exist between long-estranged siblings, and, at worst, something that was of no concern to anyone other than the two of them. She reputedly said 'of what consequence was one's behaviour, provided that it made nobody else unhappy?'[15]

~&

In an attempt to push matters to a head, even to provoke an elope-ment, Byron headed to Six Mile Bottom in early September, but he did not succeed in convincing Augusta to leave her husband and family and embrace a nomadic life of sin with him. Instead, disappointed but with his corporeal passions suitably enflamed, he headed to Cambridge and got wildly drunk with Scrope Davies. A letter that he wrote to Augusta subsequently ruefully talked of having 'swallowed' six bottles of claret and burgundy in less than three hours, 'which left him very unwell & me rather fever-ish'.[16] He referred to his 'long-evaded passage' abroad, as he did in a letter the same day to Murray, but no further mention was made of Augusta accompanying him. Byron loathed her husband, saying that she had embarked on an 'abominable marriage' and that 'she married a fool, but she *would* have him',[17] but these senti-ments were dictated as much by petulance and disappointment as genuine contempt for a man too ephemeral to be a fitting target of his anger.

For all the difficulties he faced, both practical and moral, Byron would not cease his pursuit of Augusta, whom he tried to see at all costs, to the point of asking the Websters to invite her to their house, Aston Hall in Yorkshire, while he was visiting. The loca-tion was familiar; it was where their father had entertained his mistress Lady Carmarthen. The awkwardness of this history, as well as having two lovers under one roof, seemed not to concern him, and he was vexed by her inability to attend. While he contin-ued to trade intellectual barbs with Annabella and physical ones with Frances Webster, he claimed to Lady Melbourne that he was unable to love anyone else, justifying himself by claiming 'I had a very fair & not *discouraging* opportunity at one time', referring to his cautious semi-proposal to Annabella, but the 'the feeling it was an effort spoiled all again'. Characterizing himself as a man who took against society, he darkly declared '*here* I am – *what* I am you know already'.[18]

At times, his correspondence was so self-consciously dramatic that the line between him and the protagonists of his poems seemed non-existent. Even Annabella was involved; unconscious of his actions, she received a letter from him that claimed 'the great object of life is Sensation – to feel that we exist – even though in pain – it is this "craving void" which drives us to Gaming – to Battle – to Travel – to intemperate but keenly felt pursuits of every description.'[19] A less humourless woman might have laughed at the verbose pomposity therein.

Although he was initially angered by Augusta's refusal to accompany him to Aston Hall, his irritation soon passed, so much so that he reassured her in a letter in October that he was 'not in the least angry',[20] and around this time changed his will so that she was one of its beneficiaries, along with his cousin George Byron. He even made jocular allusion to his affair with Frances, saying that he had been prevented from writing more fully 'by a thousand things' and that 'you do not know what mischief your being with me might have prevented'.[21] She remained constantly in his thoughts, although he prudently referred to her with asterisks rather than by name in his journal entries at the time; he noted on 16 November 1813 that he wrote his poem *The Bride Of Abydos* 'in four nights to distract my dreams from **' and on 24 November that 'I am tremendously in arrear with my letters – except to **, and to her my thoughts overpower me.'*[22] He alluded to Pope's words in *Eloisa,* 'Dear sacred name, rest ever unreveal'd', even as he referred to his own circumspection as he wrote 'at least even here,

---

* It should be noted that the protagonists of the poem, Selim and Zuleika, were originally brother and sister, but Byron prudently changed this detail.

my hand would tremble to write it'. [23]

Augusta responded in kind. When she received a copy of *The Bride Of Abydos,* she wrote to Byron on 29 November 1813, enclosing a lock of her hair – from her head, rather than her pubic area *à la* Caroline – and sent the message 'partager tous vos senti-mens, ne voir que par vos yeux, n'agir que par vos conseils, ne vivre que pour vous, voila mes voeux, mes projets & le seul destin qui peut me rendre heureuse.'* As a declaration of her love and con-stancy, it was as bold and unequivocal a statement as Byron's had been. He treasured the keepsake, writing on it 'la Chevelure of the *one* whom I most *loved*'.[24] As the giddy jolt of his love for Augusta spurred his creativity – he also wrote *The Corsair* in November, of which Annabella, innocent of the circumstances that had led to its creation, said 'in knowledge of the human heart & its most secret workings surely he may without exaggeration be compared to Shakespeare' – he both feared and half-relished the possibility of exposure and scandal. While incest, unlike sodomy, was not a capital crime, and was said to take place in some of the highest homes in the land, he had made enough enemies already to know that the consequences for him would be disastrous.

Reunited, the two siblings fled to Newstead at the beginning of 1814, arriving there on 17 January. Augusta was pregnant. It was the first time that she had seen her father's family home, and the three weeks that the two spent there, snowed in, were an idyl-lic time for them both, free to enjoy themselves. Byron informed Lady Melbourne, in one of his increasingly infrequent letters to her, that 'we never yawn or disagree, and laugh much more than is suitable to so solid a mansion; and the family shyness makes us more amusing companions to each other than we could be to any one else'.[25] While she was unimpressed by his 'kind of feeling' for

* 'To share in your feelings, to see only with your eyes, to act only on your advice, to live only for you, that is my only desire, my plan, the only destiny that could make me happy.' As so few of Augusta's letters to Byron survive, the existence of this revealing one is fortunate.

Augusta, which she categorized by its 'mixture of the terrible',[26] Byron staunchly defended his sister-lover, saying 'you are quite mistaken however as to *her*, and it must be from some misrepresentation of mine that you throw the blame so completely on the side least deserving and least able to bear it'.[27]

With Byron happy for once, the ceaseless need for creativity that had driven him the previous year was temporarily stopped. As he wrote to Murray, 'though shut up – *snow*bound – *thaw*bound – & tempted with all kinds of paper – the dirtiest of ink – and the bluntest of pens – I have not even been tempted by a wish to put them to their combined uses'.[28] Yet the fantasy of playing man and wife together in their ancestral home had to come to an end in February. Augusta was by then seven months pregnant, and had to return home for her confinement once the roads were cleared of snow. Likewise, his other mistress, literary fame, beckoned once more; *The Corsair* had been published on 1 February and had sold an impressive 10,000 copies on its first day of publication; Murray wrote to his star author in delight to claim that this was 'a thing unprecedented & the more grateful to me too as every buyer returns with looks of satisfaction & expressions of delight… you can not meet a man in the street who has not read or heard read the *Corsair*'.*[29]

Attacked by the Tory press, specifically the papers *The Courier* and *The Morning Post*, for a perceived slight on the Prince Regent in his poem 'Lines to a Lady Weeping', Byron wrote to Lady Melbourne to shrug off the attacks, claiming 'all these externals are nothing to *that within*, on a subject to which I have not alluded'. Except, of course, to her. It was a dangerous game for someone who was so present in the public sphere to be conducting a liaison with Augusta; the mild scandal that would have occurred were she someone else was nothing compared to what would happen if the truth of their highly intimate relationship was to emerge.

* It sold 25,000 copies by the end of the month.

Augusta returned to Six Mile Bottom, where Byron visited her for a few days in early April. Here, she gave birth to a daughter, Elizabeth Medora, on 15 April 1814, nine months after the first, intense period of her renewed intimacy with Byron. No definitive conclusion can ever be reached as to the identity of the child's father. Even her unusual middle name could either be an allusion to the heroine of *The Corsair* or the horse that had won the Epsom Oaks race the previous year. Or both, of course.

However, there remains a long-standing belief that the girl was the result of their tryst, a belief shared by Augusta and Byron. He wrote to Lady Melbourne shortly after the child was born with a carefully studied air of detachment:

> It is 'worth while' – I can't tell you why – it is *not* an ape and if it is – that must be my fault – however I will positively reform – you must however allow – that it is utterly impossible I can ever be half as well liked elsewhere – and I have been all my life trying to make someone love me.[30]

The reference to the ape was an allusion to the medieval belief that a product of incest would be monstrous: a suitably tasteless joke with which Byron hoped to neutralize the shock. When Elizabeth was christened the following month, Byron was the child's godfather. What Leigh made of his brother-in-law and wife's intimacy is unknown; he was probably so busy with his gambling and philandering that he barely noticed.

Byron, meanwhile, was caught between ecstasy and guilt. Writing to Moore, he sent him some lines 'which cost me something more than trouble' which amount to a *cri de coeur* about his relationship with Augusta. They have a passionate charge that feels both spontaneous and deliberate, as if he was casting himself in the role of one of his creations:

I speak not, I trace not, I breathe not thy name,
There is grief in the sound, there is guilt in the fame:

But the fear which now burns on my cheek may impart
The deep thoughts that dwell in that silence of heart.
Too brief for our passion, too long for our peace,
Were those hours – can their joy or their bitterness cease?
We repent, we abjure, we will break from our chain –
We will part, we will fly to – unite it again!
Oh! thine be the gladness, and mine be the guilt!
Forgive me, adored one! – forsake, if thou wilt –
But the heart which is thine shall expire undebased,
And *man* shall not break it – whatever *thou* mayst.[31]

Given the intensity of his feelings, and his willingness to confide them in others, it is extraordinary that, even after learning of Byron's actions, Lady Melbourne still viewed him as a suitable match for her niece. Her intervention in this matter was the crucial one for both parties, whose epistolary relationship might have eventually spluttered out otherwise. Nonetheless, her motives in persisting with the marriage were complex. While she saw herself as a mentor to her young protégé, she was also a matchmaker of the most elevated kind, arranging matches between those who she favoured with little heed as to the compatibility of the two that she brought together. The combination of the clever, cold and reserved Annabella and the complex, licentious Byron was never a likely one, and Lady Melbourne's knowledge of the events in his life the previous year – especially those involving Augusta – would usually preclude a conscious attempt to bring the two together. Yet she had not earned her nickname of 'the spider' for nothing. Constructing an intricate web of intrigue, the union of the two – one unsuspecting, the other distracted – would be another demonstration of her power and influence.

Nonetheless, why Byron chose to marry Annabella when he had his pick of women in England is unclear. When he wrote to her, shortly after he began his affair with Augusta, to say 'if you hear ill of me, it is probably not untrue, though perhaps exaggerated',[32] he trod a delicate path between warning her of his bad reputation, and taking a perverse pleasure in hinting at his actions without being explicit about them. His affections lay entirely with Augusta, but the opportunity of pursuing another appealed both to his vanity and sense of the absurd. When his attentions were redoubled after the birth of Elizabeth, it seems clear that he acted with a mixture of prudence and recklessness. He knew that Annabella represented 'the sensible choice', and he came to loathe her for who she was.

It is hard not to feel sympathy for Annabella in this situation. When she wrote to Byron, accepting his hasty offer of marriage, to say 'if I *can* make you happy, I have no other consideration', she was being as sincere and open as she could. Likewise, when she stated 'the fear of not realizing your expectations is the only one I now feel',[33] she had little idea of the extent to which the task was unachievable for anyone, save Augusta. However, there was little chance that his half-sister would abandon her family and embark on a scandalous elopement with Byron. Despite spending a happy time together in June and July in Hastings and London, as well as at Newstead, in a state of what Augusta called 'glorious uncertainty',[34] both knew that such snatched pleasures were never going to transform into a viable union between the two of them. Byron acknowledged this to Moore, when he said 'I am in some respects happy, but not in the manner that can or ought to last'.[35] Therefore he proposed out of despair, and Annabella would suffer as a result.

❧

Byron received word of the acceptance of his suit and, after his initial violent reaction, had to respond to it. Ironically, before he heard from Annabella, he had been in an excellent, atypically calm temper; afterwards, Augusta described him as exhibiting 'a deep & serious gratitude', saying 'well, after all, Heaven has been kinder to me than I deserve'. If this reaction seems to refer to Annabella's letter rather than Augusta's presence, it is also telling that Augusta regarded his attitude to be a total, and as she thought, 'romantic', disregard of fortune, which she contrasted with the subsequent absorption of his deeper feelings.[36]

Byron's initial letters to Annabella, if taken at face value, certainly seem adoring: 'your letter has given me a new existence... it was unexpected, I need not say welcome – but *that* is a poor word to express my present feelings.' Describing Annabella as 'one of the first of human beings', and calling her 'one whom it was difficult *not* to love', he vowed 'if every proof in my power of my full sense of what is due to you will contribute to *your* happiness, I shall have secured my own'. Explicitly referring to his long-desired exile ('I was upon the point of leaving England without hope, without fear'), intended to mirror that of his hero Napoleon, who had been sent to Elba that year, he seemed uncertain when he stated 'I am even now apprehensive of having misunderstood you and of appearing pre-sumptuous when I am only happy.' He tried to define the basis on which their life together would work – 'our *pursuits* at least I think are not unlike... my *habits* I trust are not very anti-domestic' – and attempted to paint himself as a prodigal returned to the fold by the healing powers of love, noting that, while he had 'long stood alone in life', 'there have been circumstances which would prove that although "sinning" I have also been "sinned against"'.[37]

Byron's correspondence with Annabella is more notable for what it leaves unsaid. Even as he explicitly stated that he intended her to be 'my guide, philosopher and friend',[38] his attitude towards the marriage was one of detachment rather than wholehearted joy. Even when he wrote to Lady Melbourne formally to ask for her consent to the match – perhaps the most redundant letter he ever wrote – he stated 'I mean to reform most thoroughly and become "a good man and true" in all the various senses of these respective & respectable appellations – seriously.'[39] The edge of irony that accompanied the traditional cliché was hardly nullified by his fol-lowing statement that 'I will endeavour to make your niece happy not by my doubts but what I will deserve.'[40] It bears repeating that Byron and Annabella barely knew one another, having only met a handful of times, and even then at hectic social functions. If either harboured genuinely ardent feelings towards the other, then they sprang from a mistakenly romanticized belief.

What Augusta thought of all this can only be surmised. While she believed that Annabella would bore Byron, she also hoped that, once married to a respectable woman, Byron would indeed reform and their liaison would remain a secret. All the same, she guessed that her brother was trying to play a part for which he was less than word-perfect on the lines. She commented on his letter of acceptance to Annabella that 'this is a very pretty letter – it is a pity it should not go', and Byron, as if to spite both of them, announced 'Then it *shall* go', dispatching it on 10 September.[41] Nonetheless, as Byron prepared to leave Newstead with her, he took her to an elm behind the house, and they carved their names, as well as the date, 20 September 1814.* The gesture was a small but important one; no tree would ever be defaced with the legend 'Byron & Annabella'.

Afterwards, Augusta returned to Six Mile Bottom and her family, and Byron headed to London to ruminate on the situation in which he found himself. His letters to Annabella at this time had a businesslike and unromantic quality in their declarations of love, mainly offering excuses for any failings that she might find in him. Even as he apologized that one epistle was 'more like a *factor's* letter than anything else', he gave the impression that writing to Annabella was more of a duty than a pleasure, so much so that she replied to him to say:

> I know why you do not write – you think you have nothing to say that is worth saying, and I am in the same predicament, but I do as I would be done by, and hope that *anything* from me will give you the same pleasure as I have in *anything* from you.[42]

---

* Unfortunately, this tree has long since been cut down, although an oak remains that was reputedly planted by the young Byron in 1798.

She was to be disappointed.

Ironically, given her antipathy to the match, it was Augusta who seemed most comfortable maintaining the façade that Byron's and Annabella's engagement was a joyful union between equals. She took the initiative in contacting Annabella, writing her a witty and charming letter:

> I am afraid I have no better excuse to offer for this *self-introduction* than of feeling quite unable any longer to reconcile myself to the idea of being *quite* a *stranger* to one whom I hope *soon* to call *my sister*, and one – may I be allowed to add – whom I already love as such.

Claiming that she regarded her brother as 'the most fortunate of human beings', she apologized for the delay in writing by claiming that Byron, to whom she had meant to entrust the letter, was delayed by business.[43] Annabella's response was more measured – '[her letter was] so cordially kind that I cannot say how much I thank her... I have replied – but not much to my own satisfaction'[44] – but Byron was delighted by Augusta's intervention, praising her to Lady Melbourne as 'the least selfish person in the world... you don't know what a being she is', before going on to exculpate her by claiming that 'her only error has been my fault entirely, & for this I can plead no excuse – except passion, which is none'.[45]

Byron now had to venture to Seaham to see his fiancée for the first time since the engagement, but the proposed journey gave him no pleasure. He did his best to delay going, grimly telling Hobhouse that 'the character of wooer in this regular way does not sit easy upon me'.[46] Annabella, realizing that Byron was reluctant to travel, sought to make the situation easier by inviting Augusta as well, but she graciously declined, citing her young children. The inevitable awkwardness that her presence would have caused was not mentioned, but she sought to explain her brother's tardy arrival at Seaham by citing 'the *family shyness*', which she hinted that she possessed as well.[47]

Despite Annabella's repeated hints that his presence would be welcome, Byron's reluctance to see her persisted. Augusta even offered herself as go-between, continually assuring Annabella of Byron's continued love and desire to see her, but he remained in London until 29 October when he finally began the journey north, although not before a visit to Six Mile Bottom. At last, on 1 November, he arrived at Seaham, where he had been expected for the two previous days. As with the rest of his relationship with Annabella, the stay was not a success.

When he arrived, he treated Annabella with a deeply formal courtesy that belied any romantic feelings, with his first spoken words to her being 'it is a long time since we have met'. In a letter to her aunt reporting the visit, Annabella talked of Byron speaking 'with an animation of manner that seemed to proceed from agitated spirits', and was struck 'by an appearance of personal vanity… and by the air with which he played with his large watch-chain'.[48] Many years later, she wrote an (admittedly coloured) account of her impressions of the visit, noting on the first night that 'he is coarser, sullied, since we last met', and that 'a mysterious shadow' hung over his presence there.[49]

The 'mysterious shadow' was Augusta. Annabella later wrote that she attempted to find out whether it was true that Byron had had a three-year disagreement with her over 'some frivolous offence', and his reaction was to both acknowledge it was so, and then, 'with apparently deep condemnation of his conduct towards her', said 'you might have heard worse than *that*'. Nonetheless, he expressed contrition at the break between them, saying 'I have done all in my power since to make her amends for it.'[50] While Annabella swore that she would be 'her zealous friend', she resented what she saw as 'her perhaps superior influence', maybe unsurprisingly given that Byron 'spoke of her with an air of sorrowful tenderness', and mused, in a moment of candour, that 'no one would ever possess "so much of his confidence & affection as Augusta"'.[51]

Even allowing for the fact that Annabella's account of the disappointing Seaham visit was retrospective, it is still clear that Byron's
thoughts did not lie with his wife-to-be. He delighted in dropping
hints and suggestions of some great wrongdoing; she stated that he
made a remark that he repeated after their marriage, namely that
'had you married me two years ago, you would have saved me *that*
for which I never can forgive myself'.[52] No satisfactory explanation
was forthcoming.

Confronted with what his life as a husband was to be, Byron
expressed concern and alarm. Writing to Lady Melbourne, he
made clear his dislike of Lady Milbanke ('I can't tell why, for we
don't differ, but so it is') and seemed bewildered by Annabella,
saying '[she] is the most *silent* woman I ever encountered, which
perplexes me extremely'.[53] Doubtless the cheerfully loquacious
Goose was uppermost in his thoughts, although he did not write to
her while he was at Seaham; she complained to her friend Francis
Hodgson that 'I have not heard from him for some time, and am
uneasy about it', although she swiftly qualified this by noting 'it
is very selfish to be so, for I know he is happy, and what more can
I wish'.

Whether Augusta's words were disingenuous or indicative of a
real desire for her brother's happiness, it became quickly clear that
the marriage between Byron and Annabella was doomed. After an
attempt at public relations on 6 November ('Annabella and I go on
extremely well'), he ruefully gave Lady Melbourne a truer expression of his feelings the following week, saying 'I have grave doubts
if this will be a marriage now: her disposition is the very reverse of
our imaginings.' While allowing that 'she seems well, looks & eats
well & is cheerful & confiding & in short like any other person
in good health & spirits', he found her dull and temperamental, comparing a '*scene*' that she made to one of Caroline's forays
into hysteria, and liable to draw inferences from his every word.
He hinted that, out of a mixture of frustration and lust, he had
made love to her in some form – 'I have lately had recourse to the

eloquence of *action*' – but continued to regard her as '*self*-torment-ing, and anxious, and romantic'.[54] Annabella would later state that the 'scene' he referred to was his angry reaction when she gently tried to enquire whether something frightened him about their marriage. As she said, 'a burdened conscience or an overwrought imagination were the only causes I could conceive'.[55] Again, hind-sight might make Annabella's account unduly significant, but she rightly said that 'I had linked myself to misery if not guilt'. It would have been better for all parties had the wedding been called off, but etiquette did not allow for such common sense.

After two unhappy and tense weeks, Byron left Seaham on 16 November, bound for London and then for Augusta and Six Mile Bottom. Annabella, as if by rote, declared her love to him and wished that they were married, saying '*myself* is by no means the grave, didactic deplorable person that I have appeared to you',[56] but Byron seemed determined to end the engagement. He even went so far as to write a letter breaking it off. Augusta dissuaded him from sending it, and instead suggested that he struck a calmer and more affectionate note in his correspondence. An epistle that he wrote from Cambridge – 'I am as happy as Hope can make me, and as gay as Love will allow me to be til we meet and ever my Heart – thine' – reassured Annabella, but Byron did not believe the sentiments in it, which were as cheap as a penny ballad sold on the street. As Annabella bombarded him with declarations of love and excitement about their engagement, he tried to postpone the wedding, pleading poverty.

If he wished to make Annabella feel that he was unexcited about their union, he succeeded. Despite the grumblings of Lady Mel-bourne, who told Annabella that 'I supposed his leaving you was unavoidable, otherwise I should have scolded you for allowing him to come away', a failing she ascribed to her niece remaining 'a little in ye clouds of romance, and above the feelings of common humdrum beings',[57] Byron spent December trying to find a con-venient way of escaping the shackles of matrimony. Augusta, ever the peacemaker, attempted to reassure Annabella that she was not mistaken in her impression of her brother – 'it does my heart good to read what *you* think of him'[58] – but he tarried in town as long as he decently could, pleading the necessity of selling Newstead and dealing with his solicitor Hanson. Annabella soon lost patience, writing to complain that 'the continuation of these *unnecessary* delays creates vexation of spirit to my father and mother… I must borrow an appropriate quotation from you – 'I am a little anxious to have your answer and must conclude this'.'[59] A subsequent letter feigned amity – 'I feel nothing but sunshine in the thought of being thine – thy wife'[60] – but her implication was clear; marry me or face the consequences.

Eventually, Byron realized that there was no possibility of escape. He wrote to Annabella with grim determination – 'if we meet let it be to marry… with regard to our being under the same roof and *not* married, I think past experience has shewn us the awkwardness of that situation'[61] – and began the journey from London to Seaham Hall with all the joy of a pilgrim undergoing a reluctant penance. He had obtained a special licence from the archbishop of Canterbury on 16 December that allowed a ceremony to take place at Seaham, rather than in a church. His motivation was to avoid 'fuss and publicity', which sat oddly with his usual rapture for fame. As usual, he took a diversion via Six Mile Bottom, where he asked Augusta to accompany him to his wedding; she reluctantly declined, pleading domestic commitments and her husband's protestations of illness. Hobhouse, acting as best man, accompanied him on his odyssey. He noted in his journal that 'Byron did not arrive until three… never was lover less in haste'.[62] He grew 'more and more *less* impatient' as the journey progressed. They did not arrive at Seaham until 30 December, six weeks after his departure following his earlier visit.

Hobhouse provided a vivid account of the arrival and the eventual marriage. Describing the bride as 'rather dowdy looking', albeit with 'excellent feet', and with an 'expressive but not handsome' face, he noted that she burst into tears on Byron's much-anticipated arrival, and that he 'looked foolish in finding out an excuse for our want of expedition'. Nonetheless, after the marriage settlement was signed on 31 December (with 'a little jollity') and a mock marriage that evening, the wedding proper was fixed for 2 January 1815. The night before, it was felt that 'we had not quite so jolly a dinner as yesterday'. Byron commented to Hobhouse, 'Well, H, this is our last night – tomorrow I shall be Annabella's – *absit omen!*'* These were hardly the words of an ardent bridegroom thrilled at the prospect of matrimony.

The ceremony itself passed without incident. The couple were married by Annabella's uncle, Reverend Thomas Noel, and the bride wore a muslin gown trimmed with lace, and a white muslin jacket; Hobhouse called her attire 'very plain indeed', especially for an aristocratic bride marrying a society figure. Byron, in full morning dress with white gloves, did what was expected of him, apart from jerking slightly when he was required to say the words 'I, George Gordon…' He seemed to find the statement 'with all my worldly goods I thee endow' mildly amusing, the ever-impecunious one looking over at Hobhouse with a half smile. Annabella and her mother were both very moved. 'If I am not happy, it will be my own fault,'[63] said Annabella, but Byron retained his cool, and behaved as if little of note had occurred. Hobhouse wrote of his misery at the ill-matched pairing: 'of my dearest friend I took a melancholy leave… he was unwilling to leave my hand, and I had hold of his out of the window when the carriage drove off'. It was little surprise that he described having attended the wedding feeling 'as if I had buried a friend'.[64]

He was not alone in having a deep feeling of foreboding. Augusta later said that, at the hour of her sibling's wedding, she felt as the sea must do when hit by an earthquake. She knew that,

---

* Meaning, approximately, 'may what is said not come true'.

if the marriage was not a success, she would suffer nearly as much as her brother.[65]

9

He loves or hates us together.

ANNABELLA TO AUGUSTA,
9 NOVEMBER 1815

Byron and Annabella's marriage became unhappy straight away. After the studiedly blasé attitude that he adopted in Hobhouse's presence, Byron was unable to retain his composure in front of his wife. In her account of the events of 1815, Annabella described him as being prone to 'gloom and defiance' from the moment that their carriage drew away. He did not talk to her excitedly about their life together, but instead 'he began singing in a wild manner as he usually does when angry'. Their servants travelled on the outside of their carriage, as was customary, giving Byron a degree of privacy with which to vent his discontent. During the course of their journey to Halnaby Hall in Yorkshire, one of the Milbanke houses and the scene of their honeymoon, he told Annabella of his (and Lady Melbourne's) loathing of her mother, as well as his desire to wreak vengeance on her for rejecting his initial proposal in 1813. As a further wedding gift to his new bride, he turned to her with a bitter expression and sneered, 'I wonder how much longer I shall be able to keep up *the part I have been* playing.'[1]

That a miserable and angry Byron should take his feelings out in violent fashion on Annabella was inevitable, if inexcusable. In all of his previous dealings with the central women in his life – even Augusta – he had radiated charm when he was getting his own way, and anger when he was not. If Annabella has been blamed for her humourlessness and priggishness, being a bore hardly justified the appalling treatment she endured from the first day of her marriage. For all his fine words and intelligence, the brutishness that he visited upon Annabella throughout the year or so that they were together amounts to a serious indictment of Byron as a man.

The violence began on the first day of their union. The pioneering social theorist and feminist Harriet Martineau, who later became friends with Annabella, said of her that 'at the altar she did not know that she was a sacrifice, but before sunset on that winter day she knew it'.[2] Her happiness had been sacrificed, and the wedding had taken place under fraudulent auspices. After the horrendous journey, Annabella tried her best to adopt an air of gaiety and good cheer, but it did not convince all. Martineau recorded a butler at Halnaby saying that Annabella bore 'a countenance and frame agonized and listless with evident horror and despair', and that 'he longed to offer his arm to the young, lonely creature, as an assurance of sympathy and protection'.

She needed this protection. Byron consummated their marriage virtually through rape; according to Moore, he boasted 'I *had* Lady Byron on the sofa before dinner'.[3] Thereafter, he enquired of her 'with an appearance of aversion' whether she wished to sleep in the same bed as him, something that he detested, and claimed that 'one animal of the kind was as good to him as another', provided that she was young.[4] His actions did not stem from rational thought. Samuel Rogers asserted that there was an account in Byron's memoirs of how he awoke in the night, saw a lit taper cast a crimson glow into the room and shouted 'Good God, I am surely in hell!'[5] He was suffering his own torments, which were then inflicted on Annabella by proxy. He would later claim to Hobhouse that a depressive fit had seized him on his wedding night. The 'oppression', as he called it, lasted for an entire week.[6]

The next day, Byron no longer exhibited anger and violence, but instead offered a cold restraint that was just as forbidding. When he greeted Annabella in the library, he announced 'it's too late now – it's done – you should have thought of it sooner', and, referring to the strain of madness that galloped through his family, sneered 'you were determined not to marry a man in whose family there was insanity – you have done very well indeed'.[7] He did not spare himself, saying 'I am a villain – I could convince you of it in three words'. If this was a reference to Augusta, it was true that his sister was never far from his thoughts. She had written to him on the first day of the honeymoon, calling him 'dearest, first and best of human beings', which he relayed to his new bride with 'a kind of fierce and exulting transport'.[8]

It was now that Annabella began to realize where Byron's true affections lay. She wrote that: 'two or three days after my marriage, suspicions had indeed crossed my brain', and compared these to being 'transient as lightning, not less blasting'. When she 'innocently' alluded to the possibility of an unconscious incestuous relationship between hitherto unsuspecting brother and sister, 'his terror & rage were excessive', and he had 'an air of frantic distraction' about him, which he allayed by leaving the room, armed with his dagger, like the protagonist in a Jacobean tragedy about to commit some sinful act. Even in high emotion, Byron played the protagonist in his self-penned story, which was not aided by his 'continually lamenting her absence, saying no one loved him as she did'.[9]

Despite her suspicions of Byron and Augusta's true relationship, Annabella continued a friendly correspondence with her, helped by Augusta's sincere affection for her new sister-in-law. Writing to Annabella shortly after the wedding, she gushed 'I never can express how much I wish you & my dearest B all possible happiness',[10] which swiftly drew an invitation to join them at Halnaby and to be Annabella's 'ONLY *friend*'. It seemed as if Augusta's presence would ameliorate the difficulty that defined the honeymoon. Although she gracefully declined, citing family demands, their subsequent letters became an important lifeline for Annabella, as Augusta counselled her against taking Byron – who she termed 'the Magician' and 'baby' – too seriously and offering solace, not least her claim in one letter that 'I am going to *scold* him'.[11]

Byron, meanwhile, publicly pretended all was bliss. One letter to Lady Melbourne, addressing her self-consciously as 'dearest Aunt', claimed that 'Bell & I go on extremely well',[12] just as another offered the double-edged compliment that 'you would think we had been married these 50 years'. He lied that 'I have great hopes this match will turn out well', but he also remained keen to retain their conspiratorial relationship, stating 'recollect, *we* are to keep our secrets and correspondence as heretofore'. Other letters to his friends and to Murray were as cheery and witty as ever, deflecting any suspicion of domestic misery. Even while their life together was dictated by brooding and sudden darts of aggression on his side and hapless and clumsy attempts at affection on hers, Byron saw the importance of maintaining the pretence of its success, for Annabella's sake as much as his own.

Sometimes, there was an edge of black comedy in his actions, such as when he pronounced that he was a fallen angel possessed by an invincible force of evil.[13] Annabella's inability to take his statements as anything other than gospel indicates a literal-mindedness that Augusta certainly did not possess. Likewise, some of his more extreme superstitions, such as refusing to start anything on a Friday or never allowing Annabella to wear a black gown, were as much provocation as genuine caution. At last, the bullying and tension gradually reduced in scale, and a return visit to Seaham on 21 January saw them find a measure of peace together, heralded by Byron acknowledging that, if they avoided certain subjects, 'we *might* go on together'.[14]

Once there, Byron, although bored by the inactivity, was able to relax enough to make jokes about the 'treacle-moon' that he was undergoing, commenting to Moore that 'I am awake, and find myself married'.[15] While he parried Hanson's anxious questions of financial 'expectations' from the marriage, he came to an understanding of sorts with Annabella over the next few weeks, on one occasion going so far as to unbend enough to call her 'a good kind Pip – a good-natured Pip',* and 'the best wife in the world'.[16] This affection, fleeting though it was, sustained them throughout the early months of 1815, as they remained at Seaham prior to taking a house in London. He even allowed her to make gentle fun of his club foot, a taboo subject for anyone else. During this time, Byron wrote one of his most famous poems, 'The Destruction Of Sennacherib', as part of his *Hebrew Melodies* collection;[17] those looking for autobiographical overtones might be disappointed, unless they read something into Byron's description of how 'there lay the rider distorted and pale'.

Augusta and Annabella continued a regular correspondence, although with some restraint on both sides. When Augusta referred to her 'woes' in a letter of 2 February, she swiftly reassured Annabella that 'my "anxieties" are not about B's happiness', but were instead about the 'minor calamities' of his needing to sell Newstead to ward off financial ruin.[18] Her recollection of their visit not six months before lingered. In an attempt to cheer both Byron and Annabella, Augusta invited them on a visit to Six Mile Bottom; George Leigh was away and she longed for her brother's company. As Byron, whether out of inertia or prudence, did not reply to her, it was left to Annabella to make arrangements for a trip there. When Byron was informed of the planned holiday, he wished to go by himself, announcing that the house was not large enough to accommodate them both and their servants, and that there was nowhere nearby suitable for them to stay. Annabella, showing a stubborn side, refused to be left in Seaham or London and insisted on accompanying her husband, and they departed in mid-March. She soon regretted it.

The claustrophobia and slow pace of carriage travel did not agree with Byron, and he again expressed violent sentiments

---

* He called her 'Pip' as an abbreviation for 'Pippin', a reference to her cheeks, which, he claimed, reminded him of apples.

while on the three-day journey from Seaham to Six Mile Bottom, not least further criticism of Annabella's parents. By now understanding her husband's capricious temper, she endured it, and so he became pleasant, even lightly affectionate: until, that is, the coach approached Six Mile Bottom, and his habitual gloom again dominated him. When they arrived, he initially insisted Annabella remain in the carriage while he headed inside, to, as he put it, 'prepare Guss'. When he was unable to find her, as she was upstairs changing, Annabella accompanied him inside, where she encountered Augusta for the first time and shook hands with her. Augusta seemed shy, but received Byron with affection; he, in his turn, castigated Annabella for not having been warmer and less formal to his sister.*

After this, Annabella left Byron and Augusta together, and, seeing that he was much more interested in his sister's company than in hers, retired to bed. This became a nightly occurrence. After getting drunk on brandy, Byron then abused Annabella, alluding to his 'criminal passion' for Augusta and claiming 'now I have *her,* you will find I can do without *you*'; it later transpired that Augusta had refused to allow Byron's renewed sexual advances, driving him into a state of frenzied frustration. The next morning, Byron remarked in front of both women 'Well, Guss, I'm a reformed man, aren't I?' As Annabella later noted, 'it was plain from this that his conduct must have been very bad'.

As he cheerily discoursed on his former romantic intrigues, and forced Augusta to show off copies of some of his more torrid love letters, he expressed his contempt for his engagement and marriage: 'all the time you thought I was dying for you'. His hostility was only interrupted by moments of self-awareness, such as when

* The description of Byron and Annabella's disastrous trip to Six Mile Bottom comes from her later testimony, as quoted in *Lord Byron's Wife,* pp. 291–7. While highly coloured and biased against Byron, it is nonetheless invaluable as a blow-by-blow account of his behaviour at this extraordinary time.

Annabella, in an attempt to make cheerful conversation, remarked that she would have liked to have seen his 'tenderness of expression' when he looked down at the infant Elizabeth; she noted that 'this affected him incomprehensibly'. Even as Augusta did what she could to calm Annabella, taking long afternoon walks with her and reassuring her of Byron's love, he took delight in being as provocative as he could. One such act was to have two gold brooches commissioned, one emblazoned with an A and the other with a B, and both bearing three crosses, the symbol both used to describe each other in their letters. When they arrived, he turned to Augusta, and 'with a contempt for my ignorance and blindness', said of Annabella, 'if she knew what these meant'. She had guessed all too well. Even as he described Augusta as 'my only friend' and 'my best friend', her conscience caused her to reply, 'in a tone of suppressed wretchedness', 'I fear I've been your *worst.*'

Even if Augusta denied him sex, Byron was not to be dissuaded from carnal play, expressing an intention, as Annabella shudderingly put it, '*to work us both well*'. To this end, he lasciviously drew comparisons between their underwear, and made them engage in highly charged sex games, lying down on the sofa and taking it in turns to be kissed by his wife and sister. As Annabella observed, 'he was more warm towards her than me'. Even allowing for exaggeration, his treatment of Annabella was so cruel and capricious that it reduced her to near-despair. Not that Augusta was spared; Annabella wrote that 'he kept her in a state of misery beyond mine, I thought'. As he punished her for refusing to sleep with him, he drew her into his marriage with the cruel confidence of a man who believed an incestuous *ménage à trois* was less a perversion and more of a right.

After this dreadful fortnight, Byron and Annabella left for London on 28 March. Lady Melbourne had ensured that they were found a suitably grand and aristocratic property at 13 Piccadilly Terrace, rented at £700 a year. As they left, Byron continued to wave his handkerchief at Augusta in a demonstrative way and to, as Annabella put it, 'after-eye' her, before he anxiously asked his wife whether she liked his sister and former lover. When Annabella replied cautiously that Augusta was much cleverer than Byron had suggested, he was delighted, and expressed great pleasure in their friendship. Even as Annabella had been confronted with all but unarguable proof of a transgressive relationship, she was powerless to take action, other than, as she saw it, to obey a moral imperative to keep them 'innocent', if not apart. As she later described:

> My duty allowed me no resource but to constitute myself the guardian of these two beings, who seemed indeed on 'the brink of a precipice' – in the study of their welfare, I sought to forget my own miserable and, under an earthly aspect, most humiliating condition.

When Annabella and Byron arrived in London, Augusta headed there too. She had been appointed lady-in-waiting to Queen Charlotte, which required her to live in St James's Palace, and Byron invited her to stay with him and Annabella at 13 Piccadilly Terrace before she began her role. Augusta happily wrote to Annabella to accept the chance for a visit, archly referring to 'the wind and weathercock'[19] as an indication of her brother's mercurial moods, and she arrived at their house on 12 April. As it transpired, the first few days of Lord and Lady Byron's life in London were some of their happiest; he enjoyed his reputation as a society figure, meeting the likes of Walter Scott and the politician Douglas Kinnaird, as well as resuming his acquaintance with Lady Melbourne. Doubtless she enjoyed hearing of her protégé's new-found uxoriousness. As a public husband, Byron was superb; he doted on his wife, and appeared to be hugely content. Only in private were matters less pleasant.

Upon Augusta's arrival, the fragile peace was shattered. Byron, who had a dark premonition of what her presence connoted, left the house when she was due to arrive, and behaved coldly and dismissively towards her initially, with 'lowering looks of disgust and hatred'[20] although he was unable to maintain hostility towards his beloved Goose. Yet no such thawing greeted Annabella, who was informed, in front of Augusta, 'you were a fool to let her come. You will find it will make a good deal of difference to you *in all ways*.'[21] Even Annabella's newly discovered pregnancy did not make matters easier,* and her sorrows were exacerbated by the ill health of her uncle Lord Wentworth, whom she visited on his deathbed nearby.

Augusta would eventually stay for over two months, even after she began her duties at St James's Palace. Her presence was due both to sibling affection and out of concern for Annabella, for whom Byron's contempt seemed to have increased now that he knew she was pregnant. Staying up each night drinking and laughing with Augusta, his mood abruptly changed when he went to bed, and he would treat his wife with disdain. Rather than physical violence, he conducted himself towards her with a general hostility occasionally diversified by flashes of rage. Even when she was ill, and a miscarriage thought possible, he did not exhibit any signs of concern, but instead seemed angry with her, drawing parallels with the fecund Augusta. The flirtation and sexual power play of Six Mile Bottom continued unchecked.

Sometimes Byron's behaviour verged on the absurd. When he indulged an interest in theatre by becoming part of the management committee of the Drury Lane Theatre Royal, he stated that he had only taken the role so that he had his pick of actresses: apparently a joke, albeit a tasteless one.† Annabella was unamused. He was not helped by the ever-pressing attentions of his creditors, as constant in their way as he was inconstant in his; now he could afford a grand house and was married to an heiress, they believed he could recompense them. Even a visit from Annabella's parents

* Presumably the conception occurred in the last days at Seaham – on Byron's side, as a means of relieving the tedium.
† Byron did pursue a liaison with one actress later in the year, a Susan Boyce, whom he treated in a cavalier fashion.

at the end of April could not relieve the claustrophobia of their existence. While Byron, perhaps in deference to her pregnancy, was not physically violent with her, his mood swings and frequent drunkenness made him uneasy company. When he remarked in a letter to Moore that 'we have been very little out this season',[22] this concealed the truth that his being out of the house would have been entirely preferable to his remaining within it.

Whether or not Augusta contributed directly to the dreadful situation, Annabella decided that she 'seemed to increase his ill dispositions',[23] and so asked her to leave the house in late June. Byron's melancholy at seeing his sister – and, he believed, his ally – depart was exacerbated by Napoleon's defeat at Waterloo on 18 June 1815; while his feelings towards a man who he regarded as half-god, half-devil were as contradictory as much else in his life, his loathing of the Tory Wellington meant that he was unable or unwilling to share in the general jubilation. That he was about to become a – legitimate – father seemed of little interest to him.

Nevertheless, with Augusta removed to Six Mile Bottom to deal with her husband, now newly unemployed after the victory at Waterloo, an uneasy truce returned. Hobhouse, regarded by Annabella as a bad influence responsible for Byron 'pursuing every vice, less from inclination… than from a principle of destroying every better feeling',[24] returned on 24 July, and accompanied Byron to an auction at Garraway's on 28 July, where Newstead was finally sold for 95,000 guineas: a good deal less than the £140,000 that he had originally agreed on as a selling price in 1813. With the little money that he now had, he made a new will that month, settling everything he had after the marriage settlement on Augusta. The declaration of love was explicit, as was the calculated snub to Annabella. When he headed to see Augusta at the end of August, he showed a kindness and conciliation lacking in his dealings with his wife. Augusta wrote to Annabella on 1 September to say that Byron was 'quite well', if 'invisible', despite 'a little *sparring* about *brandy*', but that he was taking a grim delight in causing

mischief, having 'confessed almost all his *naughty fits & sayings* but
without seeming to have an idea that I might have heard them'.[25]
The unspoken implication remained that Augusta had more than
simply 'heard' them.

The visit ended atypically badly, due to Augusta defending the
Milbankes against one of Byron's hyperbolic rants about them and
so he returned to Piccadilly in poor humour. Augusta reported
to Annabella that 'he has been very disconsolate without you',
and he signed letters to her 'ever most lovingly thine', but further
tension arose from Byron's involvement with Drury Lane. Annabella considered it beneath him, whether or not the actresses were
beneath him as well; she dismissed it as 'the vocation of an *Acting
Manager*',[26] and slightingly referred to Byron as '*the Manager*'.
This attack on one of his few altruistic activities only exacerbated
the tension between them, which was not helped by Annabella's
pregnancy and their financial woes.

It had been decided that she should give birth in London, rather
than at Seaham, although this was done less for her comfort and
more for Byron's fears that the bailiffs would seize their property
were they to leave the house. In the end, the threat materialized
anyway. On 8 November, a bailiff entered the house and established a presence there. Annabella wrote to Augusta to complain
that '[I] am suffering from B's distraction, which is of the *very
worst* kind... [he] speaks to me only to upbraid me with having
married him when he wished not', before she criticized his continued drinking and inopportune absences. He even denied knowing
why the bailiff was in the house, to Annabella's scepticism. The
previous week, she wrote a document entitled 'Reflections on
Lord B's character written under a delusive feeling in its favour',
that ascribed his wickedness to those who had 'induced him to act
on wrong motives, by discrediting his right ones'.[27] Her 'delusive
feeling' came at the same time as she was making fair copies of his
poems *The Siege* and *Parisina* for the printers; her forbearance and
sympathy towards her husband did her credit.

Augusta, who knew how intransigent her brother could be, had become her greatest ally. When Annabella despairingly announced 'he loves or hates us together',[28] she knew that Byron, depressed and vindictive, was starting to slide into alcohol-induced madness. Even the offer of much-needed funds from Murray, in order to prevent him selling his library, was refused, with Byron grandly announcing that the circumstances were 'not *immediately* pressing'.[29] He was more candid with Hobhouse, pronouncing himself driven 'half-mad' by his financial difficulties, but claimed he should 'think lightly of them *were he not married*'.[30]

Matters soon worsened. Byron by then barely spoke to Annabella 'except in the most harsh & unkind manner', and Augusta arrived at Piccadilly for the second time on 15 November to act as peacemaker, this time at Annabella's explicit request. The relationship between the two women, evolving from strangers to rivals and, finally, to allies, represents one of the most remarkable consequences of Byron's increasingly unchecked behaviour. This included his asking Annabella in a hopeful manner if she had miscarried after he had been particularly vile to her.[31] While drink was in part to blame for his actions – he would later state to Hobhouse that he was '*bereaved of reason*' in this time – it hardly excused his wallowing in moral and physical squalor. It was too much for Annabella to cope with alone, and so Augusta's arrival was not just welcome, but necessary.

While Byron was again initially ungracious towards his sister, he soon became his old self around her, albeit without any sexual intent. This was directed towards his playhouse mistress Susan Boyce. Augusta was sufficiently horrified by the state in which she found the house and its occupants that she summoned their cousin, Captain George Byron, in an attempt to manage Byron's lunacy. The poet was, by now, drinking so heavily that he barely knew what he was doing, and was an infrequent correspondent; one of his few surviving letters of this time apologizes for having offended the actor Alexander Rae 'because I was heated with wine', explaining that his recollection was clouded 'through the medium of a severe headache'.[32] Augusta was therefore forced to play nursemaid to her errant brother, although he responded with little gratitude, declaring grandiloquently that 'I am determined to fling misery around me and upon all those with whom I am concerned'.[33] She responded with steadfastness and calmness and, as Annabella said, 'to defend me from his threatened violence and cruelty, she seemed to acquire a fortitude inconsistent with her timid nature'.[34]

If the imminent arrival of his child should have calmed him, it had almost the opposite effect. That he had been sanguine about it as recently as September can be seen from a letter he wrote to his friend James Webster, when he claimed 'I wish a boy of course – they are less trouble in every point of view – both in education & after life'.[35] On 9 December, the day before the child was born, Annabella remained at Piccadilly Terrace for her lying-in. Byron took the opportunity to ask her 'with the strongest expression of aversion & disgust' whether she chose to live with him any longer, and, gratified by reducing her to tears, sauntered off to the theatre. When Augusta upbraided him for his behaviour upon his return, he casually remarked 'yes, I am a fool – I always *mis-time* my questions'. He then made loud noises in the room beneath Annabella's, breaking soda-water bottles in agitation. Nerves at the prospect of becoming a father were understandable, but his behaviour seemed more an exercise in tormenting his wife than in genuine disquiet.

His daughter, Augusta Ada, was born at 1pm on Sunday 10 December 1815, and the birth was relatively straightforward. The second name was a reference to a former wife of the Byron clan – 'someone who married into his family in the reign of King John',[36] according to Hobhouse – and the first name was self-explanatory. Fatherhood did not calm the errant lord. When Byron first gazed on Ada – as she became known – he smiled initially but then, as if possessed, shouted 'oh! What an implement of torture have I acquired in you!'[37] Even as Augusta tried desperately to pretend that all was well, writing to Byron's Cambridge friend Francis Hodgson that 'B is in great good looks', his mania persisted. At times, there seemed a perverse method to his madness; he had mentioned the necessity of breaking the house up, once Annabella had given birth, to Hobhouse in late November, and expressed a desire to head abroad. This raises the possibility that his behaviour was conducted as much in an attempt to force a separation from a miserably unhappy wife as it was an uncontrollable expression of his id. Yet the effort that Byron went to in creating this ghastly household, full of unease and horror, seems beyond any deliberate plan. The madness of the Gordons seemed truly alive in him, after all.

৯৯

Regardless of the truth or otherwise of the stories that Byron attempted to rape Annabella shortly after she gave birth, and had to be forcibly prevented from doing so by the Byrons' servants,[38] the Fletchers, they show that by the beginning of 1816 Byron's reputation – still publicly high, due to the careful management of his friends – was privately in ruins. As he made wild threats that he would leave the country and take Ada with him, or give her to Augusta to be brought up alongside her half-sister, it seemed as if anything was possible. Finally, on 6 January 1816, the tide broke. He had previously drunkenly confessed to Annabella that he was guilty, or believed himself guilty, of what she called 'a dreadful crime, to which he never hears or reads an allusion without the deepest agitation, & violent struggle to suppress it'.[39] Whether it was incest, sodomy or something even worse – murder was at one point debated – Byron decided that Annabella knew too much, and that her continued presence in their house was a threat to him. With this in mind, he wrote a peremptory letter banishing her and telling her to take Ada with her. Its coldness and heartlessness are without precedent in his earlier correspondence:

> When you are disposed to leave London – it would be convenient that a day should be fixed – & (if possible) not a very remote

one for that purpose. – Of my opinion upon that subject – you are sufficiently in possession – & of the circumstances which have led to it – as also – to my plans – or rather – intentions – for the future.[40]

There seemed nothing else to be done, and so Annabella, shocked but unsurprised, assented, while crying piteously that 'although I expected it, I cannot help feeling *this – to think* that I have lived to be hated by my husband'. Knowing that she faced a legal battle, she visited Hanson to prepare the ground for the allegations that she would make against Byron. The solicitor dismissed her concerns about him as little more than anxiety attacks, saying that Byron would soon return to his health. This briefly reassured her – so much so that she wrote to her father in deceptively blithe tones on 8 January, making no mention of her marital difficulties – but Byron was as mercurial as ever. He visited her in a room where Augusta and George Byron were also present, cooing over Ada, and proceeded to act in a terrifyingly violent fashion. Augusta said 'the expression of his countenance was so shocking when he took [Annabella] from the room… that George and I were in terror til he returned and stood listening in expectation that something dreadful was about to take place'.[41] During the course of their brief *tête-à-tête*, Byron sneered at Annabella 'I believe you will go on loving me til I beat you.'[42]

Although he did not hit her, she later said 'I never apprehended *immediate* danger to my life til the 13 January.'[43] As a result of this, Annabella and Ada left 13 Piccadilly Terrace early in the morning of 15 January, bound for Kirkby Mallory in Leicestershire, the Noel family estate. The evening before she left, she had a last meeting with her husband.[44] Byron initially seemed to make an attempt at salvaging matters, saying 'you are very much mistaken if you think I don't love you', and, when Annabella wept at this, remarked with bitterness, 'I wanted to make a philosophical observation on your tears.' As a result of his increasingly insane behaviour, she said 'if ever I should be fool enough to be persuaded to return I shall never leave his house alive'. When he asked, airily 'when shall we three meet again?', Annabella replied, with justifiable scorn, 'in heaven, I trust'.[45]

All the same, it seemed as if a reconciliation might be brokered immediately after she left London. Chatty, friendly letters addressed to 'Dearest Duck' and 'Dearest B' advise him not to 'give yourself up to the abominable trade of versifying – nor to brandy – nor to any thing or any body that is not *lawful & right*'.[46] Arriving at Seaham, she wished for his presence – 'both [Father] and Mam long to have the family party completed' – and signed herself 'ever thy most loving, Pippin'.[47] The happy and loving sentiments within the letters – which were later used in Byron's defence – were a sham. She later recalled that 'I… wrote cheerfully & kindly, without taking any notice of what might revive diseased associations.'[48]

Annabella also wrote to Augusta, who remained with Byron and provided continual updates as to his health. They had summoned a Dr LeMann to examine him, either for physical or mental illness, but he offered bravado, talking 'openly, rationally and good humouredly', taking care to avoid '*ye main point*', and physical frailty; Augusta informed Annabella that she had been asked to stay for a few days. This proved a trying experience, as Byron, while complaining of liver pains, did nothing to check his heavy drinking, in which he was accompanied by Hobhouse. Augusta sourly remarked that 'one comfort is *H* looks really dying – God forgive me, I hope He will take him to a better world'.[49] LeMann concluded that Byron's ills were brought on by heavy drinking, rather than psychological disturbance; in other words, he was bad, rather than mad. When Augusta told Annabella this, her last vestige of hope expired.

While she had hidden Byron's behaviour from her parents before, Annabella now saw no possibility of a reconciliation, and so, bitterly regretting her friendly letters of the previous few days, she told them of his wrongdoing, leaving out only the detail of the incest. This was as much done to shield Augusta as out of any sense of propriety. She knew that a full disclosure would outrage her mother and father, and so it proved; even as she wrote 'for Heaven's sake don't let a whisper of my wrongs get abroad',[50] she was putting together a document at her mother's behest with a young lawyer, Stephen Lushington, in which she recorded every wrong and slight done to her at Byron's hands. This recollection has been the basis of a good deal of the criticism of Byron that has been directed at him both then and since. What is undeniably true from Annabella's perspective is that, after the disappointments and privations of her year-long marriage, the opportunity to revenge herself on her unloving husband was as tempting as the necessity of safeguarding custody of Ada.

Initial suggestions of divorce came from Annabella's father, in a letter to Byron of 29 January that suggested that 'it cannot tend to your happiness to continue to live with Lady Byron', and suggested that he obtain the guidance of a 'professional friend' in order to 'discuss and settle such terms of separation as may be mutually approved'. As Augusta decided which side to support – she wrote to Annabella, with some tact, to say 'for once in my life I have ventured to act according to my own judgement'[51] – she was torn between her friendship with 'my own dearest Sis', guilt at her own responsibility, however inadvert, for ending the marriage, and a fierce residual loyalty to her beloved brother.

Finally, she acted, believing that she could serve as go-between and peacemaker in this fraught situation. She asked Annabella to halt divorce proceedings, on the grounds that they were dictated by revenge rather than a desire for her own and Ada's wellbeing, and that Lady Melbourne, once fully informed of the situation, would act on their behalf. Augusta's intentions were undoubtedly good, but even as she suggested 'I'm a coward with *bad* people',[52] it was inevitable that there was no possibility of a reconciliation between Annabella and Byron. Had it been simply Annabella's concern, she might have prevailed, but the involvement of her parents meant that battle lines were drawn.

When Byron replied to his father-in-law's letter, it was with a mixture of feigned surprise ('I am at a loss how to answer') at proceedings and a denial of some of the charges against him. Allowing that he had had to contend with 'distress without, & disease within' over the previous year, he still claimed to be guiltless of any ill treatment towards Annabella, who he described as nearer to perfection in 'conduct, character, temper, talents [and] disposition' than anyone he had ever encountered. A touch of innate Byron arrogance manifested itself when he questioned Sir Ralph's right to act on his daughter's behalf, going so far as to say 'til I have her express sanction of your proceedings, I shall take leave to doubt the propriety of your interference'.[53] If he had any doubt of Annabella's wishes, they were soon confirmed by a terse letter that she sent to Augusta, saying 'you are desired by your brother to ask if my father has acted with my concurrence in proposing a separation. He has.'[54]

Byron appealed to Annabella directly, and stated that '[I] loved you – & will not part from you with your *own* most express & *expressed* refusal to return to or receive me'.[55] He was in a bad and depressed state. Hobhouse noted that he was 'very low indeed', and, despite knowing that Annabella despised him, wrote to her on his friend's behalf, warning that 'this dreadful thing must not be done', and putting the whole saga down to 'misunderstanding'.[56] While it is possible that Annabella regretted what she had set in motion – her maid Mrs Fletcher reported that she was in a 'paroxysm of grief' when she received Byron's letter[57] – the involvement of her parents meant that there was now no possibility of retreat.

❧

Divorce in 1816 was a virtual impossibility for a woman to obtain, and would remain so until 1857, when the Matrimonial Causes Act was introduced. Before then, it was an expensive, embarrassing and protracted process that took place in the Ecclesiastical Court, and was only granted after an Act of Parliament, and this only if the husband desired it. Therefore, whatever Annabella and her family had in mind, obtaining a formal dissolution of the marriage would be extremely difficult. Instead, a more viable option was to obtain a legal deed of separation that saw the two parties remain married but free to live apart and pursue their own lives. This tended to be the preferred option of many aristocratic families as they could continue with their adulterous affairs to their heart's content, untroubled by the cost and embarrassment of a scandalous divorce.*

As Byron realized that he was unable to broker a reconciliation of any sort with Annabella, his mood changed, and some of his old defiance returned. After he refused to accede to a quiet 'private separation', he turned to the long-suffering Hanson to act on his behalf; a mistake, as his lawyer, by now in his late fifties, was second-rate and slow in comparison with the far more able Lushington. Lack of funds also did not help him find a superior advocate. The proceedings were slated to begin on 21 February, and Lushington had acquired a treasure trove of material attesting to Byron's many failings, including his affair with Caroline and rumours of sodomy and even an inclination towards paedophilia;† the only thing not used for the time being was the incest allegation.

As the case was not heard in court, neither Annabella nor Byron testified on their own behalf, but instead provided written evidence of the state of their marriage, which, in the case of Annabella, amounted to a damning list of allegations. Byron, meanwhile, found that even his closest friends such as Hobhouse were appalled by the weight of evidence against him, not least because he had lied about accusations of infidelity and spousal cruelty before. When

* The grounds on which divorce was granted did not include straightforward adultery; cruelty, incest or rape needed to be cited. Byron could have been accused of all three.
† In the case of Lady Oxford's thirteen-year-old-daughter: see p. 143.

confronted by Hobhouse, Byron's response was that of a child discovered in a falsehood, namely to become 'dreadfully agitated – [to say] he was ruined & would blow his brains out'.[58] His friend, still loyal, took care to attempt to disprove or at least conceal the revelations, knowing that scandal sheets such as *The Morning Post* were already printing rumours about his enjoying the company of Drury Lane actresses while his wife was mysteriously absent.

After he failed in a final attempt to convince Annabella to halt proceedings (in which he both unconvincingly repeated his love for her and claimed that he was 'exposed to the most black & blighting calumnies of every kind'),[59] Byron faced his destiny, even as he knew that, as Augusta put it to his friend Francis Hodgson, 'not only will his reputation be sacrificed to this exposure, but his *life*'.[60] Knowing that sodomy was a capital crime, and one that entailed 'utter destruction & ruin to a man from which he never can recover', Augusta begged Annabella to return to her husband, claiming '*your return* might be the *saving & reclamation* of him'.[61] Yet Annabella was as set on a separation as Byron was resolved against it. Lushington was summoned to Mivart's Hotel* on 21 February and presented with the crowning piece of evidence, Byron's incestuous relationship with Augusta. Initially, Lushington was appalled and believed the accusation unprovable, but soon decided to hold it in reserve in case Byron should attempt to gain custody of Ada. An offer was made of £500 a year to Byron from the Milbanke family if he would agree to the separation. Never one to be influenced by financial concerns when those of pride were at stake, he angrily refused, claiming, in a furious letter to Annabella, that 'it appeared to me to be a kind of appeal to the supposed mercenary feelings of the person to whom it was made'.[62]

In the midst of the fracas, Augusta and Annabella continued to correspond, and even saw one another on 5 March at Mivart's, a meeting Augusta described as being shockingly grim, given that

---

* The precursor to Claridge's.

Annabella was 'positively reduced to a skeleton – pale as *ashes* – a deep hollow tone of voice & a calm in her manner quite supernatural'.[63] With Byron believing that Annabella's former governess Mrs Clermont, among others, was influencing her, Augusta saw her brother attacked on all sides, and whatever defence he could muster – at one point he considered suing for Annabella's restitution – was overwhelmed by the mounting evidence against him, which now included his wife's testimony that Byron had sodomized her during their marriage. Accurate or not, this scandalous detail led to the collapse of his defence. Defeated, he was compelled to agree to a separation, drawn up by the Solicitor General, that favoured Annabella in all financial matters and, on 17 March, the brief, unhappy marriage came to an end.

Byron, beaten and downcast, began to make plans to leave England. While there was no legal requirement for him to quit the country, he knew that many loathed him and would scheme against him.[64] It was a sensational downfall. One effect of the shaming that he endured was that he began writing poetry again, after having given it up for months. One poem that he sent to Annabella immediately after their separation, 'Fare Thee Well', depicted the end of their marriage in idealized terms. By turns moving and ridiculous, it nevertheless represented Byron mining his life for material. While some of it, especially the first verse's statement that 'Even though unforgiving, never/Gainst thee shall my heart rebel', bears little relation to the difficult, miserable turmoil of their marriage, other parts show Byron engaging in bitter introspection:

> Though the world for this commend thee –
> Though it smile upon the blow,
> Even its praises must offend thee,
> Founded on another's woe:
>
> Though my many faults defaced me,
> Could no other arm be found,

Than the one that once embraced me,
To inflict a cureless wound?

If his aim was to provoke a reconciliation with Annabella and to soften public opinion, it was unsuccessful. A truer statement of his feelings was found in his occasional lines, 'Endorsement To The Deed Of Separation':

A year ago, you swore, fond she!
'To love, to honour' and so forth,
Such was the vow you pledged to me
And here's exactly what it's worth.

Byron did little to enhance his reputation with a vitriolic poem savaging Mrs Clermont, 'A Sketch From Private Life', In it, she was compared to a snake that 'steals within your walls', and possessing 'a vile mask the Gorgon would disown'. Unsurprisingly, Annabella described it as 'blackguard beyond belief'.[65] He spent his last few weeks in England mainly at home, where he amused himself by drinking, picking irritable fights with his remaining friends and indulging in casual dalliances. He later commented that he was compared with such historical malefactors and maniacs as Henry VIII, Heliogabalus, Caligula, Epicurus, Apicius and Nero in the journals of the day; none was a flattering comparison.

When he did appear in public, he was cut by most of his former friends, although some women found him even more attractive due to the devilish air that he had about him. One flirtation, with the seventeen-year-old admirer Claire Clairmont, would eventually develop into something more, but for now he was content to escape from the miseries of his situation in carnal stupor. He was shocked out of his lethargy by a farewell meeting with Augusta on Easter Sunday, 14 April, at Piccadilly Terrace; she was heavily pregnant by Leigh and en route to Six Mile Bottom, while he awaited the separation papers before he left England forever. Both were overcome by grief, knowing that they would be parted; the considerable damage that had been done to their reputations by the ill-considered marriage made matters worse. She gave him a Bible as a parting gift; he was reduced to helpless weeping as he contemplated what he had lost. Writing to Annabella immediately afterwards, he spared nothing in reminding his estranged wife of how inferior she ever was in his affections:

> I have just parted from Augusta – almost the last being you had left me to part with – & the only unshattered tie of my existence – wherever I may go - & I am going far – you & I can never meet again in this world – nor in the next – let this content or atone.[66]

Despite everything, Annabella was heartbroken by Byron's departure, becoming listless and depressed. She wrote a poem, 'By thee Forsaken', which attempted to come to terms with her husband's actions, which vainly believed that his 'self-adoring pride shall bow', and that 'a wan and drooping peace/With pardon for unmeasured ill' would emerge. If this was a genuine belief, she was to be disappointed.

With little else remaining, Byron signed the deed of separation on 21 April, remarking as he did, 'I deliver this as Mrs Clermont's act and deed.' He left his letters with Hanson, and on 23 April he departed for Dover along with Scrope Davies. Immediately after his departure, the bailiffs took everything remaining in Piccadilly Terrace, down to his books and pet parrots.* When Byron sailed to the continent on 25 April, through a rough storm, Hobhouse, accompanied by Byron's other friend, the writer and physician John William Polidori, ran to the end of the pier. He waved until he could see Byron no longer, as the poet took off his cap and gesticulated back towards England. He would never return to it while he lived, nor see his wife or Ada again.

* His library sold for £723 12s 6d.

As for Augusta, she remained his great love, and he felt grief-stricken guilt at what he had caused her by his behaviour. He wrote several poems inspired by her, one of which, the first 'Stanzas To Augusta', he completed before he departed, but gave Murray instructions that they should not be circulated until he left. As a declaration of undying affection, mixed with commentary on the troubles he endured, it remains poignant:

> When fortune changed – and love fled far,
> And hatred's shafts flew thick and fast,
> Thou wert the solitary star
> Which rose, and set not to the last.
>
> Oh, blest be thine unbroken light!
> That watched me as a seraph's eye,
> And stood between me and the night,
> For ever shining sweetly nigh.

Byron and Augusta never met again. Yet she remained a crucial figure, the source of continued confidences and advice. Even as others captured his attention, it was the loveable, good-natured 'Goose' who remained Byron's great love. It is of her, rather than his cousin Anne Wilmot, that some of Byron's most famous lines seem most appropriate:

> She walks in beauty, like the night
> Of cloudless climes and starry skies;
> And all that's best of dark and bright
> Meet in her aspect and her eyes;
> Thus mellowed to that tender light
> Which heaven to gaudy day denies.
>
> One shade the more, one ray the less,
> Had half impaired the nameless grace

Which waves in every raven tress,
Or softly lightens o'er her face;
Where thoughts serenely sweet express,
How pure, how dear their dwelling-place.

And on that cheek, and o'er that brow,
So soft, so calm, yet eloquent,
The smiles that win, the tints that glow,
But tell of days in goodness spent,
A mind at peace with all below,
A heart whose love is innocent!

PART IV

Claire
&
Mary

10

An utter stranger takes the liberty
of addressing you.

CLAIRE CLAIRMONT TO BYRON,
MARCH 1816

Byron and Shelley met for the first time by the side of Lake Geneva in May 1816. For such a momentous occasion, the circumstances were comparatively mundane. Byron was returning from an unsuccessful attempt to rent a villa, accompanied by his travelling companion Polidori. Shelley was with his mistress Mary Godwin, and the two had arrived in Switzerland earlier that month. Polidori later recorded in his diary that '[Shelley] came; bashful, shy, consumptive; twenty-six; separated from his wife'. The meeting was brief and awkward, with Byron uneasy and embarrassed by the encounter, but he managed to invite him to dinner that evening, before nodding a dismissive farewell to his female companions. There was another reason for his diffidence. Accompanying Shelley and Mary was her stepsister, Claire Clairmont, Byron's latest conquest, and a persistent one at that.

❧

Born illegitimate, Claire claimed that her date of birth was 27 April 1798, but no firm evidence exists of this, nor of her birthplace. She alluded to Swiss heritage, although this stemmed more from romantic optimism than any factual basis.* She was christened

---

* It has recently been suggested that her father was Sir John Lethbridge, MP for Minehead and former Sheriff of Somerset, and that she was born in Brislington, near Bristol.

Jane, and lived with her widowed mother Mary and brother
Charles in Somers Town in London from an early age. They were
neighbours to the philosopher and novelist William Godwin;
Mary reputedly celebrated her first sighting of the famous writer
by shouting loudly from a balcony 'is it possible that I behold
the immortal Godwin?' His own response was a circumspect diary
entry of 5 May 1801: 'met Mrs Clairmont'.[1]

Nonetheless, the combination of his fame and her forthrightness
proved an irresistable one, and they married at the end of the year
in St Leonard's church in nearby Shoreditch. Although Godwin's
friends were dubious about the match – the mild-mannered author
Charles 'the Professor' Lamb, described her as 'a very disgusting
woman' and 'that damned infernal bitch'[2] – he wished for a swift
remarriage after the death of his first wife, the feminist writer Mary
Wollstonecraft. His book about her, *Memoirs of the Author of a
Vindication of the Rights of Woman*, had caused scandal by frankly
discussing her love affairs and suicide attempts, and had led to both
of them being demonized by wider society.* He was also keen to
provide a stepmother for his four year-old daughter Mary Godwin
and stepdaughter Fanny Imlay. With the makeshift family consisting of four children by at least three different fathers,† it was an
unconventional home life, even before the addition of a further
child, William, who was born in 1803. The nearly fifty-year-old
Godwin wrote ruefully in a diary entry that 'the maintenance of a
family and an establishment has been a heavy expense, and I have
never been able, with all my industry… entirely to accomplish this
object'.[3]

The family survived by editing and, in Godwin's case, pseud-
onymously writing books aimed at children, such as an 1805 title
Fables, Ancient and Modern, which took inspiration from Aesop

---

* A typical example was the *Anti-Jacobin Review and Magazine*, which
sneered about 'such visionary theories and pernicious doctrines' and
referred to Wollstonecraft as a 'concubine'.
† Charles and Jane may have had the same father, although it is unlikely.

and La Fontaine, among others. It was in an atmosphere of free thought rather than religious instruction that Jane was raised; despite the lack of money, she later described it as a place where:

> We took all the liveliest interest in the great questions of the day – common topics, gossiping, scandal, found no interest in our circle, for we had been brought up by Mr Godwin to think it was the greatest misfortune to be fond of the world, or worldly pleasures or of luxury or money; and there was no greater happiness than to think well of those around us, and to delight in being useful or pleasing to them.[4]

Happiness was not a condition shared by many in the family. In addition to William's financial troubles, both his daughter Mary and Fanny suffered from what he called 'a quiet modest unshowy disposition' that would today be better described as depression. Nonetheless, the girls grew up into attractive prospects; they were described by Godwin's friend Aaron Burr, then vice-president of the United States of America, as 'les goddesses'.[5] Another visitor to the house, Christie Baxter, described Jane as 'lively and quick-witted, and probably rather unmanageable'.[6] She studied at a nearby finishing school, Miss Cunliffe's establishment in Walham Green, where she studied French and music and the arts of how to be a respectable young lady. However, her true education came later.

❧

Jane first encountered the poet Percy Bysshe Shelley in October 1812, when he visited Godwin for the first time. When his visiting card had arrived, the daughters of the house, thrilled by the sight of the beautiful, intellectually daring young man, 'were on tip toe to know',[7] and the fourteen-year-old Jane developed a great affection for him. As Shelley was a married man (his wife Harriet Westbrook was only a couple of years older than Jane), no greater intimacy could or did exist between the two, and the first eighteen months of their friendship proceeded in amicable exchanges when he visited her father. A more fateful meeting would occur in March 1814 when Mary, who had been away at school in Scotland, first met Shelley. By now sixteen, she was beautiful, and possessed her mother's fire and brilliance, an entirely different prospect to the amicable but unsophisticated Harriet. Jane unwittingly played pander to the two of them, later saying 'we both used to walk with him in the Wilderness of the Charterhouse, also to Mary Wollstonecraft's tomb – they always sent me to walk some distance from them – alleging that they wished to talk on philosophical subjects'. Although she claimed 'I did not know what they talked about',[8] it soon became clear as, standing by her mother's grave on 26 June, Mary informed a thrilled Shelley that she was in love with him, something he later described by saying that 'the sublime and rapturous moment when she confessed herself mine cannot be painted to mortal imaginations'.[9]

Godwin's own mortal imagination was, perhaps unsurprisingly, not fired by his protégé declaring his feelings towards his daughter. Mary had been brought up in an atmosphere where freedom and open-mindedness were prized over repression and convention, so it was inevitable that his belated attempts to instil propriety were doomed to failure. They were not helped by Shelley wildly proposing a suicide pact, to which Jane 'filled the room with her shrieks'.[10] With no other obvious solution in sight, Mary and Shelley decided to elope and fled across the Channel together on 29 July. They took Jane with them, and, despite her mother pursuing them to Calais, they formed a *ménage à trois* of sorts and continued their journey into France. There was, on Jane's part, no romantic involvement with Shelley; when she was asked whether she was someone who had taken amorous flight, she replied 'oh! Dear no – I came to speak French'.[11] Her grasp of the language far exceeded either Mary's or Shelley's, and so her presence was invaluable. Yet it was her own emancipation as much as Mary's. For the first time, she began to see the wider world that she had only previously read about or discussed. Girlishly, she pronounced each new wonder that they beheld 'beautiful enough – let us live here'.

They proceeded to Switzerland in August, and the mountainous vistas and glorious lakes led Jane to believe that this was 'the land of my ancestors'. She was also enjoying the company she kept, saying of Shelley that it was 'as if he had just landed from heaven', although there were occasional squabbles caused by lack of money and possibly Jane's jealousy of the sexual relationship between the other two. By the end of August, Mary had become pregnant, and it was clear that the idyll could not last any longer. Returning to England in mid-September, after a brief trip to Holland, Shelley, Mary and Jane had to face the consequences of their behaviour.

Shelley, upon seeing his wife again, made it cruelly clear that he was finished with her; he had met a greater love, and described their own match as being little more than friendship. Godwin refused to welcome or acknowledge him, and the trio of Shelley, Jane and Mary were in lodgings in Blackfriars by November. Relations between Jane and Shelley had become uneasy, with the suppressed tensions of the summer emerging more fully as poverty and enforced intimacy made matters more difficult. Away from the thrills of travel and transgression, they experienced what Jane described as 'the bitterness of disappointment', and even as she wrote 'how hateful it is to quarrel – to say a thousand unkind things – meaning none',[12] she began to wonder at the life they led. One moment, she mildly contemplated the 'very philosophical way of spending the day' they enjoyed, and mused that 'to sleep & talk – why this is merely vegetating',[13] and the next they would row, leading Shelley to bemoan what he described as 'Jane's insensibility & incapacity for the slightest degree of friendship'.[14] After an especially difficult week, she returned to her mother and stepfather on 13 November, but, frustrated by their disapproval of Mary and Shelley, swiftly returned to the exiled duo. She took the name 'Claire' at this time, as an allusion to a book that she had enjoyed, Rousseau's *Julie, ou la nouvelle Héloïse*, in particular the character of the protagonist's sister and confidante.

As Mary's pregnancy continued, Shelley and Claire spent more time together, with Mary as an occasionally frustrated onlooker. Although there is no evidence that their relationship ever became sexual, Shelley enjoyed adopting the persona of the wise mentor and counsellor, and did so with rather greater dash than Godwin ever managed. Claire, meanwhile, was being exposed to revelatory new ideas when it came to the role of women and their independence. Although she had never known Mary Wollstonecraft, Shelley and her family had all been influenced by her beliefs and writings, and now they found an equally impressionable home in Claire who, while intelligent and inquisitive, lacked their sophistication.

Mary gave birth prematurely on 22 February 1815; unfortunately the baby died shortly afterwards. As she sank into what would now be recognized as post-natal depression, described by Shelley as 'wretched in health and spirits', her lover and stepsister continued to spend time together, much to Mary's resentment. A typical journal entry of hers stated that she is 'very unwell... Shelley and Clara walk out, as usual, to heaps of places'. Mary began to refer to Claire as 'the lady' or Shelley's 'friend', and eventually demanded that she leave their home. On 13 May she left for Lynmouth in Devon – it being inconceivable that she could return to her mother and Godwin – and Mary treated her departure as a blessing, writing 'the business is finished... I begin a new journal with our regeneration'.[15] Shelley had greater regret at Claire's departure, and acted as her patron, ensuring that she had the funds to begin the strange, isolated existence that she now embraced. Even as she tried to make the best of it, writing to her stepsister Fanny that 'I live in a little cottage with jasmine and honeysuckle twining over the window',[16] it was a miserably lonely life for a seventeen-year-old; she later referred to how 'day after day I sat companionless upon that unfrequented sea-shore, mentally exclaiming, a life of sixteen years is already too much for me to bear'.[17]

In early 1816, her rustication came to an end. Mary had become pregnant again shortly after her miscarriage, and she gave birth to a son, William, on 26 January. Claire's relationship with her mother and Godwin seemed to have recovered, as she returned to stay at their home in Skinner Street. However, after her exploits of the previous couple of years, a resumption of domesticity seemed impossible. Mary, she reasoned, had acquired herself a brilliant, dashing and handsome poet, so why should she not set her cap at a figure even more acclaimed and famous, albeit tainted with obloquy. There was one man who seemed to deserve her, and he had fair claim to be the most talked-about figure in contemporary society at the time, mainly for ill.

❧

Byron was morose and unhappy in late March 1816, as he prepared to leave for his European exile. When he received a letter from 'E Trefusis, 21 Foley Place, Marylebone', it gave him a momentary diversion, especially as the opening lines had an endearing boldness and directness:

> An utter stranger takes the liberty of addressing you. It is earnestly requested that for one moment you pardon the intrusion, & laying aside every remembrance of who & what you are, listen with a friendly ear. A moment of passion, or an impulse of pride often destroys our own happiness & that of others. If in this case your refusal shall not affect yourself, yet you are not aware how much it may injure another. It is not charity I demand, for of that I stand in no need: I imply by that you should think kindly & gently of this letter, that if I seem impertinent you should pardon it for a while, & that you should wait patiently til I am emboldened by you to disclose myself.[18]

There were parallels between Claire's approach and that of Caroline's first anonymous letter to him four years before, but, while her predecessor had taken care to praise the author of *Childe Harolde*, Claire made a more direct entreaty to Byron, declaring 'it may seem a strange assertion, but it is not the less true that I place my happiness in your hands'. Stressing how she wrote with 'so much fearful inquietude', she unconsciously alluded to what would become *Frankenstein* in her remark 'the creator ought not to destroy his creature'. She gave little away about herself, hinting at her virginity in her self-description of one 'whose reputation has yet remained unstained… without either guardian or husband to control', and offered 'fond affection & unbounded devotion'. Unintentionally, in the directness of her appeals to Byron's vanity, she distinguished herself from those sycophants who he dismissed as 'Miss Emma Somebody with a play entitled "The Bandit Of Bohemia"'.[19]

A more experienced woman might have waited before persisting, but Claire combined the forthrightness of the inexperienced with the passion of the ingénue. She besieged Byron again almost immediately afterwards, from the pseudonym 'GCB', saying 'Lord Byron is requested to state whether seven o'clock this evening will be convenient to him to receive a lady to communicate with him on business of peculiar importance. She desires to be admitted alone & with the utmost privacy.' Byron wrote back with a mixture of disinterest and amusement to say 'Ld B is not aware of any "importance" which can be attached by any person to an interview with him – & more particularly by one with whom it does not appear that he has the honour of being acquainted. He will however be at home at the hour mentioned.'[20]

Claire visited him at the Drury Lane Theatre on that Sunday. The meeting was a mutually pleasurable one, although Byron was more interested by her connections with the politically radical Godwin and Shelley, who had recently sent him his poem *Queen Mab*. He did not see any future in a friendship, especially as his departure from England seemed so close at hand, and therefore asked for her not to be received at his house when she called.

Claire, however, was not to be denied, especially now that her first advances had been successful. Initially, she sent him samples of her writing, namely a prose piece called 'The Ideot'. After this, she briskly suggested a sexual dalliance with an unblushing candour that finally managed to achieve her desires:

> Have you then any objection to the following plan? On Thursday evening we may go out of town together by some stage or mail, about the distance of 10 or 12 miles. There, we shall be free & unknown; we can return early the following morning. I have arranged everything here so that the slightest suspicion may not be excited. Pray do so with your people.[21]

Leaving aside the ignorance of his seducer ('your people' was a grandiose reference to the rag-tag band of servants and bailiffs who lingered at his home), Byron was amused by her boldness. The letter was delivered by hand from Hamilton Place while she waited; he replied, with polished assurance, '*Certainly* – but don't go away – in the meantime look at the Morning Post & the measured motion which will amuse you'. She delightedly scribbled on his letter 'God bless you – I *never* was so happy!'

The date that Claire lost her virginity to Byron was 20 April 1816. In a letter written to him two days before, her excitement and nervousness combined in a manner both amusing and touching, as she wrote of how 'you certainly cannot wish to betray either yourself or me to the servants'. For his own part, Byron might have replied that his staff had seen it all before in the previous few years, and that, after the scandals of his divorce, little could shock the wider public. A dalliance with a girl on the cusp of adulthood – adulterous though it technically was – barely compared to incest, sodomy or many of the other abominations of which he had been accused over the previous year. Claire, who called herself 'the most miserable & nervous of beings', looked forward to how 'a few moments may tell you more than you yet know',[22] even as he should believe her 'vicious and depraved'. He had referred to her, jokingly, as 'a little fiend', and her pursuit of him had been devilish in its persistence and ingenuity.

She later said of their first assignation that it was 'perfect'. At the time, she wrote 'I shall never forget you. I shall ever remember the gentleness of your manners and the wild originality of your countenance.'[23] Byron regarded it rather differently. The following year, albeit after many more dealings with Claire, he described the opening days of their affair to his friend Douglas Kinnaird. He called her an 'odd-headed girl – who introduced herself to me shortly before I left England… I never pretended to love her – but a man is a man – & if a girl of eighteen comes prancing to you at all hours – there is but one way.'[24]

Both knew that that brief dalliance could not last. What Claire intended to be her last letter before his departure on 23 April was dated two days before, and talks of how 'you will never find one who loved you with more serious or treated you with more gentle affection than I have & still do', ending 'my dear kind friend, I love you most truly'.[25] She also referred to a meeting between her, Byron, and her stepsister, saying 'Mary is delighted with you as I knew she would be; she entreats me in private to obtain your address abroad that we may if possible have again the pleasure of seeing you. She perpetually exclaims "How mild he is! How gentle! So different from what I expected."' Perhaps this had been Byron's intention all along; the daughter of William Godwin was, after all, a more interesting intellectual prospect than her younger stepsister.*

For Byron, Claire was a distraction from his present entanglements with Augusta and Annabella, and she would have been forgotten just as every actress, maid or simpering lady of fashion before her had been. Even as she begged him to 'write me but a

---

* Mary was also the more beautiful of the two, if contemporary portraits are to be believed.

few lines' before he left, and 'this people echoed city shall become to me the most desolate & hateful of places',[26] his hour of departure was at hand. However, his erstwhile plaything had made a decision. She would return to her adopted country of origin, Switzerland, and find Byron there once more. Even as she wrote 'I assure you nothing shall tempt me to come to Geneva by myself since you disapprove of it as I cannot but feel that such conduct would be highly indelicate', she decided that 'the moment I find protection such as I am sure would not displease you, I shall venture to go'.[27] She was in love, and fatefully so. Unbeknown to her, she had also become pregnant after her brief liaison.

❧

Once again, Claire joined Mary and Shelley as their travelling companion. The trio, along with the infant William, departed for Switzerland on 3 May 1816. The Shelleys saw their journey as mirroring that of Byron's; although the scandal of their relationship had been far quieter, they had still antagonized her parents and Shelley's family. When he commented in a letter that they intended to remain abroad in Europe 'perhaps forever', it was both a rejection of English values and a renewal of the optimism that they had felt on their previous jaunt in 1814. It remains uncertain as to how much they knew of Claire's entanglement with Byron; Mary knew of the attachment from the previous introduction, and perhaps recognized something of her own attachment to Shelley in her stepsister's admiration to the famous poet. However, even the most open-minded of liberals would have been disconcerted by the one-sided nature of the relationship.

Claire wrote to Byron on 6 May to ask 'now will you believe? And where have you been?' A better question might have been 'do you care?' She was wilfully blind to the evidence, even as she mused 'every day I ask myself this question & wonder whether amidst all the novelties you behold you ever once think of me. But no I do not expect it; I have no doubt that you think my affection

all a pretence?' She knew something of Byron's homosexual inclinations, and was sufficiently *au fait* with them to hint at how 'I had
ten times rather be your male friend than your mistress'.[28]

　She knew too little of the man to whom she was offering herself. When she moaned about her unhappiness, praised Mary as
one 'who talks & looks at you with admiration… you will I dare
say fall in love with her; she is very handsome & very amiable',
and declared 'you so hate letters & I have nothing to tell you', her
incomprehension of the wider situation was nearly total. This was
partially due to her youth, but also because of a belief that Byron
would be receptive to her silly touches of romantic subterfuge, such
as her desire that he should 'write a little note for me directed as
Madame Clairville… I have taken the name of Clairville because
you said you liked the name of Clare but could not bear 'mont'
because of that very ugly woman'.*[29] She ended by stressing the
purity of her young love ('people of eighteen always love truly &
tenderly') and boasted how 'I have been reading *all* your poems.'[30]

　Byron was only mildly interested in seeing Claire again, if at
all. There had been other distractions since her; Polidori reported
that he had regained his usual priapic swagger and 'fell like a thun-
derbolt upon the chambermaid' at an inn in Ostend.[31] However,
it was inevitable that they should meet among the small ex-pat
community of Switzerland, and so their paths crossed once again
on 25 May. Byron and Polidori arrived at the suburb of Sécheron
in Geneva, at the Hôtel d'Angleterre, and Byron, wearied by his
journey, signed his age in the register as a hundred. Claire was
also resident at the hotel and saw this strained attempt at wit. To
attract his interest, she swiftly sent him a note saying 'I am sorry
you are grown so old, indeed I suspected you were 200, from the
slowness of your journey. I suppose your venerable age could not
bear quicker travelling.' Although she ended her note by saying

* The 'very ugly woman' she refers to is Annabella's loathed governess Mrs
Clermont, indicating that Byron had discussed at least some of his past
history with her.

'I am so happy',[32] no response was forthcoming, and Byron and Polidori left the next day to search for more suitable accommodation. Piqued, Claire wrote again, complaining 'how can you be so very unkind' and suggesting a specific assignation ('will you go straight up to the top of the house this evening at ½ past seven & I will infallibly be on the landing place & show you the room… I will be sure to be waiting for you & nobody will observe you walking upstairs'),[33] but he did not appear.

A less determined woman (or girl) might have given up what was becoming an embarrassing pursuit, but Claire had a trump card, namely her acquaintance with Shelley. The next day, whether by chance or design, Byron and Polidori had their first meeting with the English trio. Although it was not a particular success, the presence of the three offered Byron distraction. In the case of Shelley, he had a young man who appeared to regard him as something of an idol, despite the relatively trifling four-and-a-half-year age gap between them. In the case of Mary, their previous acquaintance had been an enjoyable and intriguing one. And Claire was entirely available for the purposes of what he had earlier described as 'connection'. He later described his mixed feelings about her to Augusta:

> As to all these mistresses – Lord help me – I have had but one. – Now – don't scold – but what could I do? – a foolish girl – in spite of all I could say or do – would come after me – or rather went before me – for I found her here – and I have had all the plague possible to persuade her to go back again… I am not in love – nor have any love left for any – but I could not exactly play the Stoic with a woman – who had scrambled eight hundred miles to unphilosophize me – besides I had been regaled of late with so many two courses and a *desert* (Alas!) of aversion – that I was fain to take a little love (if pressed particularly) by way of novelty.[34]

After their first inauspicious meeting, Byron and Shelley's friendship strengthened quickly, with Claire and Mary included in the
bond by association. The two poets breakfasted together each day,
and then spent hours searching for suitable houses in which they
could live around Geneva. After their voyages, they dined and
drank in the evenings, long, Bacchanalian affairs in which Byron
talked, with self-awareness, about his previous exploits in London,
and discussed writers and poetry with the others. Sometimes,
he behaved in an unexpected fashion. Mary recounted how, one
night, they took a moonlit ride upon the water, and Byron cried
'"I will sing you an Albanian song, now, be sentimental and give
me all your attention." It was a strange, wild howl that he gave
forth; but such as, he declared, was an exact imitation of the savage
Albanian mode.' He ended by laughing, although whether this
was, as Mary suggested, 'at our disappointment, (when we) had
expected a wild Eastern melody', or simply at a successful hoax, is
impossible to know.[35]

Byron soon found himself a suitable house, the Villa Belle Rive,
into which he and Polidori moved on 10 June, rechristening it the
'Villa Diodati' after the name of the family that owned it. It was
here in this secluded villa* that Byron and the Shelleys continued their soirées, relishing the freedom that their Swiss sojourn
had given them to discuss new and outlandish ideas of liberty
and emancipation, as well as talk of poetry. These were led by the
men – enlightened ideas had only travelled so far – but Mary, at
least, was far from silent. It is possible that Byron and Mary might
have indulged in a sexual dalliance around this time. Shelley had
encouraged one between her and his friend James Hogg the previous year, although it may well have remained unconsummated,
and the spirit of openness and experimentation possessed the
young writers. What differentiated Mary from the other women

---

* One that he described in a letter to Hobhouse on 23 June as 'very
pretty… with the Alps behind'.

Byron knew was her intellectual self-assurance and excellent judgement of character, meaning that he respected her as an equal, an
indulgence that only Augusta so far had been granted.[36]

However, what is certain is that relations between Byron and
Claire continued. The Shelley ménage established themselves in a
cottage called the Maison Chappuis in nearby Montalègre; the villa
could easily be reached through a vineyard, allowing for regular
evening assignations. Here, Byron enjoyed being 'unphilosophized'
by the increasingly experienced Claire, although her naivete in
other areas caused him frustration and anger. In particular, Mary
later reported his 'half playful rage' caused by 'a heedless girl', who
remarked that she thought he had a little of the Scotch accent.
'Good God, I hope not!' he exclaimed. 'I'm sure I haven't. I would
rather the whole damned country was sunk in the sea – I, the
Scotch accent!'[37] Any reminder of his humble roots was a continual
embarrassment for Byron, just as any suggestion of his lameness
could only be made by those closest to him – and then rarely.

Nonetheless, relations continued, only occasionally frustrated
by the presence of the tactless Polidori.* One note sent by Claire
in June has a subtly different tone from the imploring missives of
before, indicating that she was getting her own way at least some
of the time. Asking 'if you can send M Polidori either to write
another dictionary or to the lady he loves',† she bemoaned that
'I cannot come at this hour of the night & be seen by him; it is
so extremely suspicious.' The allusion to Polidori's lover – a secret
confided in Byron and then revealed to Shelley and his friends –
indicates a shared bond, as does her note that 'I know you must be
home by ten because Geneva shuts at that hour & I will be with
you at a ¼ past ten, so remember'.[38]

It was impossible that her pregnancy could remain a secret for
much longer, and so in late June, after finding out herself the

* Byron mockingly referred to him as 'Dr Pollydolly' at times.
† A mistaken allusion to Polidori's having written a dictionary; in fact it
was compiled by his father Gaetano.

previous month, she informed Shelley. His reaction to the news, and presumably his discovery of her affair with Byron, is unknown, but it is telling that he changed his will on 24 June, which provided 'to Mary Jane Clairmont (the sister-in-law of Miss Godwin) £12,000, one half to be laid out in an annuity for her own life, & that of any person she may if she pleases to name any other, the other half to be at her own disposal'. In other words, he generously undertook to support both her and her child, an action that some have taken to be confirmation that he did undertake an earlier affair with her and believed himself to be the father. However, given that it seems clear that Claire lost her virginity to Byron,* it is more likely he instead acted out of simple altruism. Certainly, he had great affection for her; in his poem *Epipsychidion*, he described her as his 'comet beautiful and fierce,/Who drew the heart of this frail Universe/Towards thine own.'

Byron, when Shelley informed him of Claire's pregnancy, was less sanguine. He wrote to Kinnaird that his immediate reaction was to ask 'is the brat mine?', before admitting 'I have reason to think so, for I know as much as one can know such a thing – that she had not lived with Shelley during the time of our acquaintance – and that she had a good deal of that same with me.'[39]

As a result, the affair between the two spluttered to an end. Byron had made use of Claire as a copyist for his poetry as well, including the finished text of *Childe Harold*, and a letter offered her services in most regards – 'if you *want* me, or anything of, or belonging to me I am sure Shelley would come and fetch me if you ask him… can you pretext the copying… everything is so awkward. We go so soon… pray come & see us.'[40] Mary and Shelley were planning a trip to the mountains, and Claire had agreed to join them; this had also been suggested as a result of Byron asking that she be removed. The three departed on 21 July, but Byron did not say

---

* Hence Claire's comment about 'one whose reputation has remained unstained'; see p. 202.

farewell. Distracted by reports of the imminent publication of Caroline Lamb's *Glenarvon* and paranoid about being observed by visiting Englishmen, he was in despair. Their last meeting before Claire left did not go well; a letter she sent complained 'was it not a little cruel to behave so harshly all the day' and asked 'shall I never see you again? Not once again.'[41] If she was aiming to elicit any sympathy from the father of her unborn child, she was to be disappointed.

In fact, the argument of mid-July was not to be their final meeting. In early August, Mary wrote in her journal that 'S & C go up to Diodati. I do not, for Lord B did not seem to wish it.' The reason why her presence was not wished for was because she had deliberately been kept in ignorance of Claire's pregnancy until arrangements could be made for the child's upbringing. Byron, perennially impecunious and already father to Ada and (probably) Elizabeth, was hardly in a position to provide financial support. He also wished to avoid further scandal being heaped upon the Shelleys by any association with him. He was not acting out of the selfishness that he had often displayed, but out of simple pragmatism; he barely knew Claire, and it would have been dishonest for him to feign any greater feelings of amity. Nonetheless, there was 'a right thing' to be done, and it involved Augusta. Many years later, Claire wrote to Byron's friend, the writer Edward John Trelawny, that:

> He proposed to place the child when born in Mrs Leigh's care. To this, I objected on the ground that a child always wanted a parent's care at least til seven years old... he yielded and said it was best it should live with him – he promised faithfully never to give it until seven years of age into a stranger's care. I was to be called the child's aunt and in that character I could see it and watch over it without injury to anyone's reputation.[42]

Belying his family motto once again, Byron's promise – if Claire's recollection was accurate – did not come to pass. But then thoughts of creation and motherhood were much on his mind in the middle of 1816, following a strange and remarkable evening in June that saw him involved in a cathartic event. It would forever change the lives of everyone involved in it, as well as leading to one of the greatest imaginative works of literature ever conceived.

11

I had a dream, which was not all a dream.

BYRON, 'DARKNESS',
1816

June and July 1816 were unusually wet and bleak months, interspersed by storms of terrifying violence. The year came to be known as 'The Year Without A Summer'. This was partly as a result of the eruption of Mount Tamboro (in the Lesser Sunda Islands of what is now Indonesia) the previous year, which had released volcanic ash into the atmosphere, causing failing crops, widespread death of livestock and reduced temperatures throughout Europe; an ice dam even formed in the nearby Giétro Glacier in the Val des Bagnes. While the weather that initially greeted Mary, Shelley and Claire upon their arrival in Switzerland in 1814 was glorious and fine, it was very different two years later. A letter of Mary's to Fanny Imlay described how 'an almost perpetual rain confines us principally to the house'. Allowing that 'when the sun bursts forth it is with a splendour and heat unknown in England', she noted that 'the thunder storms that visit us are grander and more terrific than any I have ever seen before', and boasted that 'one night we *enjoyed* a finer storm than I had ever before beheld. The lake was lit up – the pines on Jura made visible, and all the scene illuminated for an instant, when a pitchy blackness succeeded, and the thunder came in frightful bursts over our heads amid the darkness.'[1]

The company that assembled for those June evenings at the Villa

Diodati was an eclectic one. It comprised an adulterous atheist who had been disowned by his high-born family; his mistress, daughter of a woman whose already controversial reputation had been successfully ruined by her father's memoirs of her; her pregnant eighteen-year-old stepsister; a physician prone to bouts of depression; and Lord Byron, for light relief. The only quality that all shared in their Swiss exile was a desire to hide away from the world, and to discuss its failings. That the country they inhabited was in such a poor state when it came to food resources that its government would eventually have to declare a national emergency did not impinge. They had created an Eden for themselves, and it was in this garden that they would eat from the tree of knowledge.

Appropriately, memories of John Milton hung over the Diodati. He was supposed to have visited the house in 1638, and a plaque commemorated his arrival. While Milton had travelled throughout Europe between 1638 and 1639, including Switzerland, it was impossible that he had visited the Villa Diodati inhabited by Byron, as the house had not been constructed until the early eighteenth century. Yet the name still bore immense significance; Milton's closest friend from boyhood was called Charles Diodati, and the two had studied at St Paul's together. When Diodati died in 1638, Milton stated that they were 'the most intimate friends from childhood on'.[2] The current owners were related to Diodati's uncle, the translator and theologian Giovanni, who had achieved fame through being the first man to translate the Bible from Hebrew into Italian. What he would have made of his descendants' seemingly godless tenants is hard to imagine.

It was in the spirit of literary discussion that, one night in June 1816,[3] the conversation at the Villa Diodati turned to the idea of everyone writing a frightening tale. There had been much scornful discussion of how weak contemporary horror stories were, after the discovery of a small selection of German titles, *Fantasamagoriana,* which had been indifferently translated into French. It seemed unlikely that a book as banal as the *History of the Inconstant Lover* could reduce its readers into a state of giddy terror, and so Byron announced 'we will each write a ghost story', and then gave Mary a nod of literary favour when he told her that 'you and I will publish ours together'.[4]

The participants all proposed a different form of composition. As Mary later recounted in the introduction to her revised edition of *Frankenstein*, published in 1831:

> The noble author* began a tale, a fragment of which he printed at the end of his poem of Mazeppa. Shelley, more apt to embody ideas and sentiments in the radiance of brilliant imagery, and in the music of the most melodious verse that adorns our language, commenced one founded on the experiences of his early life. Poor Polidori had some terrible idea about a skull-headed lady, who was so punished for peeping through a key-hole – what to see I forget – something very shocking and wrong of course; but when she was reduced to a worse condition than the renowned Tom of Coventry, he did not know what to do with her.[5]

Mary, however, took a different approach. As she later wrote:

> I busied myself *to think of a story* – a story to rival those which had excited us to this task. One which would speak to the mysterious fears of our nature, and awaken thrilling horror – one to make the reader dread to look around, to curdle the blood, and quicken the beatings of the heart. If I did not accomplish these things, my ghost story would be unworthy of its name.

However, writing to order was an impossibility. 'I thought and pondered – vainly. I felt that blank incapability of invention which

* Byron, naturally.

is the greatest misery of authorship, when dull Nothing replies to our anxious invocations.'

Nothing more was accomplished that evening, and instead the conversation moved on to whether it was possible that humanity would have the means to stimulate life in a previously inanimate object. This had been vaguely broached by the natural philosopher Erasmus Darwin, and was a topic that interested Polidori, with his medical background; Shelley, who had taken an interest in Darwin since his days at university; and Byron, who enjoyed any intellectual discussion, especially if it involved an element of transgression. Mary later wrote that:

> Many and long were the conversations between Lord Byron and Shelley to which I was a devout but nearly silent listener. During one of these, various philosophical doctrines were discussed, and among others the nature of the principle of life, and whether there was any probability of it ever being discussed and communicated.

The experiments of Darwin were then discussed, especially one in which, as Mary recorded:

> He preserved a piece of vermicelli in a glass case til by some extraordinary means it began to move with voluntary motion. Not thus, after all, would life be given. Perhaps a corpse would be reanimated; galvanism had given token of such things: perhaps the component parts of a creature might be manufactured, brought together, and endued with vital warmth.[6]

The following evening, literary discussions were put to one side, as Polidori, who was regarded as something of a buffoon by the group, attempted to perform a play he had written. Although its success was restricted by the author's being confined to a couch after spraining his ankle in the vineyard earlier that day, it was generally agreed that, as a piece of dramatic art, it 'was worth nothing', but the conversation of the previous evening continued to intrigue its participants, and Mary wrote that 'Shelley and I had a conversation about principles – whether man was thought merely to be an instrument'.

After awaking the previous days to be asked 'have you thought of a story?' and being 'forced to reply with a mortifying negative', Mary began to think of her horror story in a different light. Those suggested by the others had been fantastical inventions, sometimes (as in Shelley's case) revealing a greater comfort with imagery and language than with story, and at others, as in Polidori's, offering an unintentionally penetrating psychological insight into his own interests in voyeurism that might have amused Freud later in the century. Byron's brief story, known as 'A Fragment of a Novel', or simply 'A Fragment', was set in Turkey and based on an incident in which, while travelling with Hobhouse, his friend had suffered from a combination of venereal disease and diarrhoea. In its modified form, Hobhouse became Augustus Darvell, a dying aristocrat who, after expiring, rapidly decomposes. The story was little more than an anecdote, although Polidori claimed that Byron's intention, had he finished it, was to make Darvell return in vampiric form.* Polidori later took up the mantle and wrote his own novel, *The Vampyre*, which was first published in 1819; to add to the cross-pollination, it was initially mistakenly attributed to Byron.

Yet, for Mary, her greatest fears were not those of abstract bogeymen, but something arising from within. As she wrote, 'invention... does not consist in creating out of void, but out of chaos; the materials must, in the first place, be afforded: it can give form to dark, shapeless substances, but cannot bring into being the substance itself'.[7] This could be linked to any creative impulse: 'invention

---

* Ironically for a man whose myth may well have inspired the fictional Count Dracula, Byron wrote 'I have a personal dislike to vampires, and the little acquaintance I have with them would by no means induce me to reveal their secrets'.

consists in the capacity of seizing on the capabilities of a subject, and in the power of moulding and fashioning ideas suggested to it'.

For Mary, there were many subjects that she could turn into imaginative form. The most obvious was the trauma caused by the death of her premature baby daughter the previous year, which had led to depression. As she wrote in her journal, 'tis hard, indeed for a mother to lose a child',[8] and 'whenever I am left alone to my own thoughts, and do not read to divert them, they always come back to the same point – that I was a mother, and am so no longer'.[9] Reading was a diversion, but it could also produce its own anxieties and fears, so much so that she had remarkably vivid fantasies. One particularly upsetting one came when she dreamed 'that my little baby came to life again; that it had only been cold, and that we rubbed it before the fire, and it lived. Awake, and find no baby. I think about the little thing all day.' With affecting understatement, she ended her journal entry 'not in good spirits'.

Her lack of fecundity was in painful contrast to Shelley's wife Harriet, who had given birth to his son in late 1814; a second, William, followed in early 1816, but the fear of sudden loss caused by death remained present. Yet hers was not the only preoccupation with childhood. After fathering a bastard with a servant girl when he came of age, Byron had become the unwilling father of a child by his loathed wife Annabella, probably another as the incestuous product of a liaison with Augusta, and was about to be informed that his brief affair with Claire was the progenitor of yet one more. None of his offspring had arisen out of the 'conventional' basis of a normal marriage, any more than Mary's late daughter had. It is possible that Mary believed the child's death to have been a judgement on her and Shelley for his abandonment of Harriet, or, more fancifully, that it represented a punishment to the entire Godwin-Wollstonecraft clan for their repudiation of the natural order of things. Although she, unlike Shelley and Godwin, never made any public profession of atheism, it seems a fair description of her lack of religious views.

At last, an idea struck, in the early hours of 16 June, and the elements coalesced in frighteningly graphic manner. Mary recorded how 'I placed my head on my pillow, [but] I did not sleep, nor could I be said to think. My imagination, unbidden, possessed and guided me, gifting the successive images that arose in my mind with a vividness far beyond the usual bounds of reverie.' What she saw 'with shut eyes, but acute mental vision' was a scene horrific in both detail and in implication:

> I saw the pale student of unhallowed arts kneeling beside the thing he had put together. I saw the hideous phantasm of a man stretched out, and then, on the working of some powerful engine, show signs of life, and stir with an uneasy, half vital motion. Frightful must it be; for supremely frightful would be the effect of any human endeavour to mock the stupendous mechanism of the creator of the world. His success would terrify the artist; he would rush away from his odious handiwork, horror-stricken. He would hope that, left to itself, the slight spark of life which he had communicated would fade; that this thing, which had received such imperfect animation, would subside into dead matter; and he might sleep in the belief that the silence of the grave would quench for ever the transient existence of the hideous corpse which he had looked upon as the cradle of life. He sleeps; but he is awakened; he opens his eyes; behold the horrid thing stands at his bedside, opening his curtains, and looking on him with yellow, watery but speculative eyes.[10]

In the midst of life, we are in death. Mary's description of what would become *Frankenstein* is as vivid and terrifying as any of Henry Fuseli's nightmarish paintings from the late eighteenth century, such as *The Nightmare* or *The Night-Hag visiting the Lapland Witches*. It has an artist's attention to its detail (not least the 'yellow, watery but speculative eyes') and a writer's careful interest in *mise-en-scène*. The character often forgotten about in the description is 'the pale student of unhallowed arts', who, Mary notes, is 'kneeling', as if in obscene mockery of his usurpation of the divine 'creator of the world'. It is the early chapters of the book presented in miniature; already, the detail is there that the artist would flee his 'odious handiwork', and that, rather than glory in his success, he would be 'horror-stricken'. This character will become Victor Frankenstein, tragic anti-hero and modern-day Prometheus, and protagonist of what would become a legendary novel.

In her preface to the revised edition, Mary wrote about the book many years later, in significantly different personal circumstances. By then Shelley had died, as had Byron and Polidori, and her reputation was in the gutter, with her husband's family having disowned her. Therefore, along with trying to make her narrative more conventional, there is the possibility of the story being exaggerated. Nonetheless, the details of what occurred after she had her dream still feel of a piece with her contemporary journal entries. As she opened her own eyes in terror, she wrote how 'the idea so possessed my mind, that a thrill of fear ran through me, and I wished to exchange the ghastly image of my fancy for the realities around'.[11] Awaking in the dismal and freezing summer would hardly have calmed her nerves, and 'the dark parquet, the closed shutters with the moonlight struggling through' seems vivid, as if the memory had remained as constant in her mind for years as the recollection of holding her dead baby.

Fear, and its clinging adherence to imagination, is best suppressed by being shared. A frightening story told out loud is immediately a less dreadful one than one kept in the dark corners of the psyche. Therefore, Mary's next response was an entirely explicable one. As she mused 'if I could only contrive (a ghost story) which would frighten my reader as I myself had been frightened that night', she knew that she had the means of expressing her miseries and fears in a story; as she put it, 'what terrified me will terrify others; and I need only describe the spectre which had haunted my midnight pillow'. What had begun as an idle provocation of Byron's, occasioned by a well-worn book of unfrightening ghost stories, had turned into a twofold opportunity for Mary. Not only could she begin to exorcise some of the trauma that she had suffered through a cathartic exercise in creation, but she could produce an imaginative work that would enable her no longer to be a figure in the corner, ignored by the men as they drank their brandy and sought to outdo one other in wit and learning, but instead to show that she was their intellectual equal, perhaps even their superior.

Therefore, the next morning, Mary was able to announce to the breakfasting Byron and Shelley that 'I have thought of a story'. She then sat down and began to write her narrative, starting with the words 'it was on a dreary night of November'. This was soon discarded as an opening, whether one takes the 'official' beginning of the book – 'I am by birth a Genevese' – or the start of the first letter that commences the narrative, 'You will rejoice to hear that no disaster has accompanied the commencement of an enterprise which you have regarded with such evil forebodings.' The latter might almost be a dig at Byron and the circumstances under which the story's creation began.

❧

Reading *Frankenstein* as the sum of its influences, it is clear that the weeks that Mary spent with Shelley, Claire and Byron – and even Polidori – in Switzerland were crucial to its genesis, both in 1816 and with her lover and stepsister two years before. In her journal from 1814, unimpressed by the 'horrid and slimy faces of our companions in voyage' that she had encountered, Mary had written 'twere easier for God to make entirely new men than attempt to purify such monsters as these'.[12] The 'new men' who found themselves at the Villa Diodati had their own monstrous elements, but also strove for truth. This juxtaposition between idealism and experience, or simply light and dark, permeates *Frankenstein*.

The Villa Diodati's progenitor, Milton, inspired both Shelley and Mary, as well as Byron, who said to Thomas Medwin that 'I

am too happy in being coupled in any way with Milton, and shall
be glad if they find any points of comparison between him and
me'.[13] Shelley described the poet as 'third among the sons of light',
after Shakespeare and Dante, and, like most of the Romantics, saw
him as a figure forever striving for truth, even through his darkness
visible. His republican views were taken up with delight by his
followers, just as his writing inspired theirs. Mary, meanwhile, had
been brought up with her father's belief that Milton had produced
both the greatest English poetry, along with Shakespeare, and the
greatest prose, along with Bacon. She could not fail to be inspired
by both her surroundings and the influence that the poet held over
those around her. The book's epigraph, from *Paradise Lost*, sets out
her debt to Milton from the beginning:

> Did I request thee, Maker, from my clay
> To mould me man? Did I solicit thee
> From darkness to promote me?

The obvious comparison with *Paradise Lost* is with Frankenstein
as a flawed God, with the monster as a guiltless Adam transformed into a tormented Satan by his reading a forbidden text.
When the creature finally reads it, Mary's debt to Milton becomes
unambiguous:

> But *Paradise Lost* excited different and far deeper emotions.
> I read it... as a true history. It moved every feeling of wonder
> and awe, that the picture of an omnipotent God warring with
> His creatures was capable of exciting. I often referred the several
> situations, as their similarity struck me, to my own. Like Adam,
> I was apparently united by no link to any other being in exis-
> tence; but his state was far different from mine in every other
> respect. He had come forth from the hands of God a perfect
> creature, happy and prosperous, guarded by the especial care
> of his Creator; he was allowed to converse with, and acquire

knowledge from, beings of a superior nature: but I was wretched, helpless and alone. Many times I considered Satan as the fitter emblem of my condition; for often, like him, when I viewed the bliss of my protectors, the bitter gall of envy rose within me.[14]

Although Mary Godwin was not Satan, despite the murmurings of some society matrons, she knew 'the bitter gall of envy' too well. This was not just from her semi-exclusion from the manly intellectual chat of Geneva, but also from Shelley's delight at the birth of his son by Harriet; Mary had been unable to share in his joy, writing instead in her journal that 'Shelley writes a number of circular letters of this event, which ought to be ushered in with ringing of bells, etc, for it is the son of his *wife*.'[15]

Yet even as she scorned the entangled personal affairs of the Romantics, she knew that her connection with them was vital, both for creative inspiration and for fame by association. While, of course, Byron was a 'name' – and still a valid commercial prospect despite the scandal in which he had been embroiled over the past year – there were other figures of influence who she recalled. There is a debt in Mary's creative process to Coleridge's famous description of how, opium-soaked, he had 'continued for about three hours in a profound sleep… during which time he had the most vivid confidence that he could not have composed less than two to three hundred lines.' Unlike Mary, whose dreams remained vivid, the person from Porlock notoriously dispelled Coleridge's fantasy meaning that *Kubla Khan* remained a fragment. Yet again this was a work that owed a public appearance to Byron, who earlier that year had been struck by Coleridge reciting it and had arranged for its reissue, by John Murray, within a matter of weeks. It seems impossible that this was not discussed at the Villa Diodati, or that Mary did not take note of the legend arising from it by the time of the book's republication in 1831.

Kubla Khan, however, is not Coleridge's most important influence on *Frankenstein*. In the same 1816 collection was his Gothic

fantasy *Christabel,* which was drenched in a feeling of dread when
it came to issues of maternity, not least the sceptre of Christabel's
mother, of whom Christabel says 'Woe is me!/She died the hour
that I was born'. This was a precise echo of how Mary Wollstonecraft died shortly after Mary was born, and the overtones of
maternity and creation hang as heavy over *Christabel* as they do
over *Frankenstein,* hinting at a literary cross-pollination that would
develop over the years.

There were other stylistic influences that Mary inherited from
her progenitors and contemporaries. It borrowed its epistolary
structure from Plutarch's *Lives,* and her father's books were influential, as were his political philosophies. It is no coincidence that
the creature talks of how 'I heard of the division of property, of
immense wealth and squalid poverty; of rank, descent and noble
blood.' Godwin's 1794 novel *Caleb Williams* explores themes of
pursuit and escape, as the latter part of *Frankenstein* does, and its
radical political sympathies are echoed in the fate of the creature,
shunned and despised by society. Likewise, his novel *St Leon,* with
its overarching theme of a protagonist searching for the secret of the
elixir of life, echoes Frankenstein's Promethean ambitions. It is no
coincidence that *St Leon* was greatly admired by Byron, who said
to Godwin, when he ventured that writing another novel would
kill him, 'And what matter? We shall have another *St Leon.*'[16]

Mary had also had her father read her Coleridge's *Rime of the
Ancient Mariner,** and its influence can be discerned through-
out, specifically the haunting verse cited in the book itself when
Frankenstein is fleeing the creature:

> Like one, that on a lonesome road
> Doth walk in fear and dread,

---

* There are clear parallels between the character of the wedding guest and
Captain Walton in *Frankenstein*; Walton even explicitly writes 'I shall kill
no albatross… I should come back to you as worn and woeful as the
"Ancient Mariner"'.

> And having once turned round walks on,
> And turns no more his head;
> Because he knows, a frightful fiend
> Doth close behind him tread.

The 'frightful fiend' might be the creature, who even explicitly says of himself 'I was benevolent and good; misery made me a fiend', but it could just as well be the forces of society, pitilessly hunting down those who resisted its diktats. This was every bit as true for the small group at the Diodati as it was for Coleridge's mariner, or Frankenstein, or the creature. While Byron, Shelley, Mary *et al* were hardly the subject of persecution, the half-curious, half-condemnatory observers who stayed nearby and talked excitedly of 'that wicked Lord Byron and his coven' were just as dogged in their pursuit. Byron complained 'I was watched by glasses on the opposite side of the Lake, and by glasses too that must have had very distorted optics... I believe that they looked upon me as a man-monster, worse than the *piqueur*.'*[17]

Frankenstein underwent many changes between its initial appearance in 1818 and its republication in 1831, and one of the most notable is in its presentation of Frankenstein's lover Elizabeth. In the revised text, Elizabeth is presented as an adopted 'sweet orphan' taken into the family, described as 'a child fairer than pictured cherub', and one of whom Frankenstein says '[I] looked upon Elizabeth as mine – mine to protect, love and cherish.'[18] Only the hint that she was 'my more than sister' refers back to the original text, where Elizabeth is described as 'the only child of [Victor's father's] deceased sister', and where near-incest seems to be almost the norm in the sickly family. This can be discerned in the description of how 'a desire to bind as closely as possible the ties of domestic love determined my mother to consider Elizabeth

---

* A 'piqueur' is a servant who ran before the carriage to clear the way; in other words, the lowest of the low.

as my future wife'. It seems probable that there were some candid conversations at the Villa Diodati about Byron's relations with Augusta, as the description of Elizabeth, both in terms of physical appearance and in character, seems to echo her idealized forbear:

> She was docile and good tempered, yet gay and playful as a summer insect. Although she was lively and animated, her feelings were strong and deep, and her disposition uncommonly affectionate. No one could better enjoy liberty, yet no one could submit with more grace than she did to constraint and caprice. Her imagination was luxuriant, yet her capability of application was great. Her person was the image of her mind; her hazel eyes, although as lively as a bird's, possessed an attractive softness. Her figure was light and airy; and, though capable of enduring great fatigue, she appeared the most fragile creature in the world.

In the revised version, Elizabeth has been transformed into a blonde-haired, blue-eyed girl whose character is barely discussed. While this makes her altogether less interesting, perhaps, eight years after Byron's death, Mary felt that a tactful move might be to expunge the echoes of incest. In any case, in both incarnations of the book, the love affair between Victor and Elizabeth remains unconsummated; had Byron's own love for Augusta remained in a similar state, the greatest part of his downfall may never have occurred. In *Frankenstein*, parenthood takes on a perverse aspect; this could have been influenced by Byron's difficult relations with his mother and non-existent relationship with his father, and also his ambivalent attitude towards his own fatherly role, as well as Mary's dealings with William Godwin, and her mother's legacy.

Finally, there is the most tantalizing autobiographical association of all, namely Byron-as-Frankenstein. He was always supportive of the book, describing it (with faint condescension) as 'a wonderful work for a girl of nineteen'[19] in a letter to Murray in 1819, but never sought any comparison with the protagonist; that would be

330

Lord Byron, by Thomas Phillips (1770–1845). The most notorious man of his age, Byron scandalized society with his poetry and love affairs before he died fighting for Greek independence at the age of 36.

Catherine Gordon, by Thomas Stewardson. Byron's long-suffering mother believed in her son's essential goodness and integrity, even as he castigated her as a drunken harridan.

Newstead Abbey, by F. O. Morris, 1880. Byron's ancestral home, inherited along with his title, was his greatest joy; he declared to his mother that 'Newstead and I stand or fall together'. Its sale caused him enormous grief.

Caroline Lamb, by Thomas Phillips. The wild and undisciplined Caroline was Byron's most notorious mistress, and her habit of cross-dressing both excited his pan-sexual appetites and appalled the great men and women of society, including her husband Lord Melbourne.

Augusta Leigh, artist unknown. Byron's half-sister enjoyed an incestuous relationship with him that led to the birth of a child, Elizabeth Medora, who was probably his; she remained his greatest love and confidante after his self-imposed exile in 1816.

Annabella Milbanke, 1812, by Charles Hayter (1761–1835). Annabella married Byron after a mainly epistolary courtship and regretted it almost immediately. Later in life, she attempted to present herself as the custodian of her husband's legacy.

Claire Clairmont, 1819, by Amelia Curran (1775–1847). Claire was one of Byron's many mistresses, but her devotion to him turned to contempt when he ignored her and refused to let her see their illegitimate daughter, Allegra.

Mary Shelley, by Richard Rothwell (1800–68). One of the few women in Byron's life who he did not have sexual relations with, Mary enjoyed a mutually fulfilling intellectual rapport with him, and was inspired to write *Frankenstein* during their 1816 sojourn in Lake Geneva.

The Funeral Of Shelley, 1889, by Louis Fournier (1857–1917). This highly romanticized depiction of the cremation of Shelley on the beach at Viareggio contains numerous inaccuracies; Mary Shelley did not attend the event, and Byron left early, repulsed by the scene.

Teresa Guiccioli, engraving, 1833, by H. T. Ryall after a drawing, 1833, by William Brockedon (1787–1854). Byron's final mistress, the aristocratic Italian Teresa Guiccioli came to represent a domestic stability that he found himself unable to be content with.

Allegra Byron, unknown artist. Byron's illegitimate daughter with Claire spent much of her short life in a convent after he tired of the responsibility of caring for her; she died of a 'convulsive catarrhal attack' brought on by typhoid in 1822.

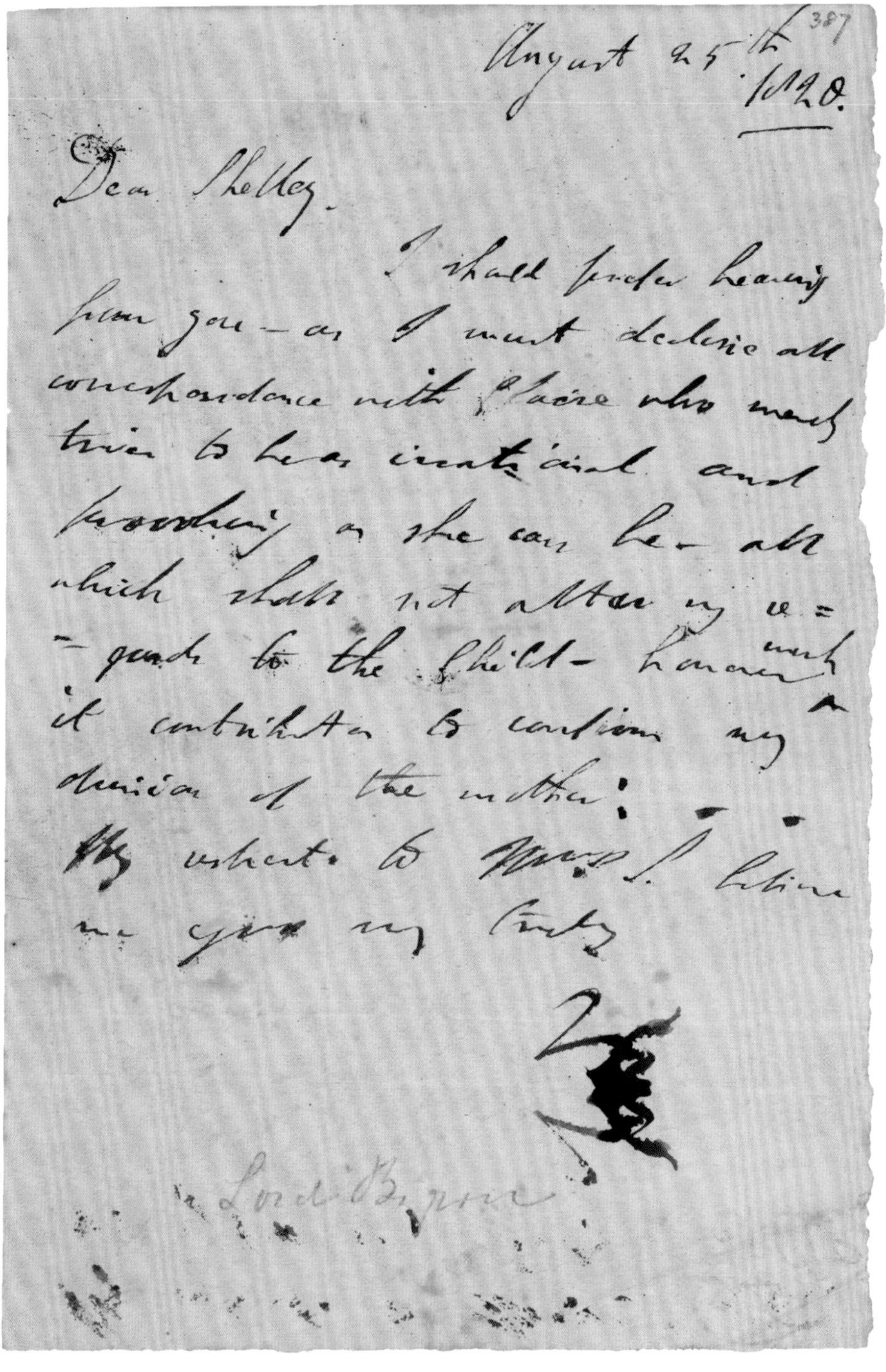

August 25th 1820

Dear Shelley,

[handwritten letter, largely illegible]

Lord Byron

A letter from Byron to Shelley, August 25 1820. Byron's refusal to have any dealings with Claire, who was Shelley's sister-in-law, caused a rift between the two; here, he describes his former lover as one 'who merely tries to be as irrational and provoking as she can be'.

Ada Lovelace, by Margaret Carpenter (1793–1872). Byron's legitimate daughter Ada never knew her father, but became increasingly fascinated by his legacy as she grew up, much to her mother Annabella's horror and dismay. She was also a pioneer in the field of computing and was nicknamed 'the bride of science'.

Elizabeth Medora Leigh, unknown artist. Augusta's daughter Medora led an unhappy and troubled life beset by exploitation both sexual and social, and died of scarlet fever after finding a small measure of happiness.

posterity's doing. While there is no association between the two characters as explicit as there would be between Byron and the character of Lord Raymond in Mary's 1826 novel *The Last Man*,* it is worth remembering Claire's comment in her April 1816 letter to Byron that 'my folly may be great, but the creator ought not to destroy his creature'. Whether or not Claire or Byron repeated this to Mary, Byron thought of Promethean folly throughout 1816. He even composed his own poem, *Prometheus*, which talked of how:

> Thy Godlike crime was to be kind
> To render with thy precepts less
> The sum of human wickedness
> And strengthen Man with his own mind.

This had also an echo in the third canto of *Childe Harold,* when art, creation and life are all yoked together:

> 'Tis to create, and in creating, live
> A being more intense, that we endow
> With form our fancy, gaining as we give
> The life we image, even as I do now.

Mary, who wrote a fair copy of these lines in June 1816, knew about Byron's interest when she subtitled her book *The Modern Prometheus*. She also knew that such descriptions as Victor attempting to 'animate the lifeless clay', explicitly inspired by the myth, would have been familiar to any reader of Byron, or Greek mythology. While Byron was in no sense a scientist,† the manner in which he stood *contra mundum* mirrored that of Frankenstein. If Byron had risen one day to find himself famous, it was equally the case that

---

* Raymond is a nobleman dedicated to the liberal promotion of freedom and love, and fights on behalf of the Greeks against the Turks.
† In this regard Byron differed from Shelley, who wrote admiringly about science in his poem *Mont Blanc*.

Victor Frankenstein, waking exhaustedly after the toil of creation, would find himself infamous.

᠊᠊᠊᠊᠊᠊᠊᠊᠊᠊᠊᠊᠊᠊᠊᠊᠊᠊᠊᠊᠊᠊᠊᠊

The eventual creation of *Frankenstein* was no less laborious for Mary than the events described within the book would be for its protagonist. A terse journal entry from 24 July 1816 simply stated 'I write my story'. Thereafter, 'write' became the standard journal entry. As she continued to compose her tale, she carried on talking with Byron and Shelley, with the arrival of Matthew 'Monk' Lewis* on 18 August further stimulating discussion. One of these conversations took place that day; as Mary wrote, 'we talk of ghosts; neither Lord Byron nor Monk Lewis seem to believe in them; and they both agree, in the very face of reason, that none could believe in ghosts without also believing in God'. Her reaction was to argue that 'I do not think that all the persons who profess to discredit these visitations really discredit them, or, if they do in the daylight, are not admonished by the approach of loneliness and midnight to think more respectably of the world of shadows.'

Mary was not the only one thinking of shadows. While she suffered from frightening visions and lucid dreams, Byron was in the midst of his *annus horribilis*. Even as he attempted to be sanguine about the publication of *Glenarvon*, he knew that his reputation was suffering further damage. He wrote to Augusta in August and talked angrily of its author, saying 'who can care for such a wretch as Caroline, or believe such a seventy times convicted liar?'[20] The tenor of his letters around this time was nervy and angry, especially when it came to Annabella; not only did he instruct Augusta 'do not mention her again', but he asked Hanson 'when you see my daughter – tell me how she is – and how she looks – but do not mention to me nor allude to any other branch of that family'.[21] Even as he hinted that he might return to England the following

---

* Lewis was so named because of the success of his 1796 Gothic novel *The Monk*.

spring, he sank into a depression that was only partially eased by his friendship with the Shelleys, and had been worsened, if anything, by his involvement with Claire.

Byron's own response to the grim summer of 1816 was to begin 'Darkness', a poem that reflected both the sense of doom and apocalypse felt by those assembled in Switzerland, and his own personal despair. There had even been a prediction by one Italian scientist that the world would be plunged into darkness forever on 18 July, and amid the panic engendered by this pronouncement, Byron produced his own examination of man being undone by nature. As with *Frankenstein*, it began with a vision:

> I had a dream, which was not all a dream.
> The bright sun was extinguished, and the stars
> Did wander darkling in the eternal space,
> Rayless, and pathless, and the icy earth
> Swung blind and blackening in the moonless air;
> Morn came and went—and came, and brought no day,
> And men forgot their passions in the dread
> Of this their desolation; and all hearts
> Were chilled into a selfish prayer for light.

A 'selfish prayer for light' is what lies behind the creation of both Victor Frankenstein's monster and any other artistic endeavour. The echoes of the opening of *Paradise Lost* can be felt strongly here as well, specifically the description of how 'As one great Furnace flamed, yet from those flames / No light, but rather darkness visible'. For Byron, as for Milton and Mary, human nature was a weak and fallible thing that could be manipulated, and even as 'the brows of men by the despairing light / Wore an unearthly aspect', there was no disguising Byron's pessimism in his bald statements that 'no love was left / All earth was but one thought – and that was death / Immediate and inglorious.' As he contemplated the world around him, he meditated on the end of man without especial sorrow:

The world was void,
The populous and the powerful was a lump,
Seasonless, herbless, treeless, manless, lifeless—
A lump of death—a chaos of hard clay.
The rivers, lakes and ocean all stood still,
And nothing stirred within their silent depths;
Ships sailorless lay rotting on the sea,
And their masts fell down piecemeal: as they dropped
They slept on the abyss without a surge—
The waves were dead; the tides were in their grave,
The moon, their mistress, had expired before;
The winds were withered in the stagnant air,
And the clouds perished.

While Victor Frankenstein attempted to give animation to 'lifeless clay', for Byron the end of humanity represents nothing more than 'a lump of death' and 'a chaos of hard clay'. Betrayed and scorned by all but a few, among them his beloved 'more than sister', impending fatherhood aroused little more than cynical indifference. Yet an odd catharsis lurked. Just as Frankenstein's creature declares at the end, 'with sad and solemn enthusiasm' that 'I shall die and what I now feel be no longer felt… my spirit will sleep in peace; or if it thinks, it will not surely think thus',[22] Byron ends 'Darkness' with triumphant exaltation, as if to imply that, 'thus sitting, thus consulting, thus in arms', the end of humanity was a consummation most devoutly to be wished:

Darkness had no need
Of aid from them – She was the universe.

It would not be long until darkness, in female form, would once again re-enter Byron's life.

12

*I shall love you to the end of
my life and nobody else.*

CLAIRE TO BYRON,
29 AUGUST 1816

After the incursions of fantastical monsters and prying eyes, it became clear that the Shelleys' Swiss idyll could not last. On 29 August 1816, Shelley, Mary, Claire, the Shelleys' child and their nurse left Geneva, bound for Bath, where they arrived in late September. Claire was by now four months pregnant, and pining for her child's father; however, Byron chose to maintain an attitude of lordly distance, alternately bored and irritated by her. She had written to him shortly before they had left Switzerland, and piteously said that 'I should have been happier if I could have seen and kissed you once before I went, but now I feel as if we had parted ill friends... my dreadful fear is lest you quite forget me... I shall love you to the end of my life and nobody else.' A lighter note was struck in her edict that Byron should 'beware of any excess in wine'.[1]

When Claire arrived back in England, she realized the disparity between her romantic ideals and the drab reality she faced. Unmarried, pregnant by a notorious blackguard who had no intention of supporting her or even responding to her, and kept away from her parents for fear of their reaction to yet another scandal, she was in an unenviable situation. Shelley gently patronized her, claiming in one letter to Byron that 'Claire is about to enjoin me some messages that are better conceived than expressed.'[2] Nevertheless, fearing for her mental state, he begged Byron to take an interest, asking 'if you do not like to write to C, send me some kind message for her'.[3] None was forthcoming; however, this was insignificant in comparison to greater tragedies that would overwhelm the family.

Claire's stepsister Fanny Imlay left the family home in London on 9 October, bound for Bristol. It was assumed that she was intending to join Mary and Claire in Bath, but instead she wrote Mary a doom-laden letter that caused great alarm, resulting in Shelley heading to Bristol to search for her. She was not found, but he was told that she had left for Swansea instead. When he arrived there, he discovered that she had committed suicide at the Mackworth Arms hotel, dying of an overdose of laudanum. She left a pitiable note, in which she desired 'the blessing of forgetting that such a creature ever existed'.[4] Her father took this literally, and saw to it that, despite an account of her death being published in the local newspaper, the *Cambrian*, her sad end was all but ignored. When asked what had happened, Godwin claimed that she had died of a fever.

It is impossible to know what led to Fanny's decision to kill herself, although she had probably inherited her mother's residual depression. It is also likely that, in comparison to Mary and even Claire, she felt underappreciated and ignored. Claire's attitude to the death, initially at least, was as dramatic as her pronouncements usually were. She mourned that 'her death was attended by such melancholy consequences as… can never be forgotten… I never passed such wretched hours. Everything is so miserable that I often wish myself quite dead.'[5] Had this been the only item of despair that visited their household, it would have made for a grim and miserable autumn, but even worse was to come.

In eloping with Mary, Shelley had abandoned his wife Harriet. While he had attempted to justify his desertion in philosophical and intellectual terms, his specious arguments failed to convince Harriet of the righteousness of his actions; they had probably done little to justify his actions to himself, either. Therefore, when he wrote to his former publisher Thomas Hookham in mid-November, he made an enquiry about her more out of guilt than genuine interest. He was appalled by Hookham's reply, which stated that, after disappearing on 9 November, Harriet's body had been found in the Serpentine on 10 December. While the inquest had returned a verdict of 'found drowned', there was the grim detail that she was 'far advanced in pregnancy'. The family believed that she had been the lover of an army captain who had been posted overseas, and, unable to bear the loneliness and shame of being the mother of a bastard, decided to kill herself.

◦❧

Claire, herself on the verge of giving birth, saw the situation with balance and compassion. She understood both Shelley's grief and what had driven Harriet to suicide. He, however, was consumed by a mixture of anger and guilt, and began to behave irrationally. He blamed those around Harriet – rather than himself – for her mental state, and described them as 'her abhorred & unnatural family' and 'detestable', and reserved an especial loathing for her sister Eliza, whom he called 'the beastly viper'.[6] Eliza had done little other than help Harriet, but Shelley was in no mood for niceties or restraint. His paranoia was such that he believed that the Westbrooks intended to snatch custody of his children by Harriet, and so, hastily and without romance, he compelled Mary to marry him in a mistaken belief that their wedding would legitimize their claim on the other children. They wed at St Mildred's church in the City on 30 December. The only man completely happy with the outcome was Godwin, who considered it a great boon to have gained the son of a baronet as a son-in-law. Mary Shelley, meanwhile, exhibited what her new husband described as 'her real attributes of affectation, prejudice and heartless pride'.[7]

Shelley confided in Claire in a manner that he would not have employed with any another, the legacy of their long and close friendship. He wrote to her after the 'o'er hasty marriage' to acknowledge her 'loneliness and low spirits which arise from being entirely left', and explicitly said that 'nothing could be more

provoking than to find all this unnecessary'. Claire later told Trelawny that 'Harriet's suicide had a beneficial effect on Shelley – he
became much less confident in himself and not so wild as he had
been before.'[8] This beneficial effect was not one that appeared to
comfort his new wife, who was all too aware that their union had
taken place out of necessity rather than from love.

A similarly loveless response was elicited from Byron early the
next year, after Claire had given birth to their child on 12 January
1817. As he knew that Byron would not respond to Claire, Shelley
acted as go-between, and informed him that 'I have good news
to tell you… Claire is safely delivered of a most beautiful girl.'[9]
Byron, whose only response to impending fatherhood had been
to note the imminent arrival of a 'Baby B' in a letter to Augusta in
mid-December, remained silent, other than a dismissive reference
to her in another letter to Augusta in late May. In it, he made light
of his paternal bonds, and said 'it seems that I have got another
– a *daughter* – by that same lady whom you will recognize by
what I said of her in former letters – I mean *her* who returned to
England to become a Mamma incog – & whom I pray the Gods
to keep there'.[10]

As Claire wrote him increasingly baroque and furious letters
that swung between vitriol and pathos,* his silence gave its own
answer. She wished her daughter to be called Alba, both a reference
to the Spanish and Italian words for 'dawn' and to the Shelley's
pet name for Byron, Albé;†[11] the child had 'pretty eyes of a deep
dazzling blue'. After the drama prior to her birth, calm prevailed,
even as the Shelleys sought to conceal the baby's illegitimacy by the
device of it belonging to 'a friend in London'.[12] Shelley attempted
to involve Byron in his daughter's life, hinting that 'Claire would

---

* As in one where she demanded 'write me a nice letter, & tell me that
you *like* me will be very pleased to have a little baby of which you will take
great care'.
† Alba is also the Gaelic term for Scotland; perhaps this was intended as a
subtle dig at Byron's much-suppressed Scottish heritage.

be the most rejoiced of all of us at the sight of a letter written by you' despite making it clear that 'I do not tell her that I write to you now'.[13] He emphasized the beauty and intelligence of Byron's child, and fruitlessly tried to arrange for Byron to pay a visit to them in England.

For Claire, 1817 was a happy time, despite Byron's continuing absence. She stayed on a small estate in Marlow that Shelley had leased, Albion House, and spent her time looking after her daughter, attempting to write poetry (albeit without any noticeable success) and playing the piano. The only difficulty was the arrangement that she and Shelley had entered into with Byron for Alba's upbringing, but that seemed remote, especially as the father had so little interest in his daughter. Nevertheless, in the summer he sent for her, and demanded that Alba live with him. Mary, about to give birth to another baby in September, knew that this would cause upset. She wrote to Shelley to say 'Claire, although she in a blind kind of manner sees the necessity of it, does not wish her to go and will instinctively place all kinds of difficulties in the way.'[14] They were therefore faced with an unpleasant dilemma as they considered where their loyalties lay; to her nineteen-year-old stepsister and her daughter, or to their lordly friend. While their sympathy lay instinctively with Claire, it seemed clear that Byron's right to look after his daughter could not be denied. Additionally, removing the child from the country would reduce the risk of scandal, something that they had not been short of over the previous months.

Therefore, it was decided that, early the next year, Claire and the Shelleys would head to Italy, where Byron now lived, in order to hand over the girl. Byron asked that the child be christened 'Allegra', rather than Alba, and so, on 9 March 1818, his daughter was baptized and named Clara Allegra. The choice of first name, unsurprisingly, was Claire's.[15] Shortly before her departure for Italy, Claire wrote to Byron to tell him about his daughter on her first birthday. The language and extremity of the sentiments expressed indicated that giving her child up was unlikely to be easy:

My affections are few and therefore strong – the extreme solitude in which I live has concentrated them to one point and
that point is my lovely child. I study her [with] pleasure all day
long – she is so fond of me that I hold her in my arms til I am
nearly falling on purpose to delight her. We sleep together and
if you knew the extreme happiness I feel when she nestles close
to me, in listening to our regular breathing together, I could tear
my flesh in twenty thousand different directions to ensure her
good.[16]

Claire, who elsewhere referred to Allegra as 'all my treasure', was
understandably mistrustful of Byron. She described the 'various
and ceaseless misgivings that I entertain of you', and worried that
'suppose that in yielding her to your care I yield her to neglect
and coldness?' This neglect was something that she returned to
later, when she piteously wrote 'when I fear for her residing with
you… it is lest I should behold her sickly & wasted with improper
management, lest I should live to hear that *you* neglected her'.

   The Shelleys and Claire left for Italy on 11 March 1818, accompanied by their children and nursemaids. After passing through the
'airy and agreeable' Calais and 'most beautiful' Lyon, they arrived
at Milan on 4 April. Claire's journal talks happily of her adventures, such as her visiting Lake Como, reading Molière and playing
chess with Shelley in the evenings. The wider purpose of her journey went unremarked until 21 April, at least by her. Meanwhile,
Shelley and Byron were exchanging fraught correspondence about
arrangements for Allegra's custody. Shelley invited Byron to Lake
Como, and tried, unconvincingly, to play the host; he suggested
'I don't know where you could find a heartier welcome – little
Allegra might return with you'.[17] Byron's response, dated 17 April,
does not survive, but it is clear from Shelley and Claire's replies
that it peremptorily demanded Allegra's immediate removal to
Venice, and that Byron had no interest either in seeing Claire, or
having any further relations with her.

Possibly unbeknown to Shelley, Claire had also written to Byron in understandably emotive terms. She stated that 'I cannot part with my child never to see her again... tell me that you will come and see Shelley in the summer or that I may then be somewhere near her – say this and I will send her instantly.' Appealing to his friendship with Shelley, she responded to Byron's obvious dislike of her ('you say you will not visit him while I am there') with misplaced optimism as she implored him to show some compassion, writing 'why might not the father & mother of a child whom both so tenderly love meet as friends?' That she still loved him, despite everything that had occurred, was clear; she referred to him as 'my dearest friend' and ended by saying 'I still pray for your happiness & health'.[18] It is unlikely that Byron cared; he was more concerned with a significant recent loss, of which he said to Murray 'the time is past in which I could feel for the dead – or I should feel for the death of Lady Melbourne, the best & kindest & ablest female I ever knew'.[19]

Shelley attempted to intercede between the two. As he felt some responsibility for the grim situation – or, as he put it, 'the deep interest I have ever felt for all the parties concerned' – he tried to prompt his friend's compassion. He attempted to 'err on the side of kindness, [rather] than of rigour', and to elicit Byron's sympathy for Claire, arguing that 'rank, and reputation, and prudence are as nothing in comparison to a mother's claims'. He did not spare the poet either in matters philosophical ('your conduct must at present wear the aspect of great cruelty, however you justify it to yourself') or practical ('the expenses of which you speak have been in our family so extremely trifling... [that] perhaps you will be kind enough not to place me in so degrading a situation, as to estimate a matter of this kind').*[20]

---

* Byron had offered to pay for the expenses involved in the first year of looking after Allegra.

Shelley's careful brinksmanship had no effect other than anger-
ing Byron, and so he abandoned the role of go-between. By then,
he had sent Allegra with her nurse to Venice, and he attempted to
placate her father, claiming that 'the correspondence from which
these misinterpretations have arisen was undertaken on my part
solely because you refused to correspond with Claire'. He absolved
himself of further responsibility, saying 'I am sorry that I misunderstood your letter; and I hope that on both sides there is here an
end of misunderstandings.'[21]

It was relatively easy for Shelley to say of Claire that she was
'wretchedly disconsolate', and that 'I know not how I shall calm
her'. Her own suffering was greater. She was compelled to abandon her daughter to a man who had rejected her, and this would
be a torment for the rest of her life. Over fifty years later, she still
recalled how '[Allegra] was the only thing I had to love – the only
object in the world I could call my very own: and I had never parted
from her from her birth, not for an hour even.'[22] On 27 April 1818,
she wrote yet another unanswered letter to Byron, in which she
implored him to 'write us a line on her safe arrival – to let me know
she is well'. Alternating between pathetic humility ('if I have been
faulty I have suffered enough to redeem my error') and desperate
passion ('my dearest Lord Byron best of human beings, you are the
father of my little girl, and I cannot forget you'),[23] she had debased
herself to miserable effect.

⤜⬦

It is easy to argue that Claire was naïve in not believing that Byron
would behave differently towards her than he had with previous
lovers. His life and art were complemented by a magisterial lack
of respect for the women around him, with a few exceptions, and
a naïve, inexperienced girl was never going to be the one to alter a
long-established pattern of behaviour. Yet Byron's callousness was
a character trait that he had possessed since childhood. In order
to protect himself from the consequences of his own, and others',

behaviour, he had built an impregnable suit of armour, concealing his depression and insecurity underneath a carapace of hard-living and equal hard-heartedness. Claire was little more than the latest in an ever-expanding line of women who had served his purposes for a short time, to be cast off and forgotten about.

Her refusal to fade quietly into the ether irritated him. He complained to Hobhouse from Venice that 'Shelley has got to Milan with the bastard & its mother – but won't send the child – unless I will go & see the mother – I have sent a messenger for the child – but I can't leave my quarters.'[24] By the time that Allegra arrived in Venice on 2 May, it merited nothing more than a postscript in another epistle to Hobhouse, in which he said 'my bastard came three days ago – very like – healthy – noisy & capricious'.[25] In the last two categories, at least, she took after her father. Claire, meanwhile, besieged him with letters, begging to be allowed to see her daughter. They went unanswered and without any acknowledgement.

At last, Shelley and Claire headed to Venice in order for her to see Allegra again, leaving on 17 August. Byron, who was busying himself with the finest courtesans that the city could provide, was not *in situ*, but had left the child with the Hoppners, the con-sul-general and his wife. Shelley described Allegra to Mary as being 'so grown you would hardly know her – she is pale & has lost a good deal of her liveliness, but is as beautiful as ever though more mild'. Shelley had decided that Claire's reunion with her daughter should be kept secret, as Richard Hoppner warned '[Byron] often expresses his extreme horror at her arrival, & the necessity which it would impose of him of instantly quitting Venice'. When Shelley met Byron, permission for Allegra to spend time in Florence was refused, on the grounds that 'the Venetians will think that he has grown tired of her & dismissed her, & he has already the repu-tation of caprice'. Byron also believed, probably correctly, that a reunion with Claire would lead to 'a second renewal of affection & a second parting'. Although he tried to be reasonable, and allowed 'after all, I have no right over the child', it was clear that he was more interested in talking to Shelley of literary matters, as he made 'great professions of friendship & regard for me'.[26]

During their encounter, Byron invited Mary, Claire and the rest to stay at a villa he had taken at Este, not far from Venice. He would not be there, dashing any hopes Claire had of a reunion. Shelley happily accepted the invitation, both for Claire's sake and for Mary's, but disaster soon intruded. The difficult, hot journey to Este gave Shelley and Mary's daughter Clara dysentery, and, after a few weeks' suffering, the child died while Shelley was engaged in an unsuccessful attempt to find a doctor. Mary, he informed Claire, was 'in the most dreadful distress' and in 'a kind of despair'.[27] She sank into a restless depression at her second loss of a child, compounded by her blaming both Shelley and Claire for having placed Clara in this situation, all in order for Claire to spend time with her own daughter. The relationship between the stepsisters, frequently fraught, was damaged further by the girl's death.

Claire's sadness was mitigated by her joy at being able to spend time with Allegra, but Byron, believing that she might attempt to abscond with the child,* asked that she be returned to him in late October. The previous month, he had written to Augusta in irritation at the temporary return of Claire into his life to say '[Allegra's] mother (whom the devil confound) came prancing the other day over the Appenines – to see her child'. Irritated that this unlooked-for development, as he put it, 'threw my Venetian loves (who are none of the quietest) into great combustion', Byron made a blackly humorous reference to the likely outcome of another meeting; 'I declined seeing her for fear that the consequence might be an addition to the family.' He ended the letter, after recounting yet another

---

* A letter written much later to Trelawny suggested that Byron jokingly remarked of Allegra 'she will grow up a very pretty woman and then I will take her for my mistress', leading Claire to consider removing Allegra from his custody and fleeing to Australia, 'where I would set up a school and earn our breads'.

affair, with his usual complaint: 'you see Goose – that there is no quiet in the world'.[28]

When Allegra was reunited with her amorous father, the Shelleys and Claire continued to travel around Italy; in contrast to the gaiety of their journey earlier that year, they now ventured 'in silence and tears'. Illness was rife, with Shelley undergoing 'intense bodily suffering',[29] and matters were not helped by a rash decision of his once recovered to adopt a Neapolitan orphan as a consolation for Mary. The child was named Elena, and Shelley forged a document declaring that Mary had given birth to the girl in December 1818, and then saw to it that the child was placed with a foster family, with the eventual intention that she could become part of their own clan. Far from bringing Mary and Shelley closer together, this parody of family life simply served to remind her of what she had lost earlier in the year.* It was a grim connection between Mary and Claire that 1818 was the year in which both of them lost a daughter, even if Allegra still lived.

⚬❧

Mary's depression lingered through 1819, although it was temporarily ameliorated by her discovery that she was pregnant again in April; she eventually gave birth to a boy, Percy Florence, in November. However, as they carried on living in Rome in the early part of the year, omnipresent tragedy again visited the family as her three-year-old son William caught malaria and, after what his mother described as 'dreadful anxiety' being visited upon his family, died on 7 June. The loss of two children in a year reduced Mary to a helpless sense of worry and impotence, as well as grief. Death seemed to stalk the Shelleys with inexorable determination. Ironically, Mary had written to her friend Maria Gisborne just two months before

* The deception also led to a blackmail attempt from a former servant of theirs, Paolo Foggi, who had been party to the forging of the document; it took legal intervention to silence him.

to express her happiness at their life in Rome, saying 'nothing but the malaria would drive us from it for many months'.[30] Now, she was reduced to despair, and told another friend, the painter Amelia Curran, that 'I shall never recover [from] that blow... everything on earth has lost its interest to me.'[31]

Claire felt a similar sense of loss to Mary. She wrote to Byron in May to ask about his plans for Allegra's education, which eschewed the romanticism of her previous letters for both bitterness ('I knew what a very unnatural thing you would think it that I should inter-fere with my own child') and world-weary cynicism ('I hope that in making my unhappiness you have found your own happiness'). Her greatest fear was for Allegra, as she knew that the child was entirely dependent on her mercurial father; the letter ended with the injunction 'visit Allegra oftener than you have'.[32]

Despite his absences from his daughter's life, Byron was fond of her. He had said of her the previous year that she was 'much more Lady Byron than her mother... is it not odd?'[33] and he wrote to Augusta in September, half-jokingly and half-proud, to say:

> Allegra is here with me – in good health – & very amiable and pretty, at least thought so. She is English – but speaks nothing but Venetian... she is very droll – and has a good deal of the Byron – can't articulate the letter r at all – frowns and pouts quite in our way – blue eyes – light hair growing *darker* daily – and a dimple in the chin – a scowl on the brow.

He praised her for her 'particular liking of music', and concluded, with an air of triumph, 'is that not B. all over?'[34]

Paternal indulgence had its limits. After Allegra suffered from illness in November, Byron wrote to Hobhouse to say 'the poor child has the fever *daily*... [it] is not dangerous – but very tiresome and tedious'.[35] Byron was worried by his daughter's indisposition, but he also realized that his affairs – in both senses of the word – were incompatible with looking after a small child, especially a mischievous and headstrong one. He ignored a letter Claire wrote to him early in 1820 to complain 'it is now almost a year and a half that I have not seen Allegra', and saying 'my anxiety is now so great, so intolerable that I count the moments til I see her',[36] as he had begun to formulate a plan that was both practical and treacherous.

Claire, who was staying at Pisa, suggested that Allegra should be allowed to join her there. She attempted to appeal to Byron by saying 'I have written to Madame Hoppner on this subject and she seems to think it very proper… you will perhaps have the kindness to return an immediate answer to Mr Hoppner.' [37] Byron did indeed write to Hoppner, but his suggestion was not what Claire desired. After noting that 'Allegra is growing, and has increased in good looks and obstinacy',[38] he was explicit about what he saw as the Shelleys and Claire's mismanagement of her, writing 'I so totally disapprove of the mode of children's treatment in their family – that I should look upon the child as going into a hospital.' Allowing that she was 'sometimes vain and obstinate', but 'always clean and cheerful', Byron determined that 'in a year or two I shall either send her to England – or put her in a convent for education'. He unconvincingly stated that 'whenever there is convenience of vicinity and access – her mother can always have her with her', but his truer feelings were revealed by his statement that 'the child shall not quit me again – to perish of starvation, and green fruit – or be taught to believe that there is no deity'.[39] Even by Byron's standards, this combined hypocrisy with breathtaking cruelty.

Claire's letters to Byron over the next few months reveal both her despondency at her continued estrangement from her daughter and also a dignified and mature attitude towards her unfortunate situation that belies his dismissal of her as a ranting madwoman. Always addressing him as 'my dear friend', she presented herself as a mild-mannered supplicant, stressing how 'I have always been anxious to avoid troubling you unnecessarily', but clearly stating that 'I beg you to remember that I did not part with her at

Milan until I had received your formal & explicit declaration that
I should see my child at proper intervals.'[40]

Byron informed Claire via the Hoppners that he did not wish
her to see her daughter. Her calm, if anguished, reply stressed both
that Allegra would not be exposed to Shelley's apparently atheistic
influence* but also that 'this letter is an appeal to your justice since
every feeling of kindness towards me seems to have died within
you'.[41] The obvious answer – that whatever 'kindness' he exhibited
towards her took place out of boredom and opportunism – was
not made, but nor was any other response. Byron continued to
ignore her letters, believing that she was not worthy of being dealt
with on equal terms. Besides, by now he had a new and impressive
mistress, Teresa Guiccioli, who occupied his attention. Claire was
nothing more than a plaything who had long outlived her interest.

When she discovered the extent of his contempt for her from
a letter he wrote to Shelley (now lost), she responded with anger
rather than humility. Making her feelings about her troubled relationship with Byron clear, she stated 'I have said before, you may
destroy me, to torment me, but your power cannot eradicate in my
bosom the feelings of nature, made stronger in me by oppression
& solitude.' Surrounded by death and despair, Allegra represented
a longed-for source of hope, and Byron's refusal to allow her to see
her was devastating. She tried to suggest that 'you have a security in
the strength of my affection for my daughter which is better than
bonds & promises',[42] but she knew that she was howling into the
wilderness.

Meanwhile, Byron was angered by what he regarded as Claire's
arrogance and presumption that she should have any role in
her daughter's upbringing. Writing in man-to-man fashion to

---

* Claire did praise him by saying 'I must always feel grateful for his kindness… & every day convinces me more of his moral virtue.' Those who
have believed that some greater intimacy lay between Shelley and Claire
can proffer this as evidence, as well as letters in which he openly longed for
'your sweet consolation, my own Claire'.

Hoppner in September, he talked of 'the most insolent letters' that he had received, and metaphorically threw his hands in the air, as he bemoaned 'see what a man gets by taking care of natural children!' He sneered at Claire as an 'atheistical mother', and saw her as an impediment to Allegra's happiness, saying 'if Claire thinks that she shall ever interfere with the child's morals and education – she mistakes – she never shall – the girl shall be a Christian and a married woman'. He concluded the letter in heartlessly blunt style: 'to express it delicately – I think Madame Claire is a damned bitch – what think you?' Hoppner's response has not survived, but it seems unlikely that the British consul-general would have chosen such insulting language to describe a countrywoman of his.

By now, Claire was used to life in her adopted country, as were the Shelleys. Mary wrote to Maria Gisborne of how 'we are tired of roving',* and Claire had settled into life in and around Florence. Byron and Shelley's friend Thomas Medwin, who encountered her in November 1820, wrote of how 'she might have been mistaken for an Italian, for she was a brunette with very dark hair and eyes'. Allowing that 'she was not strictly handsome at that time, for she had had much to struggle with', Medwin still believed that 'she was engaging and pleasing, and possessed an *esprit de société* rare among our countrywomen'. However, the fragile sense of calm that she exhibited was to be shattered within months.

On 19 January 1821, Byron wrote in his journal both that he felt 'rather in low spirits' and that he had 'thought of a plan of education for my daughter Allegra, who ought to begin with her studies'.[43] This soon crystallized, with him telling Hoppner the next month that 'Allegra is well – but not well disposed – her disposition is perverse to a degree'. He had made up his mind to do something that he had wished for Caroline and Claire, among others; she would be sent to a convent for her education.[44] Once the idea had come to

* She is probably alluding to Byron's 1817 poem 'So, we'll go no more a-roving'.

him, he acted swiftly, entering Allegra into the convent school of San Giovanni Battista in Bagnacavallo, in the province of Ravenna, on 1 March. He had few scruples about his decision, believing it the best thing for both Allegra and himself, but he underestimated the ferocity of Claire's reaction when she was informed of her daughter's removal. Typically, he did not tell her directly, but instead left it to Shelley to pass on the unwelcome news.

Claire noted in her journal of 15 March that she had 'spent a miserable day' when she learned what had become of Allegra. For a few days, she stewed in angry frustration, and then she wrote a letter full of vitriol to her former 'dear friend'. She attacked convents as being adverts for 'the state of ignorance & profligacy of the Italian women', which led to their becoming 'bad wives & most unnatural mothers', and condemned Byron for having sentenced their daughter to 'a life of ignorance & degradation'. She openly repented of her previous infatuation with him, and scornfully wrote 'I alone, misled by love to believe you good, trusted to you, & now I reap the fruits'. [45]

She instead proposed that Allegra be removed from the convent and educated in England. Although this was close to Byron's own earlier idea, her suggestion of it was enough to make her quixotic tormentor reject it. He, meanwhile, appealed to the presumably weary Hoppner for moral support, asking him 'whether I do or do not deserve such a piece of objurgation', and claimed 'I had no resource but to place [Allegra] for a time in the convent... where she will at least have her learning advanced & her morals and religion inculcated'. His desired religion for her was Catholicism – 'which I look upon as the best religion as it is assuredly the oldest of the various branches' – and he was resolved his action, even as he contradicted his earlier statements by stating 'I by no means intended nor intend to give a *natural* child an *English* education'. The convent, 'the best I could find for the present', would have to do instead. As for 'the promise made at Geneva' that Claire would continue to be involved in her daughter's upbringing,

Byron blithely rewrote history, lying 'I have no recollection [of it] – nor can I conceive it possible to have been entered into'.[46] By abnegating responsibility, he could cast himself in the role of kind, caring father, doing the best for his child, rather than the heartless and callous monster that Claire had come to believe him to be. It was a bravura performance, but the leading man was in danger of forgetting his lines.

Her daughter's forced removal caused Claire hideous sorrow. Her journal entries around this time indicate her misery; on Thursday 12 April, she wrote 'very unhappy all day' after receiving news of Byron's refusal to allow Allegra to be sent to school in England, and this carried on until late in the month, when she wrote on 30 April that she had 'very low spirits & suffer from headache'. She had just turned twenty-three, but her birthday was 'odious' to her. Like Mary, she suffered from severe depression, and her unhappiness lasted for months afterwards, with diary entries tersely reading 'low spirits' or 'I am in bad spirits'. She referred little to Byron, save one cryptic note, 'Hint for Don J – as much as one can love, who hates himself'. By then, the first two cantos of Byron's epic satire *Don Juan* had been published, and the next three would appear in August that year. Although it was issued anonymously, few remained ignorant of the author's true identity.

Although Hoppner suggested to Byron that Allegra might have been happier at school in Switzerland, her father was insufficiently concerned about his daughter's wellbeing to uproot her. In fact, he replied to Hoppner that 'it is some consolation that both Mr & Mrs Shelley have written to approve entirely my placing the child with the nuns for the present', and that 'no one but the amiable Claire disapproves of it in the natural circumstances'. That the child's mother was unhappy did not impinge on Byron's justification of his actions, especially as he pontificated that 'it has always appeared to me that the moral defect of Italy does *not* proceed from a conventual education', and that, in a dig at his own country, 'in England the only homage which they pay to virtue – is hypocrisy'.[47]

He confirmed his decision to Hoppner in another letter later that month, in which he stated '[Allegra] is so happy where she is, that perhaps she had better have her *alphabet* imparted in her convent'. Only a vague intimation that 'I will take some decisive step in the course of the year'[48] hinted at any equivocation.

The only first-hand news that Claire received of her daughter came when Shelley visited her while he stayed with Byron at Ravenna in August that year. Her brother-in-law reported that the girl was 'grown tall & slight for her age', and, although she was 'much paler', with a 'somewhat altered' face, she 'has a contemplative seriousness which, mixed with her excessive vivacity which has not yet deserted her, has a very peculiar effect in a child'. He hinted that this was due to the 'very strict discipline' that she was under, and also took care to lambast her Catholic upbringing, describing it as 'such trash' for such a 'sweet creature'.[49] Only when he was about to depart did her livelier side emerge in running around and shouting. She also asked Shelley when her father should visit, and to bring 'la mammina' – a reference to Teresa Guiccioli, with whom she had become acquainted, rather than her actual mother.[50] Her father remained neglectful. Allegra wrote a poignant letter shortly after Shelley's visit, in Italian, to her 'dear Papa', saying 'I should like so much a visit from my Papa as I have many wishes to satisfy. Won't you come to please your Allegrina who loves you so?'[51] Byron responded neither to his daughter nor the abbess at the convent, but scrawled on the letter, which he then sent to Hoppner, that while he believed it 'sincere enough', he believed she wished to see him primarily 'to get some parental gingerbread – I suppose'.[52] Incomprehension when it came to the women in his life was mixed with contempt.

Although Byron and Claire never met again, there was a curious encounter of sorts between the two in November 1821. Byron was travelling from Ravenna to Pisa, and Claire, not wishing to be in his vicinity, left for Florence on 1 November. She wrote in her journal that 'just before Empoli… we passed Lord Byron and his travelling train'. For a brief moment, Claire again caught sight of the man who had been her great love and greater nemesis. He was travelling in some style, with several wagons including every-thing from furniture and clothing to a large menagerie of animals; Shelley had described these as encompassing everything from horses and dogs to monkeys and peacocks. As Claire glimpsed the lordly coach and four draw past, crowned by the pale majesty of its inhabitant, she felt no lost love or new hatred, only fear that Allegra had been abandoned entirely in the convent so that Byron could be rid of another encumbrance.[53]

Claire next contacted her former love in February 1822. Driven to frustration by her continued inability to see her daughter, she announced that she wished to leave Italy to continue her 'disagree-able and precarious course of life', but that before she did, she wanted to be reunited with Allegra. She knew that Byron would not listen ('I am sensible how little this letter is calculated to per-suade'), so all she could do was to appeal to him as 'the author of my happiness in the far off place to which I am obliged to go', and to hope that her 'dear friend' would not 'make the world dark to me as if my Allegra were dead'.[54] She was right in thinking that Byron would ignore her letter, as he had her others, and so con-sidered more drastic action, namely kidnapping Allegra from the convent. This would involve Shelley forging a letter of permission from Byron, and, when it was suggested, he wrote angrily to her to criticize 'the thoughtless violence of your designs', and denounced the plan as 'pregnant with irredeemable infamy', and liable to lead to a challenge of a duel from Byron when it was discovered.[55] To Claire's deep disappointment, the plan was abandoned. In retro-spect, it would have been better had it gone ahead.

❧

Italy in 1822 was not a place where the young and vulnerable thrived. Illness was rife, as was demonstrated by the premature deaths of Mary's two children, and medical care was patchy and often inefficient. If a small boy or girl caught any of the diseases that stalked the country, their chances of survival were low, regardless of the wealth or stature of their parents. Claire knew of the risks that Allegra faced by remaining in the convent, but, without Shelley or anyone else to assist her in surreptitious skulduggery, she was powerless to act.

In early April, there was an outbreak of typhoid in the convent at Bagnacavallo. Normally caused by contaminated food or water, the disease was often fatal. The inhabitants of the convent took refuge in prayer, but it was not enough. Allegra contracted a fever on 13 April, and despite being repeatedly bled by the doctors, who believed she had suffered a consumptive attack, her strength never returned. A report on 14 April that she was out of danger was inaccurate. Five days later, Allegra died of 'a convulsive catarrhal attack',[56] without either her mother or father present. She was only five years old.

It was a sudden end to a short and eventful life, and greeted with sorrow by all. Byron wrote to Murray three days later to describe her death as 'a heavy blow for many reasons, but [it] must be borne, with time',[57] and announced his intention of having her buried in Harrow. He wrote in a less businesslike manner to Shelley the next day, when he described Allegra's end as 'stunning and unexpected', and hinted that his true feelings would have to be concealed beneath a façade of calm, saying 'I have borne up against it as I best can, and so far successfully, that I can go about the usual business of life with the same appearance of composure, and even greater.' While refusing to take any share of the blame – 'I do not know that I have any thing to reproach in my conduct' – he nevertheless hinted at submerged guilt, writing 'it is a moment when we are apt to think that, if this or that had been done, such event might have been prevented... I suppose that Time will do his usual work – Death has done his.'[58]

While not an apology, this was the closest Byron came to acknowledging that his actions with Allegra had been thoughtless or callous. Nonetheless, when he wrote to Shelley, he was probably not aware that Claire remained ignorant about the fate of her daughter. She had written to Mary on 9 April to say 'I am truly uneasy for it seems some time since I last heard any news from Allegra… I fear she is sick.' Knowing how distraught she would be at the news, Shelley and Mary attempted to delay telling her, until a chance remark in conversation revealed Allegra's fate on 30 April. Her worst fears, hinted at in her February letter to Byron, were confirmed; all was lost.

There is no entry in Claire's journal of 1822 between 13 April and 6 September. However, these five months were not merely spent in grief; as she later wrote, 'I found a stern tranquillity in me suited to the time'. This 'stern tranquillity' was effective enough a façade for Shelley to inform Byron the following month that 'Claire is much better; after the first shock, she has sustained her loss with more fortitude than I had dared hope'. He was only partially correct. She had sublimated her bitterness and anger into a controlled calm that would last for most of the rest of her life. She would never marry, nor have any further children.

She was kept in ignorance as to Byron's wishes for their daughter's burial, and it would be years until she discovered her whereabouts in Harrow Church.* In the meantime, she had to content herself with a lock of her daughter's hair and a miniature. Ironically, these small trinkets were the keepsakes that she had longed for during Allegra's life, and frequently petitioned Byron for.

❧

Claire would outlive both Shelleys and Byron. She died on 18 March 1879 at the age of eighty, having metamorphosed from a giddy, romantic girl into a bitter spinster, for whom every mention of Byron's name was anathema. She never forgave him for his treatment of both her and Allegra, saying of him late in life that 'never, never, neither here nor in eternity can I, nor will I, forgive

---

* As Allegra, the 'natural child', could not be buried in the church, she was placed in an unmarked grave near the church's entrance.

the injuries he inflicted upon my defenceless child', and that her daughter was 'the only thing I had to love – the only object in the world I could call my very own'. And yet she maintained what she called 'a profound silence with every one on the subject of her wrongs', refusing to offer Byron's biographers the satisfaction of her side of *l'affaire sensationelle.* When Leigh Hunt attempted to elicit her recollections of Byron for his book *Lord Byron and his Contemporaries,* she replied with circumspect tact:

> I think if I were near you, I could readily persuade you to omit all allusion to Clare [sic]… poor Clare has been buried in entire oblivion, and to bring her from this, even for the sake of defending her, would I am sure pain her greatly and do her mischief. Would you permit this part to be erased?[59]

And yet one recently discovered document appears to give the lie to Claire ending her days in silence. A fragment of autobiography that she wrote late in her life attacked both Byron and Shelley, criticizing them as nothing more than 'monsters of lying, meanness, cruelty and treachery'. She reserved especial contempt for Byron, of whom she said 'Lord B became a human tyger slaking his thirst for inflicting pain upon defenceless women who under the influence of free love… loved him'.[60] The loathing of Byron is understandable, but the criticism of Shelley seems initially out of character; after all, their relationship had been a close and apparently harmonious one. And then one remembers Shelley's relief that, after learning of Allegra's death, Claire was able to remain stoic and not to cause a series of embarrassing scenes. For all his talk of freedom and emancipation, Shelley remained quintessentially English in his belief in social propriety. Had he not refused to aid Claire in her scheme to abduct Allegra, she might even have survived.

While Claire sought to remove herself from the orbit of Byron's friends and family as far as she could, Mary took a different tack. She continued to associate with them, and their friendship became especially important after Shelley's death in a sailing accident on 8 July 1822; Byron, acting with a charity and kindness that had been largely absent in his dealings with lovers, ensured that he offered her all the help that he could on behalf of his friend, a man he described to Thomas Moore as a 'clear living flame', and one about whom 'the world was ill-naturedly and ignorantly and brutally mistaken'.[61] Mary would repay this generosity by maintaining relations with many of those in Byron's life, and would do so until her death on 1 February 1851. One of these people would be the woman who was not only central to Byron's final years but, through her actions after his death, would begin the task of maintaining his legacy.

PART V

Teresa

13

This will be my last adventure.

BYRON TO RICHARD HOPPNER,
3 JULY 1819

As a rule, Byron treated women dismally, but excuses have been made on his behalf. He has been called a typically representative upper-class Englishman of the time, emotionally repressed and sexually ambiguous. His status as a rake has been viewed as something noble, even heroic: his blackguardly characteristics merely the finer shadings of a lordly temperament. The poetry, some argue, is indivisible from the life. Character assassination of the various significant people in his life then begins. Caroline was insane; Annabella, a frigid bore; Claire, ludicrously naïve and obsessive; his mother, controlling and drunk, etc. Yet smearing those around him does little to redeem Byron's cruel and sometimes horrifying behaviour. Instead, it has to be asked whether there was anyone who he treated in a normal and decent way. Reports of his casual generosity to servants and strangers are legion, and Augusta was placed on a pedestal, but even she could suffer from his mood swings and manipulative games. Lady Melbourne, the very grandest of *grande dames*, was similarly exalted, but she seems more a partner in game-playing than a genuine friend and mentor. Which leaves Byron's last mistress, Teresa Guiccioli, in the unique role of 'Byron's true love'. As so often with roles, the reality behind the mask is a complex one.

Teresa was born in Ravenna in 1800,* the second daughter of Count Ruggero Gamba. He was a wealthy aristocrat who was also a keen adherent of the liberal politics of the day. Accordingly, he believed that his daughters should grow up educated, and so Teresa was sent to the convent school of San Chiara in nearby Faenza. Here, she acquired a reputation both for quick-witted intelligence and a strong will. San Chiara was unusual in that it offered girls a liberal education that included teaching its pupils rhetoric and eloquence, as well as a grounding in classical literature. This dangerously forward-thinking establishment was closed down by the Catholic church in the 1820s, on the grounds that a little learning was an extremely dangerous thing for young women.

Teresa, however, had already been inculcated with this knowledge, which would later prove useful; her father had proudly once said of her that she 'had been born with a book in her hand'.[1] She had other attractions as well, including shining blue eyes, flowing golden hair and an exquisitely formed mouth, which compensated for her short stature and disproportionately sizeable bust. This self-aware Eve had to be matched to a suitable Adam, but the match proposed was an unlikely one. The bridegroom found for Teresa was Count Alessandro Guiccioli, forty years older than her and already twice married. Guiccioli, a scion of one of the great Ravenna families, was said to be 'possessed of uncommon talents and a subtle intelligence',[2] and had amassed a considerable fortune through a previous advantageous marriage to a much older woman, the Contessa Placidia. He also had attachments to the world of crime, and had spent a brief period imprisoned in the fortress of Castel Sant'Angelo in Rome in 1814. As luck would have it, the man who was to testify against him, a landowner named Domenico Manzoni, was stabbed before his case could be tried, leading to Guiccioli's release. Byron wrote of him that 'they are

---

* The precise date is unknown, although some chroniclers have guessed at its being 1 January. MacCarthy suggests that she was in fact born in 1799 and that she had falsified her age.

liberal with the knife in Ravenna, and the Cavaliere Conte G- is shrewdly suspected of two assassinations already... these are but *dicerie** and may be true or not.'[3]

Regardless of whether there was any veracity to the stories of murder, Guiccioli was certainly a match for any Italian man when it came to displays of virility. He spent much of his first marriage to the Contessa seducing the maids, and, when his wife objected, exiled her to a remote villa, where her most significant action was to draw up a will in her husband's favour before conveniently dying. The mistress who replaced her, Angelica Galliani, drily described by the local vice-legate in a report as 'a young woman of some attractions',[4] gave him six illegitimate children. He married Angelica in an unsuccessful attempt to legitimize these children, and, when his wife died in 1817 while he was at the opera, he was left with a mixture of seven legitimate and illegitimate children, none of whom were even approaching their majority.

Thus, a third wife was needed, and his roving (if apparently short-sighted) eye fell upon Teresa, whom he encountered for the first time in her parents' home in late 1817. She was young, pure, fair and 'sweet seventeen'. He was old, and no stranger to vice. At the Palazzo Gamba Guiccioli examined her 'as if about to buy a piece of furniture',[5] before he concluded that she would suit his purposes. A dowry of 4500 *scudi* – a comparatively small sum, equivalent to around £10,000 in today's money – was agreed, and the bargain concluded. The notice of marriage, drawn up on 20 January 1818, allowed that 'the Cavaliere promises and guarantees to his spouse the Contessa in case of her widowhood – which God avert – a decent and comfortable provision from the Guiccioli fortune, so long as she lives a widow's life, and the interest on her dowry remains with the Guiccioli family',[6] but this was less generosity and more another form of control. Apart from anything else, it appeared that the indefatigable Count intended to last forever.

* Rumour or gossip.

The first year of their union was unexceptional. Guiccioli spent the dowry immediately, 'in such a manner as to attain the level of the other good families of the city',[7] and drew up a series of maxims for Teresa to obey at all times. These included the injunction that she should 'determine always to be a solace to me, and never a trouble', that she had to be 'satisfied with modest amusements and suitable provision', and that she must be 'true and frank, so that she will have no mysteries from me, and that I may always see into her heart'. Finally, and one imagines Guiccioli chortling merrily as he wrote this, she was commanded 'let her be faithful and beware of any appearances to the contrary'. No such demand of fidelity was made of Guiccioli, nor would it have been expected of him.

At first, Teresa appeared to be deeply in love with the count. The letters that she wrote him were addressed to 'my adorable husband and friend', and spoke of how 'you are all my soul, you are the greatest good I have on earth and I feel that I could not live without you'.[8] Even allowing for the formal exaggeration that an educated woman would have maintained in letters to her spouse, there is the hint of real passion in her description of how 'my family's love has become nothing for me... I send you a kiss as different from the one I sent my brother as fire is from light'. She stressed her virtues of thrift and prudence, and made every attempt imaginable to play the role of dutiful and adoring wife.

This did not last. Before long, Guiccioli's bullying and controlling nature showed itself, and her letters soon exchanged the intimate *tu* for the impersonal *voi*, as endearments and expressions of love gave way to household minutiae. Wearily, she commented that 'I shall not take the risk of interfering in any domestic matter without a sign from you... [I feel] sure that it is all the same to you whether I am there or not.'[9] She found Guiccioli's stepchildren an irritation, as they treated her more like a servant than a stepmother, and her husband offered no assistance. She might also have heard wider rumours of his true nature, as well as seeing it for herself; one police report described him as possessing 'a sordid, miserly spirit', and her letters referred to 'his *strange* habits', as well as making much of his so-called 'eccentricity'.[10] She began to feel trapped and frustrated. Even the arrival of a child did not help; the infant, a boy, died in November when he was just four days old. Another distraction was all too necessary, and she took a lover, a former army officer named Count Cristofo Ferri. His aristocratic appellation was probably false; she described him subsequently as 'a licentious brazen satyr' and 'not a count, but a peasant, not a gentleman, but a horse driver'. A more attractive prospect had to present itself, and he duly did.

꙳

Byron and Teresa first encountered one another in 1818, at the house of Countess Albrizzi. However, the meeting was an unremarkable one, and it was not until the following April that they were formally presented to one another at a salon of Countess Maria Benzoni's in Venice. Teresa and Guiccioli had arrived in the city two days before, and she was tired from the journey and reluctant to attend, not least because she was mourning the deaths of her mother and sister. Byron, who had come to the salon with his friend Alexander Scott, was in similarly downcast mood. Teresa later wrote that 'Lord Byron, too, was averse from forming new acquaintances, and was unwilling any more to expose himself to their consequences'.[11] This could be described more bluntly; Byron complained to Murray that 'I was in a state of great exhaustion... and I was obliged to reform my "way of life" that was conducting me from the "yellow leaf" to the ground with all deliberate speed.'[12]

Byron claimed in the same letter that he was better 'in health and morals', but this resolution was tested when he was introduced to Teresa by Countess Benzoni. Although he initially demurred, saying 'you know very well that I don't want lady acquaintances; if they are ugly, because they are ugly – and if they are pretty, because they are pretty',[13] Scott persuaded him to meet her. The countess introduced him as the 'peer of England and its greatest poet',

and Byron responded with his usual self-effacing charm, employing his underlook once more and what Teresa later called 'one of
those charming smiles that Coleridge admired so much and called
the Gate of Heaven'.[14] She was enraptured, not least by 'the extraordinary melody of his voice, in his beauty', and after talking with
him about literature, Ravenna and Venice, she thought of him as
a 'celestial apparition whom it seemed to her that she had already
seen and loved before, having seen him in her imagination'. When
the time came to part, her fatigue and unhappiness were replaced
by a new emotion, as 'she rose to leave as if in a dream… these
mysterious attractions are too shaking to the soul and make one
afraid'. Teresa, like so many before, was smitten.

There was little delay in the consummation of their mutual
affection. The day after they had first met, Byron asked to see her
alone, after her husband had retired to bed, and Teresa agreed, on
the condition that he respected her status as a married woman. On
that occasion, she managed to maintain her wedding vows, but he
saw her again the next day, and seduced her in a gondola; as she
subsequently described it, in a later 'confession' to Guiccioli she
made of their affair, 'my strength gave way – for B was not a man
to confine himself to sentiment. And, the first step taken, there
was no further obstacle in the following days.'[15] Her much-prized
honour was swept away, replaced by unlooked-for happiness.

Byron, for once, shared these feelings. He boasted to Hobhouse
with studied casualness that 'I have fallen in love with a Romagnu-
ola Countess from Ravenna', saying 'she is pretty – but has no
tact – answers aloud – when she should whisper – and this blessed
night horrified a correct company at the Benzona's – by calling out
to me "Mio Byron"'.[16] Nonetheless, he was beguiled by her, which
presented a dilemma. He asked rhetorically 'what shall I do! I am
in love – and tired of promiscuous concubinage – & have now an
opportunity of settling for life.'

The relationship between Teresa and Byron was a more complicated one than those with his English mistresses. He was tacitly

offered the office of a *cavalier servente*, effectively the role of a married woman's constant companion and public 'friend'. Although there was the pretence that this was a respectable and noble position that allowed the cuckolded husband to retain his dignity, all parties involved knew that the role of the *cavalier* was that of a lover. Another, more slangy, term for the office was '*cicisbeo*'. Byron had even written about the practice in satiric fashion in his 1817 poem, *Beppo*:

> Besides, within the Alps, to every woman,
> (Although, God knows, it is a grievous sin)
> 'Tis, I may say, permitted to have *two* men;
> I can't tell who first brought the custom in,
> But 'Cavalier Serventes' are quite common,
> And no one notices nor cares a pin;
> And we may call this (not to say the worst)
> A *second* marriage which corrupts the *first*.*

They were initially together for only a week or so, during which time they had 'four continuous days' of 'the *essential* part of the business'. Whether Guiccioli was aware of the nature of his wife's entanglement with her *cavalier* is impossible to know. However, even if he knew that he was a cuckold, he dealt with the affair with the suave assurance of a worldly man who was above petty jealousy. There were indications that he felt something other than delight at Teresa's new friendship; Byron noted that, when she called '*mio Byron*', the count was 'embarrassed', and it was unlikely to have been a coincidence that, a few days after their initial encounter, Guiccioli decided that he and Teresa should leave Venice for their country estate at Cà Zen near Ravenna. When she was told of the news, a distraught Teresa headed to the opera house to tell Byron

---

* Byron was presumably also aware that former *cicisebi* were known as *spiantati*, or 'cast offs'.

of her imminent departure. The production he was attending was none other than Rossini's *Otello*, which made for grim irony. However, when Guiccioli appeared a couple of hours later, there was no evidence of the green-eyed monster; instead, he greeted Byron with suave assurance, and even invited him to visit them in Ravenna before taking Teresa home. For once, the great seducer was outmatched, if not outclassed.

After her departure a couple of days later, Byron did all that he could to maintain close contact, even at a remove. He was aided in this by Teresa's obliging former governess Fanny Silvestrini, who remained her mistress's intimate confidante and friend. The less generous might refer to her as a pander. Nonetheless, she was an invaluable go-between, archly referring to Byron as 'Mylord' whenever she had cause to convey any news of him to Teresa. She was wholly aware of his affection for her mistress, at one point informing her that 'I will tell you that he loves you with the greatest enthusiasm and ardour, of which the most susceptible heart is capable', and that Byron had declared 'this is not a mere flash nor a whim, but a true sentiment – and that you have made on him an impression that can *never* be erased'.[17] Teresa was equally besotted, and allowed Fanny to inform Byron that 'the most afflicted Teresina, on leaving here, begged only one thing of me – that I should try to see Mylord… in order to bring her back more vividly to his memory'.[18]

Fanny was assisted by two more accomplices, a former priest in Ravenna, Padre Spinelli, and Byron's secretary and general *consigliere*, Lega Zambelli. With five people involved in the organization of a love affair there were inevitable complications. Many of Teresa's early letters bemoan the absence of any correspondence from her new lover; one said plaintively:

> What is the matter… that you do not write to me? Have you not had the opportunity… if you could imagine a thousandth part of the joy that one of your letters would have given me,

and of the pain that your silence causes instead, I am sure that you would be seized by such pity for me that you would loathe yourself and call yourself cruel![19]

If this sounds reminiscent of the passion and insincerity of Caroline's correspondence, the idea had occurred to Byron as well. He wrote to Kinnaird to compare Teresa to 'a sort of Italian Caroline Lamb, except that she is much prettier, and not so savage', and offered some wry commentary on the country that he had made his adopted home, saying 'she has… the same noble dis*dain* of public opinion – with the superstructure of all that Italy can add to such natural dispositions. To be sure they may go much further here with impunity.' Only in his belief that her affair with him was 'her first outbreak since marriage' was Byron mistaken, but the thuggish Ferri was no match for the English lord. He ended the letter to Kinnaird with the uncharacteristically frank admission that 'I am damnably in love – but they are gone – gone – for many months – and nothing but Hope – keeps me alive seriously'.[20]

Byron wrote to Teresa in Italian, in an altogether different style from the witty, colloquial manner in which he corresponded with others. While his linguistic skill was adequate for his purpose, he felt that he had to apologize for his mistakes, claiming 'the more barbarous my style, the more will it resemble my Fate away from you'. He grandly declared that 'you, who are my first and only love, who are my only joy, the delight of my life… you have gone away – and I remain here alone and desolate'.[21] This was not entirely true; a letter of the next month to Murray talked ruefully about 'a rendezvous with a Venetian girl' named Angelina, whose eighteen years belied a remarkable confidence about matters sexual. Falling into the Grand Canal 'and not choosing to miss my appointment by the delays of changing', he was asked why he could not divorce Annabella, 'my mathematical wife'. Byron's answer, 'that the status of cuckoldom was not quite so flourishing in Great Britain as with us here' was not enough for his pert temptress, who responded by briskly asking 'can't you get rid of her?', and, when Byron incredulously asked 'you would not have me *poison her*?' simply 'made me *no answer*'.[22] Passion and the potential for violent death were inextricably linked, and the chance of something similar happening to Byron at Count Guiccioli's hands, especially given his reputation, remained a risk.

Byron continued to correspond with Teresa, but underneath his high-blown declarations of undying love and passion – 'I kiss you with all my soul – a thousand and a thousand times'[23] – a petulant dissatisfaction at not being able to get his own way was beginning to creep into his letters. Although Teresa had suffered a miscarriage at the beginning of May, he wrote to Kinnaird's brother Charles with little sympathy, saying 'it was my intention to have left Venice tomorrow… but the Lady has miscarried… what the deuce should I do in the mean time without the possibility of seeing her'. Announcing his intention to depart on 20 May 'and leave the rest to the protecting deities', Byron's bravado disguised any deeper concern he felt. Nonetheless, his epistle ended in high style, as he mused 'if they open our letters at the post, they will be edified by the correspondence, it is all hitherto about whores and rogues'.[24]

Despite Guiccioli's invitation to Ravenna, Byron hesitated before making the journey, whether out of respect for Teresa's marital state, her indisposition or simply out of prudence. The previous men he had cuckolded, most notably William Lamb, had not been insignificant figures, but were bound by a certain English reserve. In a country where poisoning and assassination were seen as common means of removing obstacles, Byron knew that to openly continue his relationship with Teresa beneath her husband's roof was laden with danger.

In his heightened emotional state, he wrote to Augusta in more explicit terms than he had done since he left England. Talking of how 'we have now nothing in common but our affections & our relationship', he went on to say 'I have never ceased nor can cease to feel for a moment that perfect & boundless attachment which bound & binds me to you – which renders me utterly incapable of *real* love for any other human being – what can they be to me after *you?**[25] Whether or not Byron meant what he wrote, it sat uneasily with the similar sentiments that he expressed to Teresa, and no doubt conveyed to Angelina and any other women he wished to impress. Lasting sincerity was seldom in Byron's purview.

Eventually, at the beginning of June 1819, he headed to Ravenna. Still unsure of what the upshot would be, he commented to Hoppner that 'I am proceeding in no very good humour – for La Guiccioli's instructions are rather calculated to produce an éclat – and perhaps a scene… now to go to cuckold a papal count, who, like Candide – has already been "the death of two men, one of whom was a priest"'.[26] His bad mood had arisen because he felt that his summons reduced him to the level of the anxious *cicisbeo*, with Teresa's infrequent and often contradictory letters leaving him uncertain as to under what auspices he was going to her. He complained to Hobhouse that 'the die is cast, and I must (not figuratively but *literally*) pass the Rubicon… everything is to be risked, for a woman one likes'.[27]

It was not to be the final risk that he took.

∽

Able to switch between personal irritation and poetic ardour, Byron began writing a love lyric for Teresa, 'Stanzas to the Po', in which he viewed the river as the conduit that lay between the two of them, simultaneously keeping them apart and uniting them. He later claimed that the poem was written 'in red-hot earnest', and it has a romantic charge that feels drawn from experience, as well as from literary skill:

> The current I behold will sweep beneath
> Her native walls, and murmur at her feet;

* Augusta passed the letter to Annabella, remarking 'he is surely to be considered a maniac'.

Her eyes will look on thee, when she shall breathe
The twilight air unharmed by summer's heat.

She will look on thee,—I have looked on thee,
Full of that thought; and from that moment, ne'er
Thy waters could I dream of, name, or see,
Without the inseparable sigh for her!

It is a mark of his contradictory character that Byron could write this poem on 2 June and then complain to Hoppner, the same day, of his 'not very good humour'.

When he finally arrived at their chosen rendezvous point of the theatre in Ravenna on 10 June, he was disappointed not to be greeted by Teresa. Instead, he was met by the Secretary General of the province, Count Giuseppe Alborghetti, who shocked Byron by mistakenly informing him that Teresa was at death's door. Just as he was about very publicly to lose control of his emotions, declaring 'if the lady should die, I hope I will not survive her', salvation came from the *deus ex machina* appearance of Guiccioli, who greeted his wife's lover with the welcome news that Teresa, although weak and still suffering from the effects of her recent miscarriage, was not in danger. He then escorted Byron to the city's only hotel, the insalubrious Albergo Imperiale, and promised the *cavalier* that he might visit Teresa shortly. Then he departed, and left a disconsolate Byron with the knowledge that, for the first time since he had quit England, he was no longer master of his situation.

When Byron and Teresa were finally reunited on the evening of 11 June, the meeting was unsatisfying. The combination of her illness and their inability to talk privately, given the presence of Guiccioli and other relations of hers, left both in a sense of frustration and misery. Byron returned to his hotel and wrote to her in anguish: 'it is impossible for me to live long in this state of torment – I am writing to you in tears – and I am not a man who cries easily. When I cry, my tears come from the heart, and are of blood.' His comparative lack of fluency in Italian saw his usual wit and sophistication desert him. A central problem was that Byron, hitherto so assured a seducer, was in turmoil; he plaintively begged Teresa 'pray instruct me how I am to behave in these circumstances – I am not clear as to what it is best to do'. As usual, his primary concern was himself; even as he pleaded 'I am afraid of compromising you', he exclaimed 'if you knew what it costs me to control myself in your presence!'

A melancholy pattern formed. Byron continued to visit Teresa twice a day, chaperoned and constrained. Even as the local worthies besieged the famous poet, he cared little for worldly favour. This atypical abeyance of the limelight led one aristocrat, Conte Giulo Rasponi, to sneer that 'the common opinion is that the Palazzo Guiccioli has impressed him more than the Rotonda and the ruins of Theodoric'.[28] Frustrated, bored and without any care for the gossip that his presence attracted, Byron suggested flight to Teresa. He wrote desperately: 'if trouble arises there is only one adequate remedy, that is, to go away together – and for this a great love is necessary – and some courage. Have you enough?'[29] Her answer was inevitable, and even as she described his plea as 'a masterpiece of passion, of devotion, and of generosity',[30] she was restricted by her role as princess in the tower, complete with Guiccioli as the jailer.

She was well enough the next day for the two to take a carriage drive together to Rimini, which Teresa described as being 'green and fresh from the dews of the morning'. Byron, she thought, was 'happy and melancholy at the same time',[31] and, after an idle remark of hers about how the setting reminded her of the eighth canto of Dante's *Purgatorio*, he began writing his response, the *Prophecy of Dante*. The parallels between their situation and that of Paolo and Francesca, the passionate yet ever-parted lovers, seemed both irresistible and comically hyperbolic. Even as Byron wrote imploring letters virtually every day, the situation seemed to have arrived at an impasse. As for Guiccioli, the principal obstacle to their union, he remained an enigma. Byron wrote to Hoppner to muse 'I can't make *him* out at all', but knew the potential danger of his situation, blackly noting 'if I come away with a stiletto in my gizzard some fine afternoon – I shall not be astonished'.[32]

Teresa's health showed no firm signs of rallying, and Byron commented in a letter to Webster in early July that 'her symptoms threaten consumption – but I hope better'.[33] He was more explicit to Hoppner, and talked of how 'her symptoms are an obstinate cough of the lungs – and occasional fever etc… she bears up most *gallantly* in every sense of the word – but I sometimes fear that our *daily* interviews may tend to weaken her… I cannot tell you the effect [her illness] has upon me'.[34] Nonetheless, her illness had sent him into a philosophical state of mind, and he outlined a decision he had made:

> I have done with the passion forever – it is my *last* love – and as to libertinism – I have sickened myself of that as was natural in the way I went on – and I have at least derived that advantage from the vice – to *love* in the better sense of the word – *this* will be my last adventure.[35]

Even as he behaved towards Claire with callous disregard, he vowed that Teresa would occupy his attentions from then on. He knew that his health had been worn down by years of self-indulgence; as he said to Webster, 'my size is certainly increased considerably… my hair is half grey, [and] though not gone, seems going, and my teeth remain by way of courtesy'. He exaggerated, but the dashing rake who cut a swathe through London's salons and boudoirs alike had been replaced by a prematurely middle-aged man, limping to his would-be mistress's door for his twice-daily interviews. These, however, produced the usual connection; Byron boasted to Scott that 'our amatory business goes on *well* and *daily* – not at all threatened by extraneous matters or the dreaded consumption'.[36]

Others tried to intervene. Teresa's brother Pietro hinted to her of

Byron's English wickedness, not least his poor treatment of his wife, which led to her angry reply that 'I have had constant proofs of the extreme goodness of his heart!'[37] And Hoppner, fearing that Byron would make himself ridiculous – or worse – counselled against his involvement, advising that 'when she is sure of you', he would be cast aside. Byron ignored these hints, and instead concentrated on spending time with Teresa during her recovery. Yet, for the first time since Mary Chaworth, he felt a painful jealousy towards her other attachments, and wrote in anguish 'what is that man doing every evening for so long beside you in your box?' His old self-indulgence reappeared when he declared 'do not fear, tomorrow evening I shall leave the field clear to him', and that 'you have made me despicable in my own eyes – and perhaps soon in those of others'. That Byron was perfectly capable of making himself look ridiculous, even despicable, went unremarked. Teresa, for her part, described this letter as 'magnifique – passionné – sublime mais *très injuste*'.[38] It seems unlikely that a woman slowly recovering from a severe illness, believed by some to have been life-threatening, wished to torment her lover by provocative public flirtations with her husband.

At last, Teresa's health recovered, and she and Byron went for long, exhilarating rides in the countryside together, returning in the late afternoon and then heading to the theatre or to a salon together. They were also able to indulge their mutual passion in the palazzo itself; Byron later gloatingly reminisced about '*those* moments – delicious – dangerous – but *happy* in every *sense...* those rooms! The open doors!'[39] Their conspicuous adherence to one another produced comment. One gossip wrote 'Mylord's love was becoming ever more intense, and more noticeable in a small town. The time chosen for his calls was especially noticed with some criticism, as coinciding with the business or siesta times of the husband, when the wife was most at leisure.'[40] Yet Guiccioli remained serenely unbothered by Byron's presence in his home. Even when he was informed that there was an irreverent sonnet circulating that mocked him as an 'old bird', who should 'hang his horned head' as 'the wife her falcon has a cuckoo made', he kept calm. The only concession that Guiccioli made to the gossip was to arrange a visit for he and Teresa to his property the Palazzo Savioli, in Bologna; however, it was made clear that Byron was more than welcome to visit them there. This he dutifully did, arriving in the city on 10 August, with the intention of playing out the next act in this peculiar drama.

The relationship between Byron and Guiccioli had become oddly amicable. If Guiccioli was unaware that the younger man was cuckolding his wife, he was naïve or simply unobservant, neither of which seems likely. Instead, he wished to keep 'Mylord' in his power as surely as Teresa was, indulging him while nevertheless reminding him of his own superiority in his native country. He asked Byron for a loan, which, according to Teresa's varying accounts, he was either granted or refused, depending on its size. His significant influence can be seen in a letter from Byron to Murray asking whether Guiccioli might be appointed consul or vice-consul for Ravenna. The count's motivation for asking for this was to improve his troubled relations with the papal government. Claiming that his motive was 'a British protection in case of new invasions', Byron allowed that '*my interest* is rare',[41] but it is remarkable that he should go so far on behalf of his mistress's husband. The usual irreverent note was struck when Byron asked that he himself be made British consul at Ravenna 'that I may make him my Vice'.

However, Guiccioli repaid Byron generously for his actions, even inviting him to move into the Palazzo in his absence. This was not as obvious an act of access as it initially appeared, however, as Guiccioli and Teresa left for a visit to his estates, interrupting what she called 'this sweet existence' of languid days of reading, riding and lovemaking. Byron, frustrated by his new-found celibacy, decided on an unambiguously possessive action. He would return to Venice, this time with Teresa in his company. While she claimed her reason for travelling there was to visit his physician, citing a feared prolapse of the womb, none were fooled. Byron wished to return to his adopted city, with Teresa as his acknowledged mistress. Nonetheless, Guiccioli gave his permission, and the two departed in late August.

An idyllic journey followed, with a detour to Petrarch's house in Arquà a particular highlight. They signed the visitors' book there, and Byron may have enjoyed the parallel with defacing the tree at Newstead with his and Augusta's names. Their happiness was only marred by an unexpected reunion with their old acquaintance the Countess Benzoni at Padua; Byron said of her and her own *cavalier servente* Count Giuseppe Rangone that 'they had an embarrassed and comical look about them – they seemed to be wondering whether I deserved their blame or their protection'.[42] The countess knew that Byron had overstepped the accepted protocol when it came to the public flaunting of his relationship, and could only wonder what the consequences would be.

In a token attempt at silencing gossip, Byron and Teresa took separate lodgings when they arrived in Venice. However, this proved to be ineffectual; it was soon reported to Guiccioli that 'owing to the fatigue of the journey, [Teresa] would postpone her removal to the lodging which had been prepared, and would stay instead in the house of Lord Byron, who had kindly prepared an apartment'. Byron, tiring of being the object of intrigue, proposed that they instead visited a villa that he had taken in nearby Mira; Teresa asked and received permission from Guiccioli to accompany him there. They arrived at Mira in late September, and soon settled into a happy pattern of writing, piano playing and, of course, sex. Byron was writing the third canto of *Don Juan*, but Teresa said of it that it was 'no occupation for him, but just a distraction'.[43] He cheerily mused to Hobhouse that 'I have been an intriguer, a husband, a whoremonger, and now I am a Cavalier Servente – by the holy! it is a strange sensation'.[44] He was also buoyed by a visit from Moore, who was impressed by Teresa's 'intelligence and

amiableness'. Even the imminent arrival of Guiccioli at the end
of October did not destroy the romance. Teresa wrote nonchalant
letters to her husband from what she called her 'earthly paradise'
in which she knowingly praised Byron, saying 'I cannot tell you
all the attentions of Mylord'. These left Guiccioli in little doubt
as to what these intimate attentions involved. Even an admonitory letter from her father, warning her against 'this most seductive
young man', and what the world would say about his 'honourable' intentions, made no difference. Teresa was in love, with a
brilliantly desirable man, and that, surely, had to be sufficient.

It was not. Byron may have adopted a high camp persona to ask
Hoppner 'I should like to know *who* has been carried off – except
poor dear *me* – I have been more ravished myself than anybody
since the Trojan war',[45] but he had other concerns, ranging from
the relatively poor commercial performance of the early cantos of
Don Juan to the imminent reappearance of Guiccioli. And then,
on 28 October, he was soaked in a violent rainstorm, leading to
him being bedridden with a fever two days later, just in time for
his romantic rival's arrival on 1 November. Guiccioli had not
arrived merely to collect his wife, but to correct her as well. He
brought with him a series of 'indispensable rules' designed for
her wifely education, including 'let her be completely docile with
her husband', 'let her receive as few visitors as possible' and 'let
her not cause trouble between her husband and her father, or
anyone else'. It was a pointed reference to recent events, but an
emancipated Teresa refused to be cowed, responding with her own
'clauses in reply to yours', which included the final statement 'to
receive, without discrimination, any visitor who may come'. Battle
was joined.

Byron was surprised to find that, when he had recovered from
his illness, Guiccioli came to him in near-supplication, or, as he
put it to Hobhouse, 'he actually came to *me*, crying about it, and
I told him "if you abandon your wife, I will take her undoubtedly... but if, as you say, you are really disposed to live with, &

like her as before, I will not only not carry further disturbance into your family, but even repass the Alps'".[46] This was smart brinks-manship on Guiccioli's part. He had recently intercepted a letter from Gamba to his daughter, offering advice on how to placate her husband, and, rather than further antagonize Teresa's lover, he drew him further into his confidence. Eventually, Byron prevailed upon Teresa to return to Ravenna with her husband, and, after she departed, resolved to depart, saying to Kinnaird 'I shall quit Italy... I have done my duty, but the country has become sad to me; I feel alone in it.'[47]

Byron was distracted in November 1819 by both his love affair and his daughter Allegra's fever, which, although not life-threatening, was sufficiently irksome for him to describe it as 'very tiresome and tedious'. Without these, he might have returned to England, leaving Teresa either to play the role of a dutiful wife, or to find another *cicisbeo*. He told her that 'I am afraid on the one hand of compromising you forever by my return to Ravenna – and its consequences; and on the other hand of losing you – and myself – and all that I have known or tasted of happiness by not seeing you ever again'.[48] Apparently duty rather than pleasure was his guiding conviction, as he wrote to Teresa the next week to inform her 'I am going away in order *to save you*; and I leave a land that has become unbearable without you'. Yet he did not leave, despite going so far as to pack his boxes and prepare to depart Venice on 9 December. It was as if he was waiting for a divine intervention of some kind that would tell him which way to turn.

Finally, the revelation came. When Teresa had returned to Ravenna with Guiccioli, she fell ill again with a resumption of her previous fever. This time her father, fearing that Byron's absence from her side would lead to her falling into a final decline, begged him, with Guiccioli's acquiescence, to head to Ravenna. Byron wrote to Teresa with unconcealed glee to crow that 'love has won... I shall return – and do – and be – what you wish'.[49] He arrived in Ravenna on Christmas Eve, to a relieved and joyful reception from Teresa, and the open approval of his presence from both her husband and father. It seemed that he was triumphant.

Subsequent events might have made him question whose triumph it had really been.

14

The eve of evolutions and revolutions.

BYRON TO MURRAY,
22 JULY 1820

Byron had returned to Ravenna with the lordly assurance of a prince returning to his kingdom, even if his fiefdom remained the Albergo Imperiale. As seemed his due, the New Year's Eve party that Teresa's uncle Marchese Cavalli threw doubled as the poet's formal reception into high society. If Teresa's aim was to show off her lover, she certainly succeeded. Byron archly commented that 'if she seemed to glory in the Scandal, it was not for me to be ashamed of it'.[1] The first time that he had been in the city, he had skulked around between snatched assignations with his lover, but now he was able, as he said, to 'look as much like a *cicisbeo* as I could on so short a notice'.[2]

The idea of a domesticated Byron – tamed by an Italian woman, to boot – would have amused his enemies in England, and he was all too aware of the shift in his situation. He mused to Hoppner 'I have not decided anything about remaining at Ravenna – I may stay a day – a week – a year – all my life', and seemed uncertain about his movements, saying 'I hardly know anything beyond what I have told you.'[3] He soon wearied of his provincial life; early favourable comparisons of Ravenna with the 'Sea-Sodom' of Venice soon gave way to boredom and listlessness, which was noticed by Teresa. She commented that 'Lord Byron began to play his role with pleasure, indeed, but not without laughing at it a little. One would almost have thought that he was a little ashamed.'[4] Life in England seemed abstract and distant, with Byron docile in his new world. The death of George III on 29 January 1820, which might once have drawn a tirade of satirical invective, led to him merely commenting to Murray 'one can't help being sorry'.[5] Yet if he had sympathy for his late king, little was left for his friends; discovering that Hobhouse had been imprisoned for writing an anonymous Radical pamphlet, he shrugged and remarked 'serves him right'.

It was Guiccioli, ironically, who adopted the guise of friendship where Byron was concerned. The count suggested that the Albergo was no place for a man of the poet's stature, and offered him the second floor of Palazzo Guiccioli instead as his permanent residence. If it was a trap, it was at least an elegantly baited one, and Byron weighed the convenience and ease of access to Teresa against the bizarre state of living under his rival's roof. He decided that the Palazzo was sufficiently tempting, and moved himself, his daughter Allegra, his servants, animals and goods under his rival's roof.

It was a strange time. Byron's impatience was obvious when he wrote to Murray that 'the greatest outward respect [in Ravenna] is to be paid to the husbands – and not only by the ladies – but by their Serventi'.[6] The Palazzo belied its grandiose name by being a cramped building with one central staircase, meaning that such assignations as Byron and Teresa undertook were noticed by half the household. Far from the closer proximity increasing their ardour, it became harder and harder for the two to meet, and what notes survive reveal both parties' frustration at the situation. An extra source of misery for Byron was that Guiccioli continued to sleep with Teresa, leading to the most intimate of households. Byron mused gloomily that 'the familiarities of that man may be innocent – but decent they are not'.[7] He seemed oblivious to the irony inherent in a situation where the adulterer resented his lover's husband as the indecent one.

His irritation soon spread to Teresa, whom he came to believe was equally guilty of deceit. He complained to her that 'it would matter little to me who comes or goes, if you showed the sincerity that unfortunately cannot exist in your circumstances, in the present state of Italian morals'.[8] As the weeks crept by, he poured what little energy he had into *Don Juan*. Hints of his dissatisfaction can be seen throughout the poem, such as this observation from the third canto:

> In her first passion woman loves her lover,
> In all the others all she loves is love,
> Which grows a habit she can ne'er get over,
> And fits her loosely – like an easy glove.

Even as he boasted to Hobhouse, recently released from a rather grimmer incarceration, that 'I have settled into regular Serventismo – and find it the happiest state of all',[9] Byron was arguing with Teresa. He wrote tense and unhappy notes, complaining of enforced loans to Guiccioli and justifying arguments with her; the *cavalier* complained 'remember always that you are the one who wants to break off our relationship – and not I – and that I have never wronged you in word, or deed, or thought'.[10] Writing to the courtesan Harriette Wilson, he equivocated over his present state; he allowed that 'I am not miserable, and am perhaps more tranquil than ever I was in England', but still held that 'in answer to your wish that I shall tell you if I was "happy", perhaps it would be a folly in any human being to say so of themselves, particularly a man who has had to pass through the sort of things which I have encountered'.[11]

Finally, three days later, the two months' truce that had existed in the Palazzo Guiccioli came to an end. In a moment of suspicion, or frustration, Guiccioli broke into Teresa's writing desk, and read her correspondence with her lover. There was little ambiguity about its contents. Had he been a younger or more idealistic man, it is probable that he would have demanded a duel, or horsewhipped the adulterer. As it was, the only swords crossed were metaphorical.

Teresa, in a panic, declared to Byron 'I will die, before I cease to be your true friend!',[12] but her sacrifice was not necessary. Guiccioli had acted in a manner unbecoming a gentleman, and Byron's dismissal of him to Teresa ('after having done what he has done – no vileness – no wickedness – on his part would surprise me – or anyone else')[13] – was dictated by his assurance that he, as the *cavaliere*, was in the stronger moral position than the cuckolded husband, who lowered himself to break into desks with all the desperation of a thief in the night.

Nonetheless, Guiccioli felt compelled to act, and so confronted Byron; he stated that his intimacy with his wife had become 'displeasing' to him and asked him to discontinue his visits to her. Byron was outwardly calm and conciliatory, but also mystified. He wrote to Teresa that 'he has known – or ought to have known, all these things for many months... is it only now that he knows of your infidelity? What can he have thought – that we are made of stone – or that I am *more* or *less* than a man?'[14] Byron may have proposed to act in a gentlemanly way and leave Teresa to repair relations with her husband, as she had attempted to do once before, but his apparently selfless actions were undercut by self-regard. He wrote an admonitory note to Teresa in which he not only insisted 'it is better for you in every way to be with Alessandro', but, claiming a status as 'your *true* and sacrificed friend', announced 'the time for deciding was before leaving Venice, to which unhappy place you will remember how, and how much I implored you not to force me to return'. It was with glee that Byron ended his letter 'behold the consequences!'[15] He had abnegated responsibility before, but offering a moral perspective on the matter was a new touch of hypocrisy that seemed to fit with his *cavaliere* persona.

However, salvation was at hand in the form of Count Gamba. Hearing of his son-in-law's poor treatment of Teresa from her, he became incensed, and, after being dissuaded from challenging him to a duel, drew upon his influence with the pope, Pius VII, in order to bring about a divorce between Guiccioli and Teresa. The petition that was asked for was humiliating for Guiccioli in the extreme; not only did it ask for the return of her modest dowry and an annual allowance of 1200 scudi, but it absolved Teresa of any responsibility for the breakdown of the marriage, leaving Guiccioli as the guilty party. There was another factor in the divorce; once Teresa was separated from her husband, she would be free to associate with Byron without fear of public scandal. From her perspective, she could obtain everything that she had ever wanted.

Her lover was more circumspect. He alternated between regarding Teresa as his de facto companion, even going so far as to suggest that he would become her husband 'when circumstances permit', and more customary detachment. Knowing that Teresa had continued to have relations with Guiccioli had made him jealous. In one letter, he referred angrily to her 'yielding to his false blandishments and dotardly caresses'.[16] That she had little choice in the matter did not interest Byron. Nonetheless, his involvement in the affair led him to worry about more than propriety. He breezily remarked to Murray that 'the Countess Guiccioli is on the eve of being divorced on account of our having been taken together quasi in the fact – & what is worse that she did not deny it', and, after a typically waspish observation on sexual mores ('his not wishing to be cuckolded at *threescore* – when everyone else is at *one*') got to the point; he was frightened of the possibility of Guiccioli taking revenge. Remembering what had befallen the murdered landowner Manzoni, Byron made light of the situation ('I am warned to be on my guard as he is very capable of employing "Sicarii"* – this is Latin – as well as Italian… but I have arms… thinking that I can pepper his ragamuffins'),[17] but he knew that the risk of retribution from Guiccioli was high. As he shrugged that 'one may as well end that way as another', Byron knew that his options were narrowing. Fidelity and constancy had never seemed appealing hitherto, but now they threatened to become his destiny.

* 'Dagger men' or assassins.

A further movement in this direction occurred on 12 July 1820, when Byron discovered that a papal decree approving Teresa's annulment on the grounds of Guiccioli's 'extraordinary usage' had been passed. Byron wrote to Moore, with amusement and jubilation, that Guiccioli 'swore that he thought our intercourse was purely amicable, and that *I* was more partial to him than to her, till melancholy testimony proved the contrary'. Allowing that 'I am, of course, in an awkward situation enough',[18] Byron had not been given *droit de seigneur* over Teresa but instead had to tolerate her return to her father's house, where he could only see her under great restrictions. It was almost a worse situation, especially as the decree made it explicit that Teresa was expected to live 'in such laudable manner as befits a respectable and noble lady separated from her husband'.[19] Teresa meekly acceded, replying to the decree by saying 'the favour accorded me by the clemency of the Holy Father gives me back the peace I had lost and assures me a comfortable subsistence'.

Many men in this situation would have simply accepted defeat, returned to England, and attempted to rebuild their lives there. Byron was not one of them.

❧

Teresa's final day as a married woman was as unusual as the rest of her marriage. A thwarted Guiccioli had tried everything to ensure that his wife – or, as he regarded her, his chattel – was not allowed to leave, including asserting that the only obstacle to their happy lives together was his jealousy of Byron. This failed, and eventually he was reduced to mere pettiness. He tried to frustrate her departure, planned for 15 July, by giving orders that none of the horses be allowed to leave Palazzo Guiccioli. This led to the near-comic spectacle of the newly divorced Teresa and Guiccioli having dinner together in the presence of their servants. One of them commented that the two 'made conversation on indifferent matters, with the courteous manners characteristic of both of them'. After a couple of hours of this courtesy, Teresa had had enough, and, accompanied only by her maid and footman, left the house surreptitiously by rented carriage, bound for her father's country house at Filetto.

Bizarrely, Byron was still a guest at the palazzo, along with his daughter, servants and animals, but after the departure of Teresa his position seemed untenable. Guiccioli asked him to leave, and Byron cheerily refused. His reasons were unclear; either he enjoyed tormenting his host or he simply could not be bothered to uproot his makeshift household. Guiccioli, rather than ejecting Byron by force, accepted the status quo and made no further demands of departure. It may have suited his purposes to keep a careful watch on Byron's movements; in any case, Byron and Teresa did not see each other for weeks, even as they continued to correspond in lightly domestic fashion. Byron instead enjoyed the opportunity to write, to spend time with Allegra and to walk in the countryside, unbothered by the need to skulk around Teresa's bedroom door for secret assignations.

Nonetheless, trouble remained. Although he put on a show of unconcern when writing to Teresa about Guiccioli, saying 'you need not be afraid of violence against me',[20] Byron remained paranoid about the possibility of a sudden attack. He reassured Teresa, having sustained a small hand injury while holding a firearm, that 'I assure you that it was only for amusement that I discharged my pistols in the Pineta and not in self-defence against an assassin',[21] but casual violence was rife. Two days before, Byron had jauntily told Murray that there had been 'three assassinations last week here and at Faenza'. The death of a dissolute English poet and aristocrat, especially one whose name had been linked with a scandalous divorce, might not have been especially surprising.

Relief came when Byron encountered Teresa's brother Pietro 'Pierino' Gamba in Ravenna. After he had returned from Rome, Pierino had warned his sister against her scandalous attachment, but when he finally encountered the man that she loved, he was nearly as captivated as she was. It is possible that Byron was drawn to him sexually as well as socially, although he took care to praise him for his views and courage rather than looks; he described him as a 'very fine, brave fellow', who was 'wild about liberty'.[22] Byron, who was becoming increasingly politicized, had found soulmates in the Gamba family, whose dedication to the revolutionary society of the *Carbonari* excited and inspired him. Many of his subsequent actions stemmed from a determination to live up to their trust and belief in him; he was even inducted into the Ravenna branch, the Cacciatori Americani [sic], and made head of it. Had his English friends seen him essentially become a proto-Mafia chieftain, they might either have laughed incredulously, or been entirely unsurprised. He was delighted by the situation, boasting to Murray that 'the 'Mericani call me the *capo*',[23] and generally revelling in the drama. Additionally, his association with the rebellious underworld meant that, had Guiccioli wished to remove this troublesome poet from society, he would have been checked by the thought of repercussions.

Despite the attractions of banditry and rebellion, Byron's feelings for Teresa remained constant, to his surprise. When he confided in her that Guiccioli 'has set spies upon me', he stressed both his bravery – 'I nearly came to blows with a man in the pine-forest… I lost patience and made him understand that if he did not go on his way – it would be the worse for him'[24] – and his love for her. Finally, after weeks of separation, they began to arrange clandestine assignations from the middle of August at her father's home in Filetto. How far Count Gamba welcomed Byron's visits to his daughter is hard to assess, but Byron's new-found friendship with Pierino meant that he was soon regarded as an honoured guest. His charm and charisma made him a far more welcome match for Teresa than Guiccioli ever was.

There were issues at hand other than romance. Whether or not Byron, the *capo* himself, actually took active part in revolutionary activity or not remains uncertain. Teresa later said that he instead saw himself as a moderate figure who favoured carefully reasoned argument rather than impetuous action, but this was only partly true. Byron saw himself as a leader of men, and created a persona for himself as a central figure in the proposed Carbonari uprising. However, knowing that his letters were analysed by the Italian secret police, he sought to play down his own involvement, even as he claimed to Murray that 'we are here upon the eve of evolutions and revolutions... the Neapolitans are not worth a curse... [but] the rest of Italy, I think, might stand'.[25] Although Byron attended meetings of would-be revolutionaries at Ravenna and Filetto, he became frustrated with the absence of cohesive thought and bold deeds.

Instead, he enjoyed spending time with Teresa and her family, gradually inveigling himself into the Gamba dynasty. He boasted to Moore that 'I have lived in the heart of their houses, in parts of Italy freshest and least influenced by strangers – have seen and become (*pars magna fui**) a portion of their hopes, and fears and passions, and am almost inoculated into a family.'[26] He even wrote an insolently familiar letter to Guiccioli, complaining that the Count had misreported his age to another, and mocked him by saying 'if I, in drawing up a memorandum of *your history*, were to make you out to be a man of *seventy*, adding one seventh to your age, you would not assuredly be pleased, and I will certainly not bear this injustice'.[27] Guiccioli's response to this impertinence regrettably does not survive.

Teresa continued to pine for the absent Byron. One letter, anticipating a meeting, saw her declare that 'this hope, and every other that concerns you, makes me feel still capable of pleasure', even as she rebuked him for his gift of a scandalous book, Benjamin Constant's *Adolphe*. The novel, which concerned a doomed and all-consuming love affair between its titular protagonist and an older woman, Ellénore, led Teresa to complain 'how much this book has hurt me' and 'for pity's sake, Byron, if you have other

---

* 'In which I played a great part'.

books like it, don't send them to me!' When she was not being
befuddled by suggestive literature, Teresa enjoyed spending time
with Allegra, who was staying nearby at the Villa Bacinetti, and
in organizing summer parties and picnics. During one of these,
an eclipse took place, and Teresa recalled how Byron's observation
of the phenomenon led to him seeing 'with the eyes of his soul
the incomprehensible and indescribable beauties of the Infinite
Universe'.[28] That he blithely resumed playing a game of bowls a
moment later might indicate that his philosophical speculations
were of a limited nature.

All this time, Byron distracted himself from the composition of
Don Juan with idling. Teresa proposed, not entirely seriously, that
the two of them should indulge in angling as a pastime, saying
'yes, my love, I should like to be a fisherwoman – always, however,
on condition that you would be a fisherman – or at least that you
would not disdain to love and live with your fisherwoman'.[29] Under
the faintly strained faux-childishness (Byron was also referred to,
probably to his chagrin, as 'my very naughty Ducky O'), an edge of
desperation could be detected. With his revolutionary ambitions
thwarted, and his literary ones less successful than hitherto, Byron
was in search of greater distraction than Teresa could offer. The
wry dismissal with which he responded to her frivolities – 'Fishing
and the Fisherwoman! Always something new…'[30] indicated that
he was unimpressed by the prospect of retiring from the madding
crowd, rod grasped in hand.

Relations between Guiccioli and Teresa, non-existent since the
divorce and her flight, were re-established after the death, of sun-
stroke, of his eldest son Ferdinando in mid-September. Although
she candidly admitted that 'I had no cause to love your son;
perhaps, indeed, some to hate him', she hinted that he might turn
his tragedy to some good, telling him 'you will the more readily
be able in future to render great services to your country, because
being freed from more personal claims to turn your mental energies to more glorious thoughts… you will come to fill that place

in Society which you now do not fill'.[31] Teresa and Guiccioli's renewed correspondence wounded Byron, always jealous by nature, although he made light of it after a couple of weeks' brooding. He blustered that 'Pierino may perhaps have exaggerated what I said in a moment of ill-humour', and blamed his mercurial temperament on 'melancholy', saying 'when I have that disease of the spirit – it is better for others that I should keep away'.[32] The following day he explained this further, likening his sadness to 'a temperamental illness – which sometimes makes me fear the approach of madness – and for this reason, and at these times, I keep away from everyone – not wanting to make others unhappy.'[33] Byron had made his excuses not to prepare for a future desertion, but as an explanation of his conduct, a courtesy that few others in his life had ever been treated to.

His interest in revolutionary ideas continued. He wrote a 'noble letter', intended for the Neapolitan people, in which he offered both money and himself in the purpose of 'sharing the destiny of a brave nation defending itself against the so-called Holy Alliance, which but combines the vice of hypocrisy with despotism'.*[34] Whether battling the forces of conservative thought in England or the unholy union of Russia, Austria and Prussia, Byron relished the opportunity to stand as a champion of liberty and freedom. This impressed Teresa, who praised his 'generosity' and 'modesty', along with his 'greatness of soul', exclaiming 'one can only feel compassion for anyone who could remain indifferent after reading it, for God would have deprived him both of intelligence and heart!'[35] Nonetheless, the letter was never made public, only surviving in a draft sent to her; its bearer, a Giuseppe Gigante, ended up literally swallowing the sentiments inside it when arrested by the

---

* The Carbonari, on behalf of the Neapolitan people, were fighting a primitive guerrilla war against the 'Holy Alliance'; their intention was to install their own constitutional monarch and not be ruled from afar. The movement had a certain amount of success in 1820, but collapsed entirely early the following year.

Austrian police force. Byron's grand desires and prosaic reality had collided, with bathetic results.

∾

Teresa was not afraid to criticize Byron. While he might have expected her to praise his poems without reservation, she was unimpressed when he sent her a copy of a new French translation of his work. While Byron described the quality of the version to Murray as an 'abominable travesty', Teresa had greater concerns about some of the poems included. She described 'Fare Thee Well', his poem inspired by Annabella Milbanke, as giving 'the impression of a guilty man *asking for pity*', an incisive and accurate piece of analysis, and was similarly dismissive of 'A Sketch From Private Life', his attack on Annabella's governess Mrs Clermont. Teresa stated that the poems showed 'a certain weakness of character' in their existence, and that 'there is more than talent, tenderness and love; more than was proper towards a woman who had offended you... your *Farewell* in particular does not give any idea of your independent character'. She signed herself 'your true friend and lover for ever',[36] and elicited a rare conciliatory response from Byron, who acknowledged 'perhaps you are right – we will talk about it when we are together'.[37]

When he was not occupied with thoughts of revolution or poetry, Byron had to contend with more everyday matters, such as blackmail. Teresa's former governess and gossip Frances Silvestrini, no longer involved in the intimate details of the couple's relationship, had sought to put her knowledge of their affair into the public domain, unless she was to be paid off. Byron, made aware of her demands, damned her as 'false, sly, arrogant, corrupt, pedantic, toadying and a liar', wished that she head straight to hell, and sneered at her 'forced compliments' about him.* Nev-

---

* Byron seems to have become over-excited in the use of some of his language and so the letter has been torn, perhaps in an attempt at censorship.

ertheless, Silvestrini's threats were representative of the difficulty that they faced. Now that Teresa was divorced from Guiccioli and conducting a more or less open relationship with her *cavaliere*, it might have been a wise move to remove other sources of scandal or intrigue from their lives. Yet Byron was unable to live a quiet and peaceful life of domestic contentment.

A police report of the time described the influence and position that Byron had acquired for himself in Ravenna. His habit of walking around with fully armed servants may have been an act of simple pragmatism, in fear of an attack by Guiccioli's hired ruffians, but it also enabled him to be seen as a figure of stature, one who associated with 'the bad characters who form his society', and 'the first revolutionary in Ravenna'. He was said to hand out money 'in order to create a following', and was regarded as a dangerous and subversive presence. Infamy followed him just as doggedly as it had done in England. The key difference this time was that it had arisen from politics, rather than from a woman.

Teresa, while supportive of Byron's activities, remained in Filetto in some trepidation. Byron believed that there was a planned move by the authorities to place Teresa in a convent, as an attack on both her family and him. One of the conditions of the divorce settlement had, after all, been that she should live 'respectably' at her father's home. He praised her for being 'sufficiently heroic and obstinate', and also stated that 'I have seen the correspondence of half a dozen bigots on the subject, and perceive that they have set about it, merely as an indirect way of attacking part of her relations, and myself.'[38] Nonetheless, he knew that he had some powerful enemies, and conceded 'of course I would accede to a retreat on my part, rather than a prison on hers, for the former only is what they *really* want'.[39] He attempted to reassure her, saying 'it is unjust to attack a woman for a man's misdoing… they are attempting to rid themselves of my presence in the papal states'.[40]

As a result of over-exertion, Byron suffered poor health at the beginning of November, and a series of brief, apologetic letters to Teresa hint at his distraction. Revolutionary zeal had cooled as he continued work on *Don Juan,* as well as convincing Teresa's family that their relationship was a respectable one akin to that of brother and sister – although Byron's relationship with Augusta had set an unfortunate precedent in this regard. If anything, he was bored; one letter apologizes for a lack of previous correspondence 'because there was nothing new to say'.[41] Byron's accustomed state was not one of ennui and frustration, and this conveyed itself to Teresa, who became disillusioned with him. He felt the need to apologize for his detachment and physical distance, as can be seen by his statement to her that 'if I did not love you – if I *wished to get rid of you without blame*… the most certain way would be to *visit you*'.[42] The self-aware humour only went some of the way towards explaining her irritation, and, finally, she left Filetto for Ravenna in late November, heading to her father's house there. Here, at last, she and Byron would be in close and intimate contact. That he continued to live at the Palazzo Guiccioli added a perverse touch to the continuation of the love affair.

At the beginning of 1821, Byron had his thoughts resting on fate. The bloody death of a local military commandant, a matter of a couple of a hundred paces from his door, reminded him of the ever-present possibility of his own end; Guiccioli and his assailants were never far away. He was sufficiently affected by the man's death to write to a number of correspondents about it, including Augusta, Annabella and Murray. His hatred towards his wife had abated sufficiently for him to venture a couple of bleak jokes, suggesting 'it would have been too great a peace-offering after nearly five years – to have been gracious in the manner, as well as the matter… communications between *us* – are like "dialogues of the dead" or "letters between this world and the next"'.[43] About to turn thirty-three, he wished to cement his position in public consciousness by sending his existing memoirs to Moore. While requesting that they not be published in his lifetime, he stated that 'my first object is the truth, even at my own expense'.[44] His interests lay in creating another account of himself, seeking to extend beyond the libertine and misanthrope of repute. He even began a journal again for the first time since 1816, although it only lasted a couple of months. His feelings of boredom were made explicit in his entry of 6 January, when he asked 'what is the reason that I have been, all my lifetime, more or less *ennuyé*?'[45]

He added that, although he was 'agitated', he was '*not* in depressed spirits'. This comparative lull in excitement was down to the more harmonious relations that he enjoyed with Teresa throughout the first half of 1821. In their closest proximity for months, they saw one another daily, giving their relationship a domestic quality that both enjoyed. Teresa was pleased that, as she lived in 'a dwelling even more noble and comfortable than the one she had left in Palazzo Guiccioli', she could be 'happy and cherished by her whole family', just as Byron's own happiness was 'increased by finding himself also the object of the regard and liking of the whole town'.[46] After taking a perverse pride in being the most notorious man in London and Venice, Byron had found a niche for himself, accepted and even beloved by his adopted people. Even as he debated the idea of marrying Teresa and making a commitment that might have seemed unthinkable even a few years before, he allowed himself to relax in her company, enjoying evenings of listening to her play 'simple popular airs' on the piano or harp, or engaging in political or social discussion.

It was not all calm at home. After her criticism of his earlier poetry, Teresa was upset by the attacks Byron received after the first two cantos of *Don Juan* were published, and his attempts to tell her that the latest three cantos – 'written under a *gentler* influence' – were of a less controversial nature made little impression. She begged him not to continue writing something that could only damage his reputation, and, either in an attempt to humour her or because he saw the sense in what she was saying, Byron promised that '[I will] not write any more of *Don Juan* until you yourself authorize it'. While this might have begun as an indulgence, it became conviction; by July he was prepared to write to Murray to inform him that 'you will therefore look upon these three cantos as the last of the poem… the reason of this is not at first obvious to a superficial observer of foreign manners, but it arises from the wish of all women to exalt the *sentiment* of the passions'.[47] This led Teresa to thank him in exalted terms, claiming that 'never shall I be able to express to you the satisfaction I feel, so great is the sentiment of joy and trust with which this sacrifice you have made has inspired me'.[48]

For all the literary discussion and amity at home, political intrigue remained the watchword on the streets of Ravenna. Although there were more rumours and whispers than actual action, an uprising against the Austrians seemed likely at any time, and, had it happened, Byron no doubt had visions of himself leading a Neapolitan army to glory. His hopes were not to be realized. Due to a combination of the better-equipped Austrian army and the lazy, ill-disciplined Neapolitans, the nascent rebellion had been put down by 23 March, with the Austrians occupying Naples. Byron still attempted to preach revolution, but his heart was no longer in it. When Teresa declared 'the Italians must now return to making operas', he quipped '*that* and macaroni are their forte', and 'motley their only wear'. Although 'there are some high spirits among them still',[49] he knew that these 'high spirits' could just as easily manifest themselves in underhand acts of street violence as in noble revolt; he noted that 'a German spy… was stabbed last week… the moment I heard that he went about bullying and boasting, it was easy for me, or anyone else, to foretell what would occur to him'.[50]

In this half-soporific, half-paranoid climate, Byron had few certainties, other than his love for Teresa. Yet it seemed impossible that she and her family should escape suspicion, and, on 10 July, Pierino was arrested, although Teresa, warned beforehand, had managed to destroy any incriminating documents in his rooms. Nonetheless, the hitherto untouchable Gamba family were now enemies of the state, and Count Gamba was given orders to leave Ravenna within a day. A consequence of his departure was that

Teresa, living under his protection, had to accompany him to an uncertain destination. If the family's enemies had devised this banishment as a ruse to expel Byron, it was an elegant one. Either he would be parted from Teresa and a scandalous extra-marital affair would come to an end, or he would accompany the family into exile and deprive the authorities of the need of directly confronting a popular and high-profile figure, whose death or imprisonment could turn him into a martyr for a disaffected people. It is even conceivable that Guiccioli had a hand in the situation, viewing it as a satisfactory means of solving a problem that had occupied his attention for too long.

As usual, Byron's enemies had underestimated both his resilience and stubbornness. Gamba asked Teresa to join him in his journey, and instructed her to 'strength your spirit' and to 'take courage, for your good and for ours',[51] but this sent her into paroxysms of anguish and misery that led her to beg Byron, whom she described as 'the only tie that still holds me to life',[52] to come to her aid. He did so, acting out of both love for her and realization of the dangers inherent in the unsettled country. He wrote to Gamba, and successfully pleaded for Teresa to be given a brief stay of execution, before suggesting to his mistress that she would be better placed in Bologna with her old tutor Professor Costa, before heading to the safer environs of Florence. She agreed, and left a few days later, only to fly into a fit of panic at the thought of losing Byron. His response, written as if in frustration, told her to 'calm yourself and continue your journey, in the certainty that we shall see each other again soon', as well as stressing that her 'unreasonable grief' could lead to 'real folly', and that her stated intention of returning to Ravenna 'really makes me think that you wish to be put in a *convent* – as was threatened'.[53] A further letter of a few days later chastized her for being 'not very kind' in remaining in Bologna, and again raised the probability of her being sequestered unless she was to accede to his suggestions. Eventually, she left in early August, frightened and confused by the situation.

Byron continued to be comfortable in Ravenna, despite commenting in a letter to Hoppner that all his friends were either 'exiled or arrested'.[54] He was sufficiently sure of his own safety to consider a move to Geneva for both himself and Teresa's family, claiming that all he wished for was 'tranquil asylum and individual freedom'. However, he soon abandoned this idea, stating to Pietro that 'the idea of returning to Switzerland is most unpleasant – for many reasons – which you will become well aware of when we are there and it will be too late'. Recollections of his dealings with Claire were vivid, not to mention the 'canny and rascally' inhabitants of the country; he described how their interests lay in 'money – and deceitfulness – and avarice'. Meanwhile, his correspondence with Teresa once she was safely removed did not smack of fear or panic. He wrote placidly that 'I don't see anyone – I live with my books and my horses', and, while he assured her 'that I love you as I have always loved you', hinted at either complacency or boredom by saying 'true love says little'.[55] She was less sanguine about the situation, and Byron complained to Pierino that 'Teresa writes to me like a lunatic – as if I wished to give her up, etc… assuredly I would not have taken so much trouble for a woman from whom I was planning a separation'.[56]

It seems likely that Byron was sincere. Had he wished for a parting from Teresa, he had had numerous occasions to arrange a schism between the two, and his affronted remark to her that 'I have always been faithful and loyal to you and to all your family' was as accurate as he could have allowed. However, he had not allowed for Teresa's greater feelings of love, powerfully expressed when she complained to him that 'I feel as if I were in a desert, and alone, quite alone'. She pronounced herself tormented by 'the saddest thoughts, the most horrible visions', such as 'the sight of a funeral, the cry of a night-bird'. She did not record whether these premonitions included seeing a weakened and feverish figure lying on his deathbed less than three years hence, far from her and Italy.

A source of relief for Byron was the arrival of Shelley on 6 August

1821. Swiftly resuming their friendship, Shelley felt that Byron had become a better and more amenable person than before, something that he ascribed to Teresa. He wrote to Mary to say that '*La Guiccioli* has been an inestimable benefit to him'.[57] Even the bizarre circumstances under which he was inhabiting his mistress's former husband's house did not seem especially unlikely to Shelley, who pronounced his friend's apartments 'splendid', and accepted at face value Byron's boast that Guiccioli was one of the noblest and wealthiest men in the region. The two men spent their time riding, walking and talking, and Byron enlisted Shelley's help in an attempt to persuade Teresa against a Swiss exile. He was happy to do so, telling her of the 'monstrous' and 'infamous' accusations that had been levelled at them during their stay of 1816, and making it clear that 'accustomed as you are, Madame, to the gentle manners of Italy, you can hardly conceive what an intensity this social hatred has reached in less happy climes'.[58] Although the allusion to 'gentle manners' had unfortunate overtones, given her current state of exile, Shelley's intervention was successful. His assistance was not given entirely out of altruism. He hoped that Byron and Teresa would form the nucleus of a community in Pisa that he wished to found, which would be a more developed version of the loose group that they had formed in Switzerland.

While the friendship between the two men remained, hairline cracks formed. Shelley resented what he saw as Byron's reluctance to exert himself in any fashion that did not interest him, describing it bitterly to Mary as 'the canker of aristocracy'.[59] One of these areas was Allegra's upbringing, in which Shelley found Byron frustratingly uninvolved. He noted that she referred to her *mammina*, but this was Teresa, rather than Claire, who had showed more love and attention towards her quasi-stepdaughter than her father ever did. Eventually, Shelley left Ravenna for Florence, where he met Teresa for the first time on 21 August. She wrote to Byron that 'your friend pleases me very much… his countenance is full of goodness and talent', although she worried that 'his health seems to be very poor', and asked 'but how, dear friend, how is it possible to be so thin, so worn out?'[60]

For all Byron's apparent indifference to others, he did care about Shelley, and Teresa. Yet he longed for an escape from his ennui, and a greater involvement in revolutionary politics seemed a more seductive idea than any mistress. Pierino, with his youthful fire and vigour, had inspired him, and he mentioned to Moore in passing that 'I wanted to go to Greece lately… with T's brother, who is a very fine, brave fellow'. On this occasion, he was frustrated by 'the tears of a woman… and the weakness of one's own heart', which he pronounced 'paramount to these projects'.[61] But the idea would linger, to eventually fateful effect, for the remainder of his life.

15

I know that we shall never see each other again.

TERESA GUICCIOLI TO BYRON,
MAY 1823

The wanderlust that had always driven Byron seized him again, like a fit, in late 1821. After he decided that remaining at Count Guiccioli's palazzo was no longer a desirable state of affairs, he left Ravenna on 29 October, bound for Pisa and Teresa. There had been several delays, due to his usual prevarications, but eventually he departed, bound for a house that Shelley had found for him, the Casa Lanfranchi on the Lungarno.* He left behind a selection of his unwanted animals from his menagerie, including 'a goat with a broken leg, an ugly peasant dog [and] two ugly monkeys'.[1] Allegra, of course, remained in the convent at Bagnacavallo. Ravenna much regretted its famous inhabitant's departure, and Teresa later told Moore that 'his arrival in that town was spoken of as a piece of public good fortune, and his departure as a public calamity'.[2] On his journey, Byron found time to write a poem that expressed his love for Teresa, 'Stanzas Written on the Road between Florence and Pisa.' The final two stanzas reveal his ambivalence about his public fame compared to the private rapture that he now felt:

> Oh FAME!—if I e'er took delight in thy praises,
> 'Twas less for the sake of thy high-sounding phrases,

---

* An upmarket area of Pisa situated close to the River Arno.

Than to see the bright eyes of the dear one discover,
She thought that I was not unworthy to love her.

There chiefly I sought thee, *there* only I found thee;
Her glance was the best of the rays that surround thee;
When it sparkled o'er aught that was bright in my story,
I knew it was love, and I felt it was glory.

As he travelled to Pisa, he passed Claire Clairmont, recipient of neither love nor glory, although he remained unaware of how near he came to his former and passed-over distraction. He was more impressed by an encounter with her near-namesake Lord Clare, an old Harrow friend; he described it as 'a new and inexplicable feeling, like rising from the grave'.[3]

When Byron arrived in Pisa, whispers of his fame soon passed round the town. One university student, Francesco Domenico Guerrazzi, wrote that there was a rumour 'that an extraordinary man had arrived [in Pisa], of whom people told a hundred different tales, all contradictory and many absurd'. Noting that he possessed 'an evil genius, but a more than human intellect', Guerrazzi remarked, awestruck, that 'he was said to wander through the world like Job's Satan... I wished to see him; he appeared to me like the Vatican Apollo'. Byron had shifted in the past few years from mere notoriety and scandal to legendary status, and, despite his boredom and ill health, seemed to be more than an ordinary man.

When Byron arrived, he and Teresa resumed their roles as man and mistress. For the first time, their situations were reversed; although it was her native country, she felt like the outsider amid the exclusive set of Byron, the Shelleys and the others. They dismissed her, in the words of Mary, as 'a nice pretty girl without pretensions, good-hearted and amiable', and, in Shelley's harsher description, as 'a very pretty, sentimental, innocent, superficial Italian, who has sacrificed an immense fortune for the sake of Lord

Byron; and who, if I know anything of my friend, of her, and of human nature, will hereafter have plenty of leisure and opportunity to repent her rashness'.[4] Teresa, for her part, called Shelley 'a remarkable man… an unequalled combination of contrasts and harmonies, both physical and moral', but was less impressed by his wife, damning her with the intimidating sobriquet *'une femme supérieure'*.[5]

In any case, Teresa's relationship with Byron began a more relaxed phase, as he enjoyed playing the host among his friends, including Medwin, who used his anecdotes and witticisms as material for his later book *Conversations With Lord Byron*. Teresa would later ridicule this book as 'partly indiscreet and partly untrue', down to such statements as her having black hair and Byron having peacocks as part of his menagerie. Then again, she may have been overawed by Medwin's obvious admiration of her; he gushingly proclaimed that 'it is impossible to see without admiring, to hear the Guiccioli speak without being fascinated… grace and elegance seem component parts of her nature'. Perhaps she was offended by Medwin's description of Byron as 'very much attached to her, without actually being in love'.[6] Whether this was entirely true or not, it clearly stung Teresa, not least because it helped explain his actions over the next eighteen months.

At the beginning of 1822, Byron's circle was completed by the arrival of the sailor and adventurer Edward John Trelawny. Byron happily told Teresa that 'I have today met the personification of my Corsair', although when she expressed a desire to become acquainted with this dashing, dark-haired, almost piratical figure, he was equally quick to warn her 'you will not like him'.[7] Perhaps he feared the competition. Many women admired Trelawny, including Mary, and he later proposed marriage to Claire, who refused him but would maintain a long friendship and correspondence with him instead. He and Byron's other guests conducted a series of symposia, talking of politics and poetry with a lightheartedness that stood in contrast to the seriousness with which

Byron had conducted his revolutionary activities with Pierino. Teresa, meanwhile, adjusted to her new and more subservient role in their relationship. One of the first concessions that she made was to allow Byron to continue writing *Don Juan*, only asking that he spare 'further attacks, like those on the two earlier cantos, written *pendant les mauvais jours de Venice*'.[8] Byron responded to this permission with suave sarcasm, telling (an undoubtedly relieved) Murray that 'I obtained a permission from my Dictatress to continue it – *provided always* it was to be more guarded and decorous and sentimental in the continuation than in the commencement'.[9]

As before, Byron, Teresa and those around them were watched by the Italian secret police, and the simmering tension erupted in a skirmish on 24 March. A group that included virtually all of Byron's circle – including Shelley, Teresa and Pierino – had spent an afternoon shooting and were returning to Pisa when a local dragoon named Stefano Masi pushed past them on the road. Affronted, Byron and the others embarked upon a furious row with Masi once they returned to the city, which soon turned into an ugly physical brawl. At the end of this brawl, one of Byron's servants, believing his master was in danger, stabbed Masi with a rake, and the dragoon was seriously injured. The story both scandalized and intrigued the locals – it was asked, 'have those assassins been arrested, or are they still walking about the town?'[10] – but Teresa, terrified by the unwanted attention that the fight had engendered, begged him to keep a lower public profile, saying 'no one else will tell you that the most precious of all these lives is the one that is in the greatest danger: yours, my Byron'.[11]

Although there was a police investigation, none of the people of 'quality' were detained, although their servants were interrogated at length, and Teresa's footman Maluchielli was briefly imprisoned. Although none of the members of Byron's set were ever accused of any crime, a sentiment of ill will spread between them that damaged, if not destroyed, the amicable feeling of fellowship that had grown over the previous months. And then, amid the bleak atmosphere of mistrust and suspicion that lingered, Teresa informed Byron that Allegra had died.

∾

The loss of his 'natural' daughter had a grim effect on Byron. He began to consider his failings as a father, and informed the writer Lady Blessington:

> Let the object of affection be snatched away by death, and how is all the pain ever inflicted on them avenged… while [Allegra] lived, her existence never seemed necessary to my happiness; but no sooner did I lose her, than it appeared to me as if I could not live without her.[12]

Death was the price of self-knowledge. He withdrew from Teresa's company, but even as he spurned her sympathy, he wrote in his journal 'how much more severely would the death of Teresa afflict me with the dreadful consciousness that while I had been soaring into the fields of romance and fancy, I had left her to weep over my coldness or infidelities of imagination!' He ascribed this to the 'weakness of our natures',[13] as he shrank back into a melancholy state. There were occasional fleeting distractions – a visiting American artist, William Edward West, painted both him and Teresa, and he enjoyed a reunion with his 'earliest and best' friend Lord Clare – but little relieved his depression, leading West to comment, of Byron's habit of drawing in breath in a trembling manner, 'whenever I had observed this in persons of whatever age, I had always found that it came from sorrow'.[14]

It was left to Teresa to try to cheer Byron, which kindness she claimed 'made the world a Paradise for me'.[15] It did not bring about a similar result for Byron. Instead, he resolved to leave Italy, writing to Moore to say that he was 'fluctuating between [South America] and Greece… I should have gone, long ago, to one of them, but for my liaison with Countess G. *She* would be delighted to go too, but I do not choose to expose her to a long voyage, and a residence in an unsettled country.'[16] Byron had been living with Teresa's brother and father in Montereno in Tuscany since the end of June, along with his friend Leigh Hunt and his wife Marianne. The close-knit circumstances led to tense relations between the inhabitants, exacerbated by an incident in which one of Byron's servants, excited by his master's free thinking and revolutionary speech, 'began declaiming against the rich and the aristocracy, and speaking of equality and fraternity', as Teresa put it. This led to confusion, and a fight, and Pierino being slightly injured, and the arrival of the local police. The result, inevitably, was that the Gamba family were blamed for causing trouble, and were ordered to leave the town, and headed to Pisa.

By now, Teresa and Byron were living in sin, as a result of which the Vatican had rescinded the order that Guiccioli should provide her with an allowance; they were liable to be arrested for their conduct. And then a greater blow struck. On 13 July 1822, Teresa and her maid were awoken by the arrival of Mary Shelley, 'as white as marble', and frantic with worry about her husband's whereabouts. He and his friend Edward Williams had sailed their new boat – named, as homage, the *Don Juan* – into a terrible storm in the Gulf of Spezia five days previously, and had not been seen nor heard from since. Their shockingly disfigured bodies were discovered on 18 July on the shore at Viareggio, and, after an argument that dragged on for weeks about how they should be buried, it was agreed that they should be cremated on the beach where they had been discovered, and their ashes taken back to Pisa. The bodies, which had already been buried, were therefore exhumed and were burned in accordance with the local quarantine regulations. The cremation itself was less heroic and mythic than had been imagined, instead being both pathetic and hideous. Trelawny, who was present, described it as 'a humbling and loathsome sight', and Byron, looking on his friend's burning body, asked 'are we all to resemble that? Why, it might be the carcass of a sheep, for all I can see.'[17] After the ceremony had taken place, Byron threw himself into the water, ostensibly to see how strong the tide was. Those present feared that he had little intention of returning to land, leading to his being dragged back to shore by one of the sailors who had carried them to the beach.

With Shelley dead, and the Anglo-Italian group splintering, Byron found some solace with Teresa. When Medwin visited them, he said that 'they are now always together, and he is become quite domestic. He calls her Piccinina and bestows upon her all the pretty diminutive epithets that are so sweet in Italian.' Far from Byron being cold and detached, Medwin noted that 'his kindness and attention to the Guiccioli have been invariable'.[18] Part of this kindness consisted of attempting to find the Gamba clan a home, but an approach to the government of Lucca was fruitless, which meant that the only place that they could seek refuge was Genoa.

Before they left, Hobhouse visited Byron in Pisa. Teresa recounted how, after Byron said 'if his affection for me had not caused him to remain in Italy, saying things which would have made this earth a paradise for me, if I had not already been tormented by the possibility of losing so much happiness',[19] the arrival of his friend led to such great emotion that he was forced to sit down. Hobhouse, meanwhile, was surprised by both the slight formality of Byron and Teresa's welcome, and how Byron was 'much changed – his face fatter, and the expression of it injured'.[20] He was equally dismissive of Byron's plans to live with Teresa as, effectively, husband and wife, and caustically said of it 'this is Italian morality'. Nevertheless, Hobhouse's presence seemed a reminder of something that Byron had lost. The poet's joke to his friend on his departure that 'you should never have come or you should never leave'[21] hinted at desperate uncertainty for what the future held.

They left for Genoa on 29 September, with the unwanted Hunts trailing behind. As ever with Byron, the journey was a long and arduous one due to his insistence on transporting a veritable Noah's

Ark of animals and birds, as well as a trio of large, cackling geese, which he had originally intended to eat, but instead decided to keep, 'to test the theory of their longevity'. Teresa described these convoluted arrangements, with some understatement, as ones that 'required a great deal of time and patience'.[22] The planning, effort and expense rivalled many small military campaigns. Along the way, Byron became ill after engaging in a swimming competition at Lerici, and compared himself to Prometheus, 'just as that damned, obstreperous fellow felt chained to a rock, the vultures gnawing my midriff, and my vitals, too'.[23]

Upon the party's arrival at Genoa there was a brief peace, with the Hunts inflicting themselves on Mary Shelley at Villa Negrotto a mile away and Byron and Teresa remaining in a larger villa at Albaro, which they shared with Teresa's family. Byron never visited the Hunts, and left Teresa to head to their house to see Mary, a painful task that she dutifully undertook monthly. Without a guiding sense of purpose, Byron fell into lethargy and triviality. After a lifetime of money worries, he was now wealthy, thanks to both royalties from his poetry and an inheritance from Annabella's uncle, agreed as part of the marriage settlement. He wrote to Kinnaird to claim, without as much irony as he might once have displayed, that 'I *loves lucre*'.[24] He grew angry about perceived swindling, and even argued with Mary, telling her, that, while he was happy to supply her with money, in acknowledgement of his long friendship with her husband, he had no desire to see her again. This could either be taken as misogyny manifesting itself in predictably harsh terms, or simply a man devoid of interest in life. With his closest friends and daughters either absent or dead, he seemed to have little to motivate him.

Teresa did her best to assist Mary, offering moral if not financial support, even as the recipient of this help stated that, while 'I felt no repugnance at the idea of receiving obligations and kindnesses from a friend… a man who does not esteem me cannot be my benefactor'.[25] In truth, Byron esteemed few people, with the exception of Teresa and her family. Occasionally, local worthies such as Hill, the British minister, invited him to dinner, but the time when Byron had been the talk of London – or even of Ravenna – seemed a faint memory. Instead, he devoted himself to quiet domestic solitude, with Teresa as his companion, adviser and, where needed, ambassador. The winter of 1822 was especially poor, bringing back memories of the terrible summer of 1816, and dramatic outbreaks of lightning seemed to offer a mocking counterpoint to the stultifying routine that had claimed them. One friend of Teresa's, Signor Guiliani, reported a glittering account of a ball at the Florence carnival, with participants dressed up as ancient emperors and goddesses and festooned with diamonds and feathers. Teresa responded wistfully that 'Lord Byron had definitely given up all such futile pleasures'.[26] In their solitude, it seemed as if their mutual dependence was all that they had to look forward to as they slid slowly into a financially stable but intellectually undistinguished middle age. He could write his poems; she could learn English. But there seemed little hope of a spark being ignited. Best that way, Teresa may have felt; at least, she could reason, I have Byron close at hand, wanderlust extinguished.

And then matters changed.

❧

Byron had wished to travel everywhere from South America to London, but a mixture of inertia and a lack of opportunity had frustrated his plans. However, a chance meeting with the naval officer Edward Blaquière and a Greek government agent, Andreas Luriottis, on 5 April 1823 led him to take an interest in the situation in Greece. The uprising of the native population against the Turkish occupiers, which had seen 25,000 Greeks – a quarter of the inhabitants – slaughtered at Chios the previous spring had excited both anger and sympathy, and, following the formation of the London Greek Committee in January 1823, the largely Whig sympathizers sought to elicit a high-profile supporter to their cause.

There seemed few better equipped to stand for liberty than Byron, who was elected *in absentia* on to the committee, and they hoped that he would offer both financial and moral support.

He went even further. He wrote to Hobhouse to reveal, almost casually, that 'I entered very sincerely into the object of their journey – and have even offered to go up to the Levant in July – if the Greek provisional government think that I could be of any use.'[27] While keen to play down any idea of military involvement, he nevertheless believed that he could make a useful contribution to the struggle. The only objection, he informed Sir John Bowring, the Greek Committee's secretary, 'is of a domestic nature, and I shall try to get over it; if I fail in this, I must do what I can where I am, but it will always be a source of regret to me.'[28] In an attempt to overcome Teresa's inevitable objections, he confided in Pierino, asking that he prepare his sister for the news 'gradually, by degrees', but he knew that what he intended to do was tantamount to leaving her. As Teresa later wrote:

> A death-sentence would have seemed less terrible... [I] even, in the first moments of [my] anguish, became unjust towards Lord Byron... [I] poured out [my] misery in a letter, in which [I] accused him of sacrificing everything to his reputation, and added 'I know that we shall never see each other again'.[29]

The arguments took on a grimly unyielding aspect, laced with occasional touches of black comedy. Byron's friend Lady Anne Hardy suggested, possibly tongue in cheek, that the easiest way out of his difficulty would be for Teresa to don male attire and pose as his servant; as she said, 'were I in her place, I should try to see if I could not realize Lara's page. Would not that be heroic & troublesome to the last degree?'[30] Whether Anne knew anything of Byron's earlier proclivities or not, it was a suggestion rich in mischievous possibilities. But the delicate, refined Teresa would have been entirely out of place in the midst of revolutionary war.

That her lover was no more suited to such an environment was not openly acknowledged by anyone.

Teresa's opposition to his departure both frustrated Byron and strengthened his desire. He grumbled to Kinnaird that 'I am doing all I can to get away, but I have all kinds of obstacles thrown in my way by "the absurd womankind", who seems determined on sacrificing herself in every way... she wants to go up to Greece too!' Reflecting on both his current situation and earlier entanglements, he complained that:

> There never was a man who gave up so much to women, and all I have gained by it has been the character of treating them harshly... if I left a woman for another woman, she might have cause to complain, but really when a man merely wishes to go on a great duty, for a good cause, this selfishness on the part of the 'feminie' [sic] is rather too much.[31]

An earlier letter to Hobhouse complained about 'the absurd womankind', but took care to praise Pierino as 'a very fine spirited young fellow', who was 'very desirous to accompany me to one or other of those countries – or at any rate to go himself'.[32] Her brother's keen interest in the situation not only rendered Teresa's objections more trivial, but made Byron's own intentions seem even more noble. Finally, there was the bloody-minded sense that, as he had announced his intention in participating in the expedition, he would not back down; as he informed Hobhouse, with the petulant air of a child demanding a promised treat, 'I *will* go... damn my eye, I *will* go ashore'.[33]

It had occurred to Byron, despite his bravado, that his efforts would be pointless. He remarked to Lady Blessington with characteristic self-deprecation that:

> I am so far embarked that retreat (at least with honour) is impossible... my position excites such ludicrous images and thoughts

in my mind, that the whole subject, which, seen through the veil
of passion, looked fit for a sublime epic, and I one of the heroes,
examined now through reason's glass, appears fit only for a
travestie [sic].[34]

He went a step further as well. Teresa later said, albeit possibly with
hindsight, that 'he had a conviction that he should never return
from Greece. He had dreamed more than once, he assured me, of
dying there.'[35] Byron saw his expedition as the opportunity both
for a break from his current situation and a chance to do *something*; that this meant leaving Teresa alone and heartbroken was a
necessary sacrifice.

Circumstances favoured Byron's plans. Count Gamba's banishment was rescinded and he was allowed to return to Ravenna,
albeit with the provision that he was compelled to take Teresa with
him. This was due to the machinations of Guiccioli, who fancied
that, once Byron had tired of her, he might be able to renew his
attentions to his former wife. In either case, she needed the allowance that had been removed from her by papal decree, and so,
reluctantly, she was forced to accede. An additional reason for her
departure not being as painful as it might have been otherwise
was Byron's flirtation with Lady Blessington; although, uncharacteristically, no affair commenced, Teresa was incensed by his
affection for her. Byron complained to Anne Hardy that 'this has
plunged me into a pit of domestic troubles – for "la mia Dama",
La Contesse G – was seized with a furious fit of Italian jealousy –
and was as unreasonable and perverse as can well be imagined'.[36]
Ironically, much of his conversation with Lady Blessington was
in praise of Teresa. She later reported that 'he said that he had
been passionately in love with her, and that she had sacrificed
everything for him; that the whole of her conduct towards him
had been admirable, and that not only did he feel the strongest
personal attachment to her, but the highest sentiment of esteem'.
She then made the claim that has been repeated by sentimentalists

ever since, that 'I am persuaded this is his last attachment.'[37]

Teresa was indeed Byron's last attachment. She offered him stability, love, and intellectual compatibility. If he was originally drawn to her because she was Italian and aristocratic – he was a committed social snob when it came to his recognized lovers, as opposed to the legions of 'ordinary' women, girls and boys whom he was content merely to tup and then forget about – then it is a testament to a shift in his attitude and approach that he was mostly faithful to her, forsaking other opportunities and interests. Yet Byron still came to regard the chance of a domestic existence with Teresa, and potentially even marriage, as frustrating and unsatisfying. His decision to head to Greece, without her in pageboy attire, arose because he had had enough. After all, he had long since passed the three-year limit that he regarded as the acceptable duration of a love affair. But if he had loved anyone enough to be content, it would have been her, and his refusal to make a life with her was an indication that no woman would ever have sufficed.

The final days before Byron's departure were grim. He attempted to provide for her in his will, but, according to Teresa's own account, 'the mere idea of an act which presupposed the possibility of so terrible a misfortune caused [me] to break into such cries of pain, such applications to give up the idea, that he promised to do so'. Teresa's attachment to Byron had never been financial. As she realized that Byron really was set on his departure, and that he had settled upon a date in the middle of July to leave, she was engulfed in misery. In an attempt to placate her, Byron made an insincere promise. If all went well in Greece, he vowed, she would be sent for and could live with him there; if, instead, his task proved a failure, he would return to her and never depart again. As she prepared to head to Ravenna, she had to take consolation in what he offered, despite knowing that his leave-taking was likely to be final. She was also concerned because he looked grey and ill, rather than the handsome and vivacious man she had first met.

His final letters from Genoa were valedictory ones. Writing to one admirer of his work, a Monsieur Coulmann, he praised his father Jack as possessing 'an extremely amiable and joyous character', and described Augusta in especially glowing terms, claiming 'there is not a more angelic being upon earth'. The postscript to the letter struck an ominous note; after announcing his intention of meeting Coulmann in Paris 'should I return', he stated 'should I not return, give me as affectionate a place in your memory as possible'.[38] His ultimate leave-taking was delayed by a few days, giving Teresa faint hope that he might tire of the plan altogether. She wrote to Mary Shelley on 12 July, breathlessly, to exalt that 'I have just heard that perhaps he will not get off tomorrow. Only a few hours more! – and yet, since that moment, I have breathed a little more freely.' After several more delays occasioned by bad weather, Byron finally left Genoa on 15 July. Teresa wrote a pathetic note to her lover shortly before, to say 'I have promised more than I can perform, and you have asked of me what is beyond my strength… I feel as if I were dying, Byron, have pity on me', and begging him to 'come and fetch me, Byron, if you still want to see me alive, or let me run away and join you, at any cost'.[39] Whether the plaintive sincerity of the letter would have any effect on Byron is impossible to say, as it never reached him.

If there was a long, emotional leave-taking that occurred before Byron departed, no record survives of it. The first communication that Teresa had from him after he left were a few hurried lines at the bottom of a longer letter from Pierino, who mentioned her lover was 'very much occupied, and happy in his occupations'; Byron's contribution was 'my dearest Teresa – I have but a few moments to say that we are all well – and thus far on our way to the Levant – believe that I always *love* you – and that a thousand words could only express the same idea'.[40] If his excuse was that he was busy, it is telling that he found the time to write to none other than Goethe on the same day, at greater length, and praised him as 'the undisputed Sovereign of European literature'.[41] Thereafter, Byron headed to Greece and his stated purpose of liberation, whereupon Teresa heard little from him again, except in sporadic and brief communications, often scribbled in haste.

Teresa seemed to have lost everything. Compelled to live in Bologna with her former literature tutor and friend Paola Costa after her father was exiled to Ferrara en route to his home in Ravenna, she was unable to make any peace with her situation. Waiting anxiously for good news from her lover, she had to make do with the little snippets she received, which were as devoid of interest in her life as they were unrevealing about his own. He may have tossed her the occasional scrap of hope – 'you may be sure that the moment I can join you again will be as welcome to me as at any period of our recollection', and 'I wish… I might return quietly to Italy'[42] – but they were whirling words, without any intent behind them. Even as Pierino did his best to give a fuller account of their exploits and adventures, he was at pains to present as positive a picture of his travelling companion as possible; he omitted such details as a rage-induced fit that Byron had fallen into while they sojourned briefly at Samos.

Teresa attempted to remain as cheerful as she could in her letters to Byron. She mentioned her progress in learning English, and that she was studying philosophy. However, her correspondence seldom met with much response. In the final nine months of his life, he sent her another couple of brief postscripts to longer epistles from Pierino, one saying 'of Greece and the Greeks – I can say little – for everything is as yet very uncertain on that point', and exhorted her to remain 'tranquil, and not to believe any nonsense that you may hear'.[43] Another castigated her for not writing, but claimed, with a flash of wit, 'I hear you are turned moral philosopher – and are meditating various works for the occupation of your old age – all which is very proper.'[44] If the jokes and evasions smacked of insincerity, then it reflected his own uncertainty about the situation to which he had committed himself.

In an attempt to remedy her desperate financial state, Teresa

appealed to the newly elected Pope Leo XII to restore her allowance, as she blamed Guiccioli for its suspension 'by unknown
means, but doubtless through calumnies and intrigues'.[45] A more
liberal figure than his predecessor, Leo XII began an investigation
into Teresa's claims of poverty, and Guiccioli was questioned in
early January 1824 about the circumstances under which he had
deprived his wife of her means of subsistence. The count continued to explore the possibility of reconciliation with Teresa, on the
grounds that, with Byron exiled, she lacked the steadying influence
of a man in her life. The painful and miserable circumstances of
their divorce seemed to have left his memory. He was, however,
reminded of them by the incursion of Teresa's seventeen-year-old
brother Hippolito into the Palazzo Guiccioli, who demanded that
his erstwhile brother-in-law repay his sister's allowance. Guiccioli's
refusal, on the grounds that he would rather remarry Teresa than
pay her an allowance, did not satisfy Hippolito, nor any of the rest
of his family. After Teresa claimed, disingenuously, that she had
only spent time with Byron purely as a friend, 'two or three times a
week, for an hour, in the time which everyone gives to the *conver-
sazione*', the Vatican agreed to reinstate her allowance in April.
She might have been untruthful and her actions counter to the
sacrament of marriage, but then again so had those of Guiccioli.
The cynical might observe that they deserved one another.

Teresa heard little from Byron, and commented later to Lord
Malmesbury that she believed she was forgotten. Pierino praised
his 'monkish virtues',[46] no doubt in an attempt to allay any fears
of her lover's inconstancy, but a more concrete reassurance came
from Byron himself. Referring to her as *carissima pettegola*, or
'dearest gossip',[47] he suggested that she join him in Greece in the
spring of 1824, as he stressed his industry and efforts. He did not
mention his impending trip to Missolonghi, the main crucible
of the fighting between the Greeks and the Turks; allowing that
Teresa had to be kept informed of his movements, he wrote to his
banker Charles Barry, stressing that 'everything is *quite pacific*...

this perhaps is not the exact or entire truth, but it is as much as needs to be stated to one who will naturally be anxious about her brother, etc etc'.[48]

Pierino's letters offered similar reassurance. One from January stated 'Byron has never enjoyed such vigorous health',[49] although this was contradicted the following month by an admission that, due to his 'eating very little, only strong cheese and salad, [and] drinking a great deal', Byron was 'suddenly assailed by a strong convulsion, which prevented him from moving'. Although Pierino attempted to portray this as a call to sense, which he praised for 'the good it has done has been to make him change his way of life entirely... you see that the follies of idleness are most to be feared for him',[50] the convulsion marked the start of the final decline in Byron's health. He suggested to Augusta that the fit was epileptic, but did not confide his concerns in Teresa, preferring to write colourless and matter-of-fact notes that were either designed to reassure or simply bore her. He was more interested in the opportunity to meet Odysseus Andritzinos, leader of the forces of the Eastern Greeks. The wily Odysseus, suited to his name, made equally free with Byron's cash.

And then, suddenly, the end of the adventure came. Byron and Pierino went out riding on 9 April 1824 in Missolonghi, only for an unexpected downpour to soak them both. Upon his return home, Byron complained of severe pain and bone-shaking chills. It was decided to move him to the nearby island of Zante, where the medical attention available was more advanced, but this was made impossible by strong winds and high waves. Unable to eat or drink, he soon fell into a fever, alternating between delirium and moments of terrified clarity. He spoke of his daughter, and, more surprisingly, Annabella, but any allusion to Teresa was unclear; his words 'Io lascio qualque cosa di caro nel mondo' ('I leave something dear to the world') could have been a reference to her, but they might equally have referred to his position in Greece, his daughter(s) or his writing. Bleeding and what primitive medicine was available did nothing for him; after uttering unintelligible commands and suggestions, he died on Missolonghi early in the morning of 19 April 1824, exactly two years after Allegra.

༄

After Byron's death, the question remained of how Teresa was to be informed. Pierino, stricken with grief and guilt, told his father; Teresa's tutor Paolo Costa, hearing the news from the consul at Ancona, wrote to Guiccioli, fearing that 'the Countess may be driven by grief to commit some act which would cause grave concern to all her relatives'.[51] Guiccioli resisted the heartless pleasure he might have received from telling his former wife the news of her lover's death, but instead ensured that his son Ignazio visited Teresa to tell her of Byron's end. She received the news in near silence, without any dramatic exclamation. It may be that she had already heard it from another source, or simply that the confirmation of all her worries sent her into a near-catatonic state. As Byron's friends squabbled about everything from the preservation of his body to any outstanding loans or gifts he had promised, Teresa faced a miserable existence as his widow without even the consolation of the title.

Following Byron's death, Teresa faced further sorrows. Pierino never returned to Italy, instead remaining in Greece and becoming a colonel in the army, before dying of typhoid in 1827. Her father, meanwhile, remained in exile in Ferrara, and was not allowed to return home until 1831, after which Teresa's younger brother Vincenzo also died, of consumption. She might justifiably have thought that she was paying a harsh penalty for abandoning her wedding vows and for lying about her relations with Byron, and this may explain her extraordinary decision to return to Guiccioli in July 1826.

The count had laid siege to his former wife for more than half a decade, alternately cajoling and seducing her into coming back to him. As she was without money or social standing, she decided to agree to a reconciliation, and wrote in her journal that 'I allowed myself to be persuaded by his protestations, hoping that time and experience might have produced some change in his character, and I went to join him in Venice, hoping to find a situation that would at least be bearable.' She made one condition, however, insisting on signing a primitive pre-nuptial contract that suggested that 'in case this reunion should not prove to be to our mutual satisfaction', they would once again be able to separate, and Teresa retain her former allowance.

The reunion, unsurprisingly, was not a success. Guiccioli proved not to have changed at all, engaging in a shamelessly public liaison with a Venetian prostitute, and a subsequent letter of Teresa's refers to his actions of this time being 'of so strange and evil a nature, that they can only be confessed to one's priest or lawyer, but should not be made known to the public'.[52] If his more licentious behaviour was dictated by a desire to punish her, it is understandable, but he had overstepped the mark, meaning that even his own children took against him. A papal bull of October 1826 not only permitted her to leave Guiccioli without any culpability, but increased her allowance to 150 scudi a month. Leaving, as before, in secrecy and haste, she drove Guiccioli into a fit of fantastical violence. Ignazio wrote to inform her that 'the hours that followed your departure were very stormy; he hurried to the police, to the patriarch... he was prodigiously discomposed not by your desertion, but by the allowance'.[53] Guiccioli, who might have contracted syphilis and thus been driven insane, attempted further outrageous actions, such as attempting to sue Teresa for slander, for making such statements as his being 'guilty towards her of the darkest perfidiousness, and a kind of immorality peculiar to himself'.[54]

Teresa later attributed Guiccioli's behaviour to 'an intense and invincible eccentricity, rather than to perfidiousness'.[55] This was not an opinion shared by Ignazio, who wrote to her to say:

My father's treatment of me has reached that ultimate point,
beyond which I cannot be hurt any more. Now I see why he
quarrelled with his mother, why he quarrelled with his brothers, why he came to destroy three wives… why no friend has
ever clasped his hand, why the government is against him, why
everybody hates him.[56]

The count finally died in 1840, a scourge to all of those who had
known him, but notable for the part he played in one of the most
unusual love triangles of the age.

As for his former wife, she now had the financial freedom to live
an existence quite different to the one she had imagined for herself
before. She travelled, spending her winters in Rome, and embarked
on a brief love affair with a young friend of Byron, Henry Fox,
who said of her that 'her frankness and sincerity are unparalleled
among all the women I have ever known'.[57] Teresa was treasured
as the last substantial link to Byron, and she was both proud and
caustic about the man she described as 'her poet', talking of his
'capricious temper, and with nothing of the passion which per-
vades his poetry'.[58] She knew that her role was to be 'Byron's last
mistress', and neither rejected the title nor overplayed it, instead
quietly assuming the dignity and state of one who deserved respect
but not adulation. She visited England in 1832, met Byron's old
friends the Pigots and former headmaster Dr Drury, and ensured
that John Murray remained a grateful recipient of Byron's manuscripts and letters.

Most significantly, she met Augusta in London during her visit.
For someone who had been 'irritated' by Byron's affection for his
sister in his lifetime, she had not been predisposed to like someone
she believed was at least her half-rival. Nonetheless, they eventually
had one three-hour-long meeting at St James's Palace, after which
Teresa informed Lady Blessington (an unlikely but sincere new
friend) that 'Mrs Leigh is the most good-natured, amiable person
in the world; and besides Lord Byron was so fond of her, that she is

a very interesting person for me.'[59] They never met again; perhaps all that needed to be said had been.

Teresa eventually married again, in 1847, to the wealthy Marquis de Boissy, and she enjoyed a luxurious and peaceful existence in Paris for the rest of her life. She was unafraid to criticize items produced in the Byron memorabilia business if she felt that they were scurrilous or untrue, with Leigh Hunt's fanciful 1858 book *Byron and his Contemporaries* coming in for particularly sustained attack. She wrote to Murray's son John to complain that 'no words are capable of expressing the disgust that [Hunt] has aroused in me... everything in this book breathes hostility, calumny, falsehood'. Her lengthy journal about Byron, *Vie de Lord Byron en Italie*, did not appear in print until the twentieth century, and then only in excerpts. Her final wish, before her death in 1873, was to see her papers and manuscripts published, for the sake of, as she put it, giving an insight into Byron's 'good and kind heart'.[60]

Teresa's intent has proved both critically valuable and personally touching. Yet it would be Byron's daughters, in a different fashion, who secured his legacy.

PART VI

Ada
&
Medora

16

*What could an unseen being be
to a child like her?*

ANNABELLA TO THERESA VILLIERS,
18 MAY 1824

Ada Lovelace was a considerable figure in her own right, as well as being Byron's daughter. As a mathematician and pioneer in the field of computing, she has rightly become known as an inspiration to generations who know little about her father. She enjoys the rare distinction of having a day informally named after her in honour of her achievements.* There is, perhaps thankfully, no 'Lord Byron Day'. Yet Ada's life echoed that of the father she never knew. Like him, she was seen as a brilliant but scandalous figure, dangerously free-thinking and combining mental acuity with behaviour that was greeted with horror. Dying at thirty-six, the same age as he did, she nevertheless left an indelible impression on those with whom she associated, those she loved and those she stood against.

As with Byron, the shining star threatens to eclipse those around it, and so Elizabeth Medora Leigh, who was either Ada's half-sister or her cousin, has been seen as a mere footnote in comparison. This is not unsurprising; not even the rashest revisionist would claim that Elizabeth possessed any of Ada's talents. Yet her unjust biographical neglect has meant that her turbulent and topsy-turvy life has been little remarked upon. Regardless of whose daughter

---

* At the time of writing this is 13 October.

she was – and the evidence has consistently pointed in one direction – the self-described 'child of your guilt' represents a similarly
fascinating study of what it was to be female, intelligent and
frustrated in Victorian England.

~&

Ada, born Augusta Ada Byron on Sunday, 10 December 1815,
entered the world inauspiciously. Not only did her father cry out
'what an implement of torture have I acquired in you!' upon first
seeing her,* but she was born in a household where her father, not
content with having tried drunkenly to rape her mother, had had
an incestuous affair with his half-sister Augusta, and had attracted
national opprobrium. Rather than merely being 'mad, bad and
dangerous to know', as his previous paramour Caroline Lamb had
sardonically described him, Byron seemed positively lethal to his
wife and new daughter. It was a relief when, before Ada was even
a month old, both she and Annabella were banished from Byron's
house, bound for her parents' home in Leicestershire.

   Byron would never see Ada again. However, his attitude towards
his daughter was one of consistent regret at this estrangement
rather than contemptuous dismissal. Augusta Leigh remarked on
11 December 1815 that 'Byron is in great good looks and much
pleased with his *daughter*, though I believe he would have preferred a *son*', and Annabella's former governess Mrs Clermont
informed Hobhouse that 'she had never seen a man so proud and
fond of his child as Lord Byron', adding that Annabella had said
that Byron 'was fonder of the infant' than she was and 'fonder
of it than you are of me'.[1] His first action was to ask about his
daughter's feet, anxious that she might have inherited his deformity, and to be relieved that they were normal. His fondness
persisted throughout his life; he later wrote of her in the third
canto of *Childe Harold's Pilgrimage* that she was 'The child of Love!

* See Chapter Nine.

Though born in bitterness/And nurtured in convulsion.' Although Annabella feared that Byron would attempt to make a claim for custody, he made no such advance, although his feelings of loss for his legitimate daughter would last the remainder of his life. Before leaving for the Continent he wrote to Annabella to enclose a ring of his, as a gift for Ada; it became one of her few tangible links with her father. In return, he received a miniature portrait of Ada, dispatched via John Murray. Byron's comment was that his daughter seemed 'stout of her age' and 'very like her mother'.[2] Later on, when he heard that Ada was ill,* he was sufficiently upset to stop writing his journal until he was reassured of her recovery. Memories of Allegra's death were still with him.

The early years of Ada's life at her family's home of Kirkby Mallory were an exercise in maintaining the appearance of order where little existed. As the only legitimate child of the most infamous man in England, she was the object of intrusive gossip and speculation. On one visit to Ely, the attention was so invasive that Annabella complained that she and her daughter were treated as if they were 'lionesses'.[3] However, Ada was in an unwelcome situation. Annabella excelled at presenting an image of herself to the world as the doting mother, but privately resented the child, referring to her as 'it' and writing to her mother Judith that 'I talk to it for your satisfaction, not my own, and shall be very glad when you have it under your eye.'[4] Describing herself in a poem she wrote as 'The Unnatural Mother', the cold, analytical Annabella was hopelessly ill-suited to offering her daughter the emotional and maternal support that the child needed. Instead, she inculcated her with an intellectual curiosity that would pay its own far-reaching dividends.

Annabella's own involvement in her daughter's life was carefully limited. Nurses and governesses did what they could for Ada's tuition, and few of them were up to the task, intimidated

---

* The ailment itself is unknown, but Byron's comment that he was 'subject to the same complaint, but not at so early an age' might be a reference to scarlet fever.

by the bright, endlessly enquiring child they were expected to deal
with. Any suspicion of an emotional attachment to Ada saw the
employee dismissed without hesitation. One such expulsion, of a
nurse named Grimes, was justified by Annabella on the grounds
that 'she teaches the child to play the hypocrite'.[5] That instructing an eighteen-month-old baby to play at hypocrisy would be a
remarkable feat indeed did not impress Annabella.

One governess, Miss Lamont, kept a journal detailing her experiences of ministering to Ada, describing how she was kept in check
with a complex system of rewards and punishments, as dictated
by Annabella. It did not help that she had a near-mania for keeping anything that might excite Ada's imaginative powers in check.
Annabella justified this to her friend Theresa Villiers by saying 'Ada's
intellect is so far advanced beyond her age that she is already capable
of receiving impressions that might influence her – to what extent I
cannot say.'[6] Miss Lamont, unable to cope with her excitable charge
and demanding mother, eventually handed in her resignation in
1821; she received a hyperbolic reference and a warning never to
discuss what had passed during the course of her employment.

It remained vital for Annabella that Ada was ignorant of her
father's influence. She took this to extremes; one large portrait of
Byron at Kirkby Mallory was kept permanently covered with a
green curtain, and on the few occasions that Augusta visited the
house, she and Ada were never allowed to be alone together. Yet
Annabella's pride at having been associated with Byron meant that
she exhibited a magnanimous forgiveness of the errant poet, at
least in public. Accordingly, Ada grew up with the understanding
that her progenitor had been *someone*, even if it was unclear exactly
what his influence had been. Annabella's occasional attempts at
poetry, such as 'To Ada', attempted to justify this dichotomy,
although with little literary success:

> Thine is the smile – and thine the bloom
> When hope might image ripened charms,

But mine is fraught with Memory's gloom –
Thou art not in a father's arms!

And there I could have loved thee best,
And there have felt thou wert so dear,
That though my worldly all were lost,
My heart had found a world more near!

There then follows talk of 'a lonely mother's bleeding breast' and 'the care of Him who saves'. While Annabella had certainly not acquired any of her husband's poetic skill, she had a greater understanding of how to present herself in society, normally as a victim who had to struggle (wo)manfully against the many hardships she had endured. Ada grew up with a mother who, obsessed with her own mortality, alternated between much breast-beating about the cruelty of fate and cold calculation about her daughter's upbringing. It is unsurprising that Ada soon began crying whenever her mother appeared.[7]

Nonetheless, Annabella summed up her eight-year-old daughter in a letter to Augusta as being essentially cheerful, and said 'of her intellectual powers, observation is the most developed – the pertinency of her remarks – and the accuracy of her descriptions are sometimes beyond her years'. Presciently, she noted that her imagination was 'chiefly exercised in connection with her mechanical ingenuity', and that her countenance was 'animated'.[8] It was less than a year after this that Byron died at Missolonghi, and Annabella told Theresa that 'Ada shed large tears – I believe more from the sight of my agitation, and from the thought that she might have lost *me,* than from any other cause – for what could an unseen being be to a child like her?'[9] The complete absence of empathy with Ada's feelings was only equalled by her self-aggrandizing belief that her daughter, alternately neglected and smothered, would be devoted to her. If Ada expressed any feelings of warmth towards her mother, referring to her in a typical letter as 'my dearest sweetest Annabella',[10] they were because they had no other outlet, save her cousin George.*

Ada's upbringing, if starved of affection, was designed to appeal to her inquisitive mind. She had an unusually advanced outlook on her appearance, telling Annabella that:

> I never yet expressed to you my opinions respecting vanity, I think it is the cause of all people's foibles and unhappiness, at least I am *quite certain* it is of *all* mine, it is the cause of jealousy, falsehood, disobedience, frivolity, anger, in short almost all the faults I can think of.

Her credo, such as it was, was expressed by her statement 'I really don't care a pin's head about anything in this world, *all* I really care about… is to live long enough and in such a way as to prove that I am really worthy to inherit eternal life.'[11]

Mother and daughter undertook a Grand Tour of sorts from 1826 to 1828, travelling through Holland, Germany, France, Italy and Switzerland, and occasionally retracing her father's steps from a few years before. Although no record survives of whether Ada met any of her father's friends or acquaintances during her travels, it seems unlikely that the young girl was exposed to any of the free-thinking, hard-living company with whom Byron had associated.

Nonetheless, when she returned to England, her horizons had been enlarged; she had developed an interest in flying and bombarded Annabella with detailed and intricate letters about her obsession and even signed herself 'your carrier pigeon'. Not even an outbreak of severe ill health, which saw her consigned to bed with near-paralysis for several months in 1829, could stunt her intellectual development or prevent the realization that she was dissatisfied with her situation. As she apologized to Annabella for

---

* The son of Augusta and George Leigh.

what had clearly been an unhappy previous letter, she commented 'do not think I am making a complaint, when I say I am aware that I am far, very far indeed from happy, but I do not in the least intend to speak in a discontented manner, in telling you this'.[12]

After her illness, Ada was not able to walk unaided by crutches until 1832, and in consequence made few friends her own age. Instead, she was obliged to act as an item of curiosity for her mother's visitors. Treated as an adult in miniature, she made an impression on some of them, including her father's biographer Moore. After he visited her and Annabella, he wrote that:

> It was very evident that [Byron's] daughter, who inherited many of her father's peculiarities, also inherited his tendencies... she absolutely refused to give a kiss to anyone but her mother, and then it was not a loving hearty kiss... she had *no* taste for poetry, but... great mathematical power... her truthfulness was I think very questionable, where her vanity which was excessive was concerned, but she was exceedingly good-natured, and in some ways kind feeling.[13]

The references to 'peculiarities' and 'tendencies' hint at the idea of the repressed Ada having a maverick spirit about her. It is possible that, in early 1833, this spirit was exercised in a brief love affair with a tutor of hers, a young man named William Turner, but before anything serious could develop the tutor was dismissed and Ada was once again confined to her home. This led to tension between her and Annabella, expressed by Ada's curt comments in a letter that 'every year of a child's life, I considered that the claim of the parent to that child's *obedience* diminishes... I consider your only claim to my obedience to be that given *by law*, and that you have no *natural* right to expect it after childhood'.[14]

However, it was not long until Ada would assuage public curiosity about her with her debut at court. She was formally presented to King William IV and Queen Adelaide on 10 May 1833, at the age of seventeen. Also present were the duke of Wellington – whom her father had caustically described as 'the best of cut-throats' in the ninth canto of *Don Juan* – and Lady Caroline Lamb's former husband, Lord Melbourne. Neither had any affection for Byron, but they and the others were intrigued by the chance to see his daughter. Annabella later wrote that Ada acquitted herself 'tolerably well', despite being 'rather nervous about the ceremony of presentation, owing to the injudicious remarks made to her respecting the difficulties & dangers of that moment'. She also remarked that 'she is going to the Court Ball on the 17th. The expectation of hearing the band, and of seeing some distinguished persons, makes her look forward to it with pleasure.'[15]

Ada's appearance at the court ball was no great success, echoing her mother's initial indifference when she first came out in 1810. Her recent illness, coupled with general shyness and an understandable reluctance to be regarded as an object of curiosity, meant that the 'assemblage of the *grand monde*', as her mother described it,[16] was underwhelming. Most found her attractive, with the exception of Hobhouse, who described her as 'a large, coarse-skinned young woman, but with something of my friend's features, particularly the mouth'.[17] Nobody made any romantic advance or proposal of marriage towards her at the ball, probably to her relief, and she returned to her mother's home, Fordhook in Ealing. However, on 5 June she attended a rather different gathering. She was invited to a soirée at the Dorset Street residence of the engineer and mathematician Charles Babbage, along with a catholic assortment of philosophers, ladies and gentlemen of fashion and those who would do to swell a gathering or two. Many simply wished to gawp at Byron's daughter, newly launched in society.

There was much admiration for Babbage's latest toy, a dancing silver robot that performed pirouettes to much applause and interest. Yet compared to his other, greater invention, this was merely whimsy and distraction. The expectant guests were informed that there was something special they could see, and so they were led in small groups into a room that had all the trappings of a place of worship, so quiet and still was the atmosphere within it. It was here, in the dust-free surroundings, that Babbage introduced his audience to his greatest invention, a 'thinking machine' known as the Difference Engine.

Most of the visitors were impressed purely by the serious purpose and ornate appearance of the machine, richly constructed in brass and steel. For Ada, it was her reveille to a purpose that she had only dimly begun to understand. Sophia Frend, who was also present that evening, later wrote:

> While other visitors gazed at the working of this beautiful instrument with the sort of expression, and I dare say the sort of feeling, that some savages are said to have shown on first seeing a looking-glass, this woman, young as she was, understood its working, and saw the great beauty of its invention.[18]

The next step of Ada's life, far away from the repression of Kirkby Mallory, had begun.

❧

Annabella and Ada remained in London for much of the rest of the year, apart from brief spells touring the country. Annabella showed Ada life at factories and horse racing, to demonstrate to her the benefits of hard work and the iniquities of gambling. She expressed less interest in Babbage's metaphysics, which she dismissed as 'the whim of the moment'.[19] After her initial hesitancy, Ada had become a capable and intelligent young woman but Annabella still demanded more from her. She drew up a document in early 1834 that offered an insight into what she wished for her daughter, as approved by the family physician, William King. This grim-sounding edict proclaimed that 'all forms of excitement [are] to be excluded from her life' except 'intellectual improvement', and 'mathematics to be concentrated upon because… her greatest defect is want of order, which mathematics will remedy'. After her brief entanglement with William Turner, Annabella was keen that her daughter be kept in check. To further this, she insisted that Ada study moral maxims as well as mathematical ones, and be found a suitably rigorous mentor.

This came in the form of Mary Somerville, the Scottish scientist and mathematician. In her mid-fifties when Ada encountered her, Mary knew something of success in a traditionally masculine profession, not only matching her counterparts but outperforming them. Her book *The Mechanism Of The Heavens*, a translation and adaptation of the French scholar Pierre-Simon Laplace's *Traité de mécanique céleste,* had been published in 1831 by Byron's publisher John Murray, and had transformed a lengthy and sprawling five-volume work into something concise and readable, as well as commercially viable. Ada could not have asked for a more suitable mentor. As she visited Mary in her home at the Royal Hospital in Chelsea, where her husband William worked as the resident physician, Ada began to develop an enquiring interest in eclectic subjects, from steam engines to minerals. Mary was a friend of Babbage, and Ada became a frequent visitor to his house where, away from the whispers of society ladies, she was able to discuss the workings of the Difference Engine at length.

Babbage, a free thinker who espoused the existence of divine miracles as readily as he argued for the significance of women-oriented magazines, was a key influence on Ada. He impressed Annabella less; she believed that the autonomous working of the engine owed something to the supernatural, and she feared that it functioned under the influence of an 'occult principle'.[20] It is easy to condemn the supposedly intellectual Annabella for her short-sightedness, but her views and incomprehension were far from unusual. As the Industrial Revolution wore on, many intellectuals began to consider the idea of machinery replacing man entirely with horror. Babbage's enemy Thomas Carlyle described how 'man's whole life has been laid open and elucidated; scarcely a fragment or fibre of his soul, body, and posessions, but has been probed, dissected, distilled, desiccated and scientifically decomposed'.[21]

Ada's participation in the debate would become one of the central features of her life and work, but in 1834, she remained an interested observer. She enjoyed a trip to the Midlands later in the year, with the new machines in the factories reminding her of Babbage's 'gem of all mechanism', and had a significant experience on 15 December, when she, Mary and Babbage spent an evening at his home, during which 'the possibility of throwing a bridge from the known to the unknown was first apprehended'. Annabella dismissed this as 'unsound and paradoxical',[22] but Ada was enthralled.

Unfortunately, the warnings of those around her that she was over-exerting her imagination came true the next year. Ada suffered a nervous breakdown of sorts while at Mary's home in 1835; her tutor described her as possessing 'an agitated look and manner', and suggested to Annabella that the excitements and stimulae to which she had been exposed were too much for her. Perhaps, Mary suggested, Ada would be better returning to the family home in Kirkby Mallory and resting there? Ada replied diplomatically while not disguising her fear. She promised to be a 'very good little girl' and expressed her horror at returning to the 'desperate tight order' that she had recently left. A compromise was reached: Ada would head to Brighton to spend time horse riding and enjoying the sea air (the catch-all cure for all disorders and distempers). She took to riding with great glee, and informed Mary to say '[I] leap to my heart's content... I assure you I think there is no pleasure in way of exercise equal to that of feeling one's horse flying under one. It is even better than waltzing.'*[23] Upon her return to London, Annabella decided that a more permanent solution to her daughter's inquisitiveness and ill health was the fitting one. She should take a husband.

❧

* Her waltz-averse father would no doubt have disagreed.

The suitor decided upon was William King, 8th Baron of Ockham, who was a friend of Mary's son Woronzow Greig as well as a descendant of the philosopher John Locke. Like Byron, he was an alumnus of Trinity College, Cambridge, and he had spent some time in Greece in the years before as secretary to the governor of the Ionian Isles. After the death of his father in 1833, he inherited his title, and, at the age of twenty-eight, was looking for a wife. The appeal of marrying Byron's daughter, who was maturing into an extremely attractive woman, was clear, even as her episodes of ill health and rumoured wilfulness presented a potential obstacle. Annabella, meanwhile, was delighted that a respectable and financially solvent man was prepared to marry her troublesome daughter. Greig introduced the two of them in late May in Warwickshire, and they found each other *simpatico*: so much so that King proposed a few days afterwards. The news was made public on 12 June 1835, much to Greig's surprise.

King was not an obvious intellectual match for Ada. Stoic and practical rather than ideological or curious, he belied his descent from Locke by being more interested in such everyday matters as crop rotation than he was in Babbage's innovations. Nonetheless, Ada would not miss the opportunity to escape from the narrow confines of Annabella's influence. If his early letters to her smack of duty rather than passion – 'I look upon such happiness as too excessive to be enjoyed otherwise than in a dream, as too splendid & too overcoming for a reality'[24] – then at least it was a mutually advantageous union, especially with Ada's dowry of £30,000 (she would receive an annual income of around £300, at his discretion). Not even Annabella's insistence that King be told about her earlier indiscretion with her tutor could interfere with the wedding, which took place on 8 July 1835 at Fordhook House, west of London. Coincidentally, Teresa Guiccioli was making her second visit to England at the same time, but she was not invited to the intimate ceremony that mirrored Ada's father's hasty union at Seaham two decades earlier.

Initially, Ada's marriage brought her and her mother (whom she referred to as 'my dear Hen' in letters) closer. Annabella no longer regarded Ada as reckless and morally dubious, but instead described her as embodying 'the singular combination of powers with which she was endowed to the best and most Christian purposes'.[25] Ada's 'most Christian purposes', in the early days of her life at Ockham Park, King's house in Surrey, were simple: to be a dutiful wife and to run the household. She fulfilled her marital obligations admirably. Having informed King that 'I do not think that there can be any earthly pleasure equal to that of reposing perfect trust & confidence in another',[26] it seemed fitting that she was pregnant by Christmas 1835. Annabella was equivocal about the news, telling her that pregnancy was an uncomfortable and miserable time. However, she also decided that it was time to allow Ada to see a portion of her past that had hitherto been kept secret. The portrait of her father, so long hidden beneath the green curtain, was restored to her, at last allowing Ada to see one of the most famous images of Byron.

While Ada had seen inferior reproductions of pictures of her father before, it was her first sighting of the portrait of him in Albanian attire by Thomas Phillips. After initially being exhibited at the Royal Academy in 1814, it had not been seen in public after its purchase by Annabella's family. The image, which remains one of the iconic representations of Byron the wanderer and adventurer, helped Ada to understand her father more fully, not least because she finally realized from whom she had inherited what she considered her over-prominent jaw. Her thanks to her mother were tactful. To have been too lavish in praise might have led to accusations of romanticizing a man who had treated Annabella appallingly, but an absence of gratitude would have been callous and heartless. If the gift was an elaborate trap for Ada in order for Annabella to ascertain the state of her feelings about Byron, it could not have been better placed.

Nonetheless, her father's influence hung over her throughout the next months of her pregnancy; it was almost inevitable that, when she gave birth to a boy on 16 May 1836 in St James's Square in London, he would be christened Byron. Unlike his forebear, everyone greeted his arrival with joy, despite the inauspicious event of an eclipse taking place on the day of his birth. He was bright, suiting Ada's desire that 'I should like to have a mathematical child'.[27] Within a few months Ada recorded in her diary that '*Little B* is more attracted I think by *motion* than anything. I think he has an experimental disposition.'[28] Another pregnancy followed shortly afterwards, and, despite an expectation that it would be a boy or 'Master King the second', a daughter, Annabella, was born on 22 September 1837. Unlike her uneventful first pregnancy, the second led to Ada becoming seriously ill, probably with cholera, and she suffered poor health for the rest of her life. She showed few signs of resentment with her sickly state; she wrote to Babbage:

> You cannot think how charmed I am with my *metaphysical* child, & how I have thought of her. If she will only be kind enough to be a metaphysician & a mathematician instead of a silly minikin dangling *Miss* in leading strings I shall love her *mind* too much to care whether her *body* is male, female or neuter.[29]

Nonetheless, Ada suffered from a 'very tedious & suffering illness'[30] until early 1838, and her only distraction during her bedridden days was to maintain her correspondence with Mary, discussing everything from mathematics to the everyday business of rearing children. Some distraction came on 30 June when William was created Earl of Lovelace, with Ada as countess. While her husband responded with pride to the round of titles and privileges that his status as a grandee afforded him (including the role of Lord Lieutenant of Surrey in 1840), Ada was less interested in becoming a society figure. Instead, she became pregnant again in late 1838 on the advice of her family physician, Dr Locock, in a misguided attempt to ameliorate her health. Although the child, a boy named Ralph, was born without difficulty on 2 July 1839,

Ada was becoming frustrated that she had turned into little more than a breeding machine. As she later said, 'I am not naturally or originally fond of children, & tho' I wished for *heirs*, certainly should never have desired a child.'[31] It was clear that she needed to restore her intellectual credentials for her own self-worth, and so she intended to resume her study of mathematics. Once again, the man to assist her was Babbage.

When she wrote to him in November 1839, it was with an odd mixture of confidence and diffidence. As she stated, 'I have made up my mind to have instruction next year in town', she owed that 'the difficulty is to find the *man*. I have a peculiar way of learning & I think it must be a peculiar man to teach me successfully.' Without explicitly asking Babbage himself to be her tutor, she hoped that 'you may be in the way of meeting with the right sort of person', and reassured him that she was committed to the intellectual demands that such a path would take, declaring 'do not reckon me conceited for I am sure I am the last person to think over-highly of *myself*; but I believe I have the power of going just as far as I like in such pursuits… at any rate the taste is such that it must be gratified'.[32] Babbage, preoccupied with his successor to the Difference Engine, the Analytical Engine, was indisposed and so unable to help himself, although he allowed that 'I think your taste for mathematics is so decided that it ought not to be checked'.[33] Instead, he recommended his friend, the logician Augustus de Morgan, who tutored her for algebra and trigonometry.

Babbage and Ada continued to correspond, and occasionally to meet, throughout 1840 and 1841. Ada flattered Babbage, saying 'I scarcely dare so exalt myself as to hope, however humbly, that I can ever be intellectually worthy to attempt serving *you*!'[34] However, Ada was no passive flutterer; her injunction in the same letter, 'now don't contradict me', nodded at her belief in her own authority, as inherited from her father. She aimed to demonstrate her intellectual prowess by boasting that she was studying Finite Differences (a form of mathematical equations first popularized by Newton

in his 1687 *Principia Mathematica*) and referred to her hope that
she might be able to work on her pursuits daily. As Babbage struggled to have his complex calculating machines given wider public
recognition (and much-needed funds), Ada believed that she might
fulfil the dual role of student and patron. As she wrote to Sophia
Frend, who had by this time added to their close-knit intellectual
world by marrying de Morgan, 'I hope before I die, to throw light
on *some* of the dark things of the world. I *may* do so; or I *may not*;
but at any rate, I shall do great good to myself & my own mind, if
I do nothing else.'[35]

However, as her intellectual horizons widened, there remained
a dark and unpleasant matter at hand, and one from which Ada
would struggle to escape. It concerned, as most things did, the sins
of her father.

~

It remains unclear as to whether Ada knew about Byron's incestuous relationship with Augusta before 1841. While she had heard
rumours of scandal and depravity attached to her father's departure from England, she was never explicit about what these were.
When she mentioned 'my own *more* than suspicions to William, I
felt ashamed at having done so', knowing that 'the very idea is so
monstrous and *hideous*'. The suspicion lingered, and she asked her
mother for clarity: 'I should like some time to know how you ever
came to suspect anything so monstrous… the natural intimacy &
familiarity of a brother & sister certainly could not suggest it.'[36]

Ada hinted that this might be the fantasy of 'a very depraved
& vicious mind', and so Annabella responded by confirming the
existence of the affair between Byron and Augusta. After Annabella
initially described the correspondence between the two as containing 'hints of something fearful & mysterious in them', even as she
believed it to be merely 'childishly fond', she then told how she
accidentally made a reference to 'as if *we were brother and sister*',
which led to Byron becoming 'pale and enraged'. She lay the blame

for the breakdown of the marriage at his anger and exclamations, even as 'he uttered more fact than fiction on these occasions'; piously, she noted that 'I had lived in a circle where I could know nothing of the signs & characteristics of vice, and I hated myself – for believing even what took place before me'. As she concluded that 'if ever I was in danger of madness, it was during that time', Annabella damned Byron, and, by extension, Ada; the dagger was most skilfully inserted in her observation that 'you have a right to the excitability which appeared in you so early'.[37] *Et tu, mater?*

There remained a further question, namely the paternity of Augusta's daughter Medora. Annabella ventured ambiguity – 'I heard him claim it as *his*, but… you will understand that I could put another construction on such expressions', and suggested his hints at having fathered a child with his sister 'made me suspect the intention of tormenting me without foundation', even as Byron had sneered 'we can amuse ourselves very well *without you*'. Annabella did not mention her assurance by Caroline Lamb that Medora was undoubtedly a product of incest.

Annabella's motives in informing Ada of Byron and Augusta's liaison, and hinting at Medora's origins, remain uncertain. Perhaps she wished to revenge herself against an absent husband by striking at the daughter who had inherited many of his traits, or perhaps she was simply unable to conceive that her actions would hurt Ada and believed that she was acting out of candour and a desire to set matters straight. Her daughter had seen the portrait of her father; now, she had to know the monstrous figure behind the façade. However, Annabella also believed Medora to be her former husband's child. It was with this in mind that she attempted to bring about a relationship between Ada and Medora, perhaps in an aim to salvage something from a situation steeped in sin.

Like most attempts at controlling human beings, it did not go to plan.

17

Do you know that is my child?

BYRON TO ANNABELLA,
MARCH 1815

Had the birth of Elizabeth Medora Leigh taken place in the pages of one of the more lurid Gothic novels, it seems likely that the child would have come into the world accompanied by lightning and other grim astral portents, along with a hunchbacked crone shouting 'It's alive!' However, reality fortunately deviates from the sensational expectations of fiction. Her arrival in the world, on 15 April 1814, was undramatic. The child was Augusta's fourth, and, like the two girls and a boy born to her before, was healthy; as Byron put it in a letter to Lady Melbourne, shortly after visiting the child, 'it is *not* an ape'.[1] Both Byron and Augusta knew that, for appearance's sake, the child had to be treated as if it was her husband Colonel Leigh's, but both believed 'Medora', as she became known, to be Byron's daughter.

Byron soon began calling the child 'Do', as a pet name; the rest of her family referred to her as 'Libby'. It was a source of amusement to him and Augusta to speculate which of the family traits she had inherited. Dark-haired like her mother, but with a round chin and strong lower lip like Byron, she bore considerably more relation to him than she did to her 'official' father. For the first few months of Medora's life, Byron was a frequent, fond presence, but after he married Annabella, his visits became less regular. The next time that he saw Medora was when Annabella and Augusta spent some time together at Six Mile Bottom. The child was treated as a pawn in the sexual games that Byron was intent on playing; Annabella later claimed that Byron turned to her, and asked 'do you know that is my child?'[2] Whether this is an accurate recollection or not, it reflects the perverse pride that Byron took in his liaison with Augusta.

Meanwhile, Medora enjoyed a reasonable standard of life, although Leigh's penchant for making unsuccessful bets on the racing stretched his wife's annual income of £800 far beyond comfortable levels. Her early years were uneventful, until the news of the death of 'Uncle By' was announced in 1824; he had died four days after Medora's eighth birthday. Unbeknown to her, her mother tried to safeguard her brother's name shortly after his death by agreeing with Hobhouse that his inevitably scandalous *Memoirs* should be burned, thereby keeping his side of his affairs hidden forever. The little information that has survived about them, mainly through his friends' testimony, suggests that they were heavy on scandal, often in some detail. Had they survived, Byron might now be regarded as a latter-day earl of Rochester, synonymous with little more than debauchery.

As she grew older, Medora became aware that relations between her aunt and her mother were strained to a point of estrangement. What she was kept ignorant of was that Annabella, egged on by her constant friend Theresa Villiers, had made it clear to Augusta long before Byron's death that 'circumstances in your conduct – indispensably impose on me the duty of *limiting* my correspondence with you'.[3] Augusta angrily replied that:

> I have been assured that the tide of public opinion has been so turned against my brother that the least appearance of coolness on your part towards me would injure me most seriously – and I am therefore for the sake of my children compelled to accept from your compassion the 'limited intercourse' which is all you can grant to one whom you pronounce no longer worthy of your esteem or affection.[4]

Even as she continued to correspond with Byron, who at one point had the idea that Augusta (and, presumably Medora) should accompany him to Europe, no further meeting occurred.

After Byron's death, the legacy of £25,000 that he left Augusta changed her circumstances considerably, as well as the promise that a portion of the £60,000 settled upon Annabella would come to the Leighs in the event of her death. This would have been more than enough to establish any girl as a desirable matrimonial prospect. Medora, at the age of twelve, could have hoped to marry an aristocrat with no knowledge of her previous circumstances, ensuring that their children, at least, would be legitimate beyond question. Unfortunately, Leigh's debts meant that the money – an extremely large sum – was all spent within a couple of years, and with no signs of Annabella sickening, there seemed little hope that financially-derived respectability was about to benefit Medora.

The only member of the family who benefited from the financial boost was Medora's sister Georgiana, who had married a distant cousin named Henry Trevanion, from Cornwall. The Trevanions were as insolvent as the Leighs, which meant that any hopes of a legacy resolving their fortunes was soon to be dashed. The family despised Trevanion as a useless spendthrift, with the exception of Augusta, who defended him (her partiality could be explained by his briefly having been her lover). Medora occasionally visited her sister and brother-in-law in the houses that they inhabited, mainly near Six Mile Bottom, but was a reluctant guest, given her antipathy towards Trevanion. It was therefore something of a blow when, at the age of fourteen, she was dispatched to live permanently with them at a grim, unprepossessing country house named Bifrons near Canterbury. The property had been leased by Annabella, who had never warmed to it, and now offered it to Georgiana and Trevanion. As Georgiana was now the mother of two young children, and given to poor health, it was felt that a more robust individual should accompany her as her helpmate. This privilege fell to Medora.

❧

After she arrived, Trevanion and Medora soon began a sexual relationship, reluctantly on her part and with priapic insistence on his. The issue of consent did not arise. With Georgiana mainly confined to bed, Medora was the subject of Henry's aggressive advances, and before long she was pregnant. As she later wrote in her autobiography, 'I was ruined – and likely to become a mother by one I had ever disliked.'[5] She was not yet sixteen. Trevanion's reaction when he discovered what had occurred was splendidly hypocritical; he demanded that she 'tell the truth to Georgiana and throw myself – and him – upon her mercy'. The confession itself led to an orgy of weeping and recrimination, with Georgiana blaming herself for having created a situation in which it was inevitable that Trevanion would wish to sleep with Medora. She forgave both her sister and husband, binding the three of them together in what became another Byronic *ménage à trois*.

Knowing that an illegitimate child would bring further scandal upon their already tainted name, they resolved to leave the country. They were able to accomplish this departure due to the unexpected intercession of Annabella. Having been alerted to Medora's pregnancy by Byron's cousin George (who in turn had heard it from Trevanion's neighbour William Eden), she decided that her duty was to assist the family in having the child away from England. Her motives in helping them financially were complex; she may have wished revenge on Augusta, who remained unaware of the situation in which two of her daughters found themselves, or she may have acted out of simple charity towards Medora, of whom she once wrote in her journal that 'I could never look at her without feeling affection'. In either case, she ensured that they could cross the Channel in January 1830, bound for Calais. The young girl, her sickly sister, Georgiana's two legitimate children and their philandering father represented a decidedly perverse parody of the nuclear family.

Medora's baby was due in April, but the exhausting travel meant that she gave birth prematurely to a boy on 19 February, and, without much in the way of medical care, the child was not expected to survive. However, much to the surprise of those around her, her son showed 'promise of living'. It would have been inconceivable for her to return to England with him and so, much to her reluctance, the boy was taken away from her. It remained unclear what happened to him; she was informed in July that the child had died of convulsions aged two months, but there was no evidence of such a fate, no more than there was any suggestion of his reaching adulthood. So much for Byron's grandson. Medora recovered from her weakened state and returned to England on 2 May, bound for a reunion with Augusta, who remained ignorant of the circumstances of what had befallen her daughter since they had parted. The obvious inference was that Augusta was almost wilfully blind to the relationship between her daughter and Trevanion, but, as could be seen by her own involvement with Byron, she was unworldly when it came to the affairs of others.

When Medora arrived back in London, she would once have expected to be presented at court and thus become a respectable society figure. However, Augusta's influence was not what it had been. No longer a lady-in-waiting, she instead relied on old friends, such as the bloated and dissipated George IV, for what little patronage she could summon. She was not helped by personal tragedy; her daughter Augusta had died in March at the age of nineteen, and her younger children, George, Frederick and Emily, suffered the combined effects of paternal negligence and maternal poverty.

If Augusta can be castigated for her oversight in failing to notice Medora's pregnancy and affair with Trevanion, she can at least be partially forgiven, given the entanglements she faced. Medora continued to be devoid of prospects, interest or amusement. Given her lack of an estate – not to mention her virginity – she was hardly in a position to attract any but the most desperate and impecunious of suitors. It was by no means an enviable position for Byron's 'other' daughter to be in, not least because the only male attention she received in London came in the serpentine form of Trevanion;

she wrote that '[he] came very often – almost daily – to visit me, and his visits were not in any way discouraged by my mother'.[6]

With Georgiana tacitly approving of her husband's liaison with her sister, Medora continued her reluctant routine of acting as her brother-in-law's concubine. Whether Trevanion knew of the misery he caused her was debatable. He was addicted to laudanum and often behaved indiscreetly under its influence, writing 'wild notes' to Augusta and hinting at how Medora 'had half my consent yesterday to have disclosed the fatal cause of my misery', although he insisted that 'it shall now and ever be a secret'.[7] Unsurprisingly, his daily visits to Medora had the usual consequence, and, in January 1831, Medora realized that she was again 'likely to become a mother'. Concealing the truth from Augusta once had been difficult but possible; doing so a second time was unthinkable.

It fell to Trevanion to inform Augusta, and her response was the cause of a critical schism within her family. As she stressed that 'you know how I have loved and regarded you as my own child [and] I can never cease to do so',[8] she blamed two people for the disastrous affair that had ensued: herself, and Medora. Asking a bemused Trevanion for comfort and support, she turned on her daughter, criticized her for having 'committed *two* of the most deadly crimes' and, lamenting the 'DREADFUL consequences' of her actions, stated 'I never knew sorrow like this… I felt you might be taken from me by death, but I was not prepared for this wretchedness'. She struck the odd unintentionally comic note ('you know that I confidently hoped and intended you to be confirmed this Easter… I suppose it is *now* hopeless'),[9] but Augusta regarded Medora as the agent of her ill fortune, with Trevanion as an innocent sucked into her carefully woven web of teenage deceit. Medora was deeply hurt by what she saw as her mother's lack of understanding, writing 'she became very cruel, though to H, the only difference she made was to increase her kindness'.[10]

A compromise was reached, and Medora was again dispatched in secret with the Trevanions in March 1831 to serve out her confinement. The locale chosen this time was near Bath. It is unlikely that Medora was told how, a half-century before, her grandfather Jack Byron had wooed Catherine Gordon by his dancing and flattery. Bath had lost something of its social cachet in the intervening years, but the potential for human misery was still just as present. This was especially true of Trevanion, Georgiana and Medora, all of whom blamed the others for the predicament in which they found themselves. They attempted to outdo one another in spite; Trevanion revealed his affair with Augusta to the two sisters, and Georgiana retaliated by informing Medora that she was the 'result of adultery and incest'.[11] Medora, who pitied rather than loathed her official father Colonel Leigh, was both shocked and oddly excited by the revelation. She seemed to grow in substance by the knowledge of her true paternity, rather than feeling shame.

As the situation worsened, Georgiana became disillusioned with her sham marriage and decided to leave Trevanion. When she informed her mother of her decision, Augusta told her husband the whole sordid story in a fit of alarm. He reacted by heading to Bath with the intent of retrieving Medora and returning her to London. When he arrived, Georgiana and Medora had a panicked interview, of which Medora later wrote 'she begged forgiveness of me and entreated me never to abandon Henry. She assured me that she would immediately procure a divorce and that then I could even marry Henry if disposed to do so.'[12] While Medora digested the extraordinary offer that her sister had made her, Colonel Leigh took her back to London and unceremoniously deposited her in a lodging house-cum-institution for unmarried mothers-to-be near Regent's Park, run by a Mrs Pollen. Here she gave birth to a still-born daughter in July 1831, but there seemed little sign of release from her confinement.

Cometh the hour, cometh the man. Trevanion, deciding that his future lay with Medora rather than Georgiana, schemed to release her, and so, after he bribed the pliable Pollen, she absconded with him to Normandy, unbeknown to Augusta. She later commented to Annabella that 'from July 1831 to June 1833 – I was left in ignorance of Elizabeth's abode – and almost of her existence'.[13] These two years were not a happy time. Trevanion resented the poverty in which they inevitably found themselves, and Medora decided to escape the situation by converting to Catholicism and entering a convent. As her sexual relations with Trevanion had continued and she was pregnant yet again, it became impossible for her to be received into orders. The only saving grace was that, with her Catholicism now a central element of her life, it gave her the reason she needed to break off relations with Trevanion. As she later put it, '[he] was not under the same roof with me and from the time I entered the convent I never was but as a sister to him'.[14] On 19 May 1834 Medora gave birth to a girl, whom she named Marie. Trevanion was named on the birth certificate as 'acting for the absent father', a typical evasion.

As Medora and Trevanion continued to live in a parody of domesticity – she described how 'Henry at this time gave himself wholly to religion and shooting; I to my child'[15] – in a decrepit manor house, Chateau Penhoët in the Breton town of Morlaix, their lack of money made for a miserable and constricted existence. Augusta gave Medora an allowance of £60 a year, but given Trevanion's penchant for extravagance (shooting was far from cheap), this proved inadequate for the two of them to live on. It also did not help that, with Medora still intent on rejecting his sexual advances, he took a mistress and, like Byron with Annabella, forced Medora into an unwilling complicity. She later wrote of how 'I pass over three years of misery, but I am willing to give every detail of what I was made to suffer, though I do not think it is absolutely necessary to do so'.[16] Medora's demeaning existence with Trevanion was intolerable, but she had few other options, as a return to England with her daughter would have been impossible. Worn down by the squalor and misery in which she found herself, she became severely ill in 1838. The doctor engaged to look after her, Monsieur Carrel, quickly assessed the situation and informed

Augusta of Medora's poor health; he also suggested that her daughter was provided with a greater permanent allowance that would give her autonomy of sorts.

Although neither Augusta nor Medora had any independent income, their relationship to Byron meant that there was believed to be a near-mythical sum of £60,000, a portion of which would be inherited by them in the event of Annabella's death. Augusta therefore drew up a deed of appointment that guaranteed Medora £3,000 out of this inheritance, an action that was meant kindly but would have severe and unforeseen consequences. Nonetheless, the money was still an abstract concept, and Medora spent 1838 and 1839 in a state of perpetual ill health, desperately trying to get what little assistance she could from her mother. Records kept by Carrel, who acted as her guardian, note that she received less than £90 between August 1838 and September 1839. It was a pathetic amount, and it seemed as if she was to be reduced to a lifetime of scraping by on virtually nothing whatsoever. In her mid-twenties by 1840, she had already seen more sorrow and degradation in her short life than most could ever imagine. She needed a supporter and a friend who could not only understand her situation, but could provide practical assistance.

❧

Enter, like an unlikely fairy godmother, Annabella. Medora had written to her in desperation in May 1840 to see if there was any possibility of being able to borrow money against the deed, and Annabella, appalled at what she heard of Medora's predicament, replied to her and suggested that they should rendezvous in France in the summer to discuss what could be done. Both parties agreed that this should be done away from Trevanion. Eventually, Annabella and Medora met in Tours on 21 August 1840. Annabella said of her that 'I found her altered beyond the possibility of recognition – and in a sort of confused and stupefied state of mind, attended at times with great excitement'.[17] Medora was in poor health, suffering from appendicitis and extreme emaciation; Annabella believed that she was in danger of dying and leaving her daughter without a mother. Her feelings towards Medora were complicated. In 1820, she had written that she felt 'the most tender affection' towards her, and she continued to feel compassion. Yet, believing that she was also the product of an unnatural liaison between Byron and Augusta, she took the attitude that Medora's sinful life had been one predestined by the circumstances in which she had come into the world. It fell to her, she decided, to take this unfortunate creature in hand. If this meant becoming more of a mother to her than Augusta ever had been, and thereby vicariously taking revenge on her rival, then so much the better.

A plan was formed. Medora was to be known as 'Madame Aubin', and a cover story constructed; she was to be a widow from a distinguished family, travelling as part of Lady Byron's entourage. Her life changed beyond recognition almost immediately. After enduring years of poverty and contempt from everyone she ran into, she now found herself heading for Paris, richly attired and staying in luxurious houses. Her relationship with Annabella swiftly became that of a surrogate mother and daughter, and she was instructed to call her benefactress 'Pip'. The last person who had done so was Byron.

Even Annabella's dread at having to tell Medora the truth about her parentage was circumvented, as she had already heard about it from Georgiana. Annabella wrote, possibly with relief, 'she was unfortunately in possession of that fact before she was connected to me, and after much embarrassment from her allusions to it, I determined on admitting it'.[18] Perhaps there was a touch of prurience in the repressed Annabella's probings. Medora later wrote that:

> She implored and sought my affection by every means, and almost exacted my confidence to the most unlimited extent. I was willing and anxious, in any and every way I could to prove my gratitude and the desire I so sincerely felt to repay by my

affection and devotion any pain she must have felt for the circumstances connected with my birth and her separation from
Lord Byron.

Annabella now had two daughters, her legitimate, brilliant Ada
and the sorrowful, wretched Medora. While the former needed to
be kept in check and repressed, the latter simply wished to escape
her dire circumstances. As Medora said of Annabella, 'she evinced
much anxiety for my health and comfort, expressed indignation
for all I had suffered, spoke of the comfort I would be to her, and
of the necessity that I should be a devoted child to her'.

Medora and Annabella took a house in central Paris, at 24 Rue
de Rivoli, and, with the distractions and excitements of the city
at her disposal, Medora began to recover. Annabella gave her gifts
and small sums of money, with the promise of a larger allowance
when she was better. If her new liberty was entirely at Annabella's discretion, this was still an improvement on her entanglement
with Trevanion. That she might have been able to have a life for
herself and Marie on their own terms, rather than on somebody
else's, seemed impossible, and there is no hint of any discontent in
any of her surviving letters.

In January 1841, Annabella unexpectedly heard from Augusta,
after ten years of silence. M. Carrel had told Augusta that her
daughter was now Annabella's ward in all but name, and, while
she stressed her 'unshakeable confidence' in Annabella's treatment
of Medora, desired to know the truth of what was happening. Poignantly, she feared that 'there are those who... consider me their
dupe... I have been too often and too cruelly deceived to be in
a position to give a very satisfactory answer to such suspicion.'[19]
Annabella, faced with a choice between compassion and cruelty,
resolved upon the latter. As she attacked Augusta with a considered
ruthlessness that she knew would devastate her, she dealt with her
in a peremptory fashion that suggested she did not expect further
correspondence from her former rival:

Could I have believed that you had a mother's affection for her, you would not have had to ask for information concerning your child… your affectionate letters to her must appear a cruel mockery to those who knew that you left her, for so long a time, only the alternative of vice or starvation. Her malady, the effect of physical and mental suffering, can be retarded only by extreme care and by her avoiding all distressing excitement… Leave her in peace!

Although she stressed that this 'advice' was given 'in no hostile spirit', but with Annabella instead claiming her desire was 'to protect her to the utmost of my power',[20] it devasted Augusta. Hurt and in a panicked state, she attempted to solicit support from her former friend Theresa Villiers. However, Annabella had prepared a case in the event of Augusta attempting to disrupt her plans, including informing William King and Ada of Medora's 'true' paternity. This did not come as a surprise to Ada, who coolly replied 'you merely *confirm* what I have for *years and years* felt scarcely a doubt about, but should have considered it most improper… to hint to you that I in any way suspected". She offered her own judgement on the affair, saying of Augusta that 'I fear *she* is *more inherently* wicked than *he* ever was'.[21]

Annabella decided that it was better for Ada to attack Augusta than her departed father, and, surprisingly, sided with her. Annabella allowed that 'I have been led to acquit *him* of some portion of the guilt by recent disclosures respecting her conduct to her child – for one who could, *as she clearly did*, connive at the ruin of a daughter, must have been capable of injuring a brother in the same way'. Thus Augusta, who was guilty of little more than self-absorption and an inability to see the complexities of her daughters' affairs, was portrayed as a homewrecking harridan whose base desires extended to the sexual corruption of her own, honourable, brother. Although this was a grotesque distortion of both Augusta's character and the facts, it suited Annabella's purposes to turn both

Ada and Medora against Augusta. With their mother and aunt isolated and powerless, she would finally have the sovereignty that she had lacked while married to their father.

One consequence of this entanglement was that Ada and her husband decided that the time had come to meet Medora. Arriving in Paris in April 1841, Byron's legitimate daughter met his disgraced one for the first time. While it had been impossible to predict how the two would react to one another, their initial encounter was a happy and harmonious one. Not only did they resemble each other, but Medora responded warmly to the Lovelaces; she wrote 'I received kindnesses and promises from both, and was made to feel that I was Ada's sister at all times, which I was really.'[22] Despite the enormous differences between the two of them in situation, birth and wealth, mainly occasioned by Ada's official position as Byron's daughter, there was soon genuine friendship between them. The two of them wandered the streets and parks of Paris, and Medora soon came up with pet names for her, William and Annabella. Ada was 'Hopeful Bird', or 'Bird', and the avian theme continued with William being known as 'Crow'. Annabella was appropriately described as 'Hen'.

While they stayed only a fortnight, the Lovelaces' visit had a huge impact on Medora. Ada was the first friend of a similar age she had ever made, and she wished to continue their new acquaintance in England. Annabella was of the same mind, not least because it was reported that Trevanion had arrived in Paris with the potential to cause trouble, and so, at the end of May, they returned to England, with Medora in tow. They would stay at Ada and William's town house at 10 St James's Square, and Medora was restored to England for the first time in a decade.

Much had changed. The railway had become a ubiquitous part of everyday life, and so journeys that would once have taken a couple of days could be taken in mere hours. Not only did this have the effect of rendering the country a more accessible place, but it allowed freedom of individual movement, given the inexpensive cost of transport on the train. The price of transport in a third-class carriage was soon fixed at a penny a mile, meaning that all but the poorest could travel around the country. Finally, there was a new monarch in the shape of Victoria. Many women hoped that the presence of the first female ruler on the throne since Queen Anne might lead to a more understanding and tolerant society.

By the summer, Annabella and Medora were ensconced in a large house in Surrey, Moore Place in Esher. Although the mansion itself offered scant entertainment, it was close enough to Ada in Ockham Park for the half-sisters to continue to socialize freely. It was during this time that Medora met Babbage for the first time, and he professed himself impressed by both her elegant and confident bearing and her obvious deference towards Annabella. There were clear differences between Ada and Medora, both intellectual and social – while Medora had none of Ada's intellectual inquisitiveness, Ada expressed a polite lack of interest in her children which was the opposite of Medora's fondness for Maria – but there were also similarities, not least a propensity towards ill health. Both had inherited the sickly Byron genes.

If Medora had finally found a measure of peace and happiness in this new family, then it seemed deserved. Nonetheless, her relationship with Annabella was still a difficult one. Whether or not Annabella planned for it to happen, the feeling of beneficent altruism in which she had taken such delight when she had rescued Medora, as she castigated Augusta for her neglect and poor morals, had not lasted. Instead, this was replaced by resentment at what she perceived as Medora's lack of gratitude. It did not matter that Medora, slowly recovering from what had been believed to be terminal poor health, did what she could to show her appreciation to Annabella. Instead, by June 1842, Annabella had drawn up a document entitled 'Remarks on E', which noted, among other things, that 'in attempting to hurt those who oppose her she will hurt herself, but this will be not from recklessness, but by miscalculation', and that 'she expects to make people serve her better by bullying'.[23]

It remains unclear how accurate these accusations were. While Medora's earlier circumstances had turned her into a nervous woman who was quick to behave defensively at any hint of a slight or attack, she had responded well to the life of comfort and amity that she and her daughter had experienced over the previous years. Her domestic life was certainly unconventional; entirely dependent on Annabella for her expenses, she was occasionally kept short – for instance, she and Marie were given an allowance of £60 a year to cover all their clothing and laundry. Had they been living in France, away from society, this would have been more than adequate, but mixing in the exalted social circles to which she was becoming increasingly accustomed, it represented either thoughtlessness or a deliberate slight on Annabella's part.

Whether Medora believed that she was being discriminated against or not, she began to realize that a continued life as Annabella's ward and 'second daughter' was untenable. As she despaired of Annabella's outbreaks of anger – she wrote 'Lady Byron's temper caused me great misery'[24] – she decided that she would be happier in a warmer country, as the doctors had suggested for her. Annabella, rather than allowing her to make her own decisions, ordered that she head to the south of France, to the town of Hyères, which had a reputation for attracting English expatriates who wished to enjoy warmer weather. She also decided that Medora would benefit from a chaperone, so, against her ward's wishes, she engaged a French maid named Natalie Beaurepaire to perform the role. There was no love lost between Natalie and Medora. The former was a committed snob who informed Medora of her wish that she had been in the employ of 'a lady whose conduct have ever been irreproachable', and Medora responded that she should 'avail herself of the opportunity of quitting me, as my life and past history were not as she would wish'.[25]

As Medora prepared to leave, she continued to argue with Annabella about money. Offered an allowance of £150 a year to support her, Natalie and Marie, Medora responded angrily, not least because Natalie would be placed in control of the finances. Yet a letter of Annabella's the next month hinted that there were more complex considerations at play than simple financial ones. Asking 'do you remember, dear E, that I asked you early in our acquaintance not to use affectionate expressions towards me?', she went on to say 'I suffered myself to believe that you had conquered the early impressions to my disadvantage which were made upon your mind and were able to love me.'[26] Ada was reluctantly drawn into the situation as go-between. She attempted to convince her mother both of Medora's gratitude and her need for more than the scanty allowance she proposed to offer her, but without success. Annabella believed that she had been generous, and besides, Medora was not her daughter, regardless of how she had been treated as one.

Final arrangements were drawn up for Medora to set off from England on 22 July. Before she left, she had the unexpected and unwelcome experience of encountering Augusta for the first time in over a decade. Although her mother did not see her, Medora described to Annabella how the experience 'shocked me – pained me', and said of her 'oh how dearly, fondly, I loved her, and had she only stifled the existence her sin gave me… Oh how horrible she looked – so wicked – so hyena-like – That I could have loved her so!'[27] Even allowing for an exaggeration designed to comfort Annabella, it seems clear that her attitude towards Augusta was contemptuous, and influenced by how she had been conditioned. Annabella was magnanimous in victory, and replied 'I could not read of that meeting without great pain, and yet I believe it best that you should see what *is*.'[28]

The final encounter between Ada and Medora took place on 21 July 1842 and proved to be an emotional occasion. Ada was aware that Medora's attitudes towards her mother's assistance could be interpreted as ungrateful, but she nevertheless continued to act as a friend and confidante towards her half sister. Consequently, she bore the brunt of Medora's railing against Annabella, later writing that 'the last half hour I was there... I was compelled to hear a discourse on the bitterness of dependence and threats of throwing herself down the throat of the first man she could get hold of to marry'.[29] Nonetheless, she exhibited a fond compassion towards Medora, and she was repaid by being entrusted with Medora's zealously guarded deed of inheritance, which she asked to be deposited with William's other important papers at Ockham.

As Medora left for Hyères, it is hard to gauge what Annabella and Ada's reaction to her departure was. Amid the conventional expressions of regret and sorrow at a parting of uncertain length was a hope that Medora's sojourn in France would be a happier and more productive one than the previous decade that she spent there. There was also a gloomy foreboding that nothing in her life had ever been straightforward, and that she, like her father, was mad, bad, and dangerous to know.

Future events would fully vindicate their concern.

18

I believe no creature ever could WILL
things like a Byron

ADA TO ANDREW CROSSE,
OCTOBER 1844

As Medora headed off to an uncertain new life in Hyères, Ada appeared to be the perfect contrast to her in all respects. Seemingly contentedly married and at the pinnacle of respectable society, her intellectual interests and close association with Babbage seemed pleasant eccentricities rather than anything more. This misread her complex and demanding character. Like her father, she was torn between a desire for change and evolution, and the strictures of society holding her back. This often took violent form; when she informed Woronzow Greig that 'I am a damned ODD animal',[1] she brusquely announced that either a devil or angel watched over her, but she could not be sure which one held sway 'and for my part, I am quite indifferent which'. Convention was merely a shackle for the so-called 'bride of science'.

The central difference between Ada and Medora was that while Medora was essentially reactionary in her views and actions, Ada was an innovator in all regards. Even so, Greig counselled caution and prudence, or, in his words *'festina lente'*, there was a greater prize afoot, as long as she might restrain herself; as he put it, 'your immediate prospect is uninviting, the self denial required is great, and the sacrifice enormous – but the end is glorious and an approach to immortality will be your reward'.[2]

Part of Ada's 'approach to immortality' lay in her scientific exploration. By the beginning of 1843 she was unafraid to make her intentions known, translating a paper by the Italian engineer Luigi Menabrea that discussed Babbage's Analytical Engine and publishing it in the periodical *Scientific Memoirs*. When she told Babbage of her actions, he was startled that she had not gone further, asking her 'why have you not written an original paper on a subject with which [you are] so intimately acquainted?' When she demurred, claiming herself to be unequal to the challenge, Babbage replied that she should not merely act as a translator for Menabrea's article, but should instead add her own thoughts and opinions.[3] It was a simple observation, but startling in its implication. Women had simply not encroached on the masculine and clubby world of scientific writing. Yet if there was anyone who could tear down the smoke-stained curtain and offer something startlingly new, it was Ada.

As she established a reputation as both a free thinker and an innovator, her debt to Babbage continued to be foremost in her mind. She described the complex algebraic equations that she dealt with as being as abstract as 'sprites and fairies',[4] but believed that she could bring rigorous examination to their study. She informed Babbage that 'science has thrown its net over me, & has fairly ensnared the fairy, or whatever she is'.[5] Fairies were a much-beloved part of the Victorian imagination, painted by the likes of Turner (in *Queen Mab's Cave*) and Millais (in his *Tempest* portrait *Ferdinand Lured By Ariel*) and read about in translations of Grimm and Hans Christian Andersen, and so Ada was faithfully reflecting contemporary mores. There was also the implication that her achievements would be more substantial and less ephemeral than something created in the world of faerie.

What Ada and Babbage achieved was considerable; the studies that they made of the 'Analytic Engine' were far beyond anything that had been dreamed of in engineering before. She was keen not to become in thrall to hubris, however. She wrote an explanatory note to Menabrea's paper that:

It is desirable to guard against the possibility of exaggerated ideas that might arise as to the power of the Analytical Engine. In considering any new subject, there is frequently a tendency, first, to *overrate* what we find to be already interesting or remarkable; and, secondly, by a sort of natural reaction, to *undervalue* the true state of the case, when we do discover that our notions have surpassed those that were really tenable.[6]

She need not have been so humble. She and Babbage have justly been praised as the pioneers of computing, and they have remained an inspiration to innovators and inventors ever since.*

Yet, at the moment of her greatest triumph, a conflict between her and Babbage threatened to overshadow their achievement. Babbage wished to add a statement to the publication criticizing the lack of government interest in his research, and to leave it unsigned. Ada, who used her initials 'A.A.L.' to denote her contributions, wished Babbage to sign his statement, to avoid ambiguity as to who was contributing what. After the British Association, the publishers of *Taylor's Scientific Memoirs*, convened a meeting to discuss what should be done, it was decided that Babbage should be compelled to affix his name to his statement, or withdraw it altogether. Babbage, in return, asked Ada to withdraw her own preface from the publication, and continued to refuse to add his name to his contribution.

If this sounds remarkably petty, it should be remembered that, in 1843, Babbage enjoyed a high public reputation as both a polemicist and controversialist. Therefore, while he was happy to be associated with Ada – and her famous father – in a private and informal context, he was reluctant to be placed on an equal footing with her in a publication of this nature, and so sought to invoke what he believed to be his right of *noblesse oblige*. He was

* For a fuller account of the collaboration between Babbage and Ada, see Dorothy Stein's *Ada: A Life and a Legacy* (1980).

to be disappointed. Ada wrote him a lengthy, heartfelt letter, in which she simultaneously praised him as 'one whose genius I not only so highly appreciate myself, but wish to see fairly appreciated by others', but also attacked his 'double-dealing'. She repeated her wish to be seen as an equal partner in any collaboration that they undertook, especially as she would solely be responsible for the practical aspects of their work, creating business plans and obtaining funding from would-be investors. As she declared that 'every year adds to the unlimited nature of my trust & hope in the Creator',[7] she left it ambiguous as to whether this 'Creator' was God, Babbage or Ada herself.

The boldness and chutzpah of the letter were dictated in equal parts by hurt feelings, laudanum and wine. The latter two had been prescribed by well-meaning doctors for her outbursts of nervous attacks. Ada prevailed, after a fashion; Babbage withdrew his statement and published it anonymously in the *Philosophical Magazine*, thereby leaving Ada to claim the credit for the translation and introduction herself. The relationship between the two did not suffer irreparably, but the previous amiable balance of master and pupil had been altered. From now on, Ada would never be a mere appendage to anyone, whether teacher, husband or mother. Instead, she would be entirely her own person.

∾

During the course of her letter to Babbage, Ada at one point apologized for the comparative ill humour of her writing, explaining it by saying 'if you knew what sad and direful experience I have had'. She referred to Medora, who had begun to make what life she could for herself in southern France. She had already received a proposition of marriage while en route, from a French officer. It was hoped that a quieter and more sedate existence awaited her in the resort of Hyères, where the population was made up of transitory visitors, the elderly and invalids. Thus, when Annabella instructed her to 'go, and buy experience',[8] it was in the expectation that there was little to compare to the whirligig of London and Parisian society.

While the pretty surroundings of Hyères charmed, the high cost of rent did not, and by November 1842 Medora and Natalie had moved away, near the grubbier seaport of Toulon. Even so, Annabella continued to consider Medora's expenses unreasonable; she wrote to criticize her for 'rendering all the money arrangements as vexacious as possible for her'[9] and openly doubted whether she had been living within the agreed sum of £150 per year. This was despite the fact that Medora had no direct involvement with her allowance, which was dealt with entirely by Natalie and her husband Victor. Annabella exercised her power in petty, niggling ways. When Medora could not supply itemized receipts for her expenditure, Annabella refused to send a promised £20 earmarked for Marie's schooling.

By the start of 1843, Medora was in as bad a position as she had been in before. Hopelessly compromised by Natalie and Victor, who took their privileged position as go-betweens to play Medora and Annabella off against one another, she eventually decided that she would be happier in Paris once again. She informed Annabella that she would be heading there 'for reasons of which Lady Noel Byron could not be ignorant'.[10] Even as Annabella wrote concerned letters wondering about the lack of communication from her – 'many an anxious hour, and under severe illness, have you of late cost me'[11] – Medora was bound for the capital. When Annabella found out that her ward had disobeyed her, her response was chillingly simple. She informed her friend Selina Doyle that 'as to my pounds, they will only follow many others into the vortex of that family'.[12] Medora was to be disinherited.

Selina and her sister Adelaide were initially receptive to Medora and her party when they arrived in Paris, believing that Annabella had sanctioned their visit. When the truth emerged, their loyalties were divided. Selina believed that Medora had behaved rashly and ungratefully, whereas Adelaide took a more sympathetic view of her actions. Nonetheless, Medora's financial position was highly precarious, with her social standing even more troubled. When Annabella discovered that she was staying in a hotel on credit, she not only wrote to the proprietor to inform him that she was not supporting Medora, but also told him 'all she could of the past history of my life that could be unfavourable and painful'.[13] Adelaide paid the hotel bill, but there was no hope of Medora's hand-to-mouth existence finding any permanent relief. Once again, she was condemned to wander, alone.

She was not helped by Ada, who, influenced by Annabella, wrote to Medora in late March to inform her that she was behaving ungratefully and that the only hope for her was to comport herself in a more respectable fashion. The inherent condescension in her letter stung; Ada, who had treated Medora as a long-lost sister when the two were on intimate terms in London and the country the previous year, had essentially withdrawn her friendship. While this hurt on a personal level, Annabella's next action was that of a chess player putting a hopelessly unmatched opponent into check. She wrote to Natalie and informed her that, as there was no longer any need for her and Victor to chaperone Medora, they should leave her and Marie to their own devices and return home.

Had they done this, Medora would have been in a catastrophic position, but Natalie instead saw an opportunity of increasing her and her husband's financial standing and influence alike. Persuading an isolated Medora that they were her true friends, they encouraged her to take legal action against Annabella with a view to securing a legally binding and permanent allowance. With the aid of a leading French lawyer, Antoine Berryer, an approach was made to Annabella. This stated that Medora should be allowed a larger advance, autonomy of person and the right to live in a place of her choosing, rather than being engaged in a demeaning exercise of cap-in-hand.

Unfortunately, Annabella had decided by now that Medora's wilfulness and lack of conformity were dictated by mental illness, probably as a cause of her parenthood, and she dispatched Ada's former tutor William King* to Paris to assess her. King was now the proprietor of a lunatic asylum near Brighton, and she hoped that, if he came to the conclusion that she was a danger to herself and others, Medora could be quietly incarcerated and her potential for embarrassment brought to an end. No allowance was made for her unfortunate daughter; perhaps Annabella simply hoped that the child would return to Trevanion and cease to be a burden on her family.

When King arrived, he offered Medora a final chance. If she agreed to return to England and live under the protection of Annabella, she might be allowed to continue to receive an allowance. Medora, utterly exhausted by Annabella's stratagems and attempts at control, refused and a lively exchange of views ensued. Her later account of the termination of the meeting shows how she 'submitted to all the abuse he was pleased to bestow', even as 'it contributed all the more to make me refuse when he said "Sign – sign – you great fool"'.[14] King returned to England without Medora, and, much to Annabella's disappointment, informed her that her erstwhile ward was ungrateful, stubborn – and perfectly sane.

Nonetheless, Medora continued to be impecunious, with her only financial support the ability to borrow on the deed of inheritance that she had acquired from Augusta. Even this proved difficult, as she did not physically have the deed and Annabella's solicitors refused to send it by post, instead insisting that she or her representative return to England to collect it. This seemed impossible for a worn-out Medora, but Natalie convinced her to allow her to head back herself with the intention of obtaining the deed, claiming that she had spoken to Berryer and that he had urged her to act in such a way. This was a lie, and it seemed to Medora that Natalie, far from being a friend and helpful companion, was yet another Judas. Were Natalie to obtain the deed, there was no guarantee that she would behave honourably; it was not impossible

---

* No relation to Ada's husband of the same name.

that she would simply use it herself for her and her husband to borrow credit against it.

The situation was a grim one, and necessitated Medora's return to England. Assisted by a friend from Hyères, Captain Joseph Barrallier, she scraped together what money she could and set off for a reckoning with Annabella. It seemed as if her destiny could only be resolved by confronting the woman who had become her tormentor. When asked by Adelaide what she should do without an income, her reply was entirely pointed: 'I shall act, and Lady B will be responsible for whatever I may do.'[15]

∾

As her half-sister headed to London, Ada was beginning to worry about her own increasing ill health. To combat her fatigue and weakness she had continued to drink a mixture of claret and laudanum, and this had had the effect of making her feel alternately disengaged and over-exuberant. By 1844, she was writing to her mother to complain that 'the least too much exercise however drives my brain far wilder than even *wine* & stimulants… I am frequently awake many hours at night, with feelings of exhaustion & hunger… I cannot but *weep* almost over my inability to see so many whom I would wish to see.'[16] Her marriage had suffered, due to her husband's inability to understand his wife's shifts of mood and temper, and her children were neglected, entrusted to tutor after tutor to relieve her of maternal responsibility.

While from a contemporary perspective it seems clear that the efforts of working with Babbage had led Ada to undergo a nervous breakdown, there was no such understanding in the mid-nineteenth century. One solution to her predicament was to attempt to bleed her, but this, although approved of by Annabella, had no effect. Ada had also developed an addiction to opium, writing in her journal that '[it] has a remarkable effect on my eyes, seeming to *free* them, and to make them *open & cool*'.[17] She openly resented her body's inability to keep pace with her mind, writing to Annabella that 'the least exertion, either mental or bodily, has effects now that I never knew before'. Ironically, a sojourn in Hyères or Paris might have done her a great deal of good, but Annabella, who seemed to regard a trip to France as punishment, made no such suggestion.

Ada's intellectual interests were not at an end. She formed an association with Andrew Crosse, a pioneer in the field of experiments in electricity, and wrote to him in a strikingly forthright tone: 'You know I believe no creature ever could WILL things like a *Byron*. And that perhaps is at the bottom of the genius-like tendencies in my family. We can throw our *whole life* and *existence* for the time being into whatever we *will* to do and accomplish.' Citing the family motto of *Crede Byron*, she boasted that 'I mean to do *what I mean to do*'.[18] No wonder that she called herself 'the bride of science', a term used of her both admiringly and dismissively.

There was another aspect to Ada's life that was a world away from the intellectual pursuits in which she indulged with Babbage and Crosse. When Annabella had taken her to a race meeting when she was younger to show her the iniquity of the activity, she had loathed it. However, in need of money, she happened upon a book of Babbage's, *An Examination of some Questions connected with Games of Chance*, and believed that she could use her intellectual gifts in a more practical and rewarding fashion than hitherto by placing a series of carefully considered bets on the horses. She chose to ignore Babbage's warning that 'the words profit, winning, gain etc must, if we wish to avoid perpetual repetition, frequently be understood to comprehend the very opposite'.[19]

Ada formed a syndicate with a shadowy collection of male acquaintances, including Crosse's son John, and began gambling in 1844, but without success. She soon incurred heavy losses, which she endeavoured to conceal from her husband. However, she was both unskilled at her chosen scheme and without the extensive private resources that she needed to cover her shortfall. Before long, she was being blackmailed by her various creditors, who, knowing that there was no legal recourse for obtaining monies owed them, believed that the surest way of getting their recompense would be by exposing a great society figure – and Lord Byron's daughter! – as little more than a common gambler.

She told her husband of her activities, and though no record survives of letters immediately after the revelation, he behaved in an admirably compassionate fashion, volunteering to meet the blackmailers and prosecute them for their actions if required. Annabella, who was dangerously ill, was kept ignorant of her daughter's activities. Had she known of them, the agony that the revelation would have caused her could have hastened her death. William's condition for paying Ada's bills was that she would abandon gambling and conduct her financial affairs with the propriety becoming Lady Lovelace. That she was expected to do this on an annual income of £300 a year seemed fanciful. While Annabella lived, Ada was simultaneously in thrall to both mother and husband for her financial requirements. To obtain a large sum of money easily, and by using her intellectual acumen, seemed the only means of allowing her to pursue the independent life that she so craved. Thus, even as she publicly disavowed her gambling career, she continued to wonder whether the possibility of making a large sum of money was within her reach. By the time that Lovelace, believing it would please Ada, suggested a visit to the races in Doncaster in 1850 to see a friend's horse run, she had determined to make good on her earlier mistakes. Like most gamblers, she was confident that one great success would change her fortunes forever.

◈

Medora, when she had arrived in London seven years earlier in 1843, had faced a similar predicament. The main difference between her and Ada was that she was desperate to obtain money, not to enjoy an elevated status of existence but simply to survive. She was faced with various difficulties from the outset, not least the endless falsehoods of Natalie and Victor. They had visited Annabella to claim not only that Medora had taken delight in informing them of her true parentage, but also that they were now so compromised by association with her that they would never again be able to obtain respectable positions in society. They also hinted, with consummate malice, that Medora was preparing to blackmail the family by threatening to reveal her true origins, thereby exposing a carefully concealed secret. The scandal would be momentous.

The casual hypocrisy is worthy of a novelist's invention, but for Medora matters were more serious. Not only was her previous advocate George Stephen now in the employ of Annabella, but her involvement with Captain Barrailler, however innocently it was intended, led to mutterings that Medora had begun yet another unsuitable love affair. In fact, a more significant attachment came about when Barrailler introduced her to the lawyer Thomas Smith, who had known Byron while both were in Greece. Smith was impressed with Medora, who he described as 'a very lively and agreeable person',[20] and, believing that she would gain a greater clarity of thought from writing down what had befallen her, suggested that she put together an autobiography. This had the benefit of allowing Medora to articulate her side of the saga, but it also represented a more refined form of coercion of Annabella; if it were to be made public, the results would be disastrous.

Unfortunately, Annabella was immovable, refusing to engage in any further communication with Medora. She also faced problems with her servants-cum-informants, firstly because Natalie attempted to take possession of the deed and would not return it to Medora until she was literally compelled to, and then because, thwarted, she and her husband attempted to sue Annabella for fraud, on the grounds that she should have informed them of Medora's shameful birth. As a result, they claimed, their names had been irreparably blackened by their involvement with such a wicked woman. Wishing to avoid a public lawsuit of this kind, Annabella considered issuing a counter-suit for libel and slander, but instead settled for an out-of-court settlement, much to her chagrin.

By this point, Medora, penniless and desperate, was reduced to writing begging letters to relations and friends of Byron's, asking for 'aid and protection'. One of these letters was sent to Hobhouse, who bluntly dismissed it in a letter by saying 'Elizabeth Medora Leigh stating herself to be *child* of Lord Byron and starving – some imposter I *hope*'.[21] At a loss for anything else to do, she took the desperate step of visiting her mother on 12 August to beg her for help; the curt response from her servant was 'Mrs Leigh is not at home.' After this humiliation, she wrote furiously to Augusta to castigate her, saying 'I was made to understand you could never have loved me, the child of your guilt, in whom you have been but a means to satisfy your ambition, a sacrifice to be made to those you feared, then to throw me on the world, destitute, homeless and friendless.'[22] Whether Augusta received the letter with a sense of contrition or anger, it made little difference. The estrangement between the two, so zealously sought by Annabella, continued. The two were never reconciled before Augusta's death on 12 October 1851.

As 1843 wore on, and Medora struggled on what little financial assistance she could glean from the begging letters she sent, a different solution presented itself. She engaged a new solicitor, Sir John Hughes, who suggested that Trevanion had evaded his paternal duties without fear of the consequences and should be made responsible for his daughter's wellbeing, if not Medora's. Trevanion replied in January the next year, dolefully saying 'I am extremely sorry that it is entirely out of my power at the moment to contribute to the education of the young girl who was the object of your letter... at the moment I find it difficult to maintain myself.'[23] Knowing that Marie was not his legitimate daughter made it easier for Trevanion to evade any legal attempt to make him responsible, and a continued residence in Brittany meant that he was beyond the reach of English law.

Knowing this, Hughes proposed a solution for Medora that he hoped would solve her problems. If she left England for France, and promised not to return, she would be allowed to borrow against her deed of inheritance. Those around her saw this as the only way of finishing the saga. While human decency or simple embarrassment would not allow them to see Medora reduced to prostitution or sent penniless to the workhouse, having her removed from their lives would be a preferable solution. She borrowed £500 from a banker, Hugh Cossart Baker, on the strength of the deed, and headed with Marie to a small town outside Paris, St Germain-en-Laye, where she placed her daughter in a convent before obtaining work as a servant at a hotel where she had formerly been a resident. At the age of thirty, those around her hoped that Medora could spend the remainder of her life in obscurity, playing down her birth and reputation in less-than-splendid isolation.

Yet she remained a Byron, and that saucily indomitable spirit could not be so easily quenched. It was during her work at the hotel that she encountered a young soldier, Jean-Louis Taillefer, and, after a brief courtship, began an affair with him that resulted in her becoming pregnant in May 1846. Leaving the hotel with Marie in late November, she headed, at Taillefer's instigation, to the town of St Affrique in southern France for her confinement. Unlike her previous pregnancies this one passed without difficulty, and a boy was born on 27 January 1847, shortly before the family moved to the village of Laepeyre in the Aveyron. He was christened Jean-Louis Elie in his father's honour, but was always referred to as Elie.

Although Medora was happy with her new situation, it was still a difficult one, not least because Taillefer left her for months at a time due to his military duties. Although they were unofficially engaged, she was unmarried and therefore an object of curiosity as she participated in rural life as best she could, helped by the financial contributions that Taillefer could make. It was still far from a comfortable existence, not least because of her lover's long absences. He was barely with her at all in 1847, and did not return until July 1848. Honouring his promise to marry her, the two wed in a civil ceremony on 23 August 1848, making her Madame Taillefer: the

368 *Byron's Women*

latest in a long and often confusing series of identities.

Medora therefore began to take on the attitudes and personality of a French provincial woman, not quite a peasant but only slightly above. She became popular with her neighbours, acquiring a piano – thereby marking herself out as someone of curiosity, on the grounds that nobody around there had ever seen or played the instrument before – and word spread that she had some mysterious aristocratic connection in England, although she never elaborated on this. Republican France remained ambivalent towards those of noble birth, but Medora was judged for who she was, rather than where she had come from.

Yet, after she had found some relief and peace, her life came to an abrupt and untimely end. In August 1849, she contracted smallpox. The chances of survival, or at least survival without hideous disfigurement, were extremely low, but she faced her end with the courage that had defined her chaotic, eventful life. Around the time of her first wedding anniversary on 23 August 1849, she wrote a will that left everything, including the notorious deed, to her husband and children. She had not forgotten the ill treatment she had received, and wrote 'I also declare here that I forgive my mother and all those who have so cruelly persecuted me, as I hope myself to be forgiven.' She died on 29 August, and was buried in the local churchyard. The entire village attended her simple funeral. The priest who conducted it later described her as 'the pious, charitable Englishwoman, whom I did not have the honour of knowing myself, but of whom everyone speaks to me with the highest praise'.[24]

❧

Ada must have known of Medora's death, given that both Annabella and Augusta were informed of it in September 1849, but there is no record of her reaction to the end of her half-sister. It is possible that she had other matters in mind, not least her own continued ill health and a growing interest in her father's legacy, which came to dominate the last years of her life.

In the middle of 1850, she and William had paid a visit to New-stead Abbey during a tour of the north of England. It was the first time that she had seen her father's much-beloved home, and although its current owner, Thomas Wildman, had renovated it, it retained much of its original aspect. Wildman was disappointed that Ada, far from being a loquacious interlocutor, spent much of her time at Newstead wandering round in a state of awe. After she initially adopted an apparently blasé attitude to her homecom-ing, she soon revealed that she had been hugely affected by her experience, as she asked Wildman about his earlier meetings with Byron. For the first time, she fully accepted her status as her father's daughter. Describing it as little less than a 'resurrection', she stated 'I do love the venerable old place & all my *wicked forefathers*.'[25]

Annabella, predictably, was affronted, saying 'if the mythic idea generally entertained of your father affords you satisfaction, do not forget, dearest Ada, how much of it is owing to my own line of conduct… I was his best friend, not only in feeling but in fact.'[26] Had Ada responded to this with a considered rebuttal, she might have destroyed the fiction that Annabella had constructed. Instead, emboldened by her discovery of her origins, she returned to the races, with the intent of making good her previous losses and establishing herself as a woman of independent means, as well as assisting Babbage financially in his bid to complete his Analytical Engine.

There was, therefore, an irony in her requiring a letter from William giving her his permission to gamble. This was granted on the understanding that she was going to act in a responsible way, given her assurances that she had discovered a mathematically foolproof means of securing victory. She had not. After a series of horrendously misconceived bets, the syndicate that she had formed had managed to lose £3,200, meaning that she was obliged to ask William for a loan in order to cover the expenses. Although he was horrified at what had occurred, especially after her previous and disastrous foray into gambling, he had little choice other than to cover her debts; the alternative would have been to make her escapades public and cause a grave scandal. However, Ada soon received news that would make her financial worries seem insignificant in comparison: she discovered that she had cancer of the womb, exacerbated by the ham-fisted previous attempts at bleeding that she had suffered at the hands of so-called 'experts'.

Although Ada had been ill for much of her life, she had seemed to be in a healthier state throughout much of the 1840s, perhaps as a result of the intellectual vigour that her work with Babbage had engendered. However, from 1848 onwards, she was susceptible to fainting attacks and spasms, and painfully heavy menstrual bleeding. When diagnosed with cancer, she took a fatalistic approach, saying to her friend the chemist Henry Bence Jones that 'I'd rather have 10 or 5 *real* years of life, than 20 or 30 such as I see people usually dawdling on, without any spirit.'[27]

She undertook the usual array of quack remedies – 'rest cures' at Leamington Spa, heavy doses of laudanum and even experiments with cannabis – but the only effect that the drugs had was to dull her senses along with the pain. Annabella, when informed by William of her daughter's illness and gambling debts, did not offer any sympathy, and stated that her present situation was a direct result of her bad habits and wilfulness. Had she submitted to her mother's instruction – by now heavily influenced by the popular evangelical clergyman Frederick Robertson – she would, according to Annabella, have found salvation. Like her father before her, Ada rejected her mother's humbug and hypocrisy. She was extremely ill, but throughout 1851 she managed to remain *compos mentis*, attempting to guide her son Byron, who had embarked on a naval career, and even continuing to correspond with Babbage.

Matters worsened at the beginning of 1852. Not only was Ada, by this time dependent on laudanum, forced to readmit Annabella to her life, but William discovered that John Crosse, Ada's former partner in the gambling syndicate, had manipulated her into various undesirable actions, not least pawning her valuable jewels for the comparatively trifling sum of £800. Crosse, who was gambling again, presupposed that the risk of his behaviour being publicly exposed was outweighed by the embarrassment of Ada's debts being brought into the open. It also seemed likely that the closeness of their relationship contained a romantic element. Although there has never been any definitive proof of this, William's request that Ada and Crosse should no longer associate with one another can be seen as a dignified response to his likely cuckolding.*

In between her lapses into incoherence, Ada prepared for the end. William wrote in his diary of how:

> She spoke freely of the future state – & how necessary a sequence it was to this world, how incomplete all here was… she considered how all lives had in the view of their creator their use and mission – that they ended when that was over – how hers might be in that predicament.[28]

Ada even planned for her burial, expressing a desire to be buried next to her father in the family vault in Hucknall Church in Nottinghamshire, thereby creating an intimacy with a man that she had never known in life. She even specified her epitaph on the monument from James 5:6: 'You have condemned, you have killed the righteous man; he does not resist you.' Whether or not this was intended as a final riposte to Annabella, it certainly hinted at a strong identification with Byron as the 'righteous man'.

Eventually, after a series of seizures and mental fits, she was forced by Annabella to undergo a form of psychological torture in which she was compelled to confess her alleged sins and submit

---

* It is, however, likely that the result of a mysterious interview between the two on 30 August 1852, after which William abandoned her bedside in a state of anger and grief, was that she made an explicit confession of adultery with Crosse, and possibly with others as well.

to her mother's every desire, most of which revolved around a late attempt at crushing her daughter's will. Barely able to comprehend what was happening, she signed documents attesting to her wickedness and lack of gratitude for all the things that her mother had done for her. At last, she died on 27 November 1852, with Annabella hissing instructions for her to surrender herself to God with more willingness than she had ever allowed herself to submit to earthly authority.

Ada's funeral was held in Nottingham on 4 December. It was well attended, with mourners including William, Greig and Wildman, but neither Babbage nor Annabella were present. Many of those in attendance were Byron aficionados who took the opportunity to see the famous vault in which he had been buried reopened. Once Ada had been buried next to her father, the vault was sealed again, ending another era of the Byron dynasty.

Had she known that, after her death, she would achieve fame and recognition as both a pioneer for computing and for the oft-overlooked achievements of women in science, one imagines that she would have smiled, and enjoyed the knowledge that her mother had been thwarted. Ada epitomized life, and the excitement and fervour of the creative spirit, every bit as brilliantly as her father did, without his capricious and violent spirit. By contrast, Annabella represented the deadening and jealous hand of the mediocrity who believes itself to be the true genius: the Salieri to her daughter's Mozart. Posterity has its own way of righting these particular falsehoods. Before Annabella died of breast cancer, on 16 May 1860, she had told the saga of Byron's sinful actions, and her own virtuous part in rejecting them, so many times that she had come to seem like a bitter, backward-looking termagant, in contrast to her daughter.

Greig's reflections were as unknowingly prescient on Ada's life's work as they were a fitting review of her life, and of her end. When he wrote: 'Your immediate prospect is uninviting, the self denial required is great, and the sacrifice enormous – but the end is glorious and an approach to immortality will be your reward', he echoed the last line of her father's lyric 'Stanzas written on the road between Florence and Pisa'. The 'glorious end' is lent a near-elegiac quality in light of Greig's later summation. It seems a fitting epitaph for both father and daughter:

I knew it was love, and I felt it was glory.

POSTSCRIPT

6 April 1838.*
A meeting between Lord Melbourne
and Queen Victoria.

'Did you know Lord Byron, Lord Melbourne?'

'I did, your majesty.'

'What manner of man was he?'

'He possessed a pretty smile, but was treacherous beyond conception.'[1]

'I had heard that he misled his fellow man.'

'And woman, on all too many occasions.'

'I am extremely sorry to hear that.'

'Including, I fear to say, my own late wife, Lady Caroline. She said of him that he was "mad, bad and dangerous to know", and I agree with the accuracy of such a description.'

'I see. Was he… well favoured in looks?'

'He was extremely handsome, yes. He had dark hair, was very lame and limped very much.'

'But was the expression of his countenance agreeable?'

'No. He had a sarcastic, sardonic expression. You might go so far as to say that it was a contemptuous expression.'

'So you would not describe him as agreeable?'

'Ah. He was indeed agreeable. If anything, he could be excessively

---

* A partially imagined dialogue. Melbourne was then fifty-eight years old; Victoria, newly crowned, only eighteen.

so. But I believe that he was fond of treachery.'

'When it came to women?'

'When it came to all things. He posed as a poet, as an aristocrat, as a lover, and then as a soldier. He broke hearts and destroyed reputations. The greatest in the land fell under his spell, for he dazzled everybody and deceived them; he could tell his story very well.'[2]

'I see.'

'Do you, your majesty? I fear that he has been regarded by many as too romantic a figure, without the judgement that his many sins deserve.'

'For he was a great sinner.'

'That he undoubtedly was.'

'I think, Melbourne, that I would like to contemplate his poems further, to gauge the measure of such a sin. Might this be arranged?'

CHRONOLOGY

7 February 1756	Jack Biron (or 'Byron') is born in Nottinghamshire.
April 1764	Catherine Gordon is born in Gight Castle.
26 January 1783	Jack's only surviving daughter with his first wife Amelia Osborne, Augusta, is born.
13 May 1785	Jack Byron and Catherine marry in Bath.
13 November 1785	Caroline Ponsonby is born in Northamptonshire.
22 January 1788	George Gordon is born in Holles Street, London.
29 January 1788	George is baptized at the St Marylebone parish church.
September 1790	Jack Byron abandons his wife and child, then resident in Aberdeen, and heads to France.
2 August 1791	Jack Byron dies in Valenciennes, aged thirty-five, of tuberculosis.
17 May 1792	Anne 'Annabella' Milbanke is born at Elemore Hall, near Durham.
July 1794	George becomes the heir-but-one to the Byron estate after his cousin is killed at the Siege of Calvi.
30 August 1797	Mary Shelley is born.
c. 27 April 1798	Claire Clairmont is born.
19 May 1798	George becomes the 6th Lord Byron upon the death of his grandfather.

August 1798	Byron visits Newstead for the first time.
*c.*1799/1800	Teresa Gamba is born in Ravenna.
1801	Caroline Ponsonby and William Lamb meet for the first time at Brocket Hall.
April 1801	Byron begins his education at Harrow.
October 1801	Catherine makes contact with her stepdaughter Augusta, although they do not meet.
3 June 1805	Caroline Ponsonby and William Lamb marry. She becomes Lady Caroline Lamb.
July 1805	Byron leaves Harrow.
24 October 1805	Byron begins his education at Trinity College, Cambridge.
November 1806	Byron's first collection of poetry, *Fugitive Pieces*, is published but almost immediately recalled from sale on the grounds that it is too scandalous.
1807	Augusta marries Colonel George Leigh.
June 1807	Byron's second collection, *Hours Of Idleness*, is published.
28 August 1807	Caroline's first child, George Augustus Frederick, is born.
December 1807	Byron leaves Cambridge, heavily in debt.
Spring 1809	Byron's third collection, *English Bards and Scotch Reviewers*, appears. It attacks the *Edinburgh Review*, which criticized *Hours Of Idleness*.
22 January 1809	Byron celebrates his coming of age in London.
29 January 1809	Caroline suffers a miscarriage.
13 March 1809	Byron takes his seat in the House of Lords.
2 July 1809	Byron departs for his Grand Tour, having drawn up a will that leaves £500 a year to Catherine in the event of his death.
Early 1810	Caroline begins a love affair with Godfrey Webster.

February 1810	Annabella arrives in London for her first season.
3 May 1810	Byron swims the Hellespont 'in imitation of Leander'.
14 July 1811	Byron returns to England.
1 August 1811	Catherine, who has been suffering ill health for some time, dies, shortly before Byron's return to Newstead.
9 August 1811	Catherine is buried at Hucknall Church in Nottinghamshire. Byron does not attend the funeral.
March 1812	Annabella and Caroline meet for the first time.
10 March 1812	The first cantos of Byron's autobiographical bestseller, *Childe Harold's Pilgrimage*, are published by John Murray; the first edition of 500 copies sells out in three days.
24 March 1812	Caroline and Byron are officially introduced for the first time by Lady Holland.
Early April 1812	Byron and Caroline begin a love affair.
13 April 1812	Byron and Annabella meet at a party.
29 July 1812	Byron attempts to break off the affair, without success; Caroline instead tries to elope with him.
October 1812	Claire meets Shelley for the first time.
8 October 1812	Byron proposes marriage to Annabella, and is rejected.
June 1813	Byron publishes his Oriental romance *The Giaour*.
5 July 1813	Byron and Caroline encounter one another at a ball, and some accounts suggest that she attempts suicide.
August 1813	Byron begins a love affair with Augusta.
January 1814	Augusta and Byron head to Newstead for the spring.
March 1814	Shelley meets Mary Godwin for the first time.

15 April 1814	Elizabeth Medora Leigh, Augusta's daughter – probably by Byron – is born.
29 July 1814	Mary and Shelley elope.
September 1814	Byron again proposes marriage to Annabella, and this time is accepted. He learns the news while at Newstead with Augusta.
2 January 1815	Byron and Annabella are married.
22 February 1815	Mary gives birth to Shelley's child, but it does not survive.
March 1815	Byron takes Annabella to meet Augusta at her home in Six Mile Bottom, with disastrous consequences.
28 July 1815	Newstead is sold at auction for 95,000 guineas.
10 December 1815	Byron and Annabella's daughter Augusta Ada is born.
6 January 1816	Byron demands that Annabella leave their house.
26 January 1816	Mary gives birth to a son, William, by Shelley.
March 1816	Claire and Byron meet for the first time.
17 March 1816	A separation between Byron and Annabella is agreed that favours her in all financial matters.
14 April 1816	Byron and Augusta meet for the last time.
25 April 1816	Byron leaves England for the Continent, and never returns.
May 1816	Byron meets Shelley and Mary Shelley for the first time.
9 May 1816	Caroline publishes her *roman-à-clef* about her relationship with Byron, *Glenarvon*.
June 1816	Byron writes 'Darkness'.
16 June 1816	Byron, Shelley and Mary come up with a challenge to write a ghost story, and *Frankenstein* is the eventual result.
October 1816	Mary and Claire's stepsister Fanny Imlay dies of a laudanum overdose.
November 1816	Shelley's wife Harriet is found drowned.

30 December 1816	Shelley and Mary are married.
12 January 1817	Claire gives birth to Byron's daughter Allegra.
1817/1818	Byron writes and publishes *Beppo*.
1818	The first edition of *Frankenstein* is published.
20 January 1818	The deed of marriage is drawn up between Teresa and Count Alessandro Guiccioli.
May 1818	Byron removes Allegra from Claire and has her live with him in Italy.
March 1819	Byron and Teresa are formally presented to one another in Venice.
June 1819	Teresa is seriously ill.
7 June 1819	Mary and Shelley's son William dies.
15 July 1819	The first two cantos of *Don Juan* are published.
12 July 1820	Teresa is granted a divorce from Guiccioli.
1 March 1821	Byron enters Allegra in the convent school of San Giovanni Battista.
19 April 1822	Allegra dies of a 'convulsive catarrhal attack' in the convent.
8 July 1822	Shelley dies in a sailing accident.
15 July 1823	Byron leaves Italy for Greece with the intention of joining the fight for independence.
19 April 1824	Byron dies of fever in Missolonghi.
1826 to 1828	Ada and Annabella undertake a Grand Tour of Europe.
1826	Mary's novel *The Last Man* contains a fictionalized account of Byron as Lord Raymond.
July 1826	Teresa and Guiccioli remarry.
October 1826	Teresa and Guiccioli separate again.
26 January 1828	Caroline dies of dropsy.
19 February 1830	Medora gives birth prematurely to a boy, who dies shortly afterwards. The father is her brother-in-law Henry Trevanion.

1831	The revised edition of *Frankenstein* is published.
July 1831	Medora gives birth to a stillborn daughter.
10 May 1833	Ada is presented at court.
5 June 1833	Ada meets Charles Babbage for the first time.
19 May 1834	Medora gives birth to a daughter, Marie.
8 July 1835	Ada marries William King, 8th Baron of Ockham.
16 July 1834	Lord Melbourne becomes Prime Minister.
16 May 1836	Ada gives birth to a son, Byron.
22 September 1837	Ada gives birth to a daughter, Annabella.
30 June 1838	William King is created earl of Lovelace, making Ada countess of Lovelace.
2 July 1839	Ada's second son Ralph is born.
1840	Guiccioli dies.
21 August 1840	Annabella and Medora meet for the first time in Tours.
April 1841	Ada and Medora have their first encounter in Paris.
1843	Ada translates and introduces a paper by the Italian engineer Luigi Menabrea discussing Babbage and his Analytical Engine.
1847	Teresa marries the Marquis de Boissy.
27 January 1847	Medora gives birth to a boy, Jean-Louis Elie.
23 August 1848	Medora marries Elie's father, Jean-Louis Taillefer, in France.
29 August 1849	Medora dies of smallpox.
1 February 1851	Mary Shelley dies of a suspected brain tumour.
12 October 1851	Augusta dies.
27 November 1852	Ada dies of cancer of the womb.
16 May 1860	Annabella dies of breast cancer.
1873	Teresa dies.
19 March 1879	Claire Clairmont dies.

ENDNOTES

Full publication details for all works cited may be found in the Bibliography.

References to Byron's correspondence may be found in Byron, *Letters and Journals*, ed. Leslie Marchand, 10 vols (John Murray, 1973–80).

Prologue

1 Byron to Murray, 10 July 1818.
2 Ibid., 26 August 1818.
3 Byron to Annabella, 31 December 1819.
4 Moore, *The Life and Letters of Lord Byron*, p 192.
5 Kinnaird to Byron, 20 Feb 1821.
6 Byron to Moore, 2 Jan 1821.
7 Hobhouse, *Hobhouse's Diary*, entry of 15 May 1824.
8 Ibid.
9 Ibid.
10 Ibid.
11 Moore, *Life and Letters*, p. 194.
12 Hobhouse, *Hobhouse's Diary*, entry of 17 May 1824.
13 Ibid.

Chapter 1

1 Marchand, *Byron*, p. 16.
2 Boyes, *Amiable Mamma*, p. 5.
3 Walpole, *Castle Of Otranto*, p. 35.
4 Eisler, *Byron*, p. 8.
5 Marchand, *Byron*, p. 12.
6 Clinton, *Memoirs*, p. 33.
7 Crane, *Kindness of Sisters*, p. 46.
8 Byron to John Murray, 7 July 1823.
9 Prothero, 'Childhood', p. 64.
10 Maurois, *Byron*, p. 26.
11 Mayne, *Byron*, p. 4.
12 Boyes, *Amiable Mamma*, p. 4.
13 Marchand, *Byron*, p. 19.
14 Parker, *Byron and his World*, p. 7.
15 Marchand, *Byron*, p. 20.
16 Boyes, *Amiable Mamma*, p. 18.
17 Catherine to Mary Urquhart, 13 November 1786.
18 Marchand, *Byron*, p. 21.
19 Ibid., p. 24.
20 Jack Byron Gordon to Frances Leigh, 21 March 1788.
21 Ibid.
22 Catherine to Watson, 22 February 1788.
23 Thomas Becket to Watson, 29 February 1788.

24 Jack Byron Gordon to Leigh, 21 March 1791.

25 Ibid.

26 Catherine to Leigh, 23 August 1791.

27 Catherine to Frances, undated but 1791.

28 Marchand, *Byron*, p. 32.

29 Medwin, *Conversations*, pp. 58–60.

30 Marchand, *Byron*, p. 33.

31 Boyes, *Amiable Mamma*, p. 40.

32 Moore, *Life and Letters*, p. 5.

33 Byron to John Murray, 16 October 1820.

34 Catherine to Leigh, 29 November 1792.

35 Boyes, *Amiable Mamma*, p. 45.

36 Catherine to Leigh, 8 December 1794.

37 Moore, *Life and Letters,* p 7.

38 Boyes, *Amiable Mamma*, p. 50.

39 Ibid.

40 Marchand, *Byron*, p. 42.

41 Boyes, *Amiable Mamma*, p. 52.

Chapter 2

1 MacCarthy, *Life and Legend,* p. 14.

2 Ibid., p. 15.

3 Eisler, *Byron*, p. 34.

4 Boyes, *Amiable Mamma*, p. 57.

5 Hanson to James Farquhar, 30 August 1798.

6 Boyes, *Amiable Mamma*, p. 59.

7 Eisler, *Byron*, p. 35.

8 Marchand, *Byron*, p. 50.

9 Byron to Charlotte Augusta Parker, 7 November 179

10 Byron to Catherine, 13 March 179

11 Marchand, *Byron*, p. 57.

12 Hanson to Catherine, 1 September 1799.

13 Byron to Hanson, November 1799.

14 Catherine to the Duke of Portland, 25 July 1799.

15 Catherine to Hanson, 27 August 1799.

16 Marchand, *Byron*, p. 60.

17 Ibid., p. 62.

18 Moore, *Life and Letters,* pp. 31–2.

19 Ibid.

20 Boyes, *Amiable Mamma*, p. 72.

21 Ibid., p. 71.

22 Moore, *Life and Letters*, p. 79.

23 Catherine to Hanson, 4 May 1801.

24 Catherine to Laurie, 21 September 1801.

25 Catherine to Augusta, 18 October 1801.

26 Laurie to Catherine, 7 December 1801.

27 Gordon, *Personal Memoirs*, pp. 332–3.

28 Catherine to Hanson, 19 January 1803.

29 Byron to Catherine, 1 May 1803.

30 Ibid., 23 June 1803.

31 Marchand, *Byron*, p. 75.

32 Byron to Catherine, 15 September 1803.

33 Catherine to Hanson,
30 October 1803.

34 Mealey to Hanson,
29 November 1803.

35 Catherine to Hanson,
7 November 1803.

36 Moore, *Life and Letters*, p. 84.

37 Byron to Augusta, 26 March
1804.

38 Lord Grey to Byron, 1808,
Meyer Davis Collection mss.

39 Byron to Augusta, 9 April 1804.

40 Boyes, *Amiable Mamma*, p. 99.

41 Byron to Catherine, 1 May 1804.

42 Catherine to Hanson, 12 May
1804.

43 Catherine to Miss Abernathy,
2 July 1804.

44 Mealey to Hanson, 30 July 1804.

45 Byron to Augusta, 14 August
1804.

46 Ibid., 25 October 1804.

47 Ibid., 2 November 1804.

48 Ibid., 11 November 1804.

49 Ibid., 18 November 1804.

50 Drury to Hanson, 29 December
1804.

Chapter 3

1 Catherine to Hanson,
23 January 1805.

2 Byron to Augusta, 30 January
1805.

3 Ibid., 23 April 1805.

4 Ibid., 5 June 1805.

5 Eisler, *Byron*, p. 84.

6 Marchand, *Byron*, p. 97.

7 Moore, *Life and Letters*, p. 72.

8 Byron to Hanson, 8 July 1805.

9 Moore, *Life and Letters*,
pp. 57–8.

10 Marchand, *Byron*, p. 100.

11 Byron to John Murray,
19 November 1820.

12 Byron to Augusta, 6 November
1805.

13 Catherine to Hanson,
23 September 1805.

14 Marchand, *Byron*, p. 102.

15 Byron to Hanson, 4 December
1805.

16 Ibid., 26 October 1805.

17 Hanson to Byron, 10 December
1805.

18 Byron to Augusta, 26 December
1805.

19 Byron to Catherine, 26 February
1806.

20 Catherine to Hanson, 1 March
1806.

21 Byron to Elizabeth Pigot,
22 June 1807.

22 Harvey, 'Prosecutions for
Sodomy', p. 941.

23 Catherine to Hanson, 4 March
1806.

24 Ibid.

25 Catherine to Hanson, 20 March
1806.

26 Catherine to Hanson, 25 July
1806.

27 Byron to John Pigot, 9 August
1806.

28 Byron to Edward Long,
9 August 1806.

29　Boyes, *Amiable Mamma*, p. 125.

30　Byron to John Pigot, 16 August 1806.

31　Catherine to Hanson, 31 January 1807.

32　Ibid., 19 March 1807.

33　Byron to Elizabeth Pigot, 13 July 1807.

34　Byron to Hanson, 20 July 1807.

35　Byron to Elizabeth Pigot, 2 August 1807.

36　Catherine to Hanson, 23 December 1807.

37　Boyes, *Amiable Mamma*, p. 135.

38　Ibid., pp. 135–6.

39　Byron to Catherine, 7 October 1808.

40　Ibid., 2 November 1808.

41　MacCarthy, *Life and Legend*, p. 63.

42　Catherine to Hanson, 25 November 1808.

43　Byron to Augusta, 30 November 1808.

44　Catherine to Hanson, 5 January 1809.

45　Byron to Hanson, 17 January 1809.

46　Catherine to Hanson, 30 January 1809.

47　Ibid., 4 March 1809.

48　Eisler, *Byron*, p. 171.

49　Boyes, *Amiable Mamma*, p. 148.

50　Catherine to Hanson, 9 April 1809.

51　Byron to Catherine 22 June 1809.

52　Ibid., 15 September 1809.

53　Ibid., 12 November 1809.

54　Ibid., 11 August 1809.

55　Catherine to Byron, 9 October 1809.

56　Ibid., 9 March 1810.

57　Ibid., 11 May 1810.

58　Byron to Catherine, 20 July 1810.

59　Catherine to Byron, 9 September 1810.

60　Boyes, *Amiable Mamma*, p. 163.

61　MacCarthy, *Life and Legend*, p. 130.

62　Byron to Catherine, 28 February 1811.

63　Catherine to Byron, 16 March 1811.

64　Byron to Hobhouse, 15 May 1811.

65　Catherine to Hanson, 23 May 1811.

66　Boyes, *Amiable Mamma*, p. 171.

67　Moore, *Life and Letters*.

68　Byron to Catherine, 25 June 1811.

69　Byron to Pigot, 2 August 1811.

70　Marchand, *Byron*, p. 286.

71　Boyes, *Amiable Mamma*, p. 174.

72　Byron to Hobhouse, 10 August 1811.

73　Byron to Francis Hodgson, 22 August 1811.

Chapter 4

1　Blyth, *Caro*, p. 16.

2　Ibid.

3　Douglass, *Lady Caroline*, p. 1.

4   Ibid., p. 2.

5   Ibid., p. 3.

6   Ibid., p. 8.

7   Ibid., p. 22.

8   Ibid., p. 23.

9   Blyth, *Caro*, p. 26.

10 Lady Spencer to Selina Trimmer, 1 June 1796.

11 *Whole Disgraceful Truth*, pp. 10–11.

12 Blyth, *Caro*, p. 31.

13 Douglass, *Lady Caroline*, p. 27.

14 Blyth, *Caro*, p. 33.

15 Ibid., p. 34.

16 *Hary-O*, p. 23.

17 Cecil, *Melbourne*, p. 57.

18 MacCarthy, *Life and Legend*, p. 164.

19 Blyth, *Caro*, p. 46.

20 Ibid., p. 48.

21 Harriet to Lord Granville, 3 January 1805.

22 Douglass, *Lady Caroline*, p. 42.

23 William Lamb to Caroline Ponsonby, 1 May 1805.

24 Harriet to Lord Granville, 2 May 1805.

25 Douglass, *Lady Caroline*, p. 46.

26 Normington, *Infernal Woman*, p. 31.

27 Ibid., p. 32.

28 Ibid.

29 Blyth, *Caro*, p. 56.

30 *Hary-O*, p. 117.

31 *Whole Disgraceful Truth*, pp. 16–18.

32 Normington, *Infernal Woman*, p. 39.

33 *Whole Disgraceful Truth*, pp. 19–21.

34 William Lamb to Lady Holland, 29 August 1807.

35 *Hary-O*, p. 229.

36 Blyth, *Caro*, p. 70.

37 Douglass, *Lady Caroline*, p. 75.

38 Ibid. p. 77.

39 *Whole Disgraceful Truth*, pp. 41–2.

40 Ibid.

41 Strickland, *The Byron Women*, p. 49.

42 Douglass, *Lady Caroline*, p. 73.

43 Normington, *Infernal Woman*, p. 59.

44 Ibid., pp. 59–60.

45 Lady Melbourne to Caroline, 13 April 1810.

46 *Whole Disgraceful Truth*, pp. 52–4.

47 Caroline to Lady Holland, 3 May 1810.

48 Blyth, *Caro*, pp. 80–1.

49 *Whole Disgraceful Truth*, pp. 65–7.

50 Douglass, *Lady Caroline*, p. 95.

51 Lady Holland to Caroline, undated but *c*. June 1811.

52 *Whole Disgraceful Truth*, pp. 67–70.

53 Ibid., pp. 71–2.

54 *Lady Morgan's Memoirs*, vol 1, pp. 440–2.

55 *Whole Disgraceful Truth*, pp. 62–4.

56 Byron to Francis Hodgson, 5 March 1812.

57 *Lady Morgan's Memoirs*, vol. 2, p. 200.

58 *Whole Disgraceful Truth*, p. 77.

59 Moore, *Life and Letters*, p. 255.

60 *Whole Disgraceful Truth*, pp. 78–9.

61 Medwin, *Conversations*, p. 210.

62 *Lady Morgan's Memoirs*, vol. 2, p. 200.

63 Ibid.

Chapter 5

1 MacCarthy, *Life and Legend*, p. 165.

2 Blyth, *Caro*, p. 89.

3 Ponsonby, *Ponsonby Family*, p. 133.

4 MacCarthy, *Life and Legend*, p. 165.

5 Ibid., p. 166.

6 Caroline to Thomas Medwin, undated but *c.* November 1824.

7 Caroline to Byron, 27 March 1812.

8 Medwin, *Conversations*, pp. 65–6.

9 MacCarthy, *Life and Legend*, p. 173.

10 Caroline to Byron, undated but *c.* spring 1815.

11 Ibid., *c.* April 1812.

12 Byron to Caroline, April 1812.

13 Douglass, *Lady Caroline*, p. 106.

14 Bishop (ed.), *Samuel Rogers*, p. 191

15 Harryo to the Duke of Devonshire, 10 May 1812.

16 Eisler, *Byron*, p. 147.

17 Byron to Hobhouse, 26 February 1808.

18 Eisler, *Byron*, p. 336.

19 Douglass, *Lady Caroline*, p. 110.

20 Blyth, *Caro*, p. 93.

21 Byron to Caroline, April 1812.

22 Caroline to Byron, undated but *c.* April 1812.

23 Normington, *Infernal Woman*, p. 84.

24 Medwin, *Conversations*, p. 216,

25 Byron to Thomas Moore, 20 May 1812.

26 Caroline to Byron, undated but *c.* October/November 1812.

27 Byron to Caroline, 19 May 1812.

28 Caroline to Byron, undated but *c.* June/July 1812.

29 MacCarthy, *Life and Legend*, p. 173.

30 Douglass, *Lady Caroline*, p. 120.

31 Ibid.

32 Villiers, *Grand Whiggery*, pp. 256–7.

33 Douglass, *Lady Caroline*, p. 122.

34 Medwin, *Conversations*, p. 326.

35 Caroline to Byron, undated but *c.* August 1812.

36 Byron to Lord Holland, 12 August 1812.

37 Byron to Lady Melbourne, 14 August 1812.

38 Ibid., 13 September 1812.

39 Ibid.

40 Douglass, *Lady Caroline*, p. 128.

41 Byron to Lady Melbourne,
13 September 1812.

42 Ibid.

43 Ibid., 28 September 1812.

44 Ibid., 18 September 1812.

45 Caroline to Lady Melbourne,
17 October 1812.

46 Byron to Lady Melbourne,
21 September 1812.

47 Medwin, *Conversations*, p. 325.

48 Lady Melbourne to Byron,
undated but *c.* October 1812.

49 *Lady Morgan's Memoirs*, vol. 2,
p. 201.

50 Byron to Lady Melbourne,
10 November 1812.

51 Douglass, *Lady Caroline*, p. 140.

52 Byron to Lady Melbourne,
23 December 1812.

Chapter 6

1 Byron to Lady Melbourne,
10 January 1813.

2 Ibid., 13 January 1813.

3 Ibid., 5 April 1813.

4 Byron to Hobhouse, 17 January
1813.

5 Douglass, *Lady Caroline*, p. 146.

6 Byron to Lady Melbourne, 19
April 1813.

7 Byron to Caroline, 29 April 1813.

8 Blyth, *Caro*, p. 152.

9 Caroline to Byron, undated but
c. May 1813.

10 Byron to Lady Melbourne,
21 June 1813.

11 Douglass, *Lady Caroline*,
pp. 152–3.

12 Byron to Lady Melbourne,
6 July 1813.

13 Blyth, *Caro*, p. 154.

14 Caroline to John Murray,
7 October 1813.

15 Ibid., 28 December 1813.

16 Ibid., undated but early 1814.

17 Byron to Lady Melbourne,
25 November 1813.

18 Ibid., 8 January 1814.

19 Ibid., 10 January 1814.

20 Ibid., 11 January 1814.

21 *Whole Disgraceful Truth*, p. 114.

22 Ibid.

23 MacCarthy, *Life and Legend*,
p. 171.

24 *Whole Disgraceful Truth*, p. 121.
No reply was ever sent to the
letter.

25 Byron to Lady Melbourne,
26 June 1814.

26 Ibid.

27 *Whole Disgraceful Truth*, p. 122.

28 Caroline to Byron, 3 June 1814.

29 Ibid.

30 Byron to Lady Melbourne,
2 July 1814.

31 Normington, *Infernal Woman*,
p. 131.

32 *Whole Disgraceful Truth*,
pp. 126–7.

33 Ibid.

34 Ibid. pp. 127–8.

35 Ibid.

36 Normington, *Infernal Woman*,
p. 138.

37 Byron to James Perry, 5 October
1814.

38 Caroline to John Murray, undated but *c.* October 1814.

39 *Whole Disgraceful Truth*, p. 129.

40 Ibid.

41 Ibid., p. 130.

42 Douglass, *Lady Caroline*, pp. 172–3.

43 Ibid.

44 Blyth, *Caro*, p. 175.

45 Byron to James Wedderburn Webster, 4 September 1815.

46 Ibid., 18 September 1815.

47 Blyth, *Caro*, p. 180.

48 *Whole Disgraceful Truth*, p. 139–41.

49 Ibid.

50 Ibid., p. 143.

51 Ibid., p. 144–6.

52 Douglass, *Lady Caroline*, p. 178.

53 *Whole Disgraceful Truth*, p. 149.

54 Douglass, *Lady Caroline*, p. 180.

55 Blyth, *Caro*, p. 193.

56 Byron to Murray, 22 July 1816.

57 Lamb, *Glenarvon*, vol. 2, p. 359.

58 Ibid., vol. 1, p. 143.

59 Byron to Moore, 17 November 1816.

60 Douglass, *Lady Caroline Lamb*, p. 192.

61 *Whole Disgraceful Truth*, p. 192.

62 Ibid., p. 198.

63 Ibid.

64 *Lady Morgan's Memoirs*, vol. 2, pp. 206–8.

65 Cecil, *Melbourne*, p. 105.

66 Douglass, *Lady Caroline*, p. 292.

Chapter 7

1 Strickland, *Byron Women*, p. 67.

2 Eisler, *Byron*, p. 353.

3 Thorne (ed.), *History of Parliament*, p 41.

4 Eisler, *Byron*, p. 353.

5 Strickland, *Byron Women*, p. 68.

6 Elwin, *Lord Byron's Wife*, p. 62.

7 Ibid., p. 86.

8 Mayne, *Life and Letters*, p. 15.

9 Strickland, *Byron Women*, p. 69.

10 Byron to Caroline, 1 May 1812.

11 Ibid.

12 Hay, *The Secret*, p. 6.

13 Ibid., p. 7.

14 Ibid.

15 *Lovelace Papers*, 9–10 April 1812.

16 Strickland, *Byron Women*, p. 70.

17 Elwin, *Lord Byron's Wife*, p. 102.

18 Annabella to Judith, 27 March 1812.

19 Ibid.

20 Elwin, *Lord Byron's Wife*, pp. 104–5.

21 Ibid.

22 Ibid.

23 Annabella to Judith, 27 March 1812.

24 Ibid., 13 April 1812.

25 Ibid., 15 April 1812.

26 Ibid.

27 Elwin, *Lord Byron's Wife*, p. 110.

28 Annabella to Judith, 26 April 1812.

29 Elwin, *Lord Byron's Wife*, p. 111.

30 Caroline to Annabella, 22 May 1812.

31 Byron to Lady Melbourne, 13 September 1812.

32 Ibid., 18 September 1812.

33 Elwin, *Lord Byron's Wife*, p. 119.

34 Byron to Lady Melbourne, 17 October 1812.

35 Ibid.

36 Byron to Lady Melbourne, 18 October 1812.

37 Elwin, *Lord Byron's Wife*, p. 161.

38 Annabella to Byron, 22 August 1813.

39 Byron to Annabella, 25 August 1813.

40 Annabella to Byron, 3 September 1813.

41 Byron to Annabella, 26 September 1813.

42 Elwin, *Lord Byron's Wife*, p. 172.

43 Ibid., p. 174.

44 Byron to Lady Melbourne, 8 October 1813.

45 Elwin, *Lord Byron's Wife*, p. 175.

46 Annabella to Byron, 27 November 1813.

47 MacCarthy, *Life and Legend*, p. 226.

48 Byron to Lady Melbourne, 30 April 1814.

49 Annabella to Byron, 14 September 1814.

50 Medwin, *Conversations*, p. 26.

51 Ibid.

52 MacCarthy, *Life and Legend*, p. 227.

Chapter 8

1 Gunn, *My Dearest Augusta*, p. 69.

2 Augusta to Byron, 2 September 1811.

3 Gunn, *My Dearest Augusta*, p. 79.

4 Byron to Augusta, 27 June 1813.

5 Byron to Lady Melbourne, 1 July 1813.

6 Byron to Thomas Moore, 8 July 1813.

7 MacCarthy, *Life and Legend*, p. 206.

8 Elwin, *Lord Byron's Wife*, p. 166.

9 Crane, *Kindness of Sisters*, p. 49.

10 Byron to Lady Melbourne, 5 August 1813.

11 Crane, *Kindness of Sisters*, pp. 49–50.

12 Byron to Lady Melbourne, 20 August 1813.

13 Byron to Moore, 22 August 1813.

14 Byron to Lady Melbourne, 31 August 1813.

15 Hoobler and Hoobler, *Monsters*, p 184.

16 Byron to Augusta, 15 September 1813.

17 Elwin, *Lord Byron's Wife*, p. 171.

18 Byron to Lady Melbourne, 28 September 1813.

19 Byron to Annabella, October 1813.

20 Byron to Augusta, 10 October 1813.

21 Ibid., 8 November 1813.

22 Elwin, *Lord Byron's Wife*, p. 181.

23 Marchand (ed.), *Byron's Letters and Journals*, vol. 3, p. 205.

24 Elwin, *Lord Byron's Wife*, p. 181.

25 Byron to Lady Melbourne, 29 January 1814.

26 Elwin, *Lord Byron's Wife*, p. 183.

27 Byron to Lady Melbourne, 13 January 1814.

28 Byron to John Murray, 22 January 1814.

29 John Murray to Byron, undated but *c.* February 1814.

30 Byron to Lady Melbourne, 25 April 1814.

31 Byron to Moore, 4 May 1814.

32 Byron to Annabella, 25 August 1813.

33 Annabella to Byron, 14 September 1814.

34 Gunn, *My Dearest Augusta*, p. 110.

35 Byron to Moore, 8 August 1814.

36 Elwin, *Lord Byron's Wife*, p. 209.

37 Byron to Annabella, 18 and 19 September 1814.

38 Ibid., 20 September 1814.

39 Byron to Lady Melbourne, 18 September 1814.

40 Ibid.

41 Gunn, *My Dearest Augusta*, p. 111.

42 Annabella to Byron, 3 October 1814.

43 Augusta to Annabella, 1 October 1814.

44 Annabella to Byron, 3 October 1814.

45 Byron to Lady Melbourne, 7 October 1814.

46 Byron to Hobhouse, 17 October 1814.

47 Augusta to Annabella, 20 October 1814.

48 Annabella to Lady Melbourne, 2 November 1814.

49 Elwin, *Lord Byron's Wife*, p. 228.

50 Ibid., p. 229.

51 Ibid.

52 Ibid.

53 Byron to Lady Melbourne, 4 November 1814.

54 Byron to Lady Melbourne, 13 November 1814.

55 Elwin, *Lord Byron's Wife*, p. 231.

56 Annabella to Byron, 19 November 1814.

57 Lady Melbourne to Annabella, 1 December 1814.

58 Augusta to Annabella, 12 December 1814.

59 Annabella to Byron, 14 December 1814.

60 Ibid., 16 December 1814.

61 Byron to Annabella, 23 December 1814.

62 Elwin, *Lord Byron's Wife*, p. 247.

63 MacCarthy, *Life and Legend*, p. 237.

64 Elwin, *Lord Byron's Wife*, pp. 248–9.

65 Crane, *Kindness Of Sisters*, p. 62.

Chapter 9

1 Crane, *Kindness Of Sisters*, p. 144.

2 Beecher Stowe, *Lady Byron Vindicated*, p. 287.

3 Eisler, *Byron*, p. 451.

4 Elwin, *Lord Byron's Wife*, p. 251.

5 Ibid.

6 Eisler, *Byron*, p. 453.

7 Ibid., p. 252.

8 Ibid., p. 254.

9 Ibid.

10 Ibid.

11 Augusta to Annabella, 9 January 1815.

12 Byron to Lady Melbourne, 7 January 1815.

13 Marchand (ed.), *Byron's Letters and Journals*, vol. 2, p. 516.

14 Elwin, *Lord Byron's Wife*, p. 273.

15 Ibid., p. 518.

16 Ibid., p. 519.

17 The poem was dated 19 February 1815.

18 Augusta to Annabella, 5 February 1815.

19 Elwin, *Lord Byron's Wife*, p. 300.

20 MacCarthy, *Life and Legend*, p. 251.

21 Gunn, *My Dearest Augusta*, p. 133.

22 Byron to Moore, 12 June 1815.

23 MacCarthy, *Life and Legend*, p. 253.

24 Gunn, *My Dearest Augusta*, p. 137.

25 Ibid., p. 138.

26 Annabella to Ralp. Milbanke, 5 September 1815.

27 Elwin, *Lord Byron's Wife*, p. 323.

28 Annabella to Augusta, 9 November 1815.

29 Byron to Murray, 14 November 1815.

30 Eisler, *Byron*, p. 475.

31 Elwin, *Lord Byron's Wife*, p. 328.

32 Byron to Alexander Rae, 19 November 1815.

33 Eisler, *Byron*, p. 477.

34 Ibid., p. 478.

35 Byron to James Webster, 4 September 1814.

36 Elwin, *Lord Byron's Wife*, p. 339.

37 Ibid., p. 337.

38 Eisler, *Byron*, pp. 478–9.

39 Elwin, *Lord Byron's Wife*, p. 340.

40 Byron to Annabella, 6 January 1816.

41 Eisler, *Byron*, p. 481.

42 Elwin, *Lord Byron's Wife*, p. 34.

43 Ibid.

44 Ibid., p. 350.

45 Gunn, *My Dearest Augusta*, p. 148.

46 Annabella to Byron, 15 January 1816.

47 Ibid., 16 January 1816.

48 Eisler, *Byron*, p. 482.

49 Augusta to Annabella, 17 January 1816.

50 Annabella to Judith Milbanke, 22 January 1816.

51 Augusta to Annabella, 29 January 1816.

52 Ibid., 30 January 1816.

53 Byron to Ralp. Milbanke, 2 February 1816.

54 Annabella to Augusta, 3 February 1816.

55 Byron to Annabella, 5 February 1816.

56 Hobhouse to Annabella, 6 February 1816.

57 Eisler, *Byron*, p. 490.

58 Ibid., p. 495.

59 Byron to Annabella, 15 February 1816.

60 Augusta to Hodgson, 15 February 1816.

61 Augusta to Annabella, 17 February 1816.

62 Byron to Annabella, 4 March 1816.

63 Augusta to Hodgson, 5 March 1816.

64 MacCarthy, *Life and Legend*, p. 276.

65 Eisler, *Byron*, p. 503.

66 Byron to Annabella, 14 April 1816.

Chapter 10

1 Gittings and Manton, *Claire Clairmont*, p. 3.

2 Ibid., p. 4.

3 Kegan Paul, *William Godwin*, p. 129.

4 Claire Clairmont to E.J. Trewlany, April 1871.

5 Gittings and Manton, *Claire Clairmont*, p. 9.

6 Ibid.

7 Marshall, *William Godwin*, p. 302.

8 Gittings and Manton, *Claire Clairmont*, p. 11.

9 Shelley to Thomas Jefferson Hogg, 4 October 1814.

10 Gittings and Manton, *Claire Clairmont*, p. 12.

11 Ibid., p. 13.

12 *Journals of Claire Clairmont,* p. 50.

13 Ibid., p. 58

14 Gittings & Manton, *Claire Clairmont*, p. 22.

15 *Mary Shelley's Journal*, 13 May 1815

16 Claire to Fanny Imlay, 28 May 1815.

17 *Journals of Claire Clairmont*, p. 69.

18 Claire to Byron, March 1816.

19 Gittings and Manton, *Claire Clairmont*, p. 26.

20 Byron to Claire, March 1816.

21 Claire to Byron, 16 April 1816.

22 Ibid., 19 April 1816.

23 Ibid., April/May 1816.

24 Byron to Douglas Kinnaird, 20 January 1817.

25 Claire to Byron, 21 April 1816.

26 Claire to Byron, 21 April 1816.

27 Ibid.

28 Ibid., 6 May 1816.

29 Ibid.

30 Ibid.

31 Marchand, *Byron*, p. 610.

32 Claire to Byron, 25 May 1816.

33 Ibid., 27 May 1816.

34 Byron to Augusta, 8 September 1816.

35 Marchand (ed.), *Byron's Letters and Journals*, vol. 2, p. 623.

36 Dunn, *Moon in Eclipse*, p. 127.

37 Marchand (ed.), *Byron's Letters and Journals*, vol. 2, p. 627.

38 Claire to Byron, June 1816.

39 Byron to Kinnaird, 20 January 1817.
40 Claire to Byron, July 1816.
41 Ibid., 16 July 1816.
42 Claire to Trelawny, *c.* 1870.

Chapter 11

1 Mary to Fanny Imlay, 1 June 1816.
2 Lewalski, *John Milton*, p. 9.
3 Probably 14 June.
4 Dunn, *Moon in Eclipse*, p. 129.
5 Shelley, *Frankenstein*, p. ix.
6 Ibid., p. x.
7 Ibid., p xi.
8 *Mary Shelley's Journal*, 9 March 1816 .
9 Ibid. 16 March 1816.
10 Shelley, *Frankenstein*, p. xii.
11 Ibid, p ix
12 *Mary Shelley's Journal*, p. 21.
13 Medwin, *Conversations*, p. 172.
14 Ibid., p. 71.
15 *Mary Shelley's Journal*, 6 December 1814.
16 *Fraser's Magazine*, vol. 10, 1834, p. 463.
17 Medwin, *Conversations*, p. 13.
18 Shelley, *Frankenstein*, p. 24.
19 Byron to Murray, 15 May 1819.
20 Byron to Augusta, 27 August 1816.
21 Byron to Hanson, 28 August 1816.
22 Shelley, *Frankenstein*, p. 191.

Chapter 12

1 Claire to Byron, 29 August 1816.
2 Shelley to Byron, 8 September 1816.
3 Shelley to Byron, 20 November 1816.
4 Gittings and Manton, *Claire Clairmont*, pp. 35–6.
5 Claire to Byron, 27 October 1816 – 19 November 1816.
6 Shelley to Mary, 16 December 1816.
7 Shelley to Claire, 30 December 1816.
8 Claire to Trelawney, 30 August – 21 September 1878.
9 Shelley to Byron, 13 January 1817.
10 Byron to Augusta, 27 May 1817.
11 Eisler, *Byron,* p. 553.
12 Gittings and Manton, *Claire Clairmont*, pp. 37–8.
13 Shelley to Byron, 23 April 1817.
14 Mary to Shelley, 30 September 1817.
15 Gittings and Manton, *Claire Clairmont*, p. 40.
16 Claire to Byron, 12 January 1818.
17 Shelley to Byron, 13 April 1818.
18 Claire to Byron, 21/22 April 1818.
19 Byron to John Murray, 23 April 1818.
20 Shelley to Byron, 22 April 1818.
21 Shelley to Byron, 28 April 1818.
22 Claire to Trelawny, *c.* 1870.
23 Claire to Byron, 29 April 1818.

24 Byron to Hobhouse, 24 April 1818.

25 Ibid., 5 May 1818.

26 Shelley to Mary, 23 August 1818.

27 Shelley to Claire, 25 September 1818.

28 Byron to Augusta, 21 September 1818.

29 Bieri, *Percy Bysshe Shelley*, p. 161.

30 Mary to Maria Gisborne, 9 April 1819.

31 Mary to Amelia Curran, 27 June 1819.

32 Claire to Byron, 18 May 1819.

33 Byron to Augusta, 3 August 1818.

34 Ibid., 10 September – 23 September 1819.

35 Byron to Hobhouse, 21 November 1819.

36 Claire to Byron, 16 March 1820.

37 Ibid.

38 Byron to Richard Hoppner, 18 April 1820.

39 Ibid., 22 April 1820.

40 Claire to Byron, 23 April 1820.

41 Ibid., 1 May 1820.

42 Ibid., 4 May 1820

43 Marchand (ed.), *Byron's Letters and Journals*, vol. 8, p. 29.

44 Byron to Hoppner, 10 February 1821.

45 Claire to Byron, 24 March 1821.

46 Byron to Hoppner, 3 April 1821.

47 Ibid., 11 May 1821.

48 Ibid., 31 May 1821.

49 Shelley to Mary, 15 August 1821.

50 Gittings and Manton, *Claire Clairmont*, p. 65.

51 Eisler, *Byron*, p. 701.

52 Marchand, *Byron*, p. 939.

53 Gittings and Manton, *Claire Clairmont*, p. 66.

54 Claire to Byron, 18 February 1822.

55 Shelley to Claire, 24 March 1822.

56 *Clairmont Correspondence*, p. 173.

57 Byron to John Murray, 22 April 1822.

58 Byron to Shelley, 23 April 1822.

59 Gittings and Manton, *Claire Clairmont*, p. 116.

60 Hay, *Young Romantics*, p. 308.

61 Byron to Moore, 2 August 1822.

Chapter 13

1 Eisler, *Byron*, p. 625.

2 Origo, *Last Attachment*, pp.24–5.

3 Byron to Hobhouse, 17 May 1819.

4 Origo, *Last Attachment*, p. 27.

5 Ibid., p. 24.

6 Ibid., p. 23.

7 Ibid., p. 25.

8 Ibid., p. 28.

9 Ibid.

10 Ibid., p. 29.

11 Quennell, *Byron in Italy*, p. 152.

12 Byron to Murray, 6 April 1819.

13 MacCarthy, *Life and Legend*, p. 354.

14 Marchand, *Byron*, p. 774.

15 Origo, *Last Attachment*, p. 40.

16 Byron to Hobhouse, 6 April 1819.

17 Fanny Silvestrini to Teresa, 19 April 1819.

18 Fanny Silvestrini to Byron, 19 April 1819.

19 Teresa to Byron, 18 April 1819.

20 Byron to Kinnaird, 22 April 1819.

21 Byron to Teresa, 22 April 1819.

22 Byron to Murray, 18 May 1819. Murray considered this letter 'too gross'.

23 Byron to Teresa, 3 May 1819.

24 Byron to Lord Charles Kinnaird, 15 May 1819.

25 Byron to Augusta, 17 May 1819.

26 Byron to Hoppner, 2 June 1819

27 Origo, *Last Attachment*, p. 61.

28 Ibid., p. 68.

29 Byron to Teresa, 14 June 1819.

30 Marchand, *Byron*, p. 793.

31 Ibid., p. 794.

32 Byron to Hoppner, 20 June 1819.

33 Byron to James Webster, 2 July 1819.

34 Byron to Hoppner, 2 July 1819.

35 Ibid

36 Byron to Scott, 7 July 1819.

37 Marchand, *Byron*, p. 799.

38 Ibid., p. 800.

39 Byron to Teresa, 4 August 1819.

40 Ibid., p. 805.

41 Byron to Murray, 12 August 1819.

42 MacCarthy, *Life and Legend*, p. 363.

43 Origo, *Last Attachment*, p. 120.

44 Byron to Hobhouse, 3 October 1819.

45 Byron to Hoppner, 29 October 1819.

46 Byron to Hobhouse, 20 November 1819.

47 Byron to Kinnaird, 16 November 1819.

48 Byron to Teresa, 25 November 1819.

49 Ibid., 10 December 1819.

Chapter 14

1 Eisler, *Byron*, p. 652.

2 Ibid.

3 Byron to Hoppner, 10 January 1820.

4 Eisler, *Byron*, p. 653.

5 Byron to Murray, 21 February 1820.

6 Ibid.

7 Eisler, *Byron*, p. 654.

8 Byron to Teresa, 4 January 1820.

9 Byron to Hobhouse, 3 March 1820.

10 Byron to Teresa, 5 March 1820.

11 Byron to Harriette Wilson, 30 March 1820.

12 Origo, *Last Attachment*, p. 170.

13 Byron to Teresa, April 1820.

14 Ibid., May 1820.

15 Ibid.

16 Ibid.

17 Byron to Murray, 20 May 1820.

18 Byron to Moore, 13 July 1820.

19 Origo, *Last Attachment*, p. 188.

20 Byron to Teresa, 23 July 1820.
21 Ibid., 24 July 1820.
22 Origo, *Last Attachment*, p. 199.
23 Byron to Murray, 4 September 1821.
24 Byron to Teresa, 8 August 1820.
25 Byron to Murray, 22 July 1820.
26 Byron to Moore, 31 August 1820.
27 Byron to Guiccioli, 21 August 1820.
28 Origo, *Last Attachment*, p. 217.
29 Teresa to Byron, 7 September 1820.
30 Byron to Teresa, 9 September 1820.
31 Teresa to Guiccioli, 15 September 1820.
32 Byron to Teresa, 28 September 1820.
33 Ibid., 29 September 1820.
34 Byron to the Neapolitan insurgents, October 1820.
35 Origo, *Last Attachment*, p. 226.
36 Teresa to Byron, 10 October 1820.
37 Byron to Teresa, 12 October 1820.
38 Byron to Douglas Kinnaird, 22 November 1820.
39 Ibid.
40 Byron to Teresa, 30 October 1820.
41 Ibid., 8 November 1820.
42 Ibid., 22 November 1820.
43 Byron to Annabella, 28 December 1820.
44 Byron to Moore, 9 December 1820.
45 Byron, 'Ravenna Journal', 6 January 1821.
46 Origo, *Last Attachment*, p. 236.
47 Byron to Murray, 6 July 1821.
48 Origo, *Last Attachment*, p. 239.
49 Byron to Moore, 28 April 1821.
50 Ibid., 4 June 1821.
51 Gamba to Teresa, 11 July 1821.
52 Teresa to Byron, 11 July 1821.
53 Byron to Teresa, 26 July 1821.
54 Byron to Hoppner, 23 July 1821.
55 Byron to Teresa, 4 August 1821.
56 Byron to Pietro Gamba, 9 August 1821.
57 Shelley to Mary, 19 August 1821.
58 Shelley to Teresa, 7 August 1821.
59 Eisler, *Byron*, p. 686.
60 Teresa to Byron, August 1821
61 Byron to Moore, 19 September 1821

Chapter 15

1 Marchand, *Byron*, p. 355.
2 Ibid.
3 Ibid.
4 Origo, *Last Attachment*, p. 294.
5 Ibid.
6 Ibid., pp. 297–8.
7 Ibid.
8 Ibid., p. 300.
9 Byron to Murray, 8 July 1822.
10 Origo, *Last Attachment*, p. 305.
11 Ibid.
12 Ibid., p. 313.
13 Ibid.
14 Ibid., p. 315.

15 Ibid., p. 316.

16 Byron to Moore, 27 August 1822.

17 Eisler, *Byron*, p. 708.

18 Medwin, *Conversations*, p. 124–5.

19 Origo, *Last Attachment*, p. 323.

20 Hobhouse to Byron, 2 March 1823.

21 Eisler, *Byron*, pp. 712–13.

22 Origo, *Last Attachment*, p. 325.

23 Ibid., p. 326. Of course, this was not the first time that Byron saw himself with Promethean overtones.

24 Byron to Kinnaird, 18 January 1823.

25 Mary to Teresa, January 1823.

26 Origo, *Last Attachment*, p. 330.

27 Byron to Hobhouse, 7 April 1823.

28 Byron to Sir John Bowring, 12 May 1823.

29 Origo, *Last Attachment*, p. 337.

30 MacCarthy, *Life and Legend*, p. 454.

31 Byron to Kinnaird, 21 May 1823.

32 Byron to Hobhouse, 7 April 1823.

33 Ibid., 19 April 1823.

34 Origo, *Last Attachment*, pp. 338–9.

35 Ibid.

36 Byron to Lady Hardy, 17 May 1823.

37 Origo, *Last Attachment*, p. 342.

38 Byron to J. J. Coulmann, 7 July 1823.

39 Teresa to Byron, 13 July 1823.

40 Byron and Pietro Gamba to Teresa, 22 July 1823.

41 Byron to Goethe, 22 July 1823.

42 Ibid., 29 October 1823.

43 Byron to Teresa, 10 August 1823.

44 Ibid., 21 October 1823.

45 Origo, *Last Attachment*, p. 367.

46 Pietro to Teresa, 14 December 1823.

47 Byron to Teresa, 14 December 1823.

48 Byron to Charles Barry, December 1823.

49 Pietro to Teresa, 14 January 1824.

50 Ibid., 24 February 1824.

51 Origo, *Last Attachment*, p. 384.

52 Ibid., p 389.

53 Ignazio Guiccioli to Teresa, 21 June 1827.

54 Origo, *Last Attachment*, p. 390.

55 Ibid., p. 391.

56 Ibid.

57 Fox, *Journal*, p. 268.

58 Origo, *Last Attachment*, p. 396.

59 Ibid., p. 400.

60 Ibid., p. 422.

Chapter 16

1 Marchand, *Byron*, p. 209.

2 Byron to Augusta, 18 October 1820.

3 Woolley, *Bride of Science*, p. 85.

4 Ibid., p. 86.

5 Annabella to Lady Noel, 8 April 1817.

6 Annabella to Theresa Villiers, *c*. September 1818.

7 Langley Moore, *Ada*, p. 16.

8 Annabella to Augusta, 1 December 1823.

9 Annabella to Theresa, 18 May 1824.

10 Ada to Annabella, 13 September 1824.

11 Ibid., 2 June 1826.

12 Ada to Annabella, undated but *c*. May/June 1830.

13 Langley Moore, *The Late Lord Bryon*, p. 34.

14 Ada to Annabella, 19 May 1833.

15 Annabella to Mrs William King, 13 May 1833.

16 Langley Moore, *The Late Lord Byron*, p. 42.

17 Hobhouse, *Diary*, 24 February 1834.

18 Toole (ed.), *Enchantress of Numbe*, p. 51.

19 Ibid., p. 52.

20 Woolley, *Bride of Science*, p. 158.

21 Carlyle, *Sartor Resartus*, Chapter I.1.

22 Langley Moore, *The Late Lord Byron*, pp. 68–9.

23 Ada to Annabella, *c*. May 1835.

24 Woolley, *Bride of Science*, p. 170.

25 Ibid., p. 177.

26 Ada to King, 28 June 1835.

27 Ada to Mary Somerville, 10 April 1836.

28 *Lovelace Papers*, 28 August 1836.

29 Ada to Babbage, September 1837.

30 Ibid., 2 March 1838.

31 *Lovelace Papers*, 12 December 1840.

32 Ada to Babbage, November 1839.

33 Babbage to Ada, 29 November 1839.

34 Ada to Babbage, 12 January 1841.

35 Ada to Sophia, 1 March 1841.

36 Ada to Annabella, 3 March 1841.

37 Annabella to Ada, 8 March 1841.

Chapter 17

1 Byron to Lady Melbourne, 25 April 1814.

2 Turney, *Byron's Daughter*, p. 29.

3 Ibid., p. 48.

4 Ibid., p. 49.

5 Leigh, *History and Autobiography*, p. 30.

6 Ibid., p. 31.

7 Trevanion to Augusta, *c*. November 1830.

8 Augusta to Trevanion, January 1831.

9 Augusta to Medora, February 1831.

10 Leigh, *History and Autobiography*, p. 31.

11 Ibid., p. 37.

12 Ibid., p. 31.

13 Turney, *Byron's Daughter*, p. 107.

14 Leigh, *History and Autobiography*, p. 32.

15 Ibid.

16 Ibid.

17 Turney, *Byron's Daughter*, p. 142.

18 Ibid., p. 148.

19 Ibid., p. 156.

20 Annabella to Augusta, 20 January 1841.

21 Ada to Annabella, 27 February 1841.

22 Leigh, *History and Autobiography*, p. 34.

23 Turney, *Byron's Daughter*, p. 181.

24 Ibid., p. 187.

25 Ibid., p. 189.

26 Annabella to Medora, 4 July 1842.

27 Medora to Annabella, 19 July 1842.

28 Annabella to Medora, 21 July 1842.

29 Ada to Annabella, 21 July 1842.

Chapter 18

1 Ada to Greig, 31 December 1841.

2 Greig to Ada, January 1842.

3 Babbage, *Passages*, p. 99.

4 Woolley, *Bride of Science*, p. 262.

5 Ada to Babbage, *c.* May 1843.

6 Menabrea, *Sketch Of The Analytical Engine*, p. 284.

7 Ada to Babbage, 14 August 1843.

8 Annabella to Medora, August 1842.

9 Leigh, *History and Autobiography*, p. 38.

10 Medora to Annabella, 5 March 1843.

11 Annabella to Medora, 6 March 1843.

12 Annabella to Selina Doyle, 14 March 1843.

13 Turney, *Byron's Daughter*, p. 212.

14 Ibid., p. 221.

15 Langley Moore, *Ada*, p. 177.

16 Ada to Annabella, 14 December 1844.

17 *Lovelace Papers*, 6 January 1844.

18 Ada to Andrew Crosse, October 1844.

19 Langley Moore, *Ada*, p. 235.

20 Turney, *Byron's Daughter*, p. 234.

21 Hobhouse to unknown correspondent, 14 August 1843.

22 Medora to Augusta, 13 August 1843.

23 Trevanion to Hughes, January 1844.

24 Turney, *Byron's Daughter*, p. 275.

25 Woolley, *Bride of Science*, p. 327.

26 Ibid.

27 Ada to H. Bence Jones, June 1851.

28 Woolley, *Bride of Science*, p. 362.

Postscript

1 Creston, *Youthful Queen Victoria*, p. 342.

2 St Aubyn, *Queen Victoria*, pp. 84–5.

BIBLIOGRAPHY

General

Bone, Drummond (ed.), *Cambridge Companion to Byron* (Cambridge, 2004)

Byron, *Letters and Journals*, ed. Leslie Marchand, 10 vols (John Murray, 1973–80)

Byron: Complete Poetical Works, ed. Frederick Page (Oxford, 1980)

Clinton, George, *Memoirs of the Life and Writings of Lord Byron* (James Robins & Co, 1827)

Eisler, Benita, *Byron: Child of Passion, Fool of Fame* (Hamish Hamilton, 1999)

Franklin, Caroline, *Byron: A Literary Life* (Macmillan, 2000)

Franklin, Caroline, *Byron's Heroines* (Clarendon Press, 1992)

Harvey, A.D., 'Prosecutions for Sodomy in England at the Beginning of the Nineteenth Century', *The Historical Journal*, 21:4 (1978), 939–48

Hobhouse, John Cam, *Hobhouse's Diary*, ed Peter Cochran (https://petercochran.wordpress.com/hobhouses-diary/, 2009)

Langley Moore, Doris, *The Late Lord Byron* (John Murray, 1961)

MacCarthy, Fiona, *Byron: Life and Legend* (John Murray, 2002)

Marchand, Leslie, *Byron: A Biography* (John Murray, 1957)

Maurois, André, *Byron*, trans. Hamish Miles (Constable, 1984)

Mayne, Ethel Colburn, *Byron* (Methuen, 1924)

Medwin, Michael, *Conversations of Lord Byron* (Henry Colburn, 1824)

Moore, Thomas, *The Life and Letters of Lord Byron* (Leavitt & Allen, 1858)

Nicholson, Andrew (ed.), *The Letters of John Murray to Lord Byron* (Liverpool University Press, 2007)

O'Brien, Edna, *Byron In Love* (Weidenfeld & Nicolson, 2009)

Parker, Derek, *Byron and his World* (Thames and Hudson, 1968)

Quennell, Peter, *Byron: the Years of Fame* (Collins, 1935)

Strickland, Margot, *The Byron Women* (Peter Owen, 1974)

Catherine Gordon

Boyes, Megan, *My Amiable Mamma* (J. M. Tatler, 1991)

Gordon, Pryse, *Personal Memoirs* (Colburn and Bentley, 1830)

Prothero, R.E., 'The Childhood and School Days of Byron', *The Nineteenth Century*, 43 (1898), 61–81

Walpole, Horace, *The Castle Of Otranto*, ed. W. S. Lewis (Oxford, 2008)

Lady Caroline Lamb

Bishop, Morchard (ed.), *Recollections of the Table-Talk of Samuel Rogers,* (University of Kansas Press, 1953)

Blyth, Henry, *Caro, the Fatal Passion* (Hart Davis, 1972)

Cecil, David, *Melbourne: A Biography* (Constable, 1954)

Douglass, Paul, *Lady Caroline Lamb* (Palgrave, 2004)

Hary-O: The Letters of Lady Harriet Cavendish 1796–1809, ed. Sir George Leveson-Gower and Iris Palmer (John Murray, 1940)

Jenkins, Elizabeth, *Lady Caroline Lamb* (Victor Gollancz, 1932)

Lady Morgan's Memoirs: Autobiography, Diaries and Correspondence, 2 vols (W. H. Allen, 1862)

Lamb, Caroline, *Glenarvon* (Henry Colburn, 1816)

Leslie, Doris, *This For Caroline* (Heinemann, 1964)

Normington, Susan, *Lady Caroline Lamb: This Infernal Woman* (House of Stratus, 2001)

Ponsonby, Sir John, *The Ponsonby Family* (Medici Society, 1929)

Villiers, Marjorie, *The Grand Whiggery* (John Murray, 1939)

The Whole Disgraceful Truth: Selected Letters of Lady Caroline Lamb, ed. Paul Douglass (Palgrave, 2006)

Annabella Milbanke

Beecher Stowe, Harriet, *Lady Byron Vindicated* (Fields, Osgood & Co., 1870)

Crane, David, *The Kindness of Sisters* (HarperCollins, 2002)

Elwin, Malcolm, *Lord Byron's Wife* (Macdonald, 1962)

Hay, Ashley, *The Secret: The Strange Marriage of Annabella Milbanke and*

Lord Byron (Aurum, 2001)

The Lovelace Papers, 29, folio 86, Bodleian Library archive, Oxford

Mayne, Ethel Colburn, *The Life and Letters of Anne Isabella, Lady Noel Byron* (Constable, 1929)

Thorne, R. (ed.), *The History of Parliament: the House of Commons 1790–1820* (Boydell and Brewer, 1986)

Augusta Leigh

Bakewell, Michael, *Augusta Leigh: Byron's Half Sister* (Chatto & Windus, 2000)

Gunn, Peter, *My Dearest Augusta* (Bodley Head, 1968)

Claire Clairmont

The Clairmont Correspondence, ed. Marion Kingston Stocking (Johns Hopkins University Press, 1995)

Gittings, Robert, and Manton, Jo, *Claire Clairmont and the Shelleys* (Oxford, 1992)

The Journals of Claire Clairmont, ed. Marion Kingston Stocking (Harvard University Press, 1968)

Kegan Paul, C., *William Godwin, His Friends and Correspondence* (Henry S. King & Co., 1876)

Marshall, Peter H., *William Godwin* (Yale University Press, 1984)

Mary Shelley

Bieri, James, *Percy Bysshe Shelley: A Biography* (University of Delaware Press, 2005)

Dunn, Jane, *Moon in Eclipse: A Life of Mary Shelley* (Weidenfeld & Nicolson, 1978)

Ellis, David, *Byron In Geneva: That Summer of 1816* (Liverpool University Press, 2011)

'Gallery Of Literary Characters, no LIII, William Godwin Esq', *Fraser's Magazine*, 10 (1834)

Gilmour, Ian, *The Making Of The Poets* (Chatto and Windus, 2002)

Hay, Daisy, *Young Romantics* (Bloomsbury, 2010)

Holmes, Richard, *Shelley: The Pursuit* (Weidenfeld & Nicolson, 1974)

Hoobler, Thomas, and Hoobler, Dorothy, *The Monsters* (Back Bay, 2006)

Lewalski, Barbara, *The Life of John Milton* (Wiley-Blackwell, 2000)

Mary Shelley's Journal, ed. Frederick L. Jones (University of Oklahoma Press, 1947)

Shelley, Mary, *Frankenstein* (Penguin Classics, 2003)

Stott, Andrew McConnell, *The Vampyre Family* (Canongate, 2013)

Theresa Giuccioli

Byron, 'Ravenna Journal', ed. Peter Cochran (https://petercochran.files. wordpress.com/2009/03/ravenna_journal.pdf)

Fox, Henry Edward Fox, *The Journal*, ed. Earl of Ilchester (Thornton Butterworth, 1923)

Giuccioli, Teresa, *Byron's Life In Italy*, ed. Peter Cochran (University of Delaware Press, 2005)

Origo, Iris, *The Last Attachment* (Jonathan Cap. & John Murray, 1949)

Quennell, Peter, *Byron in Italy* (Collins, 1941)

Ada Lovelace

Babbage, Charles, *Passages From The Life Of A Philosopher* (Longman, 1864)

Carlyle, Thomas, *Sartor Resartus* (ed. Peter Sabor and Kerry McCarthy, Oxford University Press, 2008)

Langley Moore, Doris, *Ada, Countess of Lovelace* (John Murray, 1977)

Menabrea, L. F., *Sketch Of The Analytical Engine Invented by Charles Babbage,* translated and with an introductory note by Ada Lovelace (ed. Richard Taylor, London 1843)

Stein, Dorothy, *Ada: A Life and a Legacy* (MIT Press, 1985)

Toole, Betty A. (ed.), *Ada, the Enchantress of Numbers* (Strawberry Press, 1998)

Woolley, Benjamin, *The Bride Of Science* (Macmillan, 1999)

Medora Leigh

Leigh, Medora, *History and Autobiography*, ed. Charles Mackay (New York, 1870)

Turney, Catherine, *Byron's Daughter* (Peter Davies, 1972)

Postscript

Creston, Dormer, *The Youthful Queen Victoria* (Macmillan, 1952)

St Aubyn, Giles, *Queen Victoria* (Sinclair-Stevenson, 1991)

ACKNOWLEDGEMENTS

Writing the life of one person is a difficult enough endeavour, but trying to do justice to the lives of ten is a labour that would do credit to Hercules. The research for this book has taken me all over Europe, most notably to the Keats-Shelley Memorial House in Rome; to Harrow School and Trinity College, Cambridge; to the British, Bodleian and London Libraries; to the John Murray archive; and to the Heinz archive at the National Portrait Gallery. Yet there have been many other institutions, great and small, that have assisted with my research, most notably Sussex University, where the bulk of this book was composed. I am extremely grateful to all those who assisted me in the process.

In our third collaboration, Richard Milbank has displayed the fortitude and good humour that any editor should have, coupled with incisive good sense, and has continued a smooth partnership with my publishers, Head of Zeus. My thanks also to Anthony Cheetham, whose initial discussions with me about the book shaped both its structure and my approach, and Georgina Bateman, whose assistance with research matters illustrative and otherwise has proved invaluable. Catherine Hanley brought both a keen eye and a historian's precision to the copy-edit, which has resulted in a text that I am deeply proud of, and I hope does justice to its subjects.

The book is also a tribute to my marvellous agent, Georgina Capel, whose enthusiasm for the project has lasted from our first conversation about it one lunchtime to this handsome finished product. My thanks also to her associate Rachel Conway, who has been an enormous and continually good-humoured help throughout my career. I would also like to thank the following people who have assisted, directly or indirectly, with suggestions, comments and insights: Mark Atherton, Catherine Bray, Nick Dear, James Douglass, Paul Douglass (no relation), Clara Drummond, the late Lisa Jardine, the Joneses Dan, Emrys and Nigel, Ian Kelly, Benjamin Markovits, Simon Renshaw, Sir Tom Stoppard, Toby White and Joseph Wilkins. And, of course, my longest-serving literary colleague Sophie Gregory has yet again excelled herself with suitably Byronic flair in her invaluable contributions, many of which have been percolating in conversation for a decade or more. My parents-in-law Will and Sheila Alsop have been a valuable source of kindness and insight over the years, for which I remain grateful. My thanks also to my grandparents Barbara and Raymond Stephenson and Terese Larman; in deference to them, I have toned down the four-letter words, although not, alas, the moments of shocking indecency or gravity of the passions depicted herein.

The book must, however, be dedicated to my own women, my wife Nancy and my daughter Rose Evelyn Bowie. I have every hope that the latter will live up to her initials and prove every bit as intellectually adventurous and innovative as both her illustrious (middle) namesake and the protagonists of this book. I have no need to have such hopes about her mother, who has proved herself the best of people in all conceivable regards. It is with pride, gratitude and happiness that I dedicate the book to them, the most fitting recipients for a work of this nature I can imagine.

Alexander Larman, Sussex, May 2016

IMAGE CREDITS

INDEX